Bottom Line Results from
Strategic Human Resource Planning

Bottom Line Results from Strategic Human Resource Planning

Edited by

Richard J. Niehaus

Assistant for Human Resources Analysis
Office of the Chief of Naval Operations
Washington, D.C.

and

Karl F. Price

Principal
TPF&C, a Towers Perrin Company
Philadelphia, Pennsylvania

PLENUM PRESS • NEW YORK AND LONDON

Library of Congress Cataloging-in-Publication Data

Bottom line results from strategic human resource planning / t. .ed by
   Richard J. Niehaus and Karl F. Price.
        p.   cm.
   "Proceedings of the 1991 Human Resource Planning Society Research
Symposium: Bottom Line Results from Strategic Human Resource
Planning, held June 11-14, 1991, in Newport, Rhode Island"--T.p.
verso.
   Includes bibliographical references and index.
   ISBN 0-306-44187-X
   1. Personnel management--United States--Congresses.   I. Niehaus,
Richard J.   II. Price, Karl F.   III. Human Resource Planning
Society. Research Symposium (4th : 1991 : Newport, R.I.)
HF5549.2.U5B67   1992
658.3'01--dc20   91-39739
                                                            CIP

Proceedings of the 1991 Human Resource Planning Society Research
Symposium: Bottom Line Results from Strategic Human Resource Planning,
held June 11–14, 1991, in Newport, Rhode Island

ISBN 0-306-44187-X

© 1991 Plenum Press, New York
A Division of Plenum Publishing Corporation
233 Spring Street, New York, N.Y. 10013

Printed in the United States of America

Preface

This volume is the proceedings of a symposium entitled "Bottom Line Results from Strategic Human Resource Planning" which was held at Salve Regina University, Newport, Rhode Island on June 11-14, 1991. The meeting was sponsored by the Research Committee of the Human Resource Planning Society (HRPS).

In developing the agenda, the Research Committee continued the approach used in previous HRPS research symposia. The focus of these meetings is on the linkage of the state-of-practice with the state-of-the-art. Particular attention was placed on research studies which were application oriented so that member organizations can see examples of ways to extend current practices with the knowledge presented by the applications.

The meeting had sessions on: (1) The Strategic Role of Human Resources, (2) Globalization, (3) Downsizing, (4) Quality as a Strategic Human Resource Issue, (5) Forecasting Human Resource Needs, and (6) Managing People to Build Competitive Advantage. Twenty six papers were presented with discussion periods at appropriate points in the meeting. This volume contains twenty two of these papers along with an introductory paper. A short summary is also provided at the beginning of each major subdivision into which the papers are arranged.

Thanks are in order for all who contributed to the success of the meeting. First, acknowledge should be given to the members of the Research Committee who provided assistance in preparing for the meeting and in reviewing the papers which appear in this volume. These research committee members include: Lee Dyer, Charles Fay, Normand Green, Walter Griggs, Gerald Groe, Michael Hawkins, Richard Niehaus, Karl Price, David Schweiger, Carol Schreiber, and Jo Ann Verdin. Excellent help through all phases of the development and execution of the meeting was provided by the HRPS Executive Director, Steve Noble. Helpful suggestions concerning the proceedings as well as with meeting arrangements were ably provided by Joan Kasper, Ellen Gordon and other members of the HRPS staff.

Helpful editorial assistance was provided by Patricia Vann at Plenum Press in all phases of the development of this volume. Very helpful suggestions concerning the layout and production of the book was provided by Gregory Safford at Plenum.

Particular thanks should be given to the Chairman of the Research Committee, Normand Green. A special debt is owed to Salve Regina University which provided for every need during the course of the symposium. Special appreciation is due to our wives for their patience and encouragement.

Richard J. Niehaus
Karl F. Price

Contents

Introduction

Strategic Human Resource Issues

Empowering People at the Workforce Level

Restructuring/Right-sizing

Introduction

N.W. GREEN

"Bottom Line Results From Strategic Human Resource Planning" was the title of the fourth Research Symposium sponsored by the Research Committee of the Human Resource Planning Society. The symposium was presented June 11-14, 1991 at Salve Regina College, Newport, Rhode Island. More than two dozen papers were presented by the authors. Each presentation was followed by open discussion involving all participants. Twenty-two of the papers are presented in this volume.

The focus of the symposium was the presentation of written papers - followed by open discussion. The emphasis was on the evaluation of applications to show their impact on organization performance.

Dr. Karl F. Price of TPF&C was the Scientific Director who designed, organized, and conducted the program. Following the symposium, members of the Research Committee worked with Dr. Price and Dr. Richard Niehaus in selecting the papers and arranging them into five major subject areas:

    o Strategic Human Resource Issues,
    o Empowering People at the Workforce Level,
    o Restructuring/Right-sizing,
    o Managing People, and
    o Measuring the Impact on the Bottom Line.

In the first section "Strategic Human Resource Issues," four papers consider various aspects of human resource strategic issues. One of the papers gives feedback from the HRPS Corporate Sponsors Group. Two other papers talk about the relationship between the top human resources executive and the mainstream of the business. The fourth paper talks about workforce 2000 and relating the realities of marketplace dynamics to the building of that work group.

"Empowering People at the Workforce Level" is the title of the second section. The section focuses on management's efforts to give more. The five papers in the fourth section, "Managing People," strikes the broad theme of managers, their development, and how they relate to people in the management process. In the final section, "Measuring the Impact on the Bottom Line," the focus is broadly on HR programs and the differences they can make in organizational performance.

N.W. GREEN - Boyden World Corporation, 55 Madison Avenue, Morristown, NJ 07960

Bottom Line Results from Strategic Human Resource Planning
Edited by R.J. Niehaus and K.F. Price, Plenum Press, New York, 1991

Strategic Human Resource Issues

In the first paper presented, Karl Price was on "Strategic Human Resource Issues: Perceptions of the HRPS Corporate Sponsors." The paper describes a study undertaken by the HRPS Research Committee to assess the perceptions of senior human resource management executives in large North American organizations. These executives were asked about:

- o The external and internal forces of change in their organizations;
- o How their organizations are likely to respond to change, and;
- o How their HR function will respond to the shifting priorities of their organizations.

The respondents focused on:

- o Increased competition, both global and domestic;
- o The need to improve financial performance by increasing revenues and reducing costs, and;
- o Changes in the workforce and in key technologies.

"Building Global Labor Market Dynamics Into Workforce 2000" Atwater, Nelson and Niehaus describe fundamental Workforce 2000 themes and how they were developed. A proposed role for human resource forecasting is then presented. This methodology combines the identification of key events in the early 1990s and external labor market forecast model called Availability (AVAIL) system. Key analysis and findings of three different "tracks" are examined and presented using U.S. Department of Navy data. Finally, the lessons learned from the analysis are revisited so that other organizations can replicate the framework to generate guidelines of their own decision-making processes.

Koster and Schweiger's paper is entitled "Developing the Human Resource Executive as a Strategic Partner: Turning Concept Into Reality." They present a case study that illustrates from the perspective of senior executives and strategic planners the process of developing strategic human resource partnerships. While both authors have an extensive HR involvement, the case is presented from a non-HR perspective. The case is divided into six sections:

- o Background on the case organization;
- o Characteristics important in a strategic partner;
- o The organizational infrastructure needed to implement strategic human resource partners;
- o Measures and benchmarks of effective strategic human resource partners;
- o A definition of activities needed to pull the overall strategic human resource partner effort together, and;
- o Conclusions and recommendations for HR executives.

The final paper in the section "Powerful Partnerships: Linkages between HR and the Strategic Business Activities in the Delaware Valley" was presented by David W. Danner. The paper described research on the degree to which the trend toward an "integrated linkage" between HR and strategic business activity was reflected in well-regarded, high- performing Delaware Valley organizations. Data was collected from interviews conducted with key HR persons in six major organizations in the area. The data helped describe and illustrate that linkage, how it developed, and the values organizations said the linkage brought. Observation from the data may help human resource professionals to diagnose where their own or a client organization is, and to determine what conditions, strategies, or approaches might foster more integrated linkages.

Empowering People at the Workforce Level

The first paper in this section "Focusing Borden Employees on Continuous Improvement" is a case history written by Miller, Head, and Thomas. In 1988, Borden Inc. launched an ambitious drive to reduce costs by $100 million over the 1990-94 time span through its Safety, Quality, and Performance (SQP) program. SQP is a gain-sharing program which deals with practical things that employees can do something about. While SQP saved Borden more than $15 million in 1990 alone, it is not just a cost-saving thrust. SQP represents a real culture shift aimed at involving employees and managers in a partnership for the continuing improvement of the company. The focus is on investing in people to develop their potential.

This paper describes Borden's SQP program and the company's efforts to educate, involve, and train its workforce to embrace and support a philosophy of continuous improvement. Griggs and Manring in "The Bottom-Line of Empowerment" summarize their studies of empowerment programs in four organizations representing pharmaceutical, transportation, chemical coatings, and automotive electronics industries. Their analysis is based on a framework that focuses on three spheres of organization life: structural, cultural, and personal. The analysis provides insight into why empowerment efforts often fail to impact the bottom line as much as they should. The findings of this research provide managers and HR professionals with a greater understanding of how to institutionalize empowerment as a major platform for increasing organizational effectiveness and building competitive advantage.

In "Management Practices Leading to High Work Unit Performance," Gaertner and Nollen extend the work of those who have investigated organizational climate and performance. In this paper, they conduct their analysis at the work-unit level and incorporate prior performance into the analysis. The results show an absence of relationship between perception of fairness, equity, and participation of employees, and work-unit revenue performance. Another interesting suggested result is that managers can work to change the work-unit climate, independent of prior work-unit performance and have a positive effect on current performance.

Restructuring/Right-sizing

In "Management of a Major Downsizing at a Naval Shipyard," Aguilar, Niehaus, and Sharkey present a case history of downsizing at the Mare Island Naval Shipyard. During the 1988-1990 period, the Mare Island Naval Shipyard experienced a large overall workload reduction with intermediate periods of minor growth. Between 1987 and 1990, the workforce was reduced from 10,000 to 7,200 employees. A wide variety of personnel programs were used to facilitate the workload changes while providing a way for shipyard employees to maintain an orderly life. This paper provides an operational case study of the strategic and tactical actions which were taken before, during, and after the drawdown at the shipyard.

While there is no good way to reduce staffing in an organization with all the trauma which accompanies such a process, Robert V. Stonaker takes the view that there is a right way. In his paper "Voluntarily Excessing Employees: The Right Way to Downsize an Organization" he says that a strategic approach to this growing problem is absolutely required. This is true if management hopes to maintain integrity and consistent productivity during and after the process. What one company has learned is that these ends can only be achieved through a new management mindset and considerable human resource strategic planning. This case is about Metropolitan Property and Casualty, a small but emerging company in the property and casualty insurance business, and how it downsized its home office in 1990.

In "Implementing Organizational Change: An Ordinary Effort for an Extra-Ordinary Situation" Reynierse and Leyden tell the story of a merger, the steps taken to address problem areas, and the rapid improvement that occurred following the efforts. The case describes the acquisition of Long Island Trust Company by the Bank of New York in early 1987. This acquisition more than doubled the Bank of New York's asset and deposit base in the Long Island market. The two banks with widely different cultures began to experience high employee turnover, low employee morale, customer dissatisfaction, and an erosion of the profitability, assets and deposit base.

In "Staff Reduction and the Bottom Line: Less Is Not Always More" Greller and Dory take the position that theory and practice sometimes diverge. The approaches that businesses use to improve profitability in increasingly competitive markets are a case in point. Manager's actions seem to take place in a world separated from management theory and research. Under such circumstances, the effectiveness of the approaches used are rarely assessed. Manager's often take their support from anecdotal evidence - evidence often provided by people with an interest in justifying their own past decisions. Staff reductions role as a tool for productivity improvement and profitability is a case in point examined in this paper.

Managing People

Management attention is focusing on global issues and the challenges of worldwide competition. Efforts to operate globally have heightened interest in culture differences. A study, "A Cross-Cultural Study of Managerial Attitudes Toward Executive Development: Implications for Trans-National Organizations" by Beres, Portwood, Latib, Timmons, and Chowdhury explores cultural differences among senior managers of a single, trans-national corporation. The purpose of their study is to determine if shared development and direct interaction lead to convergent attitudes. Findings suggest that the convergence may occur at the general level, while differences remain at the specific level.

A management development strategy is suggested for raising the awareness of senior managers who ignore the cultural is attention toward or away from elements of reality, such as culture, HR development strategies can significantly influence management's strategic vision.

The business and labor environment of the 80s and early 90s has surfaced issues which have made traditional approaches to labor relations less effective. A slowing economy, increased domestic and offshore competition, and the changing demographics of organized labor are resulting in cooperative and creative approaches to restructuring organizations, redesigning jobs, compensating hourly employees, and providing job security. The responses of unions and management to this environment impact the design of jobs and corresponding skill and knowledge requirements for hourly workers.

Blanchard's paper is entitled, "Hourly Training Needs: The Bottom Line Reaches the Leading Edge." The paper describes an automotive component plant and a regional business unit of an international construction materials manufacturer. They are used as examples of how union and management can work together to redesign organizations and work systems meeting both company and union needs. The change, duties, and responsibilities of hourly employees, the process of developing training components, and the results of the training are described of a redesigned work place. The paper concludes with a discussion of the implication of these case studies for other organizations.

Since 1963, the Canadian Federal Government's Industrial Adjustment Service (IAS) has provided a model of change management based on joint labor-management committees. These committees are set up as a private sector initiative to resolve labor market adjustment issues at the firm, community, and sectorial levels.

These committees are chaired by neutral third parties. Employment and Immigration Canada shares the costs of the committees with the employers and furnishes technical support. Legislation and labor market adjustment approaches modeled on the IAS are now in place in the U.S. IAS consultants are on loan to countries in Eastern Europe and South America to help establish similar programs. The background and how the process works is described by Butcher in "Industrial Adjustment Service: A Canadian Model for Change Management."

In "Employee Pay Plan Preferences in a Bank" Atchison and Zumberge take the view that organizations need to find out how employees feel about systems used to determine how much they are paid. This paper describes a study conducted at an independent bank regarding employee pay preferences. The questionnaire used for the study asked employees to choose most desirable and least desirable options regarding four areas of compensation: wage setting, pay policy, increased decision, and pay form. Results show that:

1. These employees want their pay to be based on performance;
2. They have not been convinced that pay should be tied to the company's bottom-line results; and
3. It is important to keep pay competitive with similar jobs in the marketplace.

The landscape of American business changed dramatically during the 1980s. As companies and organizations looked to rest of the 90s, most are trying to adjust to a host of different forces. For some, this translates into finding ways to survive. For others, it means focusing on the impact of globalization. For still others, it may mean merely improving already strong business results to stay competitive.

Given the premise that a high level of employee commitment is critical for companies to succeed in the 1990s; that commitment now appears to be eroding in many organizations and that it is in need of a different focus, a limited participant study was undertaken. It's purpose was to explore the issue of effectively building and maintaining employee commitment. In this paper, "Employee Commitment: The Elusive Edge" Bugbee and Davis explored three dimensions of employee commitment:

o The business and human resource factors that appear to have the most impact on employee commitment - both positively and negatively.
o The influence and impact of organizational communications activity on enhancing employee commitments; and;
o The existence of any new "social contract" between the employee and the organization, and the role it plays in building and maintaining employee commitment.

While leaders of many organizations perceive a need to have a high degree of employee commitment, honing that competitive edge has proven to be a difficult task. This study was aimed at finding answers that could help as organizations strive for that elusive edge.

Measuring the Impact on the Bottom Line

Human resource functions are using effectiveness and efficiency measures to identify needed improvements in HR practices. Efficiency measures show that HR actions maximize results with minimum input. Effectiveness measures show that results and actions are addressing important people-related business issues. Efficiency measures are primarily quantative (e.g., cost, response time, and output volume) and relate results to short-term HR activities. Effectiveness measures are more often qualitative and relate results to implementation of strategies. Often the best measures of effectiveness lie in managerial perceptions of how the HR functions fit with strategic issues and plans, its service quality and level of expense. These perceptions can be measured and presented quantatively, be must be interpreted using sound business judgment. Walker and Bechet described the measures in the paper "Defining Effectiveness and Efficiency Measures in the Context of Human Resource Strategy."

Schneier, Beatty, and Shaw in "Why Measure the CEO's Performance?" indicate their research shows that only 14 percent of companies evaluate CEO's individual performance. The majority relies instead on organization level financial results to infer how effectively the CEO performs. Yet, the studies regularly show little relationship between a CEO's compensation and the corporation's financial results. A key question then becomes, what are the CEO's accountabilities?

The authors argue that a CEO's individual performance impacts company performance and culture and can and should be measured. First, the CEO's role has broadened beyond strategy setting to include articulating a strategic vision. Second, his/her leadership, as distinct from management, skill has been shown to shape company culture and resultant financial performance. In addition, data shows that both CEO's and boards believe non-financial aspects of a CEO's performance to be critical to the CEO's success. Yet, too often the board's culture, politics and composition defer candid CEO performance appraisal. Examples are cited in the paper of CEOs who see their role as a strategic actor and values disseminator, not merely a strategic planner. Performance of their companies versus industry averages demonstrates the positive financial impact of this view of the CEO role.

In "Company Values: A Key to Managing Organizations in Turbulent Times"
McLaughlin, McLaughlin, and Lischick present a paper with four major themes:

o A company's values and beliefs are a pivotal element in its survival
  and success;
o Formal statements of values and beliefs include a wide range of
  philosophical and pragmatic material than can be analyzed and
  compared within an industry and across industry lines;
o Organizations with strong values - companies that are truly
  value-driven - outperform their competitors; and
o Successful companies appear to have distinctive values and beliefs.

The paper is presented in four parts:

o Drawing upon a three-year study of 555 large public companies,
  the first section describes the approaches companies take to
  formally state their values and beliefs;
o The second section summarizes the valuable evidence on the
  relationship of values and beliefs to performance;
o The third section presents preliminary findings on the differences
  on the prevalence and scope of the values aspired to by most
  successful companies in four industries; and
o The final section covers the unique role that values and beliefs
  can play in corporate revitalizations and illustrates the prevalence
  of statements and values in companies that achieved a turnaround
  between 1985 and 1989.

Quality programs have become an integral part of doing business in both manufacturing and service industries. Firms marketing their quality programs as part of their general advertising campaigns (e.g., Ford Quality No. 1). The use of automated manufacturing systems, just in time inventory systems, and inter-active data bases requires a high level of precision and data accuracy. Manufacturing firms are requiring their suppliers to meet stringent quality specifications. Additionally, consumers have increased their expectations about quality of such good they purchase and services they receive. Retailers such as Nordstroms's have successfully entered new markets in part because of their reputation for providing a high level of customer services. Many companies such as Rockwell International have developed quality improvement programs based on customer input.

Another aspect of the quality issue is the introduction and awarding of the Malcolm Baldridge Award established in 1987 by an act of Congress. Some firms require their suppliers to apply for the Malcolm Baldridge Quality Award. Although first established for manufacturing firms, the Baldridge Award has recently been extended to services industries as well. In order to explore the types of quality programs being offered by firms in manufacturing and services industries and to determine what role HR managers have taken in these firms, a study was sponsored by the HRPS and funded by Weyerhauser and the Equitable Corporation. The paper "Quality of Output Programs for Manufacturing and Service Industries" by Verdin and Pagano is a result of that study.

Since the initiation of a major new workforce planning effort in 1988, New York State has come a long way in developing the capacity needed to conduct long-range HR planning and analysis. One of the most practical and far-reaching efforts has been the development of a comprehensive workforce information system. This database is described, including several applications which have had a clear impact on the "bottom line." A scan of the environment which percipitated a need for this focused effort is presented. The final section of the paper "Workforce Analysis and Turnover Forecasting: Building Capacity in New York State Government" by Teigland focuses on turnover analysis and forecasting which has significant savings potential.

Heinrich's paper is on "Survey Data as a Catalyst for Employee Empowerment and Organizational Effectiveness." The paper outlines what current research and practice show about the relationship between employee commitment or attitudes, as measured by employee surveys and on-the-job performance of a workforce. It then suggests and illustrates how the level of employee commitment can have a very significant impact on the bottom line results of today's organizations. Finally, criteria for an effective employee survey, and particularly an effective process of systematically feeding back survey results to employees and involving them in the development of action strategies, is presented as a powerful management tool for achieving these bottom-line returns.

Conclusion

From the papers presented in this volume, it has been shown that bottom-line results are being produced from strategic human resource planning and implementaton efforts. Properly conceived and with appropriate senior management support, the efforts described in the twenty-two papers presented here do make a tangible contribution to the organization. These efforts are of central importance to the well being to the organization.

Strategic Human Resource Issues

This section presents four papers which consider aspects of strategic issues in the human resource management process. **Price** describes a study undertaken by the HRPS Research Committee to assess the perceptions of senior human resource executives regarding key issues facing their organizations. The respondents -- the HRPS corporate sponsors -- focused on: (1) increased competition, (2) the need to improve financial performance by increasing revenues and reducing costs, and (3) changes in the workforce and key technologies.

In the next paper **Atwater, Nelson** and **Niehaus** describe fundamental workforce 2000 themes. They propose a role for human resource forecasting and present analysis of three different "tracks" using U.S. Navy data. They conclude with a review of lessons learned from the analysis showing that one must periodically revist long term forecasts to capture significant changes to strategic assumptions.

The next paper is a case history by **Koster** and **Schweiger** that illustrates, from a senior executive viewpoint, the development of a strategic human resource partnership. The case is presented from a non-human resource perspective, which can be useful to the human resource practitioner in better understanding the senior management perspective.

The final paper, a case history presented by **Danner**, describes the different roles played by human resources in well regarded, high performing, Delaware Valley (Pennsylvania and New Jersey) organizations. Observations from the data may help human resource professionals in understanding better their current situation and of other roles that might by played in their organizations.

Strategic Human Resource Issues: Perceptions of the Human Resource Planning Society Corporate Sponsors

KARL F. PRICE

Introduction

This study was undertaken by the HRPS Research Committee to assess the perceptions of senior human resource management executives in large North American organizations about:

- o the external and internal forces of change in their organizations,
- o how their organizations are likely to respond to change, and
- o how their human resource function will respond to the shifting priorities of their organizations.

The HRPS Organizational Sponsors were selected as the sample for the survey. They represent a cross-section of large corporate organizations that, because of their sponsorship of HRPS, are likely to be concerned and enlightened about strategic human resource issues.

A questionnaire was developed by the Research Committee and administered by mail to all 105 Corporate Sponsors in late Summer of 1990. Sixty questionnaires were returned, a response rate of 57 percent. A review of the study demographics (Table 1) shows that the most of the respondents represented large organizations. Sixty-six percent had employee populations of over 15,000 employees and forty-six percent had revenues of $5 billion or more. Almost half were largely domestic, but twenty-seven percent had 30 percent or more of their employees outside of their home country. The majority of the responses represented the entire corporate entity, with only 18 percent representing a division of a larger organization.

Karl F. Price - TPF&C, 1500 Market Street, Philadelphia, PA 19102

Table 1: Demographics

	Number	%
Organization Unit		
Division	11	18%
Total organization	49	82
	60	100%
Number of Employees		
5,000 or less	9	15%
5,001 - 15,000	10	17
15,001 - 30,000	17	28
30,001 - 50,000	8	13
50,001 - 75,000	3	5
75,001 - 100,000	6	10
Over 100,000	6	10
No Response	1	2
	60	100%
Revenues		
Under $500 million	5	8%
$500 million to $5 billion	23	39
$5 billion to $25 billion	20	33
Over $25 billion	8	13
No Response	4	7
	60	100%
Employees Outside Home Country		
10% or less	26	44%
10% - 20%	5	8
20% - 30%	5	8
30% - 40%	9	15
40% - 50%	4	7
Over 50%	3	5
No Response	8	13
	60	100%

Findings

Forces of Change

When asked to identify and rank the importance of some of the internal and external forces facing their organizations, the respondents focused on:

- o increased competition, both global and domestic,
- o the need to improve financial performance by increasing revenues and reducing costs, and
- o changes in the work force and in key technologies.

Figure 1 displays the forces of change, showing with the bars the percentage of respondents who indicated that the force was ranked among the five most important. In addition a weighted score is shown to indicate the strength of the rankings. The score is calculated by assigning 5 points to a rank of 1, 4 points for a rank of 2, and so on to 1 point for a rank of 5, and then summing all the points. For example, in comparing the fourth and fifth ranked factors, we see that 33 percent ranked increased domestic competition as one of the top five factors while 57 percent

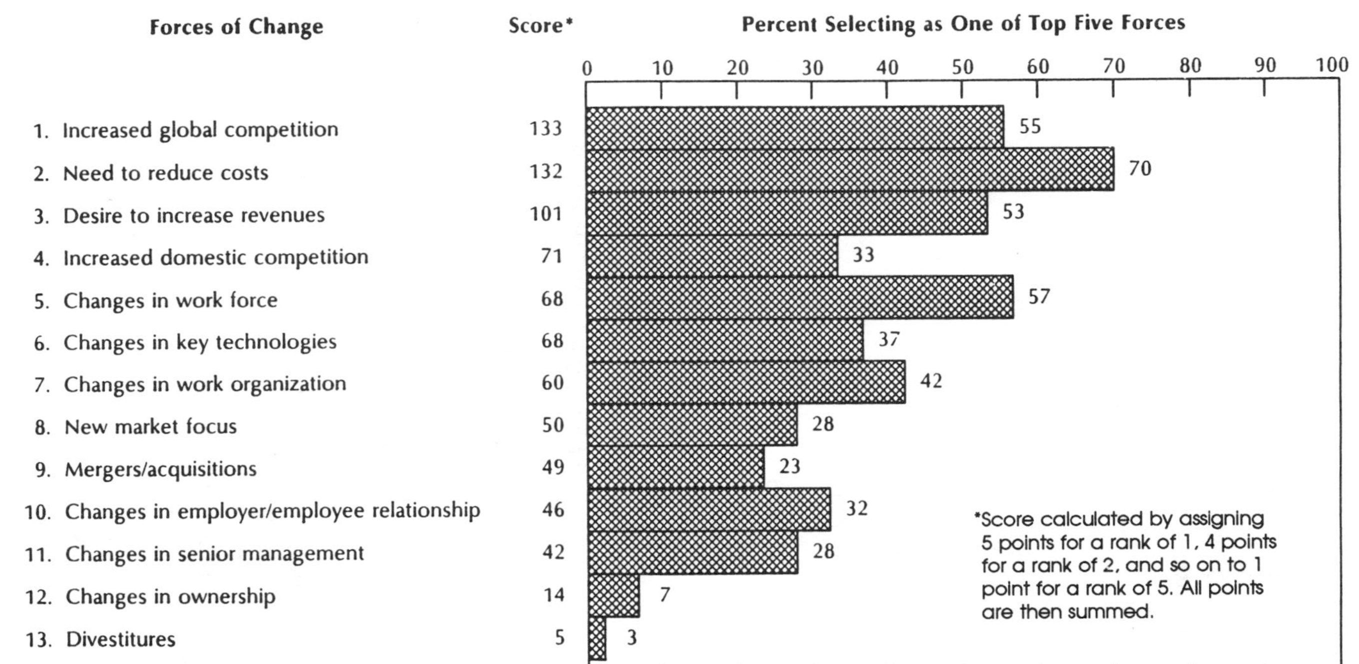

Figure 1: Forces of Change

ranked changes in the work force as one of their top five. Nonetheless, increased domestic competition has a higher score (71) than changes in the work force (68) because those who ranked it in the top five ranked it higher. For this group of organizations; mergers, acquisitions, divestitures and changes in ownership are down toward the bottom of the list.

When the demographics (Table 2) are analyzed for this question, no clear pattern is evident. An attempt was undertaken to determine if there were differences by performance by examining revenues per employee. Unfortunately, the information on industry group was not specific enough to be able to compare enough organizations within specific industries.

Organizational Response to Change

When asked to rank how their organizations were most likely to respond to anticipated pressure for change (Figure 2), the human resource executives believe that their organizations would focus on:

- o improving quality,
- o increasing productivity,
- o expanding markets both at home and abroad, and
- o lowering overhead and labor costs.

Almost three quarters of respondents indicated that improving quality and increasing productivity would be among the most likely responses that their organizations would take. Most of the other responses received a fair amount of support except for outsourcing and moving production overseas.

When the responses by demographic category (Table 3) are examined there is a fair degree of consistency across the demographic categories. The top five responses have almost universal applicability for the respondents.

Human Resource Issues

Given the importance their organizations are likely to place on improving quality and productivity, it is not surprising to find to find them listed among the top five human resource issues (See Figure 3). While 72% of respondents selected improving quality as one of the top five organizational responses, only 42% identified it as one of the top five human resource issues. This seemingly low response is contradicted by the fact that focusing on quality is expected to increase significantly over the next 2-3 years (See Figure 4).

Survey responses suggest that human resource executives believe that the key to achieving their human resource objectives, including improved quality and productivity, is through (a) attracting and retaining quality employees and (b) increasing employee involvement. The respondents also recognized the universal issue of health care cost control. They placed control of benefits costs as the second most important human resource issue facing them today.

As with the Forces of Change, there are wide differences in responses to the top five human resource issues (Table 4). Ranked six, seven and eight are issues that deal with the upgrading and development of talent at all levels of management. Respondents indicated that in today's competitive environment it is more important to improve management skills than worker skills.

Table 2: Forces of Change

Percent Selecting as One of Top Five Forces

Forces	Total Sample	Structure		Revenues				Employees						
		Div	Total Org	< 500M	500M-5B	5B-25B	> 25B	Up To 5,000	5,001 15,000	15,001 30,000	30,001 50,000	50,001 75,000	75,001 100,000	Over 100,000
1. Global competition	55%	45%	57%	20%	65%	50%	50%	55%	10%	53%	87%	67%	50%	83%
2. Reduce costs	70	91	65	60	70	60	87	55	90	82	37	100	67	33
3. Increase revenues	53	55	53	60	59	60	27	66	60	59	37	67	17	67
4. Domestic competition	33	36	33	20	35	25	62	22	30	35	50	33	17	33
5. Changes in work force	57	64	55	60	52	45	75	44	80	41	50	67	50	83

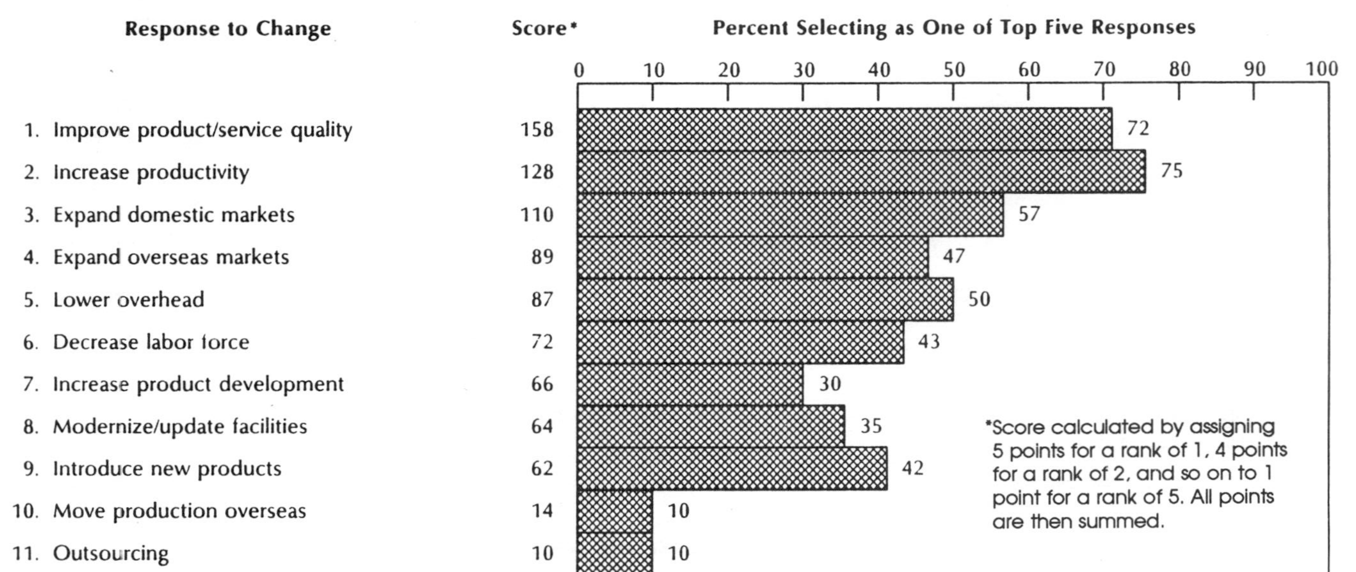

Figure 2: Organizational Response to Change

Table 3: Organizational Response to Change

Percent Selecting as One of Top Five Organizational Responses

Response	Total Sample	Structure		Revenues				Employees						
		Div	Total Org	< 500M	500M-5B	5B-25B	> 25B	Up To 5,000	5,001 15,000	15,001 30,000	30,001 50,000	50,001 75,000	75,001 100,000	Over 100,000
1. Improve quality	72%	64%	74%	80%	61%	80%	75%	67%	80%	59%	75%	100%	50%	100%
2. Increase productivity	75	82	73	100	65	70	100	89	90	59	75	67	67	83
3. Expand domestic markets	57	55	57	60	74	40	62	67	60	53	75	67	50	17
4. Expand overseas markets	47	45	47	20	52	60	25	33	20	49	75	67	83	33
5. Lower overhead	50	64	47	60	43	50	50	44	60	53	25	67	33	66

Figure 3: Human Resource Issues

Table 4: Human Resource Issues

Percent Selecting as One of Top Five HR Issues

HR Issues	Total Sample	Structure		Revenues				Employees						
		Div	Total Org	< 500M	500M-5B	5B-25B	> 25B	Up To 5,000	5,001 15,000	15,001 30,000	30,001 50,000	50,001 75,000	75,001 100,000	Over 100,000
1. Attract and retain quality employees	55%	64%	53%	60%	61%	40%	75%	55%	50%	53%	62%	100%	67%	33%
2. Control benefit costs	52	64	49	40	52	45	75	55	50	47	62	37	67	33
3. Increase employee involvement	47	46	49	20	56	55	25	33	50	53	62	0	50	50
4. Improve product quality	42	10	49	60	39	50	25	44	50	23	50	33	17	83
5. Improve employee efficiency	42	36	43	60	30	50	50	55	30	41	37	0	67	50

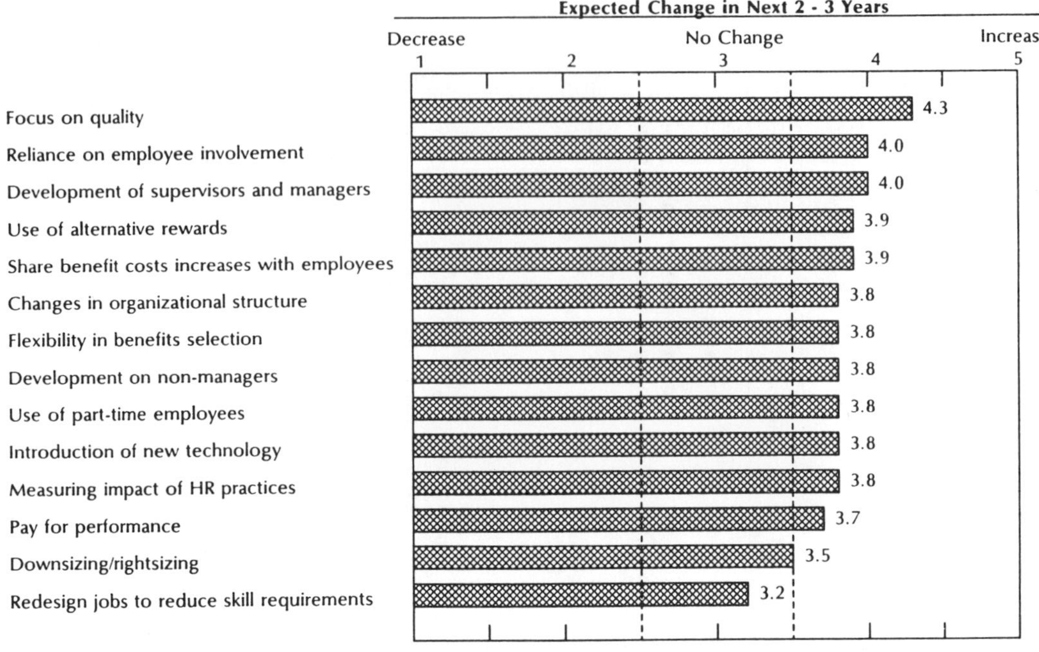

Figure 4: Approaches to Human Resource Management

Effort Expected to be Expended on Human Resource Activities

Respondents were asked to estimate how much effort will be expended on human resource management activities. They indicated that they expect to be expending more effort on almost all aspects of human resource management (See Figure 5). There is a good match between the top eight human resource issues and top eight activities that human resource executives expect to be expending more effort on over the next 2-3 years. The correlation is not perfect, because there is little variance on the effort expended. Nonetheless, the human resource executives responding to this survey seem to have internalized the issues facing them. They are allocating their resources to address the important issues.

Approaches to Human Resource Management

The human resource executives expect the next several years to be characterized by a significant amount of change (Figure 4). At the top of the list they expect an increased focus on quality throughout their organizations. The human resource executives surveyed also see an increase in the reliance on employee involvement, and to support this, an increase in the use of alternative rewards. They see increased effort spent in developing managers and supervisors to equip them to manage effectively in the changing human resource arena. Benefit costs -- an issue that simply will not go away, will demand increased attention as organizations attempt to share the increasing cost of benefits with employees.

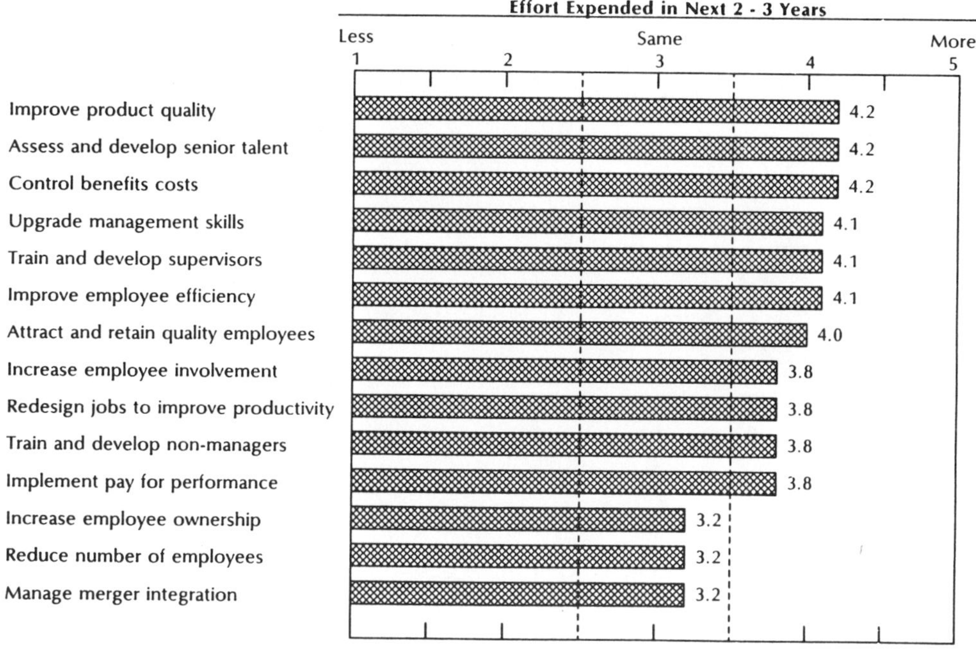

Figure 5 Effort Expected to be Expended on HR Activities

Respondents expect to face more change. They expect to expend more effort on a wide range of human resource activities in the face of organizational efforts to reduce corporate staffs.

Strategic HR Issues

It is clear that human resource executives have a major job ahead of them. They are being asked to make their organizations more responsive to the ever changing demands being placed on their businesses. They are being asked to focus on issues, like quality and productivity that historically were seen as line management issues. Organizations represented by respondents to this survey believe that the way to enhanced quality and productivity is through a high quality, involved and motivated work force. The respondents recognize their role in dealing with the basic strategic issues facing their firms. They are planning to expend the efforts of their functions on "the right things."

Building Local Labor Market Dynamics into Workforce 2000

D.M. ATWATER, J.A. NELSON, and R.J. NIEHAUS

The Building Blocks

During the mid-1980s executives and managers began to develop interest in the work force as it would exist in the year 2000. The Hudson Institute study, which was sponsored by the Department of Labor, entitled *Workforce 2000*, created an awareness that labor markets were going to be dramatically different. (See the Hudson Institute and Department of Labor (1987)). Some organizations even began to develop human resource plans to address key Workforce 2000 themes so they would have the time to make needed changes. One of the themes from Workforce 2000 which got addressed very early was to improve the basic communication skills of Hispanic workers. Since these early studies were fifteen years before the end of the century, the themes presented were often broad enough to withstand the test of time. Some of the themes presented for Workforce 2000 are already visible today.

Events are developing in the early 1990s which will certainly affect the degree of change firms will see by the year 2000. Events such as the Gulf War, cuts in federal programs and staffing, and the proposed Civil Rights Act are recognized as agents of change for the decade. While the themes from Workforce 2000, such as projected shortages of skilled workers, are still valid, some organizations seeking skilled workers may well find relief in the experienced workers being laid off by the Federal Government. Human resource planning scenarios are being reviewed and revised to include key events and their impact on bottom line programs.

Human resource forecasting also has a role to play in human resource planning for the work force in the year 2000. Counts of available workers within defined salary levels in local labor markets are being generated and used as bottom line human resource data for revisiting recruitment, training and development programs. Taking different planning views every three years has provided the U.S. Department of the Navy with information on the dynamics of local labor markets.

This paper illustrates how the themes from *Workforce 2000*, events from the early 1990s, and the dynamics of local labor markets, can be combined. At the

---

D.M. ATWATER, J.A. NELSON - William M. Mercer, Inc., 3303 Wilshire Blvd. Los Angeles, CA 90010; R.J. NIEHAUS - Office of the Chief of Naval Operations (OP-16H), Washington, DC 20370

Bottom Line Results from Strategic Human Resource Planning
Edited by R.J. Niehaus and K.F. Price, Plenum Press, New York, 1991

analytical level, these three components form "tracks" which can be used to analyze the effectiveness of recruitment, hiring, training and development.

This paper initially describes the fundamental Workforce 2000 themes and how they were developed. A proposed role for human resource forecasting is then presented. It combines the identification of key events from the early 1990s and an external labor market forecasting model, called the Availability (AVAIL) system. Key analyses and findings for the three different "tracks" are examined and presented using U.S. Department of the Navy data. Finally, the lessons learned from the analyses are revisited so that other organizations can replicate the framework to generate guidelines for their own decision making processes.

Workforce 2000 Themes

According to a recent study of work force planning among a group of "best in class" organizations, the trend in human resource planning is to address the needs of operating business units. (See William M. Mercer (October 1990)). In corporate America, this emphasis is consistent with: a one year forecasting horizon, clearer linkages between a business unit's strategic plan and a human resource plan, and a focused job classification structure to track human resources. Corporate human resource forecasting and planning functions are becoming more support service oriented. Corporate HR departments are focusing on program development when either multiple business units have common planning needs or longer term human resource issues have relevance to several business units. With such a short term orientation it is unusual to find concurrently an interest in topics related to the year 2000. Yet the level of activity has also grown over the last five years.

The Hudson Institute is recognized as starting the effort to examine changing market conditions when it completed a milestone study entitled *Workforce 2000*. The findings were published for the Department of Labor in 1987. Six strategic themes were cited to guide firms toward the year 2000:

o Stimulating World Growth,
o Improving Productivity in Service Industries,
o Improving the Dynamics of an Aging Workforce,
o Reconciling the Needs of Women, Work, and Families,
o Integrating Blacks and Hispanics Fully into the Workforce, and
o Improving Workers' Education and Skills.

While these, and other themes, are interesting and challenging, bottom line programs in companies based on such concepts require substantial interpretation. For example, Figure 1 from the Hudson Institute provides a view of expected declines in "low skilled jobs". The figure references a series of representative jobs with different skill ratings. The higher skilled jobs (3.5 and above) are shown to increase more than proportionately by the year 2000 while those below this threshold show decline. The lower the skill ratings of the jobs the larger the decline. The data presented requires interpretation to rate the skills of jobs and to determine the future needs for workers with different skills. While new jobs, or demand for workers, may be greater for higher skilled jobs, the relevance to the bottom line can differ from employer to employer.

The overall picture painted by the Hudson Institute was one of very dramatic changes in labor markets. In fact, the changes were so important that several additional follow-up studies were conducted. For example, the U.S. Department of

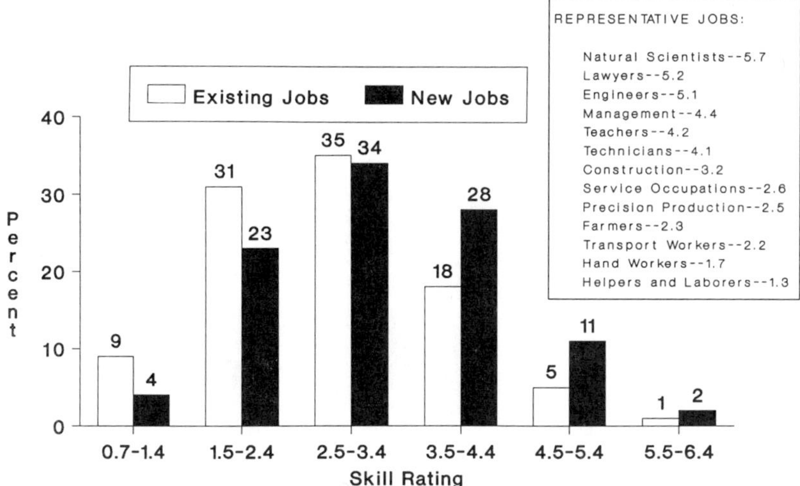

Figure 1: Expected Distribution of Jobs by Skill Rating Groups; (Source: Hudson Institute *Workforce 2000*)

Labor commissioned a study entitled *Opportunity 2000* and the U.S. Office of Personnel Management (OPM) sponsored the *Civil Service 2000* study.

The *Opportunity 2000* study listed eight factual themes to assist firms in developing their strategies for the 1990s:

o The Number of Workers Will Fall,
o The Average Age of Workers Will Rise,
o More Women Will Be On the Job,
o One-Third of New Workers Will Be Minorities,
o There Will Be More Immigrants Than Any Time
   Since World War I,
o Most New Jobs Will Be In Services and Information,
o The New Jobs Will Require Higher Skills, and
o The Challenges for Business Will Be Immense.

The Hudson Institute also identified how companies could adapt to the coming "revolution" by modifying work schedules and building specific programs for minorities, women, disabled workers, older workers, and veterans. Many bottom line human resource programs were suggested for consideration by companies.

Consistent with these themes, the *Civil Service 2000* study proposed possible programmatic responses of federal government agencies. The Department of the Navy has also done an analysis of its historical personnel data to understand better the implementation of the *Civil Service 2000* study.

A final wave of Workforce 2000 activity came from consulting companies. Studies by the Hay Group and Towers Perrin presented programmatic themes which recorded what actions or human resource programs were being put in place by corporate America. These efforts took the pulse of corporate responses to demographic and labor force trends. (See Hay Group (1990) and Spectrum (1990)).

The composite definition of Workforce 2000 used in this paper is actually a "short list" of topics compiled by William M. Mercer from its Workforce 2000

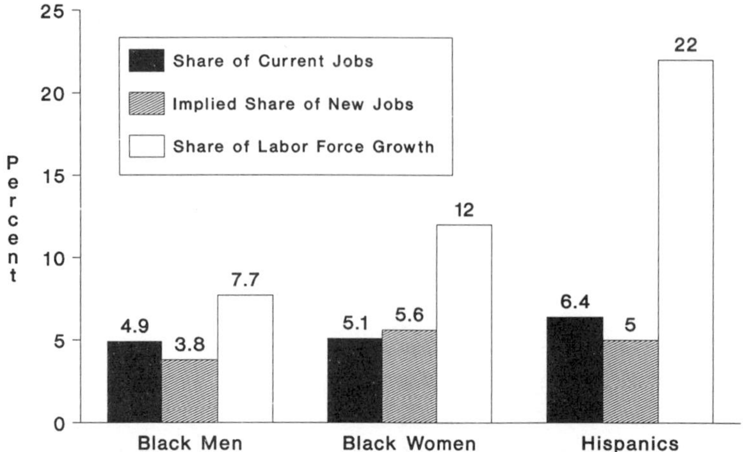

Figure 2: Labor Market Job Representation Levels for Selected Race-Groups by the Year 2000; (Source: Hudson Institute *Workforce 2000*)

seminar participants. (See William M. Mercer (August, 1990)). In the year 2000, planners predict that the work environment will be characterized by:

o Key shortages of skilled workers,
o Divergent quality of life, income and life prospects, and
o A culturally diverse workforce.

Each of these themes can be associated with earlier Workforce 2000 statements. For example, Figure 2 taken from the Hudson Institute's and Department of Labor's Executive Summary (1990), illustrates an important dimension of a more culturally diverse workforce. The chart shows that Black men and Hispanic men are not expected to get a proportionate share of new job opportunities. Their relative lack of work skills will disqualify them from new job opportunities. If these difficulties occur, they will contribute to the "have and have not" bi-polarization that is predicted for the work force in the year 2000. The challenge to firms in increasingly Black and Hispanic labor markets is how to find or train internally "qualified" Black and Hispanic men.

For women, divergent income has been documented by calculating average compensation levels relative to men. The lack of change in the average compensation ratio by sex and the means to reduce differences have been examined throughout the 1980s. (See Rosenblum (1979) and Slocum (1985)). The theme remains an important component of Workforce 2000.

These studies and numerous seminars tended to set *Workforce 2000* apart from other futuristic milestones. After re-reading the studies, the themes are insightful but very broad. Some of the themes, such as more women will be in the work force and the majority of the new jobs will be in services and information, are not really new. The historical legacy of *Workforce 2000* is likely to be that it afforded the nation an opportunity to compile and document the fundamental patterns of change in labor markets and set a point in time when they would be critically important.

A Proposed Role for Human Resource Forecasting

It is our contention that human resource planning and forecasting can be used to quantify specific job movements in local labor markets related to Workforce 2000 themes. Human resource forecasting logically follows behind and supports clarification of Workforce 2000 themes. Three actions have proven useful in developing human resource programs which can be linked to HR programs that directly affect the bottom line:

1. Build a "short list" of three key Workforce 2000 themes around which management can rally;
2. For each theme, identify at least one current external event which will affect how much can be accomplished around the theme; and
3. Generate or collect human resource forecasting information which addresses the theme when it is viewed through the external event.

Human resource planning activities thus aim to determine the speed and diversity of change for different occupations, locations and race and sex groups highlighted by Workforce 2000.

Taking the three themes from Workforce 2000 and identifying the business challenges associated with them is not a generic process. Organizations operate with a different mix of jobs/occupations, operate in different labor markets, and have different profiles of diversity in the work force. Each of the three themes identified by management needs to be focused on the organization's specific human resource situation.

The second action is to find at least one current external event which will affect the Workforce 2000 themes. These events are important because the time horizon for Workforce 2000 is almost ten years in the future while organizations are increasingly looking to take actions during their next operating cycle. The planned bottom line results, in order to be achieved, must be able to withstand numerous adjustments from outside events over the next decade. Progress will be affected by events outside the control of business units.

There is no master list of external key events which are important to all employers. the three events chosen for analysis and discussion in this paper are:

1. The availability of skilled workers from Department of Defense cutbacks;
2. The under-representation of females in higher decision-making jobs being studied by the Glass Ceiling Commission; and
3. The challenge to seniority systems from the proposed Civil Rights Act of 1991.

The analyses and findings presented here do not represent official or actual Navy plans to close specific facilities. This paper reflects no official position by the Department of the Navy or William M. Mercer on the content of the proposed 1991 Civil Rights Act or on the Glass Ceiling Commission contention that underrepresentation is present in the work force. The main purpose of this paper is to show a methodology to analyze these complex issues.

External Key Events

Shortage of Skilled Workers

The Department of Defense is developing a program to cut back on its military and civilian forces. In April 1991 base closings were announced for 31 installations. (See Weekly Federal Employees News Digest (April 1991)). Workforce 2000 themes predict increased shortages in skilled scientists, engineers, and technician jobs. When Workforce 2000 projections were originally being made, defense cutbacks were not considered. Even today, many communities are voicing concerns about the economic impacts of reductions in force and base closing on their economies. The potential upside of these reductions has not been explored. With more skilled workers leaving the Federal Government payrolls, the shortages in labor markets could be dampened. The role of human resource forecasting, in this case, is to provide information on local labor markets which can be used to examine the net effects of such reductions in force on skilled job shortages in the future.

Women in Higher Level Jobs

The underrepresentation of minorities and women in senior decision-making jobs is also being examined by the Glass Ceiling Commission of the House Education and Labor Committee. (See The Bureau of National Affairs (March 1991)). One of the key Workforce 2000 challenges is to build new work environments using flexible time and part-time workers to accommodate the increasing numbers of women in the work force.   Such efforts are not necessarily consistent with increasing the numbers of women in high decision-making jobs. Progress or change in this area is linked to reducing the differences in income between women and men.

The role of human resource planning, in this case, is to assess whether the glass ceiling is a myth or a reality. Where it is a reality, differences across geographic areas and job opportunities can be examined to focus human resource programs on business unit specific programs. Once again generic solutions are not expected to be useful to organizations.

Work Force Diversity

The proposed Civil Rights Act (CRA) of 1991 seeks to strengthen the protections offered under the original Civil Rights Act passed in 1964. (See Bureau of National Affairs (March, 1991)). One of the key provisions of the proposed 1991 CRA is the right to challenge discriminatory seniority systems. The movements of women and minorities into craft and operative jobs, where union seniority systems have historically dampened entry, is analyzed later in this paper. Trends from Workforce 2000 generally show increased availability for women and minorities in craft and operative jobs when limited numbers of new jobs will be created by companies in the next decade. In such cases, the role of human resource forecasting is to pinpoint where business realities and political/social pressures are real and high.

A selected number of themes from Workforce 2000 can realistically be examined because the effort required to do so is substantial. Current events will both accelerate and dampen the effects throughout the planning period. The roles of human resource forecasting differ for varying themes and events. Two common roles for human resource forecasting have consistently occurred. The first is to improve the ability of organizations to achieve specific business unit results. The second is to picture the dynamics of the decade ahead as a moving target.

Forecasting Methodology

The human resource forecasting methodology and tools used to study local labor market dynamics in this paper are not new. (See Atwater, Bres, Niehaus and Sheridan (1983)). The specific human resource forecasting tools are called external local labor market models. External local labor market models require detailed definitions of key concepts to be developed. The definitions provided here include: local labor markets, target groups, measurement calculations and dynamics.

In this paper, local labor markets can be either metropolitan areas or regional areas. External models estimate qualified worker and non-worker counts and representation ratios of race-sex groups within a local labor market. In contrast, Workforce 2000 themes and most external events are discussed and presented on a national level.

A specific set of jobs, human resource groups, such as race-sex groups, and a predefined forecasting horizon, such as 1996, are also prepared for the external local labor market models. Unlike Workforce 2000 groups, the jobs used in this paper are business unit specific.

Finally, a well-defined forecasting calculation is used. Availability ratios are calculated for a job group as the number of available persons in a target group divided by the total number of available persons in the local labor market. Target groups are further defined to focus on race-sex subgroups. Three points are important to remember about labor market availability measures:

1. Both workers who meet experience and wage qualifications for jobs and non-workers who are occupationally qualified and find offered wages attractive enough to begin work are counted as available;
2. Availability ratios are a closed system. If one race-sex group's numbers decrease, other groups must increase so that 100% is always the bottom line; and
3. Availability results change based on any of the definition components: geographic area, jobs defined, wages offered, forecasting timeframe, and target groups identified.

Whereas availability is a useful measure for forecasting it is not necessarily a "stand alone" labor market measure. Because it can be affected by a combination of factors including wages, geographic migration, and graduation rates from educational institutions, analyses often require more detailed follow-up analyses. It is used here because it is a proven front-end forecasting measure which is flexible enough to bridge Workforce 2000 themes and defined events. More detailed forecasting methods, such as best fit goal programming, have been used by the Department of the Navy to complete the forecasting. (See Niehaus (1978, 1985)).

Throughout this paper, we refer to the dynamics of local labor markets. The dynamics we refer to are drawn from changes in availability ratios based on projections from different points in the last decade. As shown in the findings section, important changes in local labor markets occurred between 1983 and 1985 when much of the data was being collected and analyzed for the Hudson Institute study.

There were significant changes from 1986 to 1988. In this paper, the dynamics of local labor markets refer to recorded differences between these two periods.

Human resource forecasting results used in this paper were generated using the U.S. Navy Department's Availability (AVAIL) external labor market modeling system. (For methodology see Atwater (1988)). This system is part of the Civilian Occupation Planning Estimates System (COPES). (See Atwater, Bres, Nelson and Niehaus (1988)). Descriptions of methodology, data sources, modeling variables and reports from the AVAIL system are not repeated in this document.

Because dynamics of local labor markets are the focus of this paper, two different sets of forecasting data were generated and compared. Figure 3 shows the basic comparison. In simple terms, the AVAIL model calculates external labor market results using a baseline Census snapshot for 1980, a growth calculation from a three year series of Current Population Survey (CPS) data, and Navy wage data for a benchmark period.

As shown in Figure 3, two views of external labor market conditions in 1996 were generated using the AVAIL system. The "early" view was based on growth factors calculated from the 1983-1985 CPS files. The "late" view followed by three years (1986-1988). The dynamics of local labor markets reflect differences in 1996 based on the "late" versus "early" results.

It should be noted that the next planned update of this analytical framework is expected to involve the replacement of the 1980 EEO file with the updated 1990 Census (EEO) file and another three year series of CPS files. This analytical milestone will focus on revalidation of the AVAIL model. A project is underway to separate numerical differences due to CPS data errors from "real" local labor market dynamics. As part of this analysis, the target projection date will be pushed out to the year 2000 and three comparisons will be made (the 1983-85 view, the 1986-1988 view and the new 1990 Census (EEO) base with a 1991-1993 view).

Analysis and Findings

A "track" is formed by the combination of a Workforce 2000 theme, at least one major current event and dynamic labor market information. The tracks provide decision-makers with information to develop bottom line results through specific human resource programs.

The three tracks analyzed in this paper are shown in Figure 4. A specific track is identified by reading across a line. For example, the first track addresses:

o Workforce 2000 theme: Shortage of Skilled Workers;
o 1991 Key Event: Navy Civilian RIFs of Skilled Workers; and
o Dynamic Local Labor Market Data: Groups of technicians in salary bands in over 60 local labor markets.

The second track addresses the divergent income theme for women. It seeks to determine if under-representation of women in high-level decision- making jobs is a myth or reality. The third track focuses on the cultural diversity in the work force. Specific bottom line results are cited for each of the tracks in the findings section of this paper.

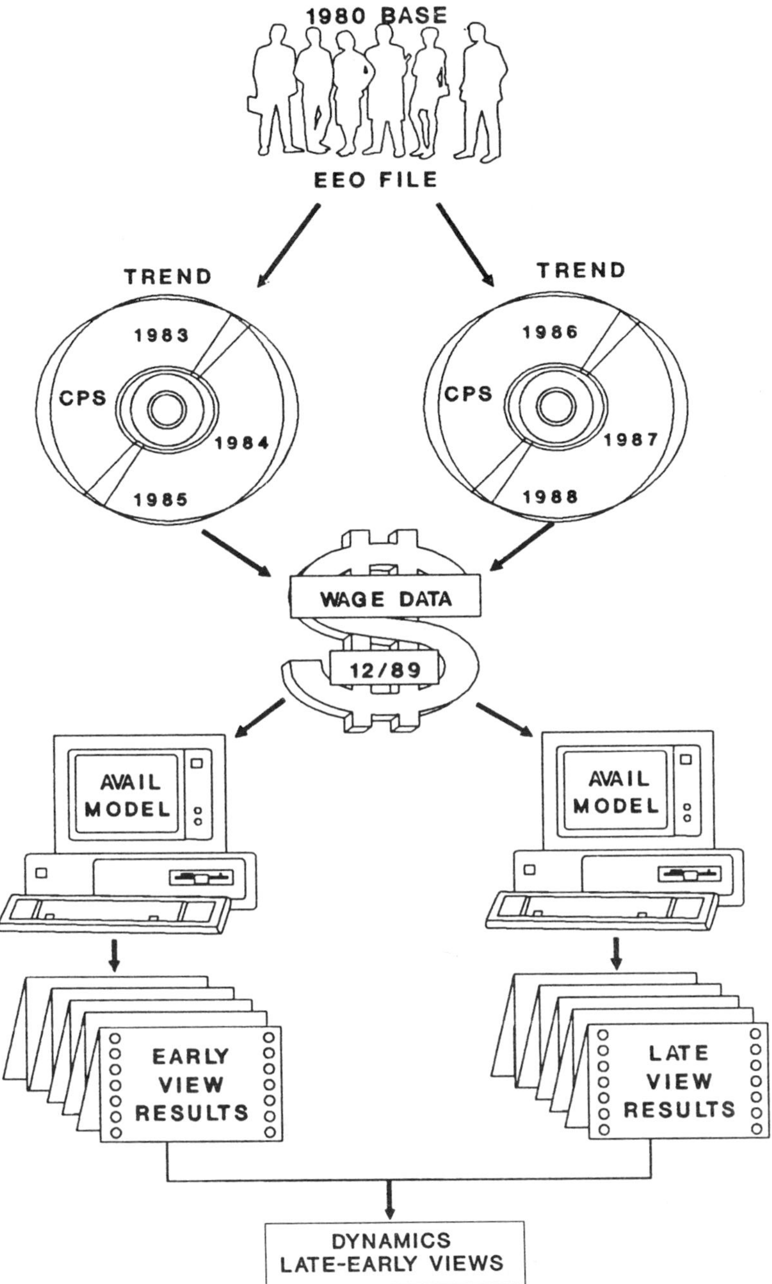

Figure 3: AVAIL Data Flows: Local Labor Market Dynamics

Workforce 2000 Theme	1991 Key Event	Dynamic Local Labor Market Data
Shortage of skilled workers	Department of Defense Reductions-in-Force (RIFs)	Technicians in salary ranges by location
Women in higher level jobs	Glass Ceiling Commission	Women in high paying jobs by location over time
Work force diversity	Proposed Civil Rights Act of 1991	Race/sex availability in crafts and operative jobs across locations over time

Figure 4: Illustrative Planning Tracks

Shortage of Skilled Workers

A key theme associated with Workforce 2000 is an increasing shortage of skilled workers. One of the first tasks managers face is to identify what skills or jobs are of interest to them. Two jobs are used to illustrate the integration of labor market forecasting and Workforce 2000: Science & Engineering technicians and Sub-Professional technicians.

In Table 1, results from ten local labor markets are presented for the two job groups. The numbers shown are the ratio of the local Navy work force to the available work force. The availability results were calculated using the 1986-1988 CPS trends. No significant differences were found using the 1983 to 1985 CPS trends and the 1986 to 1988 data.

The job groups are further broken down into pay or salary groupings, called pay grades in the Navy, so that skills can be examined. In relationship to the proposed Department of Defense base closings, the findings show possible effects on local labor markets. In particular, the following should be noted:

o Different local labor markets would have different effects. Strong effects on Scientist & Engineering Technicians do not necessarily mean strong effects on Sub-Professional technicians;

o Science and Engineering reductions would have strong effects in the high pay/skill subgroup C (Grade 9-12--approximate salary range $24,000-$45,000) with little effect in the lowest pay/skill subgroup;

o In the Sub-Professional technicians group the reductions would be most significant in the middle pay/skill subgroup B (Grade 5-8-- approximate salary range $16,000-$26,000); and

o The mix of effects across the job/skill groups varies so that bottom line effects are site or location specific.

The results show the value of job/skill specific information in local labor markets when assessments of skill shortages are being made. Good communications

Table 1: Ratio of Local Navy Workforce to Available Labor Force (as of Jan 1990)

Local Labor Market

Occupation	Pay Grade			
	A	**B**	**C**	**D**
Charleston, SC				
Science & Engineering Technicians	11.5	17.1	43.8	5.3
Sub-Professionals & Technicians	3.1	26.6	5.4	1.7
Pensacola, FL				
Science & Engineering Technicians	1.0	3.0	12.8	1.1
Sub-Professionals & Technicians	3.8	60.6	26.4	4.1
Albany, GA				
Science & Engineering Technicians	0.0	5.1	40.3	4.9
Sub-Professionals & Technicians	3.4	43.6	29.7	1.8
Key West, FL				
Science & Engineering Technicians	0.0	1.6	16.3	0.0
Sub-Professionals & Technicians	2.8	31.9	6.7	0.0
Jacksonville, FL				
Science & Engineering Technicians	2.5	5.1	13.6	3.5
Sub-Professionals & Technicians	2.9	17.8	14.1	0.7
Cherry Point–Camp Lejeune, NC				
Science & Engineering Technicians	4.1	11.7	49.9	7.8
Sub-Professionals & Technicians	3.1	35.7	7.7	2.9
Bay St. Louis–Pascagoula, MS				
Science & Engineering Technicians	2.5	2.9	18.0	1.8
Sub-Professionals & Technicians	1.1	12.1	10.4	0.0
Oak Harbor, WA				
Science & Engineering Technicians	0.8	2.1	31.1	5.6
Sub-Professionals & Technicians	2.3	15.5	6.7	0.0
Portsmouth, NH–Brunswick, ME				
Science & Engineering Technicians	9.1	8.9	31.6	4.3
Sub-Professionals & Technicians	0.4	4.5	7.4	1.4
Crane, IN				
Science & Engineering Technicians	5.3	53.4	65.5	7.3
Sub-Professionals & Technicians	0.1	18.1	9.6	0.0

Grades translate into approximate salary ranges (as of 12/89):

A: $8,500 - $16,000

B: $16,000 - $26,000

C: $24,000 - $45,000

D: $41,000 - $74,000

Source: Department of Navy
Civilian Occupation & Planning
Estimates System (COPES)

between large employers who are reducing their work forces can have solid bottom line effects. In an actual case, Mare Island Navy shipyard in Northern California used its knowledge of the local labor market to structure a successful job fair. This assessment took into account labor market conditions and maximized the placement of its skilled workers to outside employers who needed such workers.

Women in Higher Level Jobs

The representation of women in high paying jobs was studied from two perspectives. First, a range of high level decision-making jobs was examined. Then a cross-section of management jobs in the Navy was analyzed. Findings are presented in Figures 5 and 6.

The local labor market results were aggregated into seven regional areas to permit easier graphical presentations. Both tables show the availability of white women in 1996. A five year view was selected so that changes in selection, recruitment and placement would be possible if major underrepresentation levels were found.

The high-level technical and senior manager jobs for the Navy are in Grades 13-15 (approximate salary range $41,000-$74,000). This is the career level just below the Senior Executive Service (SES) jobs. Figure 5 confirms two findings:

o Representation levels for white women in scientist and engineer positions was much lower than in professional and manager positions; and

o Differences in white female representation level across regions were less than across occupations.

The results showed that women's representation levels in high decision-making jobs varied substantially by occupation. Clear definitions of which jobs are included and which are not included in the high decision making job group is required. From a litigation perspective, the standards by which the Glass Ceiling Commission and the courts will judge the success of companies in providing women access to high decision-making jobs will be significantly affected by the mix of jobs included in the senior group.

Figure 6 presents a cross sectional view of the dynamics of two salary/skill grade subgroups. One of the main issues being discussed about the glass ceiling is whether it is a myth or a reality. The data in Figure 6 would tend to support the conclusion that much of the glass ceiling issue is generational. The results in this table are differences in (growth) in representation between the late and early period forecasts for 1996. A figure such as 36.4% within Grade 9-12 (approximate salary range $24,000- $45,000) for Southern California means: the representation level of white females in junior manager and administrative specialist jobs was projected to increase 36.4% by 1996 based on updated trend data from 1983-85 to 1986- 88.

As Figure 6 shows, much higher representation increases are found for women in Grades 9-12 (approximate salary range $24,000-$45,000) jobs regardless of region. Grades 13-15 (approximate salary range $41,000- $74,000) job increases are positive but smaller. If there is an existing base of qualified managers in the Grades 9-12 pool and the number of job openings is less in the Grade 13-15 pool, the lower but positive growth rate is likely to be both reasonable and structural/ generational.

The standards by which organizations will be judged compare internal changes with external labor market changes. From an external labor market standpoint, the movement of women into high decision-making jobs is quantifiable. Based on the availability ratios, additional progress should be visible by the mid 1990s. Organizations like the Navy Department, which tracks such representations issues, have the information needed to confirm their progress, put their achievements in perspective, and hold human resource managers responsible for their actions over five year planning horizons.

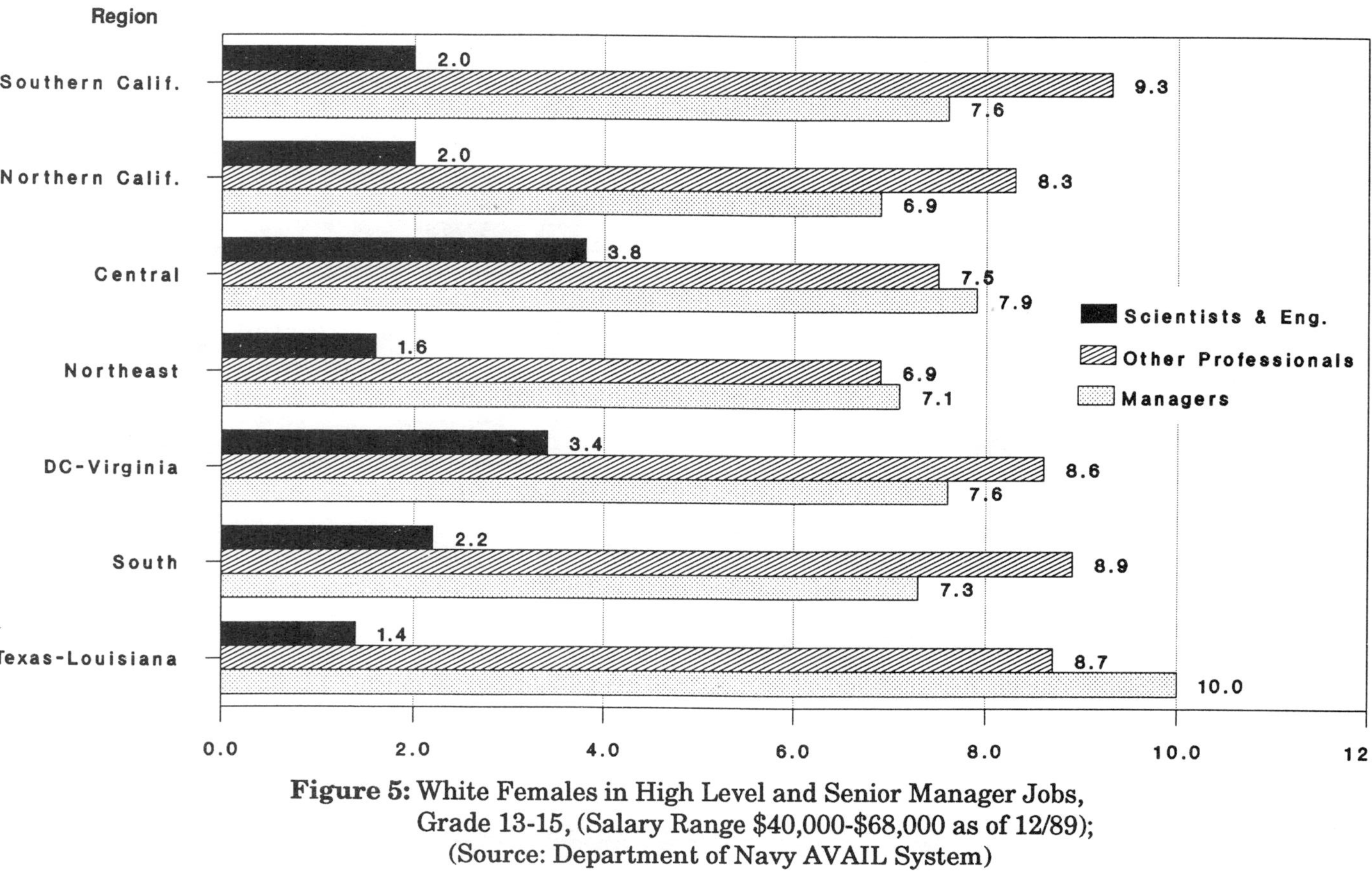

Figure 5: White Females in High Level and Senior Manager Jobs, Grade 13-15, (Salary Range $40,000-$68,000 as of 12/89); (Source: Department of Navy AVAIL System)

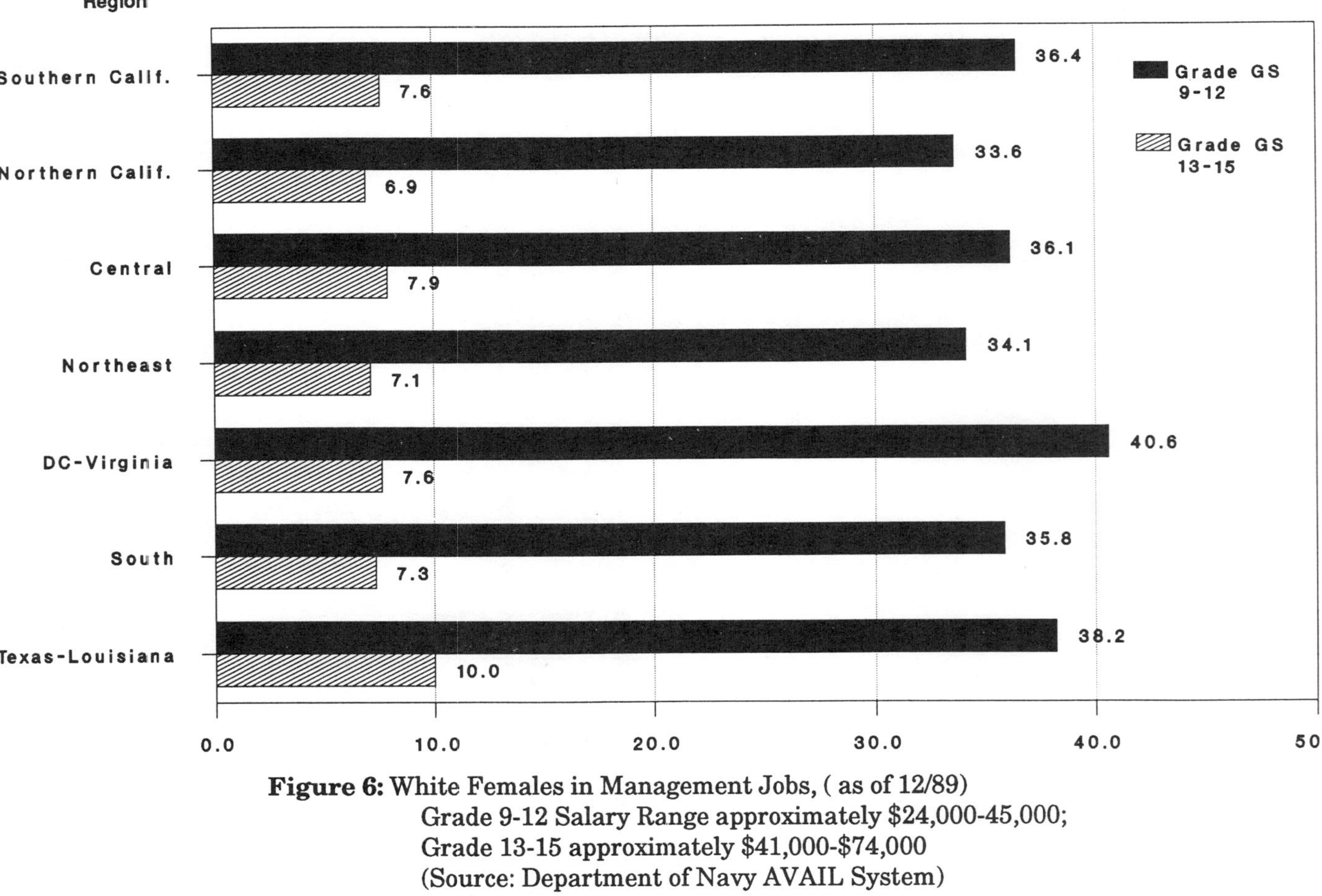

Figure 6: White Females in Management Jobs, (as of 12/89)
Grade 9-12 Salary Range approximately $24,000-45,000;
Grade 13-15 approximately $41,000-$74,000
(Source: Department of Navy AVAIL System)

Work Force Diversity

Work force diversity was examined across race groups (White, Black and Hispanic) and sex (male and female) groups. Differences between 1983-1985 trends for availability and 1986-1988 availability projections for 1996 in each of seven geographic areas were tabulated and compared. The findings shown in Table 2 highlight the largest changes in race-sex representation values. Changes varied by sex-race group and by job category across local labor markets.

The changes in representation are examined based on an expansion of rights to challenge seniority systems as proposed in the Civil Rights Act of 1991. Unlike the previous two tracks, the significance of the external event (the proposed Civil Rights Act of 1991) played a key role in the selection of the jobs and forecasting parameters for this analysis. In particular, craft and operative jobs which tend to be unionized have strong seniority system programs.

The results shown in Table 2 illustrate that a national solution to work force diversity is not reasonable. No single policy can address issues of representation for White women in the Northeast, Hispanics in Southern California and Black males in the South. The proposed challenges to seniority systems would affect companies with local facilities throughout the U.S. in different ways.

The projected declines shown for race-sex groups are even associated with different factors. In the Southern California case, the lack of qualified Hispanic workers occurs in a labor market where increasing numbers of qualified non-Hispanic workers are relocating to the region to produce a declining Hispanic representation level. Seniority systems could be inappropriately challenged if Hispanic representations do not increase in this geographic area.

White female projected declines in the Central and Northeast regions reflect expected changes in their selection for white collar jobs. Seniority systems may be challenged on the basis that they have created selection barriers in this area.

Projected declines of black males in the DC/Virginia region result from larger increases in white male availability. Projected increases in Black male representation for jobs in the South and Texas/Louisiana reflect increased concentration rather than diversification. Seniority systems may need to be modified to keep pace with these increases to avoid challenges in this labor market.

Table 2: Key Labor Market Diversity Measures in 1996

Labor Market	Race-Sex Priority	Job Priority
Southern California	-10.2% Hispanic males	Crafts
Northern California	**	**
Central	-3.5% white female	Crafts
North East	-3.5% white female	Operatives
DC/ Virginia	-8.2% Black male	Crafts
South	+4.2% Black male	Operatives
Texas/Louisiana	+7.0% Black male	Operatives

**No significant change predicted.

Source: Department of the Navy AVAIL System special reports, 1991

Each human resource forecasting result is part of a bigger picture which makes up the diversity of the work force predicted for the year 2000. Bottom line programs which accurately take into account the specifics of local labor market dynamics can expect greater success than broad, national policies/programs.

Lessons Learned

Key events in the early 1990s will alter the speed and direction of change in labor markets as the year 2000 approaches. With such changes and the needs of organizations to address job, location and race-sex specific issues, techniques such as external local labor market forecasting can play significant information roles. The results presented here do not provide a complete answer to the development of solid bottom line programs to address the important human resource issues facing business units in the 1990s. However, there are several important lessons:

o Differences in the mix of human resources across geographic areas can be important. Workforce 2000 and generic programs will not have equal effects on business units in different local labor markets;

o Job specific differences can be dramatic. Even within job group different wages/salaries and qualifications can affect predicted results. Events, such as legislation and federal programs, do affect the pace and direction of change; and

o Human resource planning and forecasting information exists to provide more than a static view every ten years of the external labor markets. These tools can provide insights into the dynamics of labor markets which focus on Workforce 2000 themes and key events.

With the release of the 1990 Census, there will be a surge of interest in external local labor market forecasting. These data will provide organizations with an excellent opportunity to benchmark their specific bottom line issues against the Workforce 2000 themes and external events of the period. Now is an appropriate time to begin to plan how to use effectively the local labor market data from the 1990 Census, Workforce 2000 themes and current events to implement human resource programs.

References

Atwater, D.M., *An Opportunity Based Modeling Approach: The Decision to Begin Work*, Los Angeles, CA; 1988.

Atwater, D., E. Bres III, J. Nelson and R. Niehaus, "A System for Estimating the Availability and Retention of U.S. Navy Civilian Personnel", OP-16H Research Report No. 50, Washington, D.C.: Office of the Chief of Naval Operations (OP-16H), 1988.

Atwater, D., E. Bres III, J. Nelson and R. Niehaus, "Navy EEO Labor Market Availability Data for the 1990's", OP-16H Research Report No. 47, Washington, D.C.: Office of the Chief of Naval Operations (OP-16H), 1986.

Atwater, D., E. Bres III, J. Nelson and R. Niehaus, "Analyzing Organizational Structure Change Using Proactive Labor Market Forecasts", OP-16H Research Report No. 49, Washington, D.C.: Office of the Chief of Naval Operations (OP-16H), 1987.

Atwater, D., E. Bres III, R. Niehaus, and J. Sheridan, "Labor Market Availability for U.S. Navy Civilian Professions in the 1980's", OP-16H Research Report No. 42, Washington, D.C.: Office of the Chief of Naval Operations (OP-16H), 1983.

Atwater, D., E. Bres III, R. Niehaus, and J. Sheridan, "Navy EEO Labor Market Availability Data for the 1980's", OP-16H Research Report No. 43, Washington, D.C.: Office of the chief of Naval Operations (OP-16H), 1983.

Atwater, D., E. Bres III, R. Niehaus, and J. Sheridan, "Human Resources Supply-Demand Policy analysis Models", in R.J. Niehaus, Ed. *Human Resource Policy_Analysis: Organizational Applications*, New York: Praeger, 1985, pp. 92-120.

Bureau of National Affairs, Inc., "Bush Administration Civil Rights Bill Introduced March March 12, 1991 with Section by Section Analysis of Proposed Legislation," *Daily Labor Report*, Washington, D.C., March, 1991.

Feurer, M.J., R.J. Niehaus, and J.A. Sheridan, "Human Resource Forecasting: A Survey of Practice and Potential", *Human Resource Planning*, vol. 7, No. 2, 1984.

Gaertner, K.N., "Managerial Careers and Organization-wide Transformations", R.J. Niehaus (Ed.), *Creating the Competitive Edge through Human Resource Applications*, New York, Plenum Press, 1987.

Hay Group, "The Hay Human Resource Forecast, 1991-2000", New York, NY, 1990

Johnson, W.B., S. Faul, B. Huang and A.H. Packer, *Civil Service 2000*, Hudson Institute, Washington, D.C., June, 1988

Niehaus, R., *Computer-Assisted Human Resource Planning*, New York: Wiley Interscience, 1978.

Niehaus, R., *Human Resource Policy Analysis: Organization Applications*, New York: Praeger, 1985.

Rosenblum, J.E., "Organizational Career Mobility: Promotion chances in a Corporation During Periods of Growth and Contraction", *American Journal of Sociology*, 85, 1979a.

Slocum, J.W. Jr., W.L. Cron, R.W. Hansen, and S. Rawling, "Business Strategy and the Management of Plateaued Employees", *Academy of Management Review*, 28, 1985.

Towers Perrin, "Workforce 2000: Competing in a Seller's Market-- Is Corporate America Prepared?", *Spectrum*, 12, September 17, 1990

U.S. Department of Labor and Hudson Institute, *Opportunity 2000: Creative_Affirmative Action Strategies for a Changing Workforce*, Indianapolis, Indiana, September, 1988

U.S. Navy Office of Civilian Personnel Management, *Navy Civilian Workforce and Civil Service 2000*, Washington, DC, March, 1989

Weekly Federal Employees' News Digest, "Special Report--Base Hit List, State by State", April 22, 1991

William M. Mercer, "Work Force Planning and Management Study," October 17, 1990.

William M. Mercer, "1990 Annual Round Table Discussion Seminar-- Workforce 2000", October, 1990

Workforce 2000: Work and Workers in the 21st Century, Hudson Institute and Department of Labor, Indianapolis, Indiana, June, 1987.

Developing the Human Resource Executive as a Strategic Partner: Turning Concept into Reality

R.S. KOSTER and D.M. SCHWEIGER

Introduction

During the past five years, many authors have questioned the role of human resource (HR) executives in business (Ulrich, 1987, 1989; Manzini, 1988). In particular, they have argued that many HR executives have failed to become respected and effective strategic partners in the business planning process -- i.e., they have not become integrally involved in strategic decision-making. Many reasons have been offered for this failure. Primary among them has been the inability of HR executives to demonstrate the contributions that human resources can make in developing competitive advantages and thus supporting business strategies.

It has been further argued that this failure stems from a lack of professional and personal competencies by HR executives. Some of the more critical competencies have been identified by Ulrich (1987). Examples of professional competencies include: (a) knowledge of the business; (b) respect within the HR department; (c) ability to anticipate change and respond proactively; (d) ability to involve and commit line managers; and, (e) the development of a data-base orientation. Examples of personal competencies include: the ability to think strategically, the development of credibility, candor, and political agility; and, true business leadership.

While the observations of these authors make sense and have furthered our understanding of strategic human resource partnerships (SHRP), they have been made primarily from the perspective of human resource professionals. Moreover, they have not fully captured what organizations actually do to make SHRP a reality.

Today's HR practitioners seem to be facing considerable difficulty converting existing SHRP concepts into reality. SHRP efforts appear to create more frustration than satisfaction. There are more failures than success. Current published

R.S. KOSTER-Boehringer Ingleheim Corporation, 90 East Ridge, P.O. Box 368, Ridgefield, CT 06977; D.M. Schweiger - College of Business Administration, University of South Carolina, Columbia, SC 29208

descriptions of SHRP narrowly represent the views of HR practitioners and/or HR academicians. Rarely do we find published views of senior executives, strategic planners, or others outside the HR function. This does not imply that the HR professional's views are necessarily wrong. On the contrary, much of what they have to say may be helpful.

However, it would be instructive to examine how those outside the HR function -- i.e., the primary users of HR -- view SHRP. In particular, how do senior executives and strategic planners look at SHRP? What do they expect from such a partnership? To answer these questions, we present a case study of how one company, the Boehringer Ingelheim Corporation (BIC), attempted to involve HR in their strategic planning process as a true strategic partner.

Focus of the Study

We present a case study to provide a more balanced perspective of SHRP. We will illustrate, from the perspective of senior executives and strategic planners, the process of developing SHRP. It is important to note that while our study is presented from a non-HR perspective, both authors have had extensive HR involvement. Previous to his current strategic planning responsibilities, Ronald Koster was in charge of HR Planning and Development for several companies (for a total of 12 years). David Schweiger has studied, consulted and taught both strategic planning and human resource management. We believe that we can empathize with, understand, and be sensitive to both the HR and non-HR side of SHRP.

Our case analysis will be divided into six sections. The first section provides background on BIC and describes the cultural and managerial conditions under which it began its SHRP efforts. This description sets the context for the SHRP effort. It also provides the reader with a benchmark against which to measure the similarities and differences between BIC and their own company.

The second section focuses on the characteristics that BIC senior executives thought were important to a strategic partner (both in general and in HR terms). The third section examines the organizational infrastructure that was needed to implement SHRP. The fourth section focuses on measures and benchmarks of an effective SHRP effort. We discuss this issue separately because of the importance of measurement in documenting the success of an organizational activity.

The fifth section examines the activities that were needed to pull the overall SHRP effort together. Particular focus is given to what BIC learned, what BIC might have done differently, and how BIC's SHRP experiences relate to the SHRP articles being published today. In the final section, we provide some concluding thoughts and recommendations for HR executives considering a similar effort.

Boehringer Ingleheim Corporation: The Organizational Universe

The reader may find BIC's organizational environment different from the one found in the organization. Much of BIC's partnership success is due to its distinct domestic and international organizational values and cultures. As such, it is important that the reader have a good understanding of "what" and "who" BIC is and what it brings to the strategic planning process. BIC is a leading U.S. pharmaceutical firm with five major subsidiary operations. These include: (1) ethical pharmaceuticals, (2) hospital generic drugs, (3) animal health care, (4) specialty chemicals, and (5) a specialty bakery business unit.

The ethical pharmaceuticals unit, the largest of BIC's operations, is the central focus of this case. It is a licensor of an international, privately-held (family owned) corporation, Boehringer Ingelheim Pharma of Canada -- a licensor of the international German corporation of Boehringer Ingelheim GmbH. This U.S. operation has been in existence for little over 20 years and at present has revenues of approximately $500 million and 2500 employees.

While the BIC operation has always had some involvement in strategic planning, it was not until four years ago that it introduced a formal planning process. The need for this process was created by several factors: rapid changes in the pharmaceutical industry and marketplace, increasing competitive pressures, rapidly changing regulatory conditions, expanding scientific technologies (e.g., biotechnology), and the establishment of a new Chief Executive Officer for U.S. operations.

The decision to adopt a worldwide, formalized strategic planning process has required BIGmbH to do this in a wide diversity of countries and cultural settings. BIC has been confronted with the challenges of establishing suitable domestic (U.S.) strategic planning processes. It has also had to deal with the challenges of achieving a well-balanced, integrated, and effective worldwide strategic planning process.

Unique to BIC's domestic structure is that many of its management philosophies, etc. have, to some degree, been influenced by the family owned structures and the philosophies of its German operations. Many of these philosophies, surprisingly, fall in the area of human resources.

In the worldwide context, the HR function holds a prominent position at the senior executive levels of most country operations. The domestic HR function holds a similar level of prominence and involvement which many U.S. organizations have yet to achieve. Being an integral part of the worldwide ethic, these HR-oriented philosophies have done a great deal to foster more meaningful HR partnerships.

Before the establishment of BIC's formalized strategic planning framework, the HR function was an integral partner in many of the company's key decision-making activities. It has, and continues to hold, active membership in several key management committees, both domestically and internationally. The HR presence filters down throughout BIC's domestic operations. There is a deep concern and interest in its employees. BIC is committed to long-term employment and development from within. It focuses on rewards for contribution, which is an integral part of its HR philosophy. In sum, employees are considered a strategic "asset" rather that a liability within BIC, and as such are automatically part-and-parcel of any strategic effort.

In essence, BIC's has a unique business environment with varied cultural perspectives and a unique management orientation to HR involvement. Such participation of HR in strategic decision-making, and BIC's need to build a suitable strategic planning environment set the stage for its development of SHRP. This is not to argue, however, that building the partnership was easy. On the contrary, a much focused effort and initiative by HR management to make the partnership a credible and respected contributor within the context of business operations and the executive decision-making framework was required. More will be said about this point later.

The Characteristics of Effective Strategic Partnership

The most important step in developing a strategic partnership is to establish its essential characteristics. Since BIC's focus on partnership was from a business-oriented perspective, it is only reasonable that it be described by the "users" involved in the strategic process -- senior executives and strategic planners.

Before describing the characteristics of an effective partner, BIC's executives established the following four premises:

1. Partnership is at the executive decision-making level of the organization.
2. Partnership members include those functional unit and business unit executives who are considered integral members of the organization's decision-making body and are involved in all aspects of the company's strategic planning process.
3. In most cases, the partnership is maintained by functional unit heads and/or business unit heads. However, additional individuals are brought into the strategic partnership process when they can contribute to the strategic planning process.
4. The company's CEO is automatically considered a partner though he may not be in direct coordination of the strategic process. In BIC's case the strategic planning process is under the guidance of a strategic planning group and the CEO delegates planning coordination responsibility to this group.

The characteristics of an effective partner are divided into two categories: (1) those which relate to any partnership, no matter the functional area; and (2) those which pertain specifically to SHRP. We first discuss general partnership characteristics.

General Partnership Characteristics

The characteristics of a general partner are divided into three areas: (1) cognitive (i.e., thinking) skills and business knowledge; (2) process (interpersonal) skills; and, (3) cultural and attitudinal orientation. Cognive skills and business knowledge pertain to a strategic partner who:

o Thinks beyond his or her immediate functional area.
o Understands the nature, language (e.g., financial, technical, marketing) of the business.
o Sees the nuances of competitive environments, external conditions, and the implications of these for the long-term direction of the company.
o Grasps the complex relationships between long-term vision, strategy, and tactics and short-term goals, action plans, programs, and activities.
o Makes difficult, risk-oriented decisions
o Generates new, innovative, and creative ideas.

Process skills pertain to a strategic partner who:

o Shares his/her views and judgments by openly presenting them, even in environments characterized by dissent, pressure from colleagues, and even the CEO.
o Discloses his/her own strengths and weakness without fear of "looking bad" to other planning partners; is willing to accurately portray existing conditions.

o Skillfully "negotiates" with colleagues and friends by disagreeing without
  taking an adversarial position; compromises when necessary; and, also
  stands his/her ground when necessary.
o Comfortably works in symbiotic relationships with other strategic
  partners.
o Leaves his/her "territorial protectionism" at the door.
o Develops and maintains professional credibility and respect with his/her
  other partners.

Cultural and attitudinal orientation characteristics pertain to a parner who:

o Comes to the strategic planning process ready to plan -- prepared, skilled,
  and comfortable with the long-term strategic planning philosophy of
  his/her organization.
o Learns from the planning experience and takes back ideas, visions, and
  long-term directions to his/her own functional area -- communicates the
  visions, directions, and targets down through the other layers of the
  organization.
o Moves beyond the "can't do" mode, because things didn't work in the past, to
  the "can do" mode of planning.
o Brings an "entrepreneurial" spirit to the planning process
o Brings "substantial effort" to the process -- passivity is not partnership.

SHRP Characteristics

Concerning the characteristics of SHRP, the executives considered all of the
general partnership characteristics to be essential. In addition, they felt the
following characteristics to be important:

o Identifies critical HR concerns, issues, problems, and opportunities both
  outside and inside the company.
o Links HR functions to the financial aspects of the business -- knows the
  financial impact of HR, understands financial statements, and accurately
  estimates   financial costs when developing ideas and suggestions.
o Links long-term, strategic HR direction with operational HR issues and
  conditions which may differ considerably across various functional areas.
o Understands how the various functions operate and sees the difference
  between individual HR functional needs.
o Has the necessary HR support services in place to implement strategic HR
  recommendations.
o Understands the organization's current and future HR strengths and
  weaknesses as well as competition HR conditions -- openly benchmarks the
  organization's capabilities against the "best-in-class" HR operating groups.
o Not only represents the people aspects of the company publicly, but also the
  company as a whole, in all areas of the business.
o Deals with sensitive executive issues responsibly, maintains is/her own
  colleagues and partners.
o Understands how education, learning, and development are linked to the
  long-term, strategic interests and needs of the business -- does not provide
  "show pieces," but rather, looks at providing functional training support

that, while not glamorous, is both critical and essential to functional business performance.

   o Properly portrays the importance of HR to the strategic, long term success and competitive position of the company in the marketplace to his or her colleagues and partners.

   o Helps "oil" the partnership process through strong interactive, group dynamics, communications, and listening skills.

   o Model good management skills..

In sum, BIC's experience suggests that strategic partnerships require a very broad and complex set of individual characteristics and that they be used when appropriate. In this section, we have attempted to present these characteristics from the perspectives of senior executives. In the next section we describe the infrastructure that BIC used to put SHRP into action.

SHRP Infrastructures

Successful strategic partnerships are built upon infrastructures which must be established before the initiation of the partnership and be continually maintained to develop it. The term "infrastructure" encompasses the critical organizational reporting relationships, policies, practices, attitudes, and commitments that support SHRP. Infrastructures may be tangible and visible, or they may be abstract and conceptual (i.e., involve subtleties such as empowerment and trust).

Regardless of their particular configuration, infrastructures are the fabric that weave the entire partnership process together and keep it that way. It is our contention that without well established infrastructures a strategic partnership, no matter what the functional area, will only be temporary and will erode when business conditions and pressures arise.

Infrastructures fall into two categories. One category pertains to strategic partnerships in general and serve as necessary pre-requisites to a functional partnership relationship. The other pertains to those which specifically relate to a particular discipline, such as HR.

General Partnership Infrastructures

The most critical aspect in the success of the partnership process at BIC was the full, dedicated, and organizationally visible commitment of the CEO. Without his open support, the partnership process would have failed. The CEO initiated the partnership and has sustained it over time.

A second critical factor is the partnership characteristics displayed by the partners themselves. When provided the opportunity to participate, the partners effectively performed. If they had missed their "window of opportunity" it would have quickly eroded the partnership environment and made future partnerships extremely difficult to create.

SHRP Infrastructures

Narrowing our focus to the HR area, BIC found that the following functional infrastructures were also necessary for an effective HR partnership. First, the organization's culture embraced SHRP as a vital and essential element in running the business. HR was seen as more than simply an administrative and support element. In particular it was an integral part of the strategic planning process.

This is not something that can be created solely by the HR executive. Without the HR philosophy having been established by the international atmosphere of the European business operations, it is doubtful that BIC's HR executive would have had the opportunity to develop an effective long- term relationship. This is not to argue that characteristics of the HR executive were not essential and necessary in developing and sustaining the partnership. Indeed, they were. However, they were not in and of themselves sufficient.

To be successful, the HR partnership at BIC had to extend beyond the strategic planning process. While its presence in the planning process was essential, its presence in other activities and decisions that took place on a day- to-day basis was also essential. The HR executive's success in key operational decision was a crucial antecedent to his/her involvement in the strategic planning process. Operational success built the executive's credibility in the organization and earned him the respect and support of other strategic partners. The HR executive had to "earn his or her spurs" so to speak in the operational arena in order to be accepted in the strategic arena.

When the opportunity arose, the HR executive had to be ready, willing, and able to plan strategically. He had to develop appropriate planning experience before he entered the partnership -- i.e., he had to first set realistic long-term goals and plans and implement them successfully within his own unit.

The SHRP also needed the infrastructures that enabled him to quickly and accurately access and use HR information external and internal to the organization to support the strategic planning process. Moreover, he had to respond to unexpected issues that impinged upon the planning process. This required the establishment and management of linkages between the HR function and the outside world; linkage between the HR function and other functions within the company; and, the ability of the HR executive to integrate strategic activities with operational activities on an ongoing basis.

After examining these infrastructures one is probably struck that nothing new is being said here. What we have identified probably seems like the essential infrastructures found in any successful organization. Maybe that is the one thing that BIC learned from the SHRP process. Successful strategic planning and partnerships are based on sound management principles.

Surprisingly, when BIC approaches its strategic partnership effort it had to determine which infrastructures (general and HR specific) were in place and being used and which were "thought" to be in place, but were actually not. The latter had to be established while the partnership effort was being developed. In the next section, we discuss one factor that is crucial to any SHRP effort, the ability to measure its impact on the organization.

SHRP Measures and Benchmarks

Have you ever heard the phrase, "If you can't measure it, don't use it." If you have not, than welcome to what some call the battle cry (or lament) of the strategic planner.

Peter Drucker has always made two critical assertions about business planning and management: (1) few factors are as important to business performance and success (whether in the short- or long-term) as measurement, and

(2) measurement often tends to be one of the weakest areas in business management

Successful strategic planning is built on reliable and effective measurement. Underlying every strategic partnership rests the issue of determining the cost-benefit contributions being made to the long-term strategic direction of the company. In most strategic partnerships, the measurement issue has been successfully addressed and even improved upon over the years. For example, marketing has many indicators for measuring contributions and success. Finance can be considered almost a role model of indices, performance ratios, and assessment formulas to gauge overall business contributions and performance. Even manufacturing and R&D have developed a wide variety of measures for strategic planning. However, HR is an area where we seem to still encounter considerable measurement difficulty. Over the years, it seems that little progress has been made by HR practitioners to promote the active development of suitable performance measures.

Jac Fitz-enz (1984) explains that HR measurement efforts have failed to materialize as one would have hoped by this time. This area of the discipline is sadly and noticeably deficient. When it comes to the SHRP process this is especially true. Because of the risks and exposures which are involved in the planning process, HR functions seem to object ardently to establishing measures and benchmarks of performance.

There still exists a myth within HR that their discipline is something esoteric, complex, subjective, and immeasurable. HR practitioners continue to believe that what they do is more of an "art" then a science and as such is incapable of being accurately measured with business-type methods. This may be one of the underlying reasons strategic planners seem to find their HR partners less than contributory and difficult to work with when compared to other partnerships.

Bottom-line orientation and anchoring is a "must" to strategic SHRP. Cassell, Juris, and Roomkin (1985) have indicated early on that suitable, bottom-line indexing is essential if we are to achieve

> "...integration between planners and policy makers, so that corporate goals, timing, availability of product, readiness, and availability of manpower can interact with economic and market forecasts, facilities, and investment plans, in order to provide an objective basis for establishing manpower requirements (and strategic HR contributions."

Strategic HR partners must recognize that in strategic planning and decision-making the dollars which flow to future investments are going to be assigned to those areas where the promise, and demonstration, of future return on earnings is the greatest. Unlike the flow of funds to changes in investment opportunities, which can occur quickly, the decision to invest in human capital and activities occurs much more slowly. As such it calls for more objective measures of past, present, and future contributions, not just subjective and behavioral descriptions. SHRP requires a measurement perspective which demonstrates the relationships between aggregate, human capital flow and contributory results. Strategic measures must be an integral part of developing the SHRP. Early on, BIC established financial indices around such areas as: labor cost, management and executive costs, health care costs, recruitment expenses, training costs, ratio of personnel cost to net sales, and benefit costs.

Currently, BIC is working to establish a greater range of measures to accomplish internal and external trend analyses for such areas as: demographics, labor profiles, educational conditions, turnover, and time differentials between capital investment and productivity contributions. BIC's SHRP effort is also working on developing measures for tracking and comparing performance contributions to overall business success and relationships between training and development investments to measurable productivity improvements.

In one key strategic activity, HR is an integral partner in implementing a company-wide overhead value analysis effort. In another strategic project, SHRP initiated an employee "ideas contribution program" to help address strategic productivity cost reductions and effectiveness improvements.

In both cases, the efforts of HR were linked to direct financial measures of contribution and were closely tracked against established financial indices over a two-year assessment period. Follow-up programs of this nature are now scheduled for other functional areas in order to continue working toward strategic control of overhead costs. These activities will also be facilitated by the HR group and will again be constructed around definitive financial measures.

A second aspect of measurement and strategic partnership has to do with strategic benchmarking. Measures are constructed to monitor and track partnership performance and contribution, benchmarking is a company's proactive effort to gain competitive advantage. Robert M. Fifer (1986) has described strategic benchmarking as:

"The assessment and analysis of industry, competitor, and best-in-class organizations in order to define accurately the business factors of success required to achieve and maintain competitive advantage and maximize shareholder value."

At some point the SHRP must be ready to benchmark his or her operations. Ideally, it is helpful if this can be done as part of the strategic planning process. Sometimes, this is not possible due to higher business priorities.

In sum, measurement and benchmarking are critical aspects of SHRP development. For the strategic HR partner it means overcoming past objections to measurement and actively pursuing the design and development of suitable measures using business-type methods. From the CEO's perspective there is an expectation, almost a requirement, that strategic partners use measures and benchmarks as part of the partnership sharing and analysis process. Strategic planners require it as part of an effective overall planning effort. The organization demands it if it is to compete realistically in the marketplace. BIC's experience has shown that measurement and benchmarking are crucial to the SHRP process and will remain so for a long time to come.

Pulling It All Together

We attempted to approach our study in a structured and logical manner. In reality the way the pieces came together and were implemented at BIC was much more dynamic and fluid. Because of this we would like to close our discussion by addressing some of the nuances of partnership development and try to "pull" all the pieces together.

We begin by summarizing what BIC has learned in general. First, BIC's experience has shown that HR strategic partnership is neither elusive nor unattainable. On the contrary, BIC has found that with the proper managerial philosophy, top management commitments, and infrastructures in place, it can be achieved.

Second, achieving any type of partnership, whether it be HR or any other functional area, is not done by the functional group alone. It has to be orchestrated, integrated, and supported by many other groups and individuals outside the particular functional area. The HR executive had to develop and cultivate sources of support to bring about a lasting partnership. Some of this was institutionally developed. BIC placed the HR executive in a senior role with direct reporting relationship to the CEO within each business unit. Moreover, HR had board level representation at the European headquarters. Other efforts to build support included the formal development of cooperative relationships such as a joint venture between HR and the Strategic Planning Group to develop HR information/ intelligence data base.

Third, BIC also learned that timing is crucial when establishing SHRP. When he timing is wrong, you cannot force the issue. There are simply too many visible and invisible obstacle in the way. Going against the flow is what produces the frustrations and failures we mentioned earlier, "tilting with windmills" only results in painful disappointments.

This is something many of today's academics and practitioners who write about SHRP may be overlooking, or down playing. They seem to ignore the organizational culture and timing issues that surround partnership development. There is almost a presumption by today's authors that the HR partnership is not happening because of the HR practitioner's personal lack of effort or preparation. We strongly disagree with position.

There are many actions that the HR practitioner can and should take to develop effective partnerships. However, it is a mistake to simply pre-suppose that the organizational culture is ready and waiting for the HR function to "get its act together." In reality many organizations have developed cultures that exclude the HR function from key business decisions and have relegated it to an administrative entity used only to implement and carry out the will of the organization at large. Until these cultures change, nothing the HR practitioner can do will bring about true partnership, no matter how hard he/she tries. This may require new senior executives who bring a different HR culture. However, do not underestimate the power of inertia.

The fourth thing learned from BIC's SHRP experience is that the required cultures and infrastructures are important to have at the outset. However, they do not have to all be fully developed or in place in order to start developing partnerships. They can grow and mature over time. In this manner, they become even more effective. All the partners may help educate and shape the role of any one of the partners, and thus further develop personal relationships.

The following two examples illustrate this development process at BIC. The first concerns business knowledge and skills. The second involves SHRP bottom line measurement.

Example 1: *Business Knowledge and Skills*

At the outset of the partnership it was critical that the partners knew the "basics" -- e.g., fundamental understanding of finance and marketing.

Other aspects could be enriched over time. For example, BIC's strategic planning function was assigned the task of updating basic business knowledge as part of on-going executive strategic planning meetings. Functional groups were required to prepare specialized informational briefings to explain their operations, review the implications of their activities (concerning to the strategic interests of the corporation), and clarify any aspect of their operation that others did not understand.

The briefing helped improve all the partner's understanding of the business -- e.g., the industry, BIC's products, marketing efforts, financial conditions, HR elements, and production situations. They also ensured that all partners were knowledgeable of the conditions and interrelationships that existed within the organization.

This process has proved exceptionally helpful to all partners and is something that they now look forward to. In this manner BIC has: trengthened the infrastructure; helped develop the business knowledge and breath of its decision makers; and created greater shared understanding of the overall dynamics of the organization. This has all been done in a non-threatening, fully supportive learning environment. BIC's strategic partners have "learned to learn" and support and cooperate with each other.

Example 2: *SHRP Bottom-Line Measurement*

Here again, BIC found that certain functional partnerships may not enter with obvious and visible contributions right from the start. To expedite efforts, BIC focused first on those that were able to demonstrate immediate and measurable contribution to strategy and business positioning. Once done, these then served as models for other areas.

For those areas that could not do this immediately, BIC partners worked with them outside the process to improve their ability. For example, when the HR executive entered the partnership process, minimal HR measurement had been undertaken. Some measures had been developed, but a number were not directly related to the strategic planning process. The HR function has been working with other partners to develop measures and is beginning to show observable signs of promise. It still is going to take some time to reach a desired level of optimal partnership operation, but BIC is making progress in the right direction.

The fifth learned element is that strategic planning and partnership development takes considerable time. At BIC, eight years were allotted to bringing about suitable strategic planning and partnership changes. While only half- way through that time frame, BIC is quite satisfied with its progress to date.

This raises a very important point. Many of today's authors portray SHRP as a revolutionary activity. At BIC, it has been an "evolutionary" process of change. At the outset of the strategic effort, this was one essential ground rule personally established by the CEO. He required that all strategic planning efforts be evolutionary in nature. Too many reliable systems and methods were in place and would be overshadowed or lost if the effort was too rapid or seen as too disruptive.

There was also the politics of change and vested interests to consider. The decision has proved to be the right one in this environment. By moving slowly and allowing sufficient time to identify better the working capabilities, BIC has been able to move the partnership along at a rate of change that has been acceptable to all partners. Change is occurring slowly, but surely.

A culture characterized by strategic planning and partnerships has been continually ingrained as part of BIC's way of managing. BIC's top management can see exceptional differences in the way it operates now and the way it operated when it first began the strategic planning process.

Finally, BIC learned that there is a "systems mentality" that tends to permeate large organizational thinking. With the advent of personal computers, elaborate information systems, and high-tech methods to business management, a systems orientation has taken on a considerable importance in recent years. By systems orientation we mean that all actions or selected strategies are fixed to, or built upon, the development of some sort of support system -- manual or computerized.

BIC has found that the strategic planning process and partnership environment can be hindered if there is too much reliance on solving strategic problems through the development of systems. Strategic planning and management, while dependent upon certain technological systems to enhance effectiveness and efficiency, is driven by non-structured methodologies and processes. Too much of a systems orientation serves only to detract from the desired innovation, creative thinking, and risk-taking that are so important to successful strategic thinking.

After about three years of effort, and many attempts at establishing various executive information systems, expert systems, systems networks, and the like, BIC has come to realize that effective strategic partnership is dependent upon individuals and relationships. Look again at what BIC's strategic partners used to describe strategic partnership. You will see that the most of those characteristics do not focus on structuring and framing elaborate "systems," but rather focus on the subjective and interpersonal dynamics of trust, communication, disclosure, negotiation, and compromise.

If one thing seems to be working for BIC, it is the ability of its strategic partners to avoid the need to form elaborate systems and rely more on their personal and interpersonal skills to solve problems. We mention this because HR is one functional area that may be succumbing to the systems mentality as a solution to creating strategic partnerships. If one looks at what authors and vendors attempt to provide, it is better systems and methodologies, rather than better ideas on how to remove attitudinal or cultural barriers. To many consultants, it is a better HR Information System (HRIS) that is going to solve the strategic partnership problems that exist today. Actually, a more elaborate system is probably going to compound the strategic partnership issue, rather than help it.

As strategic facilitators, we have learned that strategic thinking requires a host of different tools, to be used at different times and in a variety of ways. Few things are stable and repetitive in the strategic planning process. What works to help the strategic process today may not work tomorrow. As environmental, competitive, and market conditions change so must the managerial outlooks and analytical methods. Systems approach strategic planning as a relatively static process. Unfortunately, this is not the way business works and it is counterproductive if one tries to make it operate that way.

While systems are helpful, they are not a panacea. As such, BIC's experience and ours suggests that strategic partners are going to have to be ready to be more flexible in their approaches, more responsive to creating new ways of looking at their organization, and more fluid in designing support systems. PCs and information systems are not going to replace personal judgment and business experience. They are only going to help individuals do things faster and possibly more efficiently. On the other hand, systems may provide too much information too quickly which may compound the complexity of the planning process. BIC has learned over time to keep its partnerships non-systems oriented; in BIC's lexicon it refers to any systems as have to be "transparent."

In summary, we believe that much of what is written about SHRP today is valid and holds definite promise for improving the partnership process. However, improving the process is not going to "make partnership happen." Many suggestions proffered by today's authors will help "fine tune" SHRP performance and contribution. When it comes to creating true partnership, we have to address the culture of the organization and its true receptivity and commitment to including HR as a real "partner" in the total strategic effort. Only when this is achieved will real partnership be born.

Doing Things Differently

Everyone would like the chance to go back at times and do things differently. If we were to look at BIC's own partnership development activities in retrospect, the top executives are not sure that they would do many things differently. Granted, they probably would like to have seen some of the infrastructures strengthened and reinforced before the start of the partnership effort, but beyond this they would have pursued the same activities, to the same degree, and under the same time frame.

They say because they believe that what is happening at BIC is effective and in line with its particular culture and strategic directions. HR participation is well placed and contributes to the strategic activities. It has been well accepted by the other members of the strategic and is successfully linking operational HR activities with long-term strategic directions. Even though there are areas which need further growth and refinement, things seem to be working well for BIC's particular needs.

Summary and Conclusions

What has this paper been able to bring to the issue of SHRP development? We hope we have been able to show that the process of partnership development, while not easy, is also not impossible to attain. The partnership can work and does work when the culture, infrastructures, and commitments are in place.

Also, we hope that we've shown that being a partner requires personal commitment, hard work, skill development, and ability to understand and meet other strategic partner needs. While certain aspects of the SHRP are functionally dependent, just being an expert in the HR field is not enough to qualify for true strategic partnership. Time and again we have seen how executives (CEO and other strategic partners) require expertise outside of one's narrow functional arena. We need global perspectives, broad-based thinking, visionary leadership skills, group skills, and a host of other non- functional, but business related, characteristics.

Hopefully, our paper has been able to show how SHRP is really established and deveveloped within an organization. It has and will continue to be an integral part of BIC's strategic efforts. We close with the following recommendations of

BIC's HR executive who is well on his way to becoming a SHRP:

o The strategic HR partnership has to provide proactively a leadership role within the company to create and maintain productive human resource contributions.

o The strategic process at times has a tendency to be overpowered by those directly related to product flow -- i.e., marketing, research, new product planning, and production. Don't become frustrated or impatient when they appear to control "center stage." One must remember it is a "team effort" and partnership is comprised of contemporaries, not adversaries. Let them participate.

o Be an active member, participate and sell. It's easy to accommodate partnership "after the fact." The hard part is to be an active partner -- giving, sharing, listening, and analyzing.

o Know what your competition is doing. Staying up with them is not good enough, you have to pursue being better.

o Spend time with your partners, both in and out of the strategic planning sessions. Share views, know what their concerns or objections might be. Discuss your ideas and watch how many come back to you as suggestions from others during the planning sessions. The strategic process requires that partnerships have common interests and common languages. This includes HR. Helps develop your partners' HR vocabulary and language.

o You have to be a business generalist, not just a "people person." Know your other partners by "living with them." Get to know them so well that there is no difference between your perceptions of them and their environments and reality. Your contributions will only be meaningful if you truly understand their problems and needs. Avoid centralization of HR efforts.

References

Manzini, A. "Integrating Human Resource Planning and Development: The Unification of Strategic, Operational, and Human Resource Planning Systems," *Human Resource Planning,* 11, 2, 79-94.

Ulrich, D. (1989) "Assessing Human Resource Effectiveness: Stakeholder, Utility, and Relationship Approaches." *Human Resource Planning*, 12, 4, 301-316.

Ulrich, D. (1987) "Organizational Capability As a Competitive Advantage: Human Resource Professionals as Strategic Partners". *Human Resource Planning*, 10, 4, 169-184.

Fifer, Robert M. "Beating the Competition: A Practical Guide to Benchmarking" *Kaiser Associates Publication,* 1986.

Fitz-enz, Jac. "How to Measure Human Resources Management." *Saratoga Institute*, McGraw Hill Book Co., 1984.

Cassell, Juris, Roomkin. "Strategic HR Planning: An Orientation to the Bottom-linc" *Management Decision (UK),* Vol:v23n3, pgs. 16-28, 1985.

Powerful Partnerships: Linkages between HR and Strategic Business Activities in the Delaware Valley

D.W. DANNER

Introduction

The challenge of the 80's was seen as effectively linking human resource planning to business planning and strategic activities (Burack, 1986). The current literature offers the same prescription for organizations which want to be able to survive the accelerating change and instability of the business environment going into the 1990's.

How does the senior management of your organization characterize the relationship between the strategic business activity and the human resource functions? Do they see personnel supporting their primary concern with product and profitability by "getting the right people when they need them?" Or is it "we communicate our human resource needs to HR once our business strategy is established, and it is up to HR to respond with appropriate programs and services." Another perspective could be that senior management works closely with HR professionals to look at human resource implications of the business strategies. HR helps management see how it can strategically attract, position and develop the people. Or does your organization "routinely involves all functions, including human resources, in important business decisions. HR is just as much a part of the team as anyone else."

Each of the above reflects a particular management orientation toward the human resources function. Paul Buller (1988) suggests that such orientations have important implications for the status of the firm's human resources function, the nature of its workforce, and ultimately, its success. The intention of this research effort was to present and illustrate this concept for members of the Philadelphia Human Resource Planning Group. This would be done in a way that they could analyze and evaluate it, and consider its relevance for their own or a client

D.W. DANNER - Hahnemann University, Broad & Vine Streets, Philadelphia, PA, 19101-1192.

Bottom Line Results from Strategic Human Resource Planning
Edited by R.J. Niehaus and K.F. Price, Plenum Press, New York, 1991

organization. A research team chaired by the author reviewed the literature, prepared an overview and some preliminary questions. Several well-regarded and high-performing organizations in the Delaware Valley were chosen for the first interviews to determine if there were some interesting examples of the approach to test the questions. A second round of interviews was held with key HR persons in six of the companies. These companies were willing to offer more detailed information about their organization's human resource function and their strategic business activity. Two of the companies were in pharmaceuticals, two manufactured chemicals, and two were in financial services.

Prior Research

The Need: To remain competitive in a constantly changing environment, many organizations are making human resources a significant part of their long range business and strategic planning (Burack, 1986). Organizations are realizing that the success of their long-range planning and strategic approaches rests on corresponding analyses and planning by human resources which is linked to these business-related analyses. The extent to which the firm can integrate its strategic decision making and human resource functions enhances its chances for success (Buller, 1988).

The challenge to HR departments is to adapt their function to take a more strategic role in helping companies not merely to attract and retain good people, but to institute "systems and processes that enable individuals to add value" (Ulrich and Yeung, 1989). Central here is the recognition that people are a key element in the successful execution of their business strategy.

If such a linkage were attained in an organization, the planning processes of HR and those of the business units would be integrated to the extent that they influence and are influenced by each other. Tom Kelly (1989) suggests that the business strategy would give direction to HR activities, and HR issues, internal and external, would be considered in the business planning process.

Though this linkage is well defined and illustrated in the literature, organizations have been slow to realize this potential. In Nkomo's 1986 survey of 287 Fortune 500 firms, 57% reported no integration of HR planning and strategic planning. In a survey by the American Productivity Center (Rhodes, 1988), top executives did view HR's role as critical to business success. They desired a closer linkage between HR and strategic business planning. They doubted, however, about HR's ability to fill this role. A survey by TPF & C reported that only two out of twenty CEOs at high-tech firms would consult HR when considering certain strategic issues.

In summary, many developments in today's turbulent business environment seem to suggest that companies where HR is more linked with the other business functions will enjoy a competitive advantage. The slow pace of this integration in American businesses indicates that more is involved than just adopting and implementing the concept. Urgings of senior management or top planning and HR executives alone will not make it happen. The application of this approach probably will not be uniform for all companies. It will require an analysis of the fit between the firm's strategic planning and human resources linkage and its environment. The literature suggests that HR professionals along with other senior managers need to explore and better understand how the integrated linkage between strategic planning and human resource functions can contribute to long-term business success, including how that linkage can be achieved.

The Research: Buller's research (1988) on eight high-performing firms categorized the degree of integration between the strategic business activity and human resource functions, from low to high, using the four-level model proposed in the 1985 research of Karen Golden and Vasudevan Ramanujam. The four levels differ not just in their linkage between HR functions and strategic business activities but show significantly different HR activities and organizational views of HR according to level. The four levels are as follows:

ADMINISTRATIVE LINKAGE - little or no linkage between HR and strategic business functions.

HR Activities: Traditional personnel activities; day-to-day handling of logistics related to the employment function.

Organization's view of HR: relatively unimportant; view people as neither a constraint or an asset to the business.

ONE-WAY LINKAGE - a linkage exists, though not highly integrated, flowing sequentially from strategic business planning to HR. HR able to be more proactive, such as designing programs to support the business plans. HR, however, reacts to the business plans, versus influencing them. HR seen as a resource, but not a strategic business partner.

HR Activities: designs programs to support the business objectives; the linkage may be informal.

Organization's view of HR: management may view people as crucial to the success of the business, but assumes HR can always find the right people; HR director probably not on the senior management team.

TWO-WAY TWO-WAY LINKAGE - information flows both to HR planners from business planners and vice versa. A sense of reciprocity and interdependence.

HR Activities: partnerships with line managers; focus on activities to enhance profitability; HR input into important business decisions; HR and the line share responsibility for certain HR activities.

Organization's view of HR: the HR function is credible and important; seen as a strategic partner; HR input important to business decisions and strategic direction; the organization realizes that HR management is everyone's responsibility.

INTEGRATIVE LINKAGE - the interaction between HR and business managers is dynamic, frequent, formal and informal. The senior HR executive is involved in strategic decisions even when they may not involve human resources.

HR Activities: HR functions well integrated with each other; HR activities more focused on what business needs are at a particular time; senior HR executives actively involved in the company's strategic planning process.

Organization's view of HR: as business partners from more than just an HR perspective; HR executives have high credibility; HR executives are viewed as part of the management team.

Another way to contrast the relative linkage, indicated in Figure 1, is to look at certain key variables in the relationship between HR and strategic business activity. Companies interviewed for this research noted these contrasts as the linkage changed.

VARIABLE	LOW LINKAGE	HIGH LINKAGE
Business environment	stable, predictable: no felt need to change HR	change or crisis having a major HR component
HR Structure	centralized, functional structure	some decentralization, with HR staff closer to the line
HR Role	administrative orientation	consultative, not transactional; low control
HR Staff	administrative orientation	business orientation, high personal credibility; think bottom line have trust of line
Organizational Decision Making	HR represented at most organization levels, but decision made first, then check for HR implications	HR in the process at the senior levels, on day-to-day basis at mid management levels
Formal or Informal Planning Processes for Corporate or HR	may be neither in place or formal process only - lacks involvement in HR planning	formal processes include HR and line. Day to day inintegration is vital, often informal

Figure 1: Relationships between Human Resources (HR) and Strategic Business Activity

The Findings   The data from the interviews with Delaware Valley organizations are summarized below under five key questions.

1. *To what degree are the four "levels of integration" appropriate and helpful in distinguishing different patterns of linkage between the strategic business activity and HR functions and activity?*

The "levels" concept proved a helpful filter through which to view HR's relationship to strategic business activities. It highlighted some distinct differences between HR activities of the six companies and differences in the degree to which HR is involved in the strategic direction of the company. Based on the interview responses, it was possible to determine that four of the companies seemed to be between two levels, one between levels 2 & 3, three between levels 3 & 4. One of the remaining two was a level 2, the other 3.

The concept provided a perspective on the organization that went beyond "functions" to signal relationships. What circumstances within the company and in its business environment could help explain some of the different relationships observed? One helpful observation was that this integration was not necessarily universal or uniform across the organization, even in the most integrated organizations. Sometimes it appeared related to the severity of external pressures on a business line -the more stable the environment, the less push to achieve greater strategic business activity-HR integration. In other cases, senior executives in certain areas of the company viewed HR less as a strategic business partner than executives in other divisions or business lines, and the HR involvement in their areas reflected that.

Finally, the strategic business activity-HR integration also appeared to have a formal-informal continuum associated with it. In and beyond level 3, the linkage was increasingly more informal. Business planning at the higher levels became a less formal process, and the HR executive participated on the business team and in decision making as a full partner rather than as a HR representative. Nevertheless, one   company commented that while the formal processes were important on a broad level, the informal linkage was most vital to the success of the linkage.

2. *What did the linkages look like in the six companies?*

Four of the six companies appeared to be between two levels, one between levels 2 & 3, three between levels 3 & 4. The remaining two were a level 2 and a 3. Companies between levels tended to appear this way because of (a) different approaches in divisions or business lines within the company itself, or (b) differences between the approaches of the management of each of the divisions. In these cases the differences were not primarily that there was too much overlap between characteristics of the levels.

CASE 1 (level 2 organization)

The senior HR executive meets regularly with senior management in this organization, but is not involved in strategic planning. The corporate strategic planning unit is functionally and physically related to the CEO's office while HR is located in a totally different building. The two major changes in HR programs, a flexible benefits programs and a day care facility, came more from senior management direction than from HR initiatives or from collaboration between HR and senior management. There is no strong linkage within the organization enabling the business lines and HR to collaborate on issues as they emerge. Even as the more innovative programs do emerge from HR, it seldom enlists the line to enable smooth introduction and buy-in.

CASE 2 (level 2-3)

The key HR person has very limited connection at the strategic or tactical level, but has more of a role in helping prepare for the decision through process facilitation. There is discussion and reaction to the implications of strategic directions for HR. The most direct support of the strategic direction is in what HR provides to develop the people resources of the business through training and career development.

CASE 3 (level 3-4)

Business planning has become a much less formal process - natural, organic - and HR executives work hand-in-glove with management. The increasing quality and sophistication of senior HR professionals led to them being seen as strategic thinkers and as an integral part of the business team. There exists, however, somewhat of a schism in the HR activity across the company. Both the strategic, developmental and the classical technocratic HR roles are exercised, depending on the bias of the divisional executive.

CASE 4 (level 4)

In this somewhat decentralized HR environment, the divisional HR manager is a member of that division's management team. She and her staff all perform generalist functions. The support HR staff at the corporate level and in the field enable these generalists to avoid a heavy transaction load. This allows them to assume a consultative role and become part of the division's business teams.

The Division HR Manager spends approximately 90% of her time with line managers and 10% with other HR staff. The business management team appreciates this, viewing her as vital to their team, a peer and as someone who adds value beyond her HR inputs.

CASE 5 (level 4)

The Senior Vice President of Human Resources was a key player in helping his company successfully weather a major merger in the recent past. The merger was done quickly and successfully, dealing well with the people issues and the other merger-related challenges. Human Resources emerged with the image of an effective contributor to accomplishing business objectives. The VP of HR is now a senior business executive who continues to "creatively use the power of Human Resources to build the company." This is central to the vision that the organization must develop its people if a merger and the resulting organization are to be successful.

Based on their contribution, Human Resources was commissioned to head the transition management for a second merger. A new position of VP of HRD and Planning was created and placed in the executive wing since 50% of his time was spent with senior people.

Human resources uses the concept of "benchmarking," seeking to measure themselves against the best, then determines how to close the gap. Their seven point "business-oriented strategy" includes recruitment of talent, reward and recognition systems, and management of diversity programs.

Line management involves HR in their strategizing, asking "Where do we want to go? Which people will help? How can we develop them so they can help us meet our objectives? How can we get buy-in?" This may involve team-building, simulations on new ways of thinking, or a plan to develop certain people.

3. *How did these companies develop the more integrated linkages?*

The level 3 and 4 companies interviewed noted two major routes by which they developed the integrated linkage. One route was an evolutionary or gradual process. The second started with some major upheaval or change in which management recognized the need for HR's input and participation in managing the transition issues. The companies mentioned mergers, acquisitions and downsizings as examples of events which "opened the door."

Common threads in both scenarios are the (1) capability and (2) credibility of the HR professionals. Portwood(1989) observes, "Profes sionals in the HR field have been saying for some time that human resources are a strategic resource in business today. They have argued that HR professionals should be included in the strategic management activities of their firms. While the former is true, the latter must be earned through demonstration that they are prepared to make a meaningful contribution to corporate strategy and overall organizational goals." Professional competence and sophistication of senior HR professionals is key to them being perceived as strategic thinkers. Buller (1988) noted that "it appeared to be essential that the HR executive have a good knowledge of the business and be seen as capable of providing credible input into the strategic planning process."

The more gradual process of the inclusion of HR in the strategic management activities was cited by two organizations. Often, credibility was vested in a particular person, not the HR function per se. That person demonstrated an awareness of the range of issues faced by the business team, and the ability to make a contribution to the decision-making process. They acted as catalysts and process support for the planning and decision-making, being proactive and anticipative of the HR aspects of the business issues. That perceived capability and credibility, however, was not a once-and-for- all or a "given" by virtue of their position. The HR person had to continue to earn that credibility through the quality of their participation and service.

When the process of inclusion accompanies major organizational change or upheaval, the credibility and capability issues are present also. The environmental/business pressures may well highlight the strategic necessity of attending to HR issues. However, an integrated linkage will only evolve if the HR person has the competence to seize the moment and capably respond to the issues. Both the competence and up-to-date understanding of the issues in the field and an understanding of the range of issues facing the organization are fundamental. If the HR person is ready at this critical moment, he or she can achieve the credibility that lead to his/her inclusion as part of the business team.

CASE 1 gradual change

The change was gradual, but it was sponsored by an HR person who was one of top seven persons to be named to the new managing committee. Now, every division has a VP of Human Resources on the planning team. "The increasing quality and sophistication of senior HR professionals led to them being seen as strategic thinkers. Very important is personal credibility. It is implicit and difficult to measure. The HR person is 'there' and they get asked. Some get in their boss's face about issues and are proactive and anticipative. They are catalysts, process managers - which is often why they get asked. A lot of what they offer is intuitive in nature."

In general, this interviewee related, four factors helped the change take place:

o Corporate commitment to strengthening the HR function.

o The increasing sophistication of the HR team - they got better, got more invitations.

o The nature of the business became more complex and fast-moving.

o The increasing importance and variety of HR issues which severely impacted the business: e.g. restructures, technological advances.

CASE 2 business event precipitates change

After a merger, when the firm found that the cost-cutting strategy of severe staff reduction saved money but precipitated lowered quality, they decided to add a large number of employees to counter the trend. HR had been seen as too administratively oriented and having limited touch with the line or linkage to the business objectives. A task force appointed to work on the hiring included line managers, legal, marketing, and HR staff. It provided recommendations as it worked and these were often implemented as they went along.

The approach of the HR and line working together initiated the fundamental change in HR. This included a different HR mission and structure, moving it "from auditors to consultants" and to working with the line rather than separate from it, more proactive and less transaction oriented. A more decentralized HR structure emerged.

4. What are some of the values in the more integrated linkages?

Nkomo's research (1986) suggests that, when human resource planning is integrally related versus being isolated from organizational planning, and is proactive versus reactive, firms rate the contributions of the planning significantly higher than firms which were classified as using incomplete approaches. Firms perceive benefits in seven areas: contribution to organizational performance, labor cost savings, employee productivity, employee satisfactions, management development, EEO/AA goals, reducing under- and over-staffing.

Delaware Valley firms surveyed pointed primarily to two linked benefits. In the rapidly changing business environment, the linkage was vital to maintaining the competitive edge. In the face of a merger or some similar internal event, the linkage was also critical to recovering and maintaining productivity.

CASE 1

Asked about the value of the more integrated linkage to the company, the HR person indicates that, it is vital both for the success of the company and for its survival. "If the company is to survive the merger, it needs to develop its people." HR is tied to the overall strategy of the company, and the company recognizes that its people are key to realizing the strategic objectives.

The linkage also enables HR to do some things in much faster time than under its earlier, more bureaucratic structure. That change helps create the perception that HR is more "responsive" to the needs of the line and more "efficient" in fulfilling the transaction responsibilities of HR.

CASE 2

A "more effective structure for HR" was cited as a key value of the linkage. The HR staff was reduced from almost four hundred persons to one hundred, with some HR staff moving to line jobs. Significant savings resulted from better handling of transactions, now centralized. HR persons directly engaged with the line now broker services, and are perceived as more in touch with line needs.

5. How can these linkages be fostered?

The research suggests the need for an organizational "readiness" for the linkage, an evident credibility and capability in the HR function. If these two conditions exist, the HR person or division can proactively press toward greater strategic business activity-HR linkage. The caveat is that full linkage is not seen as the most appropriate, or sometimes, the most economical, strategy for every type of organization or business climate.

CASE 1

The HR person says that HR cannot 'force' itself into a linkage. "Stop asking to come to the party . . . if you haven't been invited, there is a reason. You can't force yourself on the managers. The onus is first on the professional . . . to look at his or her competencies, then to make sure management sees that you have, and can bring, those competencies. Some managers may never see it - but you can't force it. Provide the value needed every little step of the way, with every service or intervention you provide, until you become a member of the team. They will invite you, expect you to participate, if you can show that value."

CASE 2

A key to influencing how HR activity will be linked to strategic business functions is how the HR person works with his/her executive and the business area. The business area HR person interviewed in this organization said that she spent 90% of her time with the line, 10% with other HR people. She and her HR staff influence the line by:

o being familiar with the business issues impacting them
o identifying HR implications of business issues
o providing HR input that makes sense from a business perspective
o spending time in the staff meetings and business meetings of the line
o gaining personal credibility with the line managers

The formal planning processes and the documentation that accompanies them happen a couple of times a year. These formal processes are valuable in that they force those in the process to step back and take an objective look at where they are. The informal linkages and processes which occur daily on-site, however, are what drive their day-to-day decisions.

CASE 3

In this company the person representing the HR function was a key variable in fostering a readiness for a more integrated linkage. The HR executive was seen as one of the top twenty executives in the organization. The executive was involved as a real business partner from the beginning of the merger talks. He played a key role regarding the merger and in what followed from it. His personal credibility earned the position and participation in business planning, which set the stage for the role that HR was to play beginning with the merger.

CASE 4

The "trust" in the HR persons which led to their involvement in the business planning, despite only a limited and informal linkage, hinged on the following activities:

o HR consultants forced themselves into business unit staff meetings,
   reported on HR activities, asked questions and developed relationships.
o They worked with the line managers in a consultative way to solve problems and thus developed credibility.
o They took on the role of "change agents."

Summary

These comments are descriptive rather than prescriptive, not specifying any one organization ought to be doing, but noting what is working for some effective organizations under specific circumstances. Summarized under five key variables found in the research, the following comments touch on some of the research team's learnings and highlight some implications for HR practitioners.

Business Environment: Though the business environment can either precipitate or suppress the readiness or necessity for the more integrated linkage, the HR practitioner cannot postpone developing the capacity to function in the more integrated relationship until the business environment prompts it. Changes can come very quickly and the window of opportunity for HR to demonstrate the value of its participation in the strategic management process can likewise close very quickly.

Planning Processes: The key to the fully integrated linkage is that both formal and informal planning processes include line and HR. Where there is specific HR planning and strategic business planning they are more often work in "tandem" than in "sequence." To function in the more integrated linkage, the HR person must credibly offer a contribution to the planning process. Or, he/she must at least make a contribution in facilitating the process and knowing the questions which need to be asked. To function in the fully integrated setting, the HR person must know the business in such a way that s/he can serve as a full participant. In the best settings, the participation of HR with management in planning is natural and "organic."

HR Structure: One difference between the levels of linkage is the degree of centralization or decentralization of the HR function. This often determines the relationship between the HR person and the line.

The more decentralized structure allows the HR person to be more involved with the line, promotes learning the business and the needs, and focuses less on providing transactions. The more relationship to the line at all organizational levels, the greater potential for diagnosing, highlighting and being responsive to emerging HR needs in the business areas. HR must also have sponsorship and a link at the top of the organization. In the fully integrated linkage, the senior HR person has day to day access to the senior management and to the strategic business functions.

The closer relationship to the line, however, does not automatically insure the linked relationship. First the HR person earns credibility by providing the services the line needs, then there is the opportunity to demonstrate their value for strategic business activities beyond strictly a HR representation.

HR Staffing: In the less linked settings, the HR staff are more administratively oriented. In the more linked, the HR staff are more business oriented, think bottom line, and have the trust of the line. The HR executive or the organization aspiring to the fully integrated linkage will need to recognize that it is the quality of the staff as much as the structure of the function that determines whether the line will see the value of the HR contribution to the bottom line and to strategic business decisions.

HR Professional's Role: The fully integrated linkage appears to require a person who can act more as a "consultant" than as an "auditor." Persons in this research effectively filling the HR professional's role in the more integrated setting demonstrate a credibility and an array of skills and abilities beyond the stereotypical HR persons in low-linkage organizations. Some of these skills and perspectives can be learned by the in-place HR person. However, those already possessing the knowledge and skills, and above all the attitude, will be able to function strategically when the opportunity opens.

The more integrated linkage between HR functions and strategic business functions is serving several high-performing Delaware Valley organizations very well. There seems to be present some exciting prospects for the vital and effective role HR can play in an organization. The fully integrated linkage may not be for everyone, however, and the question would seem to be not whether an organization ought to have the more fully integrated linkage per se, but rather whether the linkage as it exists in their organization best serves the firm considering the internal and external conditions, and if not, what are some alternatives.

References

Buller, Paul, "Successful Partnerships: HR and Strategic Planning at Eight Top Firms", *Organizational Dynamics*, (Autumn, 1988) pp.27-43.

Burak, E, "Corporate Business and Human Resources Planning Practices: Strategic Issues and Concerns,"*Organizational Dynamics*, (Summer, 1986) pp.73-86.

Golden K. & Ramanujam, V., "Between a Dream and a Nightmare: On the Integration of the Human Resource Management and the Strategic Business Planning Process", *Human Resource Management*, Vol. 24, 1985.

Kelly, T., "Strategic Partnerships in HRM", *Personnel Administrator*,(January, 1989) pp.76-82.

Nkomo, S., "The Theory and Practice of HR Planning: The Gap Still Remains", *Personnel Administrator*, (August, 1986) pp.71-84.

Nkomo, S., "Prescription vs. Practice: The State of Human Resource Planning in Large U.S. Organizations", *Southern Management Association Proceedings*, 1984.

Portwood, James, "Process Management vs. Problem Solving: Choosing an Appropriate Perspective for Evaluating Human Resource Systems," in *Creating the Competitive Edge Through Human Resources Applications*, Niehaus, R. and Price, C., Ed., Plenum Press, 1989, pp.181-191.

Rhodes, D. "Can HR Respond to Corporate Strategy?", *The Journal of Business Studies*, March/April, 1988.

Ulrich, D. & Yeung, A., "A Shared Mindset", *Personnel Administrator*, (March 1989) pp.38-45.

Empowering People at the Workforce Level

This section concerns management's efforts to give more decision making responsibility to the working level. It is generally agreed that involving employees improves bottom line results. However, it is clear that deciding to empower employees and actually producing effective results do not necessarily go hand in hand. The three papers in this section look at various dimensions of making a successful connection between the decision to empower employees and the achievement of success.

Miller, Head, and **Thomas** in their case history on Borden, Inc., describe the Borden SQP (safety, quality, and performance) program. This case history talks candidly about some of the start-up problems encountered, how they were overcome, and the results produced.

Griggs and **Manring** present four case studies on the empowerment process. The cases are drawn from pharmaceutical, transportation, chemical coatings and automotive electronic industries. The cases provide guidance on do's and don'ts and will be useful in producing a greater understanding of how to institutionalize the empowerment process.

In the final paper, **Gaertner** and **Nollen** talk about what management can do to produce improved work unit performance. A positive finding is that managers can apparently work to change the work unit climate independent of prior work unit performance. These efforts can have a positive effect on current performance.

Focusing Borden Employees on Continuous Improvement

A.M. MILLER, J.H. HEAD, and B. THOMAS

Introduction

In today's fast-paced business arena, regular infusions of new ideas are essential to achieving and sustaining competitive advantage. While good ideas can come from almost anywhere in a company, many organizations have found it difficult to involve all employees in organized problem- solving.

Gain sharing is one method being used to encourage both employee ideas and individual commitment. In the spirit of Japanese kaizen, gain sharing taps into the natural desire of most people to want to be involved in decisions affecting their job. However, in the spirit of American incentives, gain sharing provides a modest, variable pay reward in combination with non- monetary recognition based on pre-determined measures. To be successful, the process relies on employee involvement at all levels and in-depth information sharing by management.

This paper documents the evolving gain sharing process at Borden Inc. It describes the company's Safety, Quality and Performance (SQP) program -- a gain sharing process -- and the company's efforts to educate, involve, and train its work force to embrace and support a philosophy of continuous improvement. It will outline the steps taken, the lessons learned, and the financial and employee relations results achieved since SQP was introduced.

Borden's SQP program focuses plant management and employee attention on specific improvement goals in safety, quality and performance.It takes advantage of existing company audit data and procedures in both safety and quality and provides a heavy emphasis on program monitoring and continuous improvement.

The SQP program treats employees as potential contributors by fully sharing program goals and business imperatives with them, and actively tapping their ideas for improvement. Senior managers are encouraged to become strong role models and actively lead employees toward greater participation. Employees are recognized as partners by sharing with them the financial gains made through the program. The logo for the SQP program in shown in Figure 1.

A.M. MILLER - Borden Inc., 180 East Broad Street, Columbus, OH 43215;
J.H. HEAD - Ernst & Young, 1300 Huntington Building, ; Cleveland, OH 44115;and
B. THOMAS - Frank Russell Company, P.O. Box 1616, Tacoma, WA 98401

Figure 1: Safety - Quality - Performance (SQP) Logo

Background

Borden Inc. is a diverse, multi-product, world-wide organization with operations in most parts of the free world. With 46,500 employees, Borden operates more than 240 food and non-food manufacturing facilities around the globe. The company's operations represent six distinct business areas including pasta, snacks, niche grocery, dairy, non-food consumer products, and films and adhesives. With 1990 net sales of nearly $8 billion, Borden has the objective of becoming the lowest cost producer and an aggressive marketer of brands in each of its businesses.

Today, Borden is the world leader in pasta, wall coverings, forest product adhesives and vinyl wrapping film. It operates the number two salty snacks business and the largest dairy business in the United States. In 1985, the company was perceived primarily as a dairy company with a considerable number of regional food businesses. To create this metamorphoses, the company began 1985 with a three-fold strategy to:

o Streamline, modernize and restructure manufacturing operations;
o Move aggressively on a program of precise acquisitions and internal
   development in Borden's chosen growth areas; and
o Capitalize on the knowledge and dedication of Borden people.

The concept of tapping into the employee pool of knowledge evolved into the idea of an incentive program in 1987. That year, ROSE, for Return On Shareholder Equity, was launched as a vehicle to explain shareholder equity. If employees understood shareholder equity, the logic said, people would learn to work together to improve profits.

As its centerpiece, ROSE offered a $500 to $1,000 annual bonus to salaried and non-union hourly employees, creating an award pool of $1,000,000. Up to 2,000 employees in the U.S. and Canada were eligible to win an award in the ROSE program. To receive the award, the recipient's plant had to be the best in budget

70

performance for that year, or the most improved in financial performance over prior years. As an employee motivator, ROSE was not a great success.

In a follow-up assessment of ROSE, several factors emerged as likely contributors to the program's lack of success. First, the program included several design obstacles. For one, only salaried and non-union hourly employees could participate. Of those, corporate staff (about 600 employees) and international employees (more than 10,000) were excluded and not happy about it.

Union members -- about 50% of domestic employees -- were also left out because Borden did not want to negotiate on budget or profit levels. This left the union uninvolved and alienated because salaried and non-union hourly employees in a plant could win the ROSE award while their union employees could not. Finally, few people really understood return on shareholder equity even with good communication. As a result, workers at the plant level couldn't identify with the program.

A second reason for the demise of ROSE had to do with the company's culture. In 1986, Borden was an organization of strong regional brands. That same year, the company embarked on a four year acquisition program to achieve critical mass in key industries. Borden's objective was to become number one or number two in key business segments through acquisition.

While Borden's strong regional brand acquisition strategy was good for growing the business, in cultural terms it resulted in many independent companies with diverse management skills and styles. Management talent was high, but there was little uniformity in management practice - no real cultural glue. Borden management wanted to build strong employee commitment by creating a common focus that would bridge the company's cultural gaps. ROSE was seen as a way to do that. When ROSE did not work, the company looked for alternatives.

Evolving Plan Design

In the spring of 1988, Borden began experimenting with various incentive options and processes to focus employee attention -- to create a cultural glue. During the next 36 months a gain sharing process evolved through a continuing cycle of planning, implementing, assessing and making modifications.

Initially, the design team included the company's chief administrative officer, director of safety, vice president of consumer affairs, vice president of employee relations, and four senior dairy operating managers. To provide a common focus, the team identified safety, quality and productivity as logical improvement measures. Besides being universally acceptable, there was assurance from dairy managers that data for these elements were readily available. Further, the measures were well known to managers across the dairy organization.

Plans for the revised incentive plan, a prototype gain sharing program, were ready in mid-1988. The design team introduced the concept to dairy division managers who agreed to run the program within their plants. Descriptions of the SQP process were printed and mailed out. Early results and interest were weak.

To understand why, the design team decided to step back and assess the situation. Research was conducted to understand better gain sharing principles and how they could be applied to Borden. Two additional steps, solid employee communication and manager training were identified as missing elements.

Based on this assessment, the company launched a series of informational meetings for general managers and plant superintendents in 1989. These meetings focused on the mechanics of SQP. Results began to improve and, encouraged, the company began planning a national communication effort.

As part of its initial planning, Borden decided to test the gain sharing concept and pilot a gain sharing program among its operating plants in Ireland and the United Kingdom. Included within the test group were 14 company locations, chosen because of their common English language.

To test the gain sharing idea in Ireland and the U.K., the core design team facilitated a five-day series of meetings in London. In attendance were the top management team of each of the subsidiaries. The objectives of the meetings were to:

o Educate the top management team of each division regarding the gain
   sharing concept and the plan development process;
o Clarify the strategy of the parent company and its expectations for each of
   the subsidiaries;
o Identify the next steps and set timetables for development and
   implementation; and
o Determine the reaction of subsidiary management to the concept.

Discussions with Irish and English operating management, and experience with the pilot programs offered several challenges to the core design team. Before taking the gain sharing concept overseas, Borden had designed the incentive process to reward competition between plants. In Ireland and the U.K., the team discovered that inter-plant competition would not work for several reasons:

o From a business perspective, each operating unit acted fairly
   independently. No two plants among the fourteen were enough alike to
   allow inter-plant competition.
o While there were obvious opportunities for improvements in safety, quality
   and productivity, each unit management team had different management
   styles, strategies, and levels of business management sophistication.
o There was little in the way of a human resource management
   infrastructure and few common practices in human resource
   management.

As a result, the design team adopted the concept on plant-specific design. In effect, each plant within the test group in the U.K. and Ireland developed SQP measures that reflected their own distinct businesses. Instead of competing against other plants, these plants would compete against themselves, trying to best their own prior year's record. This design shift also underscored the importance of individual managers in the gain sharing process.

Other important insights also emerged through the gain sharing pilots in the U.S dairy division and in the fourteen test plants in the U.K. and Ireland:

o While there was resistance to corporate intervention and change at various
   levels and from unit to unit, it was not perceived as insurmountable. One
   European manager offered the argument that the SQP gain sharing
   process was illegal in his country (it wasn't).
o Implementation of a structured gain sharing system could improve the
   consistency of management skills development by providing the same
   basic human resource management tools.

o For successful development and implementation, the gain sharing process
   needed to be: (a) structured, (b) simple, (c) time-phased, (d) supported by
   outside (e) consultation and corporate resources, and (f) have top
   management commitment and accountability.
o The core design team would need to moniter closely the plan development
   process and follow-up at regular intervals to provide feedback on the
   quality of the process and assure proper unit behavior.

Pilot SQP plans in Ireland, the U.K., and the U.S. in 1989 were generally successful. These plans set the stage for expanded implementation in U.S. operations during the next year.

In 1989, SQP was up and running in 120 plants, primarily in dairy, pasta and snacks in the U.S. and in Ireland and the U.K. The success of these early programs not only validated the gain sharing process, it resulted in cost savings of $5,000,000. The early programs provided a format for both organizational assessment and systematic development of the management system across all Borden locations.

During 1989, U.S. plants competed against one another for SQP awards. This aspect proved unpopular among managers and created a winners-losers paradigm. Based on the success of the SQP process in Ireland and the U.K., Borden moved toward a plant-specific design concept for all U.S. plants in 1990.

The new design allowed plants to compete against their own prior year record based on specific business objectives, historical data, and targeted improvements. With a plant specific gain sharing design and self competition, Borden introduced the notion that everybody could be a winner. In 1990, 25% of participating plants won a SQP award at some level.

SQP at Borden

Borden's SQP program as it evolved is based on five assumptions:

1 Improvements in safety, quality and performance must go hand-in-hand.
   Incremental gains must be made in all three areas to qualify for awards.
2. The gain sharing must be significant to all participants. Borden
   discovered that the minimum acceptable amounts for their employees
   were well below the $500 to $600 per employee suggested by the literature.
   For Borden employees, the amount of the award proved not as important
   as the recognition and celebration of success. Still, minimum payouts are
   built into the gain sharing design in each plant.
3. A profit center's SQP goals and budget goals are separate, that is, a center
   may achieve SQP goals but not achieve budget goals or vice versa.
4. The SQP goal must be credible to employees, that is, it must have a real
   chance for success.
5. To be shared, the SQP gains must be related to employee performance and
   they must be *real* gains.

Central to SQP is a design that tailors essential components to each individual plant or location. At each plant, specific targets for safety, quality and performance are set by management and shared with employees through plant sponsored briefing and training programs. Employees participate in finding ways to reduce accidents, improve quality and enhance performance and efficiency through locally designed suggestion systems.

SQP programs may have a duration of 6, 9, or 12 months, based on what best fits the business. Programs are scheduled to minimize gaps and to keep the motivational momentum going. Each plant general manager appoints a SQP Coordinator. The coordinator handles the employee suggestion aspects of the program, arranges employee briefings and organizes plant communications.

In SQP design, employee teamwork is recognized, and suggestions are solicited and acted on quickly. Gains in the combined safety, quality and performance targets are shared with employees through awards of up to several hundred dollars per person as follows:

SQP Measures

The first step in local program design is to select appropriate bench marks for measurement. The measures include:

Safety: The most often used bench marks for safety are:

> *OSHA Recordable injury rate:* Frequency of employee injuries
> *Vehicle accident rate:* Frequency of vehicle accidents
> *Rated plant safety inspection scores:* Machine guarding, electrical, fire and
> evacuation plans, etc.

With the help of plant safety coordinators, the plant SQP team examines its safety and develops measurable improvement goals for safety, subject to division and corporate approval. The team also develops point scales to reflect the plant's total performance. Within corporate guidelines, plants with below average safety records are required to target greater minimum improvement Plants with exceptional safety performance earn points for maintenance of those levels.

This is the scale one plant constructed to rate improvements in its existing injury frequency rate of 11.5 per 200,000 working hours as shown in Table 1. In this plant, a frequency rate of at least 11.0 per 200,000 hours was set as the minimum acceptable safety score to qualify for a SQP award. With 200 employees working 400,000 hours annually, a rate reduction from 11.5 to 11.0 would result in one less injury. At this level, the plant would be awarded 60 safety points. While cost savings of over $1.25 million have been associated with the reduction of accidents, Borden does not include these savings in the SQP results.

Table 1: Scale for Rating Improvement of Injury Frequency Rate

Frequency Rate	Points
0.00 - 5.00	90
5.01 - 7.00	80
7.01 - 10.00	70
10.01 - 11.00	60
11.01 & Over	0

Table 2: Scale for Quality Assurance Rating

Corporate QA Rating	Points
9.00 and above	90
8.75 - 8.99	80
8.50 - 8.74	70
8.40 - 8.49	60
8.39 or below	0

Quality: Quality bench marks vary depending on the kind of business. Typical quality measures using the scale in Table 2 include:

o Food plant sanitation scores based on the annual corporate inspection and quality assurance (QA) rating
o Scores of monthly internal QA ratings which focus on specific problems
o The amount of product that deviates from standard specifications
o Goods from current production which are returned or rejected by customers
o Consumer complaints which are influenced by employee performance

A food plant with a prior corporate quality assurance rating of 8.30 might target improvement on the following scale to achieve quality points. To achieve the minimum quality points to qualify for a payout (60 in this example) the plant would have to achieve 8.4 or better.

In practice, most plants would use several different quality bench marks in computing points. However, in food plants, no points would be given for improved performance in other quality areas if the plant fell below its historical corporate QA sanitation performance. As a result, no award could be earned.

Performance: Because labor is a major productivity cost item, a further reduction in direct labor costs through greater work efficiency is often one of the first targets selected. If we assume that a plant has already budgeted a 4% reduction in direct labor costs, this target may become the base improvement level for these costs. This is reflected on the scale in Table 3.

Calculating Gain Sharing: Combining the scores in all three areas -- Safety, Quality, and Performance -- dollar awards per employee are calculated using a formula. Under the program, awards for each employee must be reasonable -- about $200 per employee during a six month period. At an employee payout ratio of 20 to

Table 3: Scale for Measuring Dirct Labor Costs

% Improvement	Savings	Points
8.1 and above	$125,000	50
7.1 - 8.0	100,000	40
6.1 - 7.0	75,000	30
5.1 - 6.0	50,000	20
4.1 - 5.0	25,000	10
4.0 and below		0

Table 4: Typical Payout/points Formula

	Points		Payout
Safety	Quality	Performance	
25	25	205 =	$200
50	50	275 =	$275
75	75	345 =	$350
100	100	430 =	$425
125	125	520 =	$500

25% of the incremental gain, a plant must be able to realize SQP savings of about $800 to $1000 per employee in order to offer a reasonable incentive. A typical payout/points formula might look like the one shown in Table 4

Monetary awards are based on the lowest achievement level. For example, if a plant scores 60 safety points, it would be placed at the *lower* 50 point level on the chart. Dollar payouts are also figured in terms of the lowest achievement level. If a plant earns 50 points in safety, 50 points in quality, and 345 points in performance, the award would be $275.

Training

While the company provided training early in the SQP process, it was most often technical or informational in nature, geared to SQP program designers at the local plant level. At the end of 1989, the core team determined that technical training and information meetings had to be supplemented with broader development of the people who would be working with SQP.

Early in 1990, Borden added plant manager and SQP coordinator training. As in other elements of SQP, the training followed the four step model of plan, implement, assess, and react formed in the early stages of the process. As a result, the training process evolved from concept, through design, to pilots, to final program.

At the beginning of 1990, SQP was still somewhat new for many managers. So, training was conceived as a mixture of motivation, information, and skills instruction and aimed at plant managers and SQP coordinators. The training consisted of three modules:

Module 1: This section introduced the essentials of effective supervisor/employee communication and the key information needed by employees and their preferred sources. It also explored the primary elements perceived as important by employees in a "good working environment" and the critical information needed with SQP.

Module 2: This module focused on two types of meetings -- informational and problem-solving. Participants practiced problem-solving techniques (brainstorming, fish bone analysis, etc.) and leading an informational meeting (e.g., first quarter gain sharing progress report). This aspect of the training was important since each of the participants was asked to conduct informational meetings as a regular part of their plant promotion of SQP and as part of their training.

Module 3: This section described building an effective team through discussion of the characteristics of an effective team, recognizing and dealing with team behaviors (positive and negative), role of the team leader, etc. Through case studies and discussion, participants practiced evaluating team behavior and prescribing appropriate actions by the team leader to improve both team and individual team member effectiveness.

The training reached 192 general managers and SQP coordinators from 144 locations in 1990 and was tailored around Borden's SQP program. At each of the 11 training sessions, managers appraised the training with high marks.

Communication

In 1990, Borden launched a comprehensive communication campaign to build general awareness of SQP, its primary elements, and the benefits to employees. Plant SQP Coordinators began receiving monthly materials that could be used or adapted locally.

Based on the feedback provided during the management training in the first half of 1990, Borden commissioned a series of focus groups to assess both communication and training needs. Upward communication through these focus groups was intended to capture perceptions in the following areas:

o Understanding of the SQP program by employees including purpose, procedures, scoring, and current vs. preferred sources of information.
o Perceptions of the strengths/weaknesses of the SQP program.
o Extent to which employees support the program.
o Supervisors' experience in working with employees on key SQP program aspects such as handling suggestions, team related concerns, employee questions, and areas of employee concern.
o Perceived levels of management support for the program.

The assessment provided a mix of information reflecting the regional company diversity inherent in Borden's culture. For the most part, supervisors are enthusiastic about SQP and believe that the program enhances their work as supervisors. Most believe, as one supervisor put it, that the program "fits in with our job responsibilities" and is not an add on.

Employees view SQP as a win-win. They have the opportunity to be more involved, to contribute and to make suggestions. The company benefits from ideas generated in each of the program categories (safety, quality and productivity). In terms of plan design, the assessment offered several conclusions:

o Local management's attitude, approach, and degree of involvement are the three most critical factors to successful implementation. While managers exhibit widely differing styles, the SQP process and training provide a continuing means to influence each of the three factors.
o Information to employees about the program must be clear, non-technical and, depending on the location, available in several languages.
o In order to foster employee understanding about what constitutes a "good suggestion", feedback about ideas should be provided universally across the company.

o Ongoing training and communication relating to the program are essential.
o The term "productivity" connotes negative images of cost cutting, work speed-ups, and so on. A term such as performance is not as emotionally laden.
o Involvement by union-represented employees is important and poses no real impediment to implementation. In Borden's experience, 98% of local unions in the U.S. endorsed SQP in writing even though the terms of the program were not negotiable. So far, Canadian represented employees are the only group to reject gain sharing. Various suggestion programs are used in the Canadian SQP plans in lieu of an incentive arrangement.

Results

Assessment in 1990 influenced several changes in the SQP Program. New, simplified print communications for all employees were introduced in 1991 to help improve employee understanding of the program, particularly its scoring mechanism. Programs are now available in six languages -- English, French, Spanish, Portuguese, Italian and German.

Videotape "testimonials" from real employees now provide managers with a philosophical rationale. The key message is that SQP facilitates employee involvement in the day-to-day operations of the business. It provides people a voice and challenges them to grow.

The "P" in SQP was changed in 1991 from productivity to performance to reflect the sentiment in the field. A national monthly publication has been launched to share employee ideas with everyone.

In 1990, Borden realized savings of more than $15 million from productivity improvements alone after deducting the expenses of running the program and providing rewards. Employee suggestions are estimated to add another $3-5 million in cost savings (actual cost savings were not yet tallied for 1990 as of this writing).

The company has realized a 43% cumulative reduction in the accident rate across participating plants. At one Canadian plant, productivity has improved 16% and raw materials usage is down 10%. Absenteeism, consumer complaints, and waste are all down significantly. In 1990, there were no work stoppages by organized labor, the first time the company has been strike-free in 23 years.

Summary

For the future, Borden's emphasis has changed from the mechanics of the gain sharing process to the development of human resources. A management and employee skills training program is under development and communication, at the corporate and local levels, is undergoing constant refinement.

As Borden widens the company's SQP program to 220 plants in 1991, ongoing assessment will become critically important. SQP gains come through the creative ideas of people. The number and quality of those ideas depend heavily on the way in which people are managed. Ongoing assessment will enable the company to understand how to ensure the success of SQP in a variety of facilities and different businesses across the organization. The current target is to develop an organizational assessment process that will identify critical needs at the unit manager level. The unit manager will then be held accountable for continual assessment of his or her unit's organization effectiveness and the application of management tools to improve continually the management process.

The Bottom Line of Empowerment

W.H. GRIGGS and S.L. MANRING

Introduction

During the 1970's, the major focus of organizations was on quality. In the 80's, the focus on cost was added. The 90's require not only quality and cost, but also speed of response. Now the concept of employee empowerment is being looked at as a primary vehicle for increasing organizational effectiveness and improving quality, cost and responsiveness. Operationally, we have defined empowerment as the outcome of a congruent organizational culture and structure that supports individual and group self-initiating actions.

This research report is based on our study of employee empowerment in four organizations representing pharmaceutical, transportation, chemical coatings, and automotive electronics industries. The size of the total population involved in the four cases was 450 people, including senior and middle managers, technical professionals (scientists and engineers), technicians, and shop level operators. While the organizations differed by type of industry, structure and culture, what they have in common is a growing commitment to create a flatter organization with an empowered workforce.

In our investigation of employee empowerment, using intensive group and individual interviews, we identified several critical underlying assumptions:

o Empowered employees will find more meaning and challenge in their work.
o Increased meaning and challenge leads to stronger personal involvement and commitment to organizational goals.
o Empowered and committed employees can "self-manage" toward higher levels of quality and productivity.
o "Self-managed" employees reduce the need for layers of management and staff, thereby reducing costs and response time.

As researchers, we were struck by the apparent simplicity and straightforwardness of these assumptions. We were also curious why so many empowerment programs

W.H. GRIGGS and S.L. MANRING - GriggsManring, Inc. 63 Oakwood Drive, Chapel Hill, NC 27514

seem to founder. Our analysis provides insight into why empowerment efforts often fail to impact the bottom line as much as they should.

We based our analysis of these organizations on a framework that focuses on three spheres of organizational life: structural, cultural and personal. *Structural* factors include, the type of organizational hierarchy, policies, procedures and control systems.which are in place. *Cultural* factors reflect beliefs, norms and values about how the organization works, vis-a-vis getting things done and reaping the rewards. *Personal* factors include the freedom to act with confidence and competence; confirmation of individual worth and contribution as a team member, and a sense of belonging and having a career.

From our research, we believe that effective organizations are distinguished by congruence among cultural values, the supporting organizational structures, and the behaviors of managers and employees. Using our four case studies, we will illustrate how each of these spheres affects empowerment.

CASE 1

This large midwestern pharmaceutical company has a strong reputation for its commitment to treating people well. Like many companies, it is struggling to move from a traditional hierarchical structure and paternalistic culture to a flatter and more participative organization. The senior management leaders in information systems, engineering, and materials management took the initiative to sponsor a programmatic approach to the study of empowerment. They were particularly concerned about whether the organization's structure, culture and managerial skills and attitudes were appropriate to support the company's anticipated rapid rate of growth.

As the researchers, we were asked to carry out an in-depth survey to determine the extent to which managers (ranging from executive directors to department heads) felt "empowered" after several months of training and implementation of programs designed to increase levels of participation. Their approach placed great emphasis on consensus-style decision making. This emphasis on consensus was perceived as an important antidote to what had historically been called the "hero management style" of the company.

Through a combination of individual interviews and focus group sessions with 175 managers in three divisions, a number of structural, cultural and personal variables were identified that affected managers' sense of empowerment. These are presented and discussed below.

Structural Variables

Managers reported that a major factor which negatively affected their empowerment efforts was a general lack of focus and well-articulated goals. This was due in part to the ongoing shifting of divisional priorities, coupled with confusion about managerial role responsibilities.

Despite the high value placed on empowering individual initiative, approval processes and administrative controls remained tightly held at the top. Approval authority requiring multiple signatures governed routine travel and relative small purchases that had already been approved once in the planning process.

The strategy for human resources created many difficulties. The corporate HR strategy was to move people frequently in order to develop broad-based generalists. Managers, however, reported that the organization's commitment to rapid lateral and vertical movement was failing to provide the depth of experience required for organizational effectiveness. Rapid career moves were seen as contributing to the development of personal style as opposed to solid skills and depth of job knowledge. Managers also reported feeling less able to respond to the challenges of their own jobs because of inadequate experience in the grade.

Along with rapid movement of personnel, the organization was using tight head count control, ostensibly to avoid over staffing and the subsequent risk of layoff; however, the consequence throughout the organization was felt as increased stress due to work overload. The policy was also viewed as a short term oriented control process run from the top of the personnel organization and was out of synchronization with planning cycles and real staffing requirements. Managers felt dis-empowered when requests for staff were denied because of short term business cycle adjustments despite previous approvals in the planning process.

Managers reported difficulty in reaching clarity about what behaviors were most appropriate with the changing role of the manager (from traditional, hierarchical to facilitative, participatory). There was a lack of training and experience, coupled with the lack of an accessible personnel manual to provide basic guidelines for managerial decisions on personnel policy. This left managers in a persistent state of ambivalence about their role and authority to act on personnel matters.

Cultural Variables

Consensus management was voiced as the high value for the future, although it was actually being played out in an exaggerated form to avoid confrontation or responsibility for decisions. Despite the value placed on consensus, there were many examples of high level managers moving in to save a situation, consistent with the hero management style of the past. This conflict between word and deed was compounded by what was described as managers' excessive need to know all details of their area (in case they were asked), their aversion to risk taking (e.g., empowering their subordinates) and a fear of failure.

Managers recognized that the high emphasis placed on interpersonal communication as the dominant mode for gaining consensus had become a parody of effective communication and decision-making. Communication was seen as a process of "greasing the skids" to prepare the way for acceptance of proposals and to avoid conflict and confrontation. Meetings were characterized as more reflective of the Japanese culture, where one never hears "no" and is not sure when there is a "yes".

There was great concern that top corporate management did not adequately recognize the effects of the present rapid rate of growth that the organization was experiencing and which was causing many departments to feel they were in a survival/crisis mode. Senior leadership of the company was accused of being too focused on Wall Street and disconnected from the internal consequences of rapid growth and cultural change within the company.

Personal Variables

The perceived path to personal success took the form of style and image, i.e., having the 'right stuff' to get ahead (become a generalist). Recruiting practices placed great emphasis on interpersonal skills, appropriate dress and social activities in universities. There was strong agreement among department heads and middle managers, that too much time and energy went into developing interpersonal and stylistic competencies as opposed to concentrating on how to achieve effective results. While interpersonal competence was valued as contributing to effectiveness, excessive concern with the 'right stuff' demanded too much of an individual's time in networking and seeking personal feedback and support.

A Summary of Findings and Action Implications

This company can be characterized as placing a high value on careful planning and thoroughness in implementation of change programs. The company is equally concerned with measuring the progress and outcomes of planned change programs. The results from the study of empowerment created a new perspective and focus for further development of empowerment efforts that would enhance the core value of the organization: concern and regard for the individual.

Based on this research, the central task for this organization now is to align the structural, cultural and personal variables for greater congruence. Specifically, the structural issues that need attention are: (a) aligning approval authority with clearer definitions of managers' freedom to act; (b) transferring responsibility for head count control to managers in order to integrate staffing more effectively with planning processes; (c) increasing focus on competency development, with an attendant results orientation; and (d) introducing a more clearly defined discipline for conducting meetings, which balances attention to process with outcomes.

To overcome some of the remaining cultural barriers, the organization needs to: (1) continue to challenge the "hero manager" as the dominant managerial style; (2) increase acceptance of constructive conflict in the service of improved decision making; and (3) balance the consensus process with the needs for timely decision making. To increase a personal sense of empowerment, the organization needs to: (a) refocus its promotion policy to become more grounded in attainment of competencies that are results-oriented; and (b) become more explicit about the role of the manager in an empowered organization and to support that role with clear definitions of appropriate managerial responses.

CASE 2

This division, located in the mid-west, functions as an internal technical consulting group to the rest of a major corporation in the transportation industry. The division's mission is to introduce leading edge manufacturing technology and systems to the manufacturing divisions of the corporation. The organization is staffed with specialists in mechanical, electrical and computer engineering disciplines.

This division was recently reorganized under new leadership; the new division head was formerly with a major consulting firm. Shortly after joining the organization, the division head articulated a new mission and vision, and he restructured the organization into multi-disciplinary teams consistent with the project nature of the division. The division's new vision articulated new role definitions and behaviors of managers and professionals. Self-regulating teams were empowered to take significant initiative in working with their client systems and the rest of the corporation. Considerable emphasis was placed on these groups becoming a non-hierarchical team of collaborative professionals, very much in the model of professional consulting groups.

Some months later, we were asked to conduct focus group sessions for the entire organization of 125 people. The purpose of the focus groups was to determine how well the new mission and vision were understood, accepted and implemented throughout the division. Our findings, organized by structural, cultural and personal variables, follow.

Structural Variables

The movement from a hierarchically structured organization to project teams was considerably more difficult than originally anticipated. For example, while the vision was very clear in the new division head's mind, neither the vision nor the concrete implementation steps were clearly communicated or understood through the organization. Managers and professionals were concerned about the lack of clarity in organizational focus and planning activities. They complained of not being clear about whom they really worked for (specifically, who now had control over performance appraisals and career movement).

The professionals tended to move quickly to embrace the team concept, but they reported that many senior managers were unable to manage the behavioral change from a top-down control style to a facilitative, collaborative mode. Some senior managers reported being very uncomfortable with the new organizational structure. They were concerned about the lack of clarity regarding the new role behaviors required of them in the consulting teams. For some, the absence of "senior" titles created a perceived loss of status vis-a-vis the outside world.

There was inadequate training for effective communication, negotiation or conducting meetings, This was having a negative effect on the division's efforts to develop a stronger sense of team.

There were disagreements about how to rearrange the physical facilities, moving away from traditional offices with closed doors to open offices and/or large open meeting places. While the former were seen as "old style management", the latter were viewed as more consistent with open, collaborative teams.

Cultural Variables

The culture of the corporation was derived from its long history in heavy manufacturing. For years it had been deeply hierarchical and tightly structured. The division's culture was very similar until the arrival of the new general manager. As he redefined the mission and vision of the organization and brought in new professionals, conflicting cultural values and assumptions began to surface.

The shop personnel, who built experimental models, were treated differently from the professionals "upstairs". It became apparent that team membership was more determined by professional credentials than by the needs of the project.

The new need for an increased sense of trust, openness and risk taking was conflicted with the older norms of competition among individuals for hero badges. The influx of many new members to the organization, bringing with them other cultural norms, made it all the more difficult to reconcile differences and reach agreement on the new behavioral norms for this division. There was also concern about whether the new culture they sought to create in the division would be consistent with the older culture of their client groups in the corporation.

Personal Variables

The lack of a traditional structure increased uncertainty about individuals' performance, status and acceptance by other members of the organization. For many, the new mission and vision promised more opportunity for greater visibility and the rewards of working in a collaborative team environment. Others, more used to heavily structured systems, showed concern about the potential loss of opportunities to achieve individual recognition.

The process by which people were assigned to particular projects was not clear to all professionals. Some suspected that "project dynasties" were being created and that these dynasties were more political than competence-based.

The ongoing effort to develop a skills inventory was perceived as a useless abstraction in comparison with the pressing need to staff and develop teams. At the same time, the continued lack of clarity about the relative value and assessment of individual contributions made it difficult for some to understand how they would progress in their careers.

Because this particular organization, as well as the transportation industry in general, was in a great state of change, it was difficult for people to give their full commitment to the division or to its new mission. There seemed to be a "watch and wait" attitude instead of a sense of dedication of purpose.

A Summary of Findings and Action Implications

This organization is attempting to change dramatically its mission and mode of operation to function effectively as consultants to manufacturing in a multi-division corporation. Based on our research data, this organization needs to concentrate first on addressing the following structural issues: (a) in the absence of the former hierarchical structure, it is critical for the organization to translate its new mission and vision into clear definitions of how managers will manage their internal staff resources and relate to their external client systems; and (b) create mechanisms, including meeting protocols, project staffing procedures, and formal communication processes that are designed to reduce uncertainty and ambivalence about the role and functioning of managers and project teams.

Secondly, the organization needs to concentrate on addressing some cultural issues: (1) there needs to be a major effort to develop a common language, set of values, and expectations about behavior consistent with the new mission that are widely understood and acted upon. This is particularly critical because of the existence of several cultural streams, resulting from organizational turnover plus the different orientation of the new division head; (2) the new cultural definition, expressed in terms of language, values and expectations needs to become central in the recruiting, staffing and promotion processes; and (3) there needs to be periodic assessment of whether the organization is developing increasing congruence between the values that are expressed in the new mission and vision and the values that are acted upon.

At the personal level, (a) there needs to be an increased level of dialogue between managers and professionals regarding career opportunities and competencies required for recognition as fully contributing organizational members; and (b) senior managers need to be helped through the transition from the older hierarchical organization, which allowed them considerable role and title status, to their new role as facilitator-manager in the flatter group-oriented culture.

CASE 3

This research and development lab is part of a chemical coatings manufacturing, distribution and sales corporation located in the mid-west. The lab is staffed with Ph.D. scientists, technologists, technicians and computer specialists. Its primary mission is to provide state-of-the-art coatings for the automotive industry. The lab was recently reorganized to merge corporate research personnel with the division's development group. This recent merger created uncertainty with respect to the relative weight of "R" vs. "D". The general perception among both research and development personnel was that the mission and culture of the organization reflected a "Little r - Big D" orientation.

The organization also reflected other signs of struggle over cultural values. This struggle took the form of an "old values vs. new values" controversy. Many problems associated with lab management indicated a lack of managerial skills training and inconsistent managerial practices. These problems reflected the old values, which were associated with excessive top- down control. The new values, associated with participation and empowerment of organizational members, were being pushed by some lab directors and technicians but not by middle management.

Following the R & D merger there was a period of uncertainty about whether the lab was to be relocated to a different state (where corporate headquarters are located). During this several year period, the corporate decision was to put no money into the existing facilities of this lab, which resulted in a rapid deterioration of physical working conditions. The move issue was finally settled by the corporate decision not to move and not to consider moving the lab for at least five more years.

Under these circumstances, we were asked to undertake an intensive study of the factors that were negatively affecting morale, retention, performance and quality. We conducted a series of focus group sessions involving all 100 members of the lab to help us understand what different groups perceived as the sources of frustration. A number of structural, cultural and personal factors that negatively affected both individual and group effectiveness were identified. These are reviewed below.

Structural Variables

One restraining force in this lab effort to develop a sense of team work and personal empowerment was the felt sense of separation among the three major functions: research, development and production. Part of the difficulty stemmed from the structure of the three components, with each having their hierarchical reporting relationship to one of three directors. The division vice president was located in corporate headquarters out-of-state and although he was on site weekly, his presence was not felt as a unifying force in relation to the three components.

The nature of the work in the three components, although related, was not generally perceived as interdependent. Each component was driven by a different sense of time and priorities about the work that needed to be done. The structural difficulties were manifested in several ways, for example:

o There were no integrative communication structures that created a sense of communality of mission or priorities.

o Planning and budgeting processes were overridden by short term edicts driven by monthly fluctuations in sales. This discontinuity between time cycles required for research and the reaction to sales fluctuations created major disruptions to effective research and development management.

o The structure of jobs, which was more consistent with specialized individual task assignments, did not allow for collaborative, team based activities.

o The specialist job orientation precluded easy formation of task teams to carry out innovative and interdisciplinary projects.

o Personnel policies were perceived as being administered differentially across the components and in relation to types of jobs.

Cultural Variables

As the corporation tried to transmit corporate philosophy through policies and administrative controls, the differences between the corporate and the division culture became manifest. For example, the stated corporate philosophy was to place a high value on innovation. However, administrative controls over financial and human resources were perceived within the division as excessively restrictive, short term oriented and dysfunctional for an R & D environment. The inference drawn by division personnel was that the corporation did not value this division nor its personnel. This was inadvertently reinforced by senior management's public attention to sales volume and dollars and not to technology development.

Within the lab itself, there was an inherent clash among the three cultures: research, development and production. The intra-divisional differences perpetuated a "we-they" attitude among the three components, manifesting itself in low levels of trust and suspicions about motives or capability across the three components.

Attempts to move from a "Father knows best" culture to a collaborative "adult-to-adult" culture were inhibited by the different histories and leadership orientations of the three lab directors. The differences among the lab directors were amplified down through the organization so that at the technician level, cooperation was very difficult across department boundaries and there was a persistent theme of competition for scarce resources.

Considerable stress in the organization was the direct result of inadequately prepared middle managers who were unable to function effectively with human resource issues. Several instances were reported of personal harassment and job-related discrimination against women. At the same time, there were complaints among men and women about favoritism toward a particular ethnic group.

Personal Variables

At the most fundamental level, uncertainty about the future of this lab persisted as a dominant personal concern. The irony is that while the corporation was committed to keeping people informed about relocation plans for the lab, as the plan was on-again - off-again, people began to lose a sense of control over their personal and professionals lives. Many left, either because the lab was going to be moved or was not going to be moved. For many who stayed, there was a lingering sense of resentment toward the corporation and mistrust of the division's senior management. Other personal concerns remained on a wide range of human resource activities in the face of organizational efforts to reduce corporate staffs.

Because of the lack of clarity about the role of research in this new market driven environment, many Ph.D. professionals questioned the long term viability of their position. Without a clearly articulated technical ladder, many other technical professionals were unable to see beyond their present job to a long term technical career.

Because of inadequate attention to the formation and development of effective teams, people did not have a sense of involvement and interdependence with others. There was no real sense of cohesiveness and belonging, and the feelings of isolation and being under-valued were intensified by the poor physical condition of the facility.

People reported that they spent so much time chasing supplies and cleaning their work area that they did not have adequate time or a sense of full commitment to give to their task assignments. At the same time, the difficulty in acquiring needed equipment and resources discouraged individuals from taking initiative in expanding their scope of activity.

A Summary of Findings and Action Implications

The task now is to recreate this organization into a positive work environment. A first step is to find structural alternatives to the current "three silo" system with its attendant intergroup conflict and competition for available resources. The key issues to be addressed include: (1) creation and utilization of a mission and vision statement that defines the organization's purpose and goals and can be used as a vehicle to unify the total organization; (2) development of human resource policy guidelines for the training and development of management, in order to restore a sense of moral integrity in this organization; (3) establishment of formal communication processes that draw top managers into a closer understanding of the daily situation of the total staff; (4) creation of multi-disciplinary task teams to address both organizational as well as technical issues and opportunities; and (5) development of well-thought out training and career planning programs for lab personnel.

There are several cultural issues to be addressed that will have a profound effect on the personal commitment and sense of belonging among lab personnel. Action steps should include: (1) an intensive effort by top management to elevate the level of management integrity and active concern for providing just and fair treatment of the people in the organization; (2) concerted "symbolic" acts by management representing a sincere commitment to the people, to technology development and to improve the physical environment of the facility; and (3) a commitment to ongoing dialogues between lab personnel and division management, including the vice president, focused on the mission/vision statement and the general health and well-being of the organization.

CASE 4

This study took place in a unionized plant within an electronics division of one of the big three auto makers, located in the midwest. The plant has relatively old equipment and is under the threat of closing because of a non-competitive cost structure, compared to new plants in the south and in Mexico.

An experimental group of production workers was formed to see if the "team concept" of organizing production would lower costs and improve quality and response time to customer orders. Changes in job structure were agreed to by the union, and workers were asked to sign up for the newly restructured department. Several months into the change process, we were asked to provide a day of team building, using an outdoor group problem-solving program. We were also asked to conduct focus group sessions with the three shifts of operators to determine if the team concept was working and if the production workers felt empowered to take more initiative in managing their production areas. The targeted activities for self-management included production scheduling on the line and tool management.

At the completion of our study, we reviewed the focus group data and our recommendations with the general foreman and the production workers. However, the general foreman was transferred to another plant before the recommended action steps were initiated. Three months later the new foreman asked for a new survey to provide a fresh starting point. The results of the second survey indicated a serious erosion of positive commitment and trust among the production workers.

These two surveys and three months of direct involvement with 50 members of the organization provided the researchers with some valuable insights into the structural, cultural and personal variables that determine whether team- oriented empowerment programs can positively affect the bottom line in a production system. The highlights of our findings are reviewed below.

Structural Variables

While the production group had been organized into teams, the supporting structures of engineering, production control and line management remained in a traditional hierarchical structure. There were at least three effects of this: (1) although a basic tenet of teams is open communication across boundaries, in this situation, the hierarchical structure of the support groups precluded more open communication patterns; (2) the hierarchical reporting relationships of the support groups required longer decision cycles for establishing the priorities for action on the production floor, and (3) professionals, particularly in staff support functions, did not see themselves in service of the basic production unit. These structural anomalies resulted in the following types of situations, which greatly increased operator frustration:

1. The development of a production control system to support operator controlled machine scheduling lagged both the operators' willingness to accept the new responsibilities and management's proposed timetable for implementation.
2. Measures of production performance were poorly developed and the supporting data about performance improvements, e.g., relating to scrap, machine utilization, etc. were unavailable to production teams in the experimental area.

The proposed team concept required a considerable reallocation of production work, as well as additions of work items that traditionally had been assigned to other staff or support groups (scheduling, process control, tool management, etc.). Production workers were expected to figure out how to work together to accomplish all their task assignments and to coordinate this across three shifts. However, industrial engineering support in terms of an assessment of time units required to manage all the old plus new elements of the job in the new team configuration was not provided. This created confusion and anxiety among the operators about whether they could function in the new situation; as a result, operators regressed toward the old practice of negotiating elements of work through the union committeemen.

While there was agreement in principle that training was critical for the success of this program, there were obvious gaps in implementation, for example:

1. Operator training for new responsibilities, e.g., process control, gauging techniques, tool changes, etc. was minimal (attempts to train operators were conducted on the production floor under extremely noisy conditions).
2. Training operators for working in a team based system was limited to one or two days of class instruction about group dynamics early in the project and the outdoor team building session several months later. There were no follow-up sessions after these initial programs.
3. Training to help union committeemen and the three shift supervisors understand and appreciate the different requirements of their new roles vis-a-vis self-managed teams was not provided.
4. There was no planned communication training program which would ensure that the learning from one shift was transferred to the other two shifts or that intershift rivalry and tensions could be managed effectively.

The mid-stream turnover of the general foreman assigned to the experimental program created problems and time delays while the new foreman got on board and oriented. For the production workers, changes in management called into question the fundamental organizational commitment to the project. Secondly, the operators were concerned that the new manager would redefine the project according to personal whims without an understanding of the history of the project. Third, while the new general foreman brought a very valuable perspective and sense of excitement about the program, he had to spend time establishing himself with the production team, the shift supervisors and union committeemen, and creating effective ways to communicate, set priorities and resolve differences.

Cultural Variables

There was a minimum attempt to articulate the norms governing the traditional hierarchical organization and what new norms needed to be developed and incorporated to support the self-managed production teams. For example, the fundamental "we-they" attitudes between management and labor were only confronted superficially. The historic distrust between labor and management was never fully explored in a way that helped either party develop an increased sense of trust and confidence in the other.

Before the introduction of this self-managed team concept, operators had functioned independently of each other in relation to their bank of machines. Disputes and conflicts between operators and shifts were mediated either by supervisors or union committeemen. While many operators adopted the new norms (and preferred them), some operators on each shift were unable or unwilling to change their mode of working with their fellow operators. There were no organized efforts to help operators manage peer relationship issues consistent with their new level of interdependence.

Personal Variables

Though the staffing of the "self-managed" production unit was advertised as a voluntary process, operators reported feeling coerced by the lack of options. Management had repeatedly warned that unless this plant could show considerable cost savings, the work would be moved to plants in Mississippi or Mexico and this plant would close.

There was no pre-screening of operators, based on whether individuals preferred interdependent teams as opposed to independent work. Consequently, while some operators signed up because they liked the idea of working within teams, others signed up because they did not feel they had any real choice. This resulted in team compositions mixed between those who embraced the new mode with enthusiasm and those who were resentful and resistant. There were no organized efforts to help teams reconcile these differences.

While the old system required considerable overtime, which made this hot, dirty work more attractive to the workers who hired into this area, the perception of many operators was that the team concept would reduce the availability of overtime and substantially reduce pay checks. This loss of overtime remained a threat to operators' commitment to a full development of the team concept.

There was a lingering resentment among the operators in general about how quickly they were pushed into this new system to make up for years of managerial inattention to this plant. These feelings continued to be fueled by a lack of specific data about benchmarks and the critical "bogies" related to increased capacity, quality and cost reductions, etc. This lack of well-communicated performance criteria caused operators to distrust the objectivity of decisions about the ultimate success/failure of this experiment. Management's continued use of the threat to move the work to Mississippi or Mexico was suspected by many operators to be the actual long term plan of the company.

A Summary of Findings and Action Implications

This organization is struggling to move beyond its own history as a deeply hierarchical organization, with a "Command and Control" approach to management and a long standing adversarial relationship with labor. The company's urgency to become more competitive, in our opinion, drove the organization to shortcut several important steps in the change program that now need to be revisited.

The central task for this organization, based on this research study, is to integrate a number of structural, cultural and personal variables. Specifically, the structural issues that need attention are: (1) a redefinition of the boundaries of the work group to include support functions as well as the basic production teams. It must be clearly communicated that the engineering, production control, and tool maintenance support functions are in service of the production teams; (2) development of clear and defensible measures of production output, costs and quality and their impact on the financial health of the operation; (3) a clarification of the roles and relationships among management, production workers and the union in the context of the new work structures. In addition there needs to be a clarification of the commitment of individuals in these three groups to the new work structures; (4) the provision of more and better training for production team members, support personnel, managers and union committeemen; and (5) creation of a set of well-defined criteria that make explicit the economic and production milestones necessary for a sense of success.

To integrate this new team approach to production, several cultural/personal areas need attention: (1) management needs to examine its assumptions about the potential contributions of production workers. (Our data indicated that the production workers were far more capable of comprehending and incorporating change than management gave them credit for; operators' concerns were primarily in reaction to the poorly thought out and executed change program); (2) organizational leadership must become much more visible in terms of providing support and resources, in order to create an atmosphere of shared responsibility for the success of the program; (3) management must create and institutionalize organizational continuity vis-a-vis change programs, in order to maintain commitment of the operators and to coordinate effectively the total production and support systems; and (4) labor and management need to move away from their adversarial relationship toward an increased sense of partnership or stewardship in order to improve the competitive position of the plant.

Conclusion

How can managers and human resource professionals ensure that empowerment efforts in their organization will positively affect the bottom line? First, we believe there needs to be a large enough vision that includes comprehension and integration of the structural, cultural and personal variables in the design and implementation of empowerment programs. Through our illustrations in four organizations, we have shown the importance of giving relative weight and attention to each of the three spheres and creating a congruent organizational structure and culture that supports individual and group self-initiating actions.

Secondly, each sphere of activity - structural, cultural and personal - requires a well-articulated strategy for successful interventions, that is balanced and coherent in relation to the other two spheres, before undertaking the change program. Each of these strategies must be supported by clear measures of progress and success. Too often managers underestimate the complexity of their situation and fall into the trap of "designing on the road" with too little up front planning.

Third, empowerment efforts will fail unless senior management is involved, cares, and provides significant and ongoing indications of leadership and support, both in terms of a highly visible "umbrella", as well as the provision of adequate staffing and financial resources.

Management Practices Leading to High Work Unit Performance

K.N. GAERTNER and S.D. NOLLEN

Assuring high work unit performance has always been an important organizational task, especially during times of scarce resources and economic uncertainty. One potential source of high performance is the management practices in the work unit. Sometimes called "climate" (Litwin and Stringer, 1968), these factors include the work unit's formal and informal systems, its ways of solving problems and making decisions, its management "style", and its goals and values.

Several studies have shown organizational climate to be related to individual performance (Pritchard and Karasick, 1973; Forehand and Gilmer, 1964) and organizational performance (Hansen and Wernerfelt, 1989; Denison, 1984; Lawler, Hall, and Oldham, 1974). Moreover, Hansen and Wernerfelt (1989) found that organizational climate explained about twice as much variance in firm performance as economic variables (market share and size).

In this study we extend the work of those who have investigated organizational climate and performance in two ways; with analysis at the work unit level and by incorporating prior performance into the analysis. The work unit level is a largely neglected level of analysis. George and Bettenhausen (1990) and Gladstein (1984) are notable exceptions but their results are opposite and inconclusive. Gladstein (1984) found that climate-type factors accounted for none of the variance in work unit sales performance, but she predicted work unit performance with individual perceptions. George and Bettenhausen (1990) found a zero-order correlation between one element of work group climate and sales performance but did not report multivariate results.

The work unit is an important level of analysis for several reasons, apart from the dearth of extant field research at this level. First, as many firms are large and decentralized, the operant "organizational" level may be the work unit rather the organization as a whole. This is especially true for geographically dispersed and sometimes isolated work units.

Second, many climate perceptions are most relevant at the group level. Insofar as organizational climate results from a social learning process (Jones and James, 1979) the most proximate environment for learning is the work group. In

---

K.N. GAERTNER and S.D. NOLLEN - Georgetown University, School of Business Administration, Washington, D.C. 20057

highly differentiated firms it may not make sense to talk about organizational climate because each work unit has its own climate.

Third, group work is proliferating by using quality circles, autonomous work units, task forces, and the like. Therefore we are seeing more and more work organized as group work rather than individual work, increasing the salience of the group.

Finally, though constrained by the organization, work unit climate can be influenced by an individual manager's initiatives. Thus it is changeable and actionable and worthy of research attention.

We also extend existing research by incorporating *prior* performance in the analysis, thus controlling for a potential cause of climate. Very little previous research has been longitudinal (Lawler, Hall, and Oldham, 1974 are a notable exception) and even among longitudinal studies, prior performance is measured poorly if at all. However, it is important to control for prior performance because it may be a *cause* of work unit climate rather than caused by work unit climate (Staw, 1975).

The Research Model

We define work unit climate as the perceptions of work unit employees about the context within which work is accomplished. We do not define climate with reference to objective, externally verifiable work conditions. For our purposes, climate is the received, enacted work environment resulting from an interaction between the person and the work setting (Schneider, 1983).

Work setting contributions to work climate may come from two sources, (a) structural or input factors such as size, technology, division of labor, and (b) formalization and interpersonal or process factors such as reward system, leader behavior, and opportunity to participate. The resulting climate is the way in which these factors are received by employees.

Extant climate research suggests structural or input factors are not very strong determinants of climate perceptions (Lawler, Hall, and Oldham, 1974), while process factors are stronger. This may be because process factors are more immediate and observable by the employee while structural factors are distant and amorphous on a day-to-day basis. Therefore we look at the immediate work environment and the process by which work is managed as the source of work unit climate.

While there have been many studies involving organizational climate, very few have focused on the effect that work unit climate has on work unit performance, as we do here. Conceptually, work unit performance ought to be a function of four factors: (1) characteristics of the marketplace (such as competition, technological change, regulation), (2) characteristics of the people doing the work (their ability, experience, and motivation), (3) the physical resources available (tools and machinery), and (4) the work climate. Blumberg and Pringle (1982) refer to the last two as opportunity to perform. It is the last set of factors on which we focus our attention.

Among the climate characteristics which have been found to influence some type of performance in previous research are: (1) emphasis on performance and performance improvement (Hansen and Wernerfelt, 1989); (2) performance contingent reward allocation, especially among sales people (Podsakoff and Todor, 1985; Gaertner and Nollen, 1989); (3) efficient use of resources (Denison, 1984),

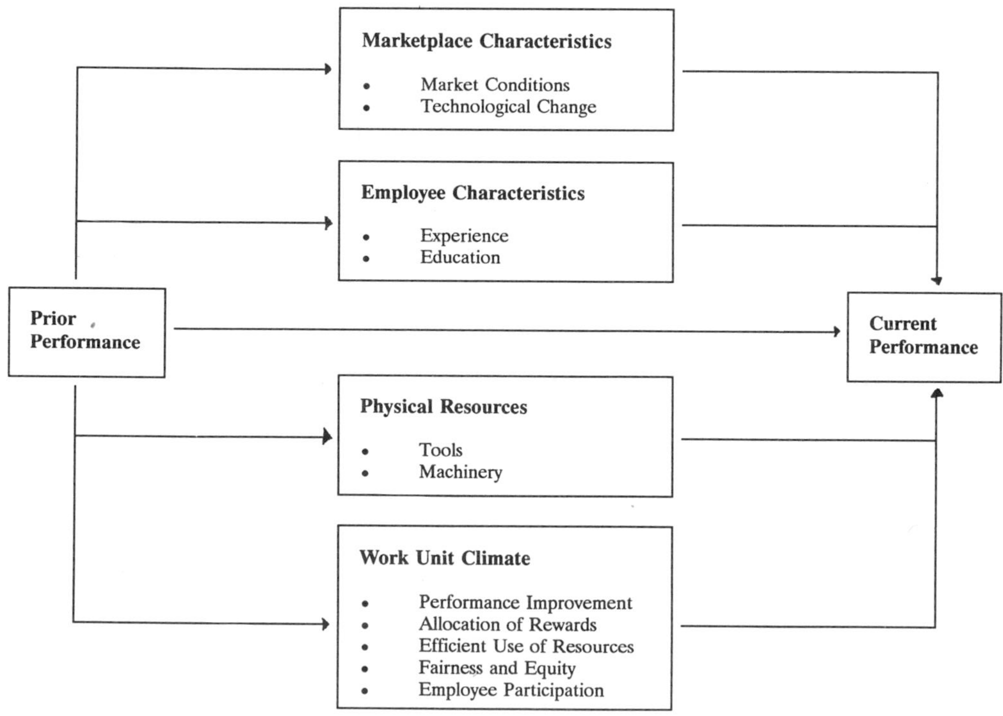

Figure 1: Model of Work Unit Climate and Work Unit Performance

(4) perceptions of fairness and equity in handling employees (Hansen and Wernerfelt, 1989; Denison, 1984); and (5) opportunity for employee participation in decisions (Gaertner and Nollen, 1989).

As shown in Figure 1, our emphasis here is on the relationship between work unit climate and work unit performance. However, we also control for some of the other factors that are likely to influence performance; employee skill and marketplace conditions. We do not include physical resources. There is not much variability among work units on this factor and they are not critical to the performance of the work units in this study.

Finally, we control for prior performance because it is likely to affect current work unit climate, marketplace position, and even possibly employee characteristics. High performing units may be (a) more dominant in their markets, (b) more able to negotiate favorable performance targets, (c) more likely to retain good employees and attract new ones, and perhaps (d) likely to influence the perceptual evolution of work unit climate. Controlling for prior performance allows us to make causal inferences with more confidence and also removes some of the confounding effects of prior performance on current performance.]

Methods

Data from 177 semi-autonomous work units in one U.S.-based multinational corporation are used in this study. The work units are located throughout Europe and Asia. They range in size from 1 to over 100 employees. Most work units have between 20 and 50 employees. Their primary functions are marketing, sales, and service, though staff departments of finance, personnel, and education are also included. Product lines range from high technology computers and integrated systems to routine business forms and paper products. No production facilities are included in this study.

Two data sources are used in the study. These sources include financial performance information collected and collated through the accounting function and employee attitudes, collected via a survey administered by the human resource function.

Defining Work Units

Our underlying rationale for level of aggregation is that work units ought to be defined at a meaningful level. Employees in a work unit should be able to identify the unit, proximity and interaction must be present, and some meaningful fate outcomes should be held in common.

Our choice of level of aggregation is based on physical location and type of work performed. The work units are (1) geographically proximate (everyone in a work unit works in the same place) and (2) functionally homogeneous. Members of a work unit report to a bonus eligible manager who is held accountable for financial results. Usually, bonus eligible managers in each function report to a location manager. Thus, these work groups are functional departments within one of twenty-one countries included in the study.

Measuring Work Unit Performance

Defining work unit performance is difficult. It depends upon so many factors that are out of the control of local managers (such as market conditions and corporate strategy regarding products). We chose two measures of work unit performance that account for at least some of the uncontrollable aspects of performance. We use two components of bonuses given to the top manager in the work unit, a bonus based on revenue and one based on return on assets. These two bonuses take into account such things as the difficulty of revenue goals, uncontrollable changes in asset base, and corporate mandates that might detract from revenue or ROA during a particular year. As such these performance measures control for marketplace factors to some degree though this control is far from perfect. The measures are:

1. *Revenue Bonus.* This measure depends on the extent to which managers meet their revenue targets. The revenue targets for managers in turn are determined at the corporate level, considering market forces. This means that the revenue bonus partially accounts for the difficulty of performance.
2. *Return on Assets Bonus.* This measure depends on work units' pre-tax income compared to their assets. It also reflects changes in assets so that managers who increase their unit's assets are not unduly penalized and managers who reduce their assets are not unduly rewarded.

In both cases we use the deviation of the work unit's bonus from the mean bonus of all units in the same function as the actual measure (See "Other Factors" section).

Defining Work Unit Climate

To ascertain work group climate we use data from the firm's survey of employees. Each work unit in the study has at least a 65% response rate to the survey. Most of the surveys were administered in 1988 and 1989. Responses were aggregated at the work unit level so that we can examine average employee perceptions of management practices and employment conditions as they relate to performance. Unless noted otherwise, questions were asked in a modified Likert format with a five point response scale ranging from (1) very positive to (5) very negative. We always reversed the attitude scales so that higher response values indicate more positive attitudes. (Because we are working with a survey the firm developed for its own use , we do not have question wordings that are widely used in the literature. Therefore, we do not diminish problems of non-comparability already existing in the literature.) The questions used are given below:

Performance Improvement Orientation:

The last performance appraisal I received was helpful to me in improving my performance.

Allocation of Rewards:

An employee where I work is much more likely to be praised for good performance than criticized for poor performance.

The better my performance, the larger my salary increase will be.

We also include the interaction between merit pay and function (sales versus all others). The purpose was to test the proposition that merit pay is more salient in direct sales work units as compared to staff and service work units

Efficient Use of Resources:

How would you rate your organization on being efficient (conducting its business in a cost-effective manner)?

We are dedicated to creating value for our shareholders and financial communities by performing in a manner that will enhance the return on their investments.

In my work unit decisions are usually made without undue delay.

Fairness and Equity to Employees:

Four questions are averaged to yield one scale measuring the work unit's treatment of employees (Cronbach's alpha = .79):

Employees where I work can get a fair hearing for their complaints.

Employees here are treated with dignity and respect.

My work unit takes a genuine interest in the welfare of its employees.

We respect the individuality of each employee and foster an environment in which employees' creativity and productivity are encouraged, recognized, valued, and rewarded.

Opportunity to Participate:

Three questions are averaged to yield a single measure of opportunity to participate (alpha = .82):

Management makes an effort to get the ideas /opinions of people like me.

Management takes action on employee ideas and opinions.

I have the freedom to use my own judgment in getting the job done.

Opportunity to Participate and Fairness and Equity are correlated above .8. Therefore the two were combined for the analysis (alpha = .902). The resulting variable is called "Employee Relations."

Other Factors:

Most other factors come from a common source, the corporation. Because this study is confined to one company, we have no variability in most of these factors and do not include them here. We do have measures of prior work unit performance, work unit function, and group composition as follows:.

Prior Performance is measured with the same performance bonus, determined by the same formula, two years before current performance (in 1987). This information is taken from financial records.

Work Unit Function is measured as the type of work done in the unit, taken from the financial reporting data. As noted earlier, we control for otherwise unmeasured and unknown characteristics of each function in the analysis by correcting the bonus data for the mean bonus received in that function. Mean ROA-based bonus was calculated for each function. A new ROA bonus was calculated for each work unit, its original bonus minus the average bonus received by all work units in that function. The same calculation was performed for revenue-based bonus. By doing this, we hoped to correct for market-related performance factors not already taken into account by the firm's bonus calculation. (We also ran the analysis without this correction. The substance of the results is no different, though less variance in performance is corrected. Therefore, our results have a less conservative bias.)

We also include a control which attempts to measure performance goal difficulty. The firm takes this into account in bonus determination, but we include it in the analysis to compensate for non-performance factors in bonus determination (such as corporate politics or use of personal likes and dislikes). In the case of ROA bonus the control is asset growth during the last year. Rapid growth in assets increases the denominator of the ROA calculation, thus making it more difficult to achieve an ROA goal (though perhaps rapid growth in assets is a sight of bad management and therefore ROA bonus ought to be low).

For revenue bonus the control is the current year's revenue objective as a percent of last year's revenue objective. This, too, is not a perfect indicator of goal difficulty. As Gladstein (1984) notes, it may be that high performing managers are simply those who are able to negotiate lower performance goals.

We have two measures of *employee characteristics* available, length of service and education. These questions were asked in the survey with categorical responses rather than actual years of service and years of education as response categories. There were no education effects so this variable was dropped from the analysis for simplicity. For length of service, we use percent of work unit employees with four to twenty years of service, assuming this is likely to be the highest performing (fully trained, not yet retiring) workforce. Means, standard deviations, and zero-order correlations among all variables used in the analysis are shown in Table 1.

Results

The first important result from this research is that the two measures of performance are not highly correlated. That is, units whose top managers received a large ROA bonus are not necessarily the same units with a high revenue bonus.

One can readily argue that these two components of overall bonus should not be highly correlated. They are, after all, meant to capture different aspects of performance. However, we also found that different climate characteristics were associated with different aspects of performance. Thus it may not make sense to talk about performance as if it were a unidimensional, global fact. Rather, we should take care in defining the type of performance under consideration because different climates affect different aspects of performance.

Revenue-Based Performance

When performance is measured in terms of meeting revenue targets, the strongest contributors to performance are: (a) managing with praise rather than punishment; (b) perceptions of deliberate (slow) decision making; (c) merit pay (especially among *non*-sales people); (d) a high proportion of employees in the 4-20 year seniority category; and to a smaller degree (e) improvement-oriented performance appraisals. Perception about fairness, equity, and participation for employees is *not* related to revenue-based performance. Finally, higher performing units had more difficult performance goals and *lower* performance in 1987. These results are shown in Table 2.

These results are not as expected on several grounds. First, we expected more employee-oriented climates to be higher performing, stemming from the opportunity for participation. Though the participation- performance relationship is problematic in the literature, it is more often found when work is complex, uncertainty is high, and required interaction is high. The work done in these work units is not routine. A good deal of it is individual sales and marketing which may not require participation and, in fact, where participation is seen as a waste of time.

Table 1: Means, Standard Deviations, and Zero-Order Correlations Among Variables [*]

		Mean	Std Dev	1	2	3	4	5	6	7	8	9	10	11	12	13
1.	Perf.-Impr. Appraisal	2.914	.418													
2.	Manage with Praise	2.983	.363	.232												
3.	Merit Pay	2.893	.527	.443	.275											
4.	Effic. Resource Use	3.025	.374	.448	.107	.254										
5.	Shareholder Value	3.741	.402	.040	.062	.056	.160									
6.	Rapid Decisions	2.573	.433	.369	.189	.157	.358	-.031								
7.	Employee Relations	3.052	.347	.265	.341	.419	.191	.065	.058							
8.	Length of Service	30.506	20.281	-.155	.107	-.034	-.014	-.130	.209	-.171						
9.	Asset Growth**	-.318	18.321	.148	.125	.095	.044	-.008	.007	.059	.038					
10.	Rev. Goal Difficulty**	1.849	50.196	-.054	-.082	.129	.028	.050	-.072	.038	.005	.275				
11.	1987 Revenue Perf.**	-.426	6.089	-.032	-.137	.082	.124	-.183	.065	.073	.193	-.145	.255			
12.	1987 ROA Perf.**	-.613	6.580	.129	.016	.073	.185	-.152	.328	-.126	.267	-.165	-.006	.549		
13.	1989 Revenue Perf.**	-.715	4.472	.091	.176	.157	.070	.099	-.032	.024	.230	.541	.101	-.091	-.048	
14.	1989 ROA Perf.**	-.667	5.647	.111	.009	.113	.183	.118	.153	-.227	.221	-.202	-.206	.051	.358	.273

[*]   Correlations greater than |.12| are statistically significant, p < .05, one-tailed test.
[**]   The means are not exactly zero because the correction for functional mean was calculated using 218 work units on which we had any valid performance data. The sample size for this analysis is 177 due to missing data from the surveys.

Table 2: Determinants of Revenue Performance

Variables	Standardized Regression Coefficients		
	Excluding Performance	Including Performance	Addition to R^2
Climate:			.018 (p = .06)
Perf.-Impr. Appraisal	.114	.102	
Manage with Praise	.169**	.139**	
Merit Pay	.115*	.123*	
Effic. Resource Use	.044	.068	
Shareholder Value	.091	.063	
Rapid Decisions	-.196**	-.192**	
Employee Relations	-.081	-.060	
Merit Pay X Staff	.128**	.128**	
Input Controls:			.082 (p < .001)
Length of Service	.265***	.295***	
Goal Difficulty	.092	.127**	
1987 Revenue Perf.		-.151*	.083 (p < .05)
R^2	.156	.175	
Adj. R^2	.105	.120	
F	3.08 (p=.001)	3.17 (p<.001)	

* $p \leq .1$ ** $p \leq .05$ *** $p \leq .01$, two-tailed test.

For interaction term, staff and service = 1, sales = 0.

Return on assets as the basis for performance shows a different pattern of results. Here the strongest contributors to performance are: (a) perception of efficient use of resources, (b) creating value for the shareholder, (c) merit pay, a seasoned but not retiring workforce, and, to a smaller degree, (d) performance.

The results are also not as expected in that perceptions of *slower* decision making are a contributor to performance when we predicted just the reverse. This may be due to the fact that these work units are all located outside the USA. They may be subject to local prevailing norms about speed (slow) and participation (low) in decisions. They may also reflect frustration by employees about too many changes from corporate headquarters, especially regarding product lines and compensation.

The third unexpected result is the interaction between function and merit pay. Staff and service units with a merit pay climate were more likely to be high performing. In sales units, perceptions of merit pay were not as strongly associated with high performance.

Table 3: Determinants of Return on Assets Performance

Variables	Standardized Regression Coefficients		
	Excluding Performance	Including Performance	Addition to R^2
<u>Climate:</u>			.122 (p < .001)
Perf.-Impr. Appraisal	.103	.086	
Manage with Praise	.045	.047	
Merit Pay	.189**	.170**	
Effic. Resource Use	.144**	.115*	
Shareholder Value	.119**	.152**	
Rapid Decisions	-.001	-.052	
Employee Relations	-.340***	-.303***	
Merit Pay X Staff	.189**	.074	
<u>Input Controls:</u>			.048 (p < .01)
Length of Service	.203***	.155**	
Goal Difficulty	-.236***	-.191***	
<u>1987 Revenue Perf.</u>		.240***	.044 (p < .01)
R^2	.247	.291	
Adj. R^2	.202	.244	
F	5.45 (p<.001)	6.17 (p < .001)	

$* \ p \leq .1$ $** \ p \leq .05$ $*** \ p \leq .01$, two-tailed test.

For interaction term, staff and service = 1, sales = 0.

ROA-Based Performance

This may be because merit pay is taken as a given in sales. However, in staff and service units, pay and performance are more difficult to link. Therefore, in these more subjective settings, the perception that pay and performance are linked is associated with higher work unit performance.improving appraisals. Employee relations is *negatively* associated with performance, high performing units having employees with perceptions of less participation and less treatment with fairness and equity. Finally, prior performance is positively related to current performance. These results are summarized in Table 3.

Some of these ROA results make intuitive sense. Efficient use of resources, creating value for the shareholder, merit pay, and a seasoned work force are all sensibly linked to high return on assets. They all represent in some way an effective use of assets in increasing revenue (and rewarding employees for same). The strong negative effect of employee relations, on the other hand, is a puzzle. It may be that employees in high ROA units feel used or feel that high ROA is being accomplished at their expense. If this is true, we would expect higher turnover in these units than others.

If we examine the proportion of employees in the low seniority categories, comparing the 1/3 highest performing and 1/3 lowest performing units, we see that the low performing units are much more likely to have a workforce with one to three years of experience than the high performing units. In the low performing units, 33.8 percent of all employees are in the one to three year category. In the high performing units only 21.5 percent of all employees are in the one to three year seniority category. This difference is statistically significant ($p < .001$). This suggests higher turnover in high performing units (which may also keep labor costs low, thus increasing ROA).

We tested each of three types of variables for significant contribution to the variance explained in performance, net of all other variables. The first block is the process variables. The second is length of service and goal difficulty. The last is prior performance. In the revenue equation the first two factors contribute significantly, increasing r^2 by about .08 each, net of all other effects. Prior performance only increases r^2 by .015.

The largest contribution to ROA-based performance is the block of climate variables, adding .12 to r^2 net of all other variables. The other two blocks contributed about .04 each to r^2 as well.

Discussion and Conclusions

Several results are particularly noteworthy in both sets of equation. The first is the absence of a relationship between perception of fairness, equity, and participation for employees and work unit revenue performance and the strong negative relationship with ROA performance. These results are not consistent with Hansen and Wernerfelt's (1989) and Denison's (1984) work, perhaps because they used different instruments and methods than we. On the other hand, the discussion above suggests that when ROA is the measure of performance employees may feel that performance is achieved at their expense, leading to high turnover.

We do not find any effect of employee relations for revenue-based performance if we consider this variable an indicator of employee-centered management. We know in leadership studies that employee-centered styles do not correlate consistently with performance, absent substantial controls for characteristics of the situation. We know from job satisfaction research that high performance is not a reliable outcome of high morale. We know from the procedural fairness literature that a climate of trust and commitment evolves when fairness is perceived. However, (as with much commitment research) the connections to performance have seldom been demonstrated (Tyler and Bies, 1990). A possible exception is in lay-off studies, where some find a positive relationship between perception of fairness and subsequent performance by survivors (Brockner and Greenberg, 1990). Nevertheless, upon reflection, it is not surprising that perceptions of fairness, equity, and participation are not related to revenue-based performance.

A second result worthy of discussion is the effect of controlling for prior performance in the analysis. Regardless of how we measure performance, controlling for prior performance did not affect the substance of the results very much. In the revenue analysis, controlling for prior performance only strengthened the goal difficulty effect. In the ROA analysis controlling for prior performance tended to decrease the size of most effects, but only slightly. The substance of the results is unchanged by the inclusion of prior performance. This is important because it suggests that managers can work to change the work unit climate, independent of prior work unit performance (or the effects of their predecessor's style) and have a positive effect on current performance. In other words, the way in which employees react to and interpret management practices makes a difference, especially for ROA performance.

Finally, we were surprised to find the two measures of performance only correlated about .27. This had rather important implications for the way in which we think about performance. How performance is defined matters almost as much as how employees are managed. Perceptions of merit pay and length of service were the only consistent results across equations. All other results were specific to the type of performance under consideration. Therefore managing for a high performance work force is very much dependent upon what one means by high performance.

References

Blumberg, M. and Pringle, CD. (1982) "The Missing Opportunity in Organizational Research: Some Implications for a Theory of Work Performance," *Academy of Management Review*, Vol. 7:, No. 4: 560-569.

Brockner, J. and Greenberg, J. (1990) "The Impact of Layoffs on Survivors: An Organizational Justice Perspective," in J.S. Carroll (Ed.), *Applied Social Psychology and Organizational Settings*. Hillsdale, NJ: Lawrence Erlbaum Associates: 45-75.

Denison, D.R. (1984) "Bringing Corporate Culture to the Bottom Line."*Organizational Dynamics*, Vol. 13 (Autumn): 5-22.

Forehand, G. and Gilmer, B. (1964) "Environmental Variation in Studies of Organizational Behavior. "*Psychological Bulletin*. Vol. 62: 361-382.

George, J.M. and Bettenhausen, K. (1990) "Understanding Prosocial Behavior, Sales Performance, and Turnover: A Group-Level Analysis in a Service Context. "*Journal of Applied Psychology*, Vol. 75 (No. 6): 698-709.

Gladstein, D.L. (1984) "Groups in Context: A Model of Task Group Effectiveness." *Administrative Science Quarterly*, Vol. 29 (No. 4): 499-517.

Hansen, G. S. and Wernerfelt, B. (1989) "Determinants of Firm Performance: The Relative Importance of Economic and Organizational Factors "*Strategic Management Journal*, Vol. 10, No. 5 (September-October): 399-411.

Jones, A.P. and James, L.R. (1979) "Psychological Climate: Dimensions and Relationships of Individual and Aggregated Work Environment Perception. "*Organizational Behavior and Human Performance*, Vol. 23: 201-250.

Lawler, E.E. III, Hall, D.T. and Oldham, G.R. (1974) "Organizational Climate: Relationship to Organizational Structure, Process, and Performance." *Organizational Behavior and Human Performance*, Vol. 11: 139-155.

Litwin, G.H. and Stringer, R.A., Jr. (1968) *Motivation and Organizational Climate*. Cambridge, MA: Harvard University Press.

Podsakoff, P.M. and Todor, W.D. (1985) "Relationships Between Leader Reward and Punishment Behavior and Group Processes and Productivity."*Journal of Management*, Vol 11, No. 1: 55-73.

Pritchard, R.D. and Karasick, B.W. (1973) "The Effects of Organizational Climate on Managerial Job Performance and Job Satisfaction." *Organizational Behavior and Human Performance*, Vol. 9: 126-146.

Schneider, B. (1983) "Work Climates: An Interactionist Perspective," in N.R. Feimer and E.S. Geller (Eds.) *Environmental Psychology: Directions and Perspectives*. New York: Praeger, pp. 106-128.

Staw, B.M. (1975) "Attribution of the 'Causes' of Performance: A General Alternative Interpretation of Cross-sectional Research on Organizations." *Organizational Behavior and Human Performance*, Vol. 13: 414-432.

Tyler, T.R. and Bies, R.J. (1990) "Beyond Formal Procedures: The Interpersonal Context of Procedural Justice," in J.S. Carroll (Ed.), *Applied Social Psychology and Organizational Settings*. Hillsdale, NJ: Lawrence Erlbaum Associates: 77-98.

Restructuring/Right-sizing

In this section, three case histories and a study focus on what has unfortunately become a necessity in current business practice. **Aguilar, Niehaus,** and **Sharkey** talk about downsizing at the Mare Island Naval Shipyard in the period of 1987-1990. The case describes a wide variety of programs used to facilitate work-load changes and, also, provided shipyard employees the ability to maintain an orderly life.

The next case is set in the Metropolitan Property and Casualty Company and describes how they downsized the home office in 1990. **Stonaker,** describes what that organization feels is the right way to downsize an organization.

The acquisition of Long Island Trust Company by the Bank of New York in 1987 is described by **Reynierse** and **Leyden**. This case describes the negative consequences of putting together two widely different cultures. In brief, the merger was a traumatic event that negatively affected almost every aspect of the business operation. Here is what management did in response.

In their study, **Greller** and **Dory** argue that many times staff reductions do not produce the lasting results envisioned. They argue that management's actions are often justified only by anecdotal evidence rather than hard data.

Management of a Major Downsizing at a Naval Shipyard

M. AGUILAR, R.J. NIEHAUS and F.S. SHARKEY

Introduction

During the 1988-1991 period, Mare Island Naval Shipyard has undergone a large overall wordload reduction with intermediate periods of minor growth consistent with ship overhaul schedules. Between 1987 and 1990, the workforce was reduced from 10,000 to 7,200 employees. A wide variety of personnel programs were used to facilitate the workload changes while providing a way for shipyard employees to maintain an orderly life, where possible. This paper provides an operational case study of the strategic and tactical actions which were taken before, during, and after the drawdown at the shipyard.

An integrated approach is shown which relates the management process with the information support system. Emphasis is on the management decisions necessary for direction and continuity to ensure a productive organization throughout the process. The decision support and modeling system was used to develop the strategic and tactical plans and to monitor and control the stream of decisions as the workforce changes unfolded. Innovative management practices were instituted to integrate necessary management decisions with employee needs at each stage of development.

Besides the quantitative issues brought out by the decision support system, considerable effort was made to include all segments and interest groups at risk during the downsizing. This paper discusses the integration of those capabilities with a variety of management practices. These include such issues as: use of job clubs, use of videos, involvement of the unions and the press, etc., to ensure that the whole shipyard community was fully informed and involved, where possible, in this turbulent process. Equal Employment Opportunity (EEO) and impact on women issues were also addressed, adding to the complexity of making the necessary transitions. The paper concludes with an examination of the need to continue the analysis and use of innovative approaches during the early post drawdown period.

M. AGUILAR, and F.S. SHARKEY - Mare Island Naval Shipyard, Vallejo, CA, 94592 R.J. NIEHAUS, Office of Chief of Naval Operations (OP-160),Washington, DC 20370

Background and Situation

Massive changes in the defense posture of the United States are underway. For a naval shipyard charged with the maintenance of nuclear submarines, the issue became how to most gracefully implement a large workload reduction while minimizing the impact on the shipyard's effectiveness and on employee livelihoods. The goal has been and continues to be to retain an adequate, skilled, core workforce during the downturn in a way that will allow the continuation of a competitive workforce. In the longer term, workload will fluctuate about a lower level average personnel strength.

A previous paper (see Aguliar, Bres, Niehaus, and Sharkey, 1990) described the Mare Island Naval Shipyard efforts to use all available tools and approaches for managing expected personnel turbulence. The idea is that any important decision should use all available information and be as forthright as possible with both management and employees. Overall management concerns remain:

o Keeping the workforce lean to compete successfully for work.
o Planning for workforce strengths to reduce personnel impacts.
o Maintaining a highly skilled workforce.
o Planning for resource availability to meet the projected workload
  in the mid 1990's.

The shipyard has participated in developing and implementing many workforce planning models to manage its workforce more effectively. This work is the result of a long-term Navy program in developing civilian workforce planning methodologies and supporting information systems (see Charnes, Cooper, and Niehaus (1972) and Niehaus (1979, 1988)). These models are part of the Computer-Assisted Manpower Analyses System (CAMAS), a Navy-wide information system to provide assistance for a variety of civilian personnel planning applications.

In the study just before the dramatic events in Eastern Europe, the shipyard faced a 30% workload drop for FY90-91, expecting a return to previous workload levels in FY95-98. However, because of the retirement of several submarines, the workload is now expected to continue to decline at reduced levels with small peaks and valleys over time. These changes illustrate the dynamic nature of workload and related workforce planning with the need to continue responding to significant unexpected changes. The need is to have a management response capability which allows the rapid evaluation of unforeseen perturbations in the workload.

Figure 1 shows the changes in workload and staff over the past several years. The accessions (hiring) and loss patterns are also shown. There have been a series of reductions over the past three years. The most traumatic was the Reduction-In-Force (RIF) of 560 personnel, implemented in September 1990. This overall tracking of workforce changes was quite helpful in formulating the strategic alternatives which were modeled using a decision support system. Originally, a much larger reduction was expected. Through much planning and subsequent management action by both the shipyard and higher level authorities, the difficult RIF actions were brought to a minimum.

Figure 2 shows several alternatives, using the different scenarios, under consideration during management discussions before the 1990 RIF action. This particular chart was developed just before the RIF. Its purpose was to focus on the workforce strategy of concern over the next few years. More descriptive information concerning the different models can be found in Aguliar, et. al. (1990). Technical

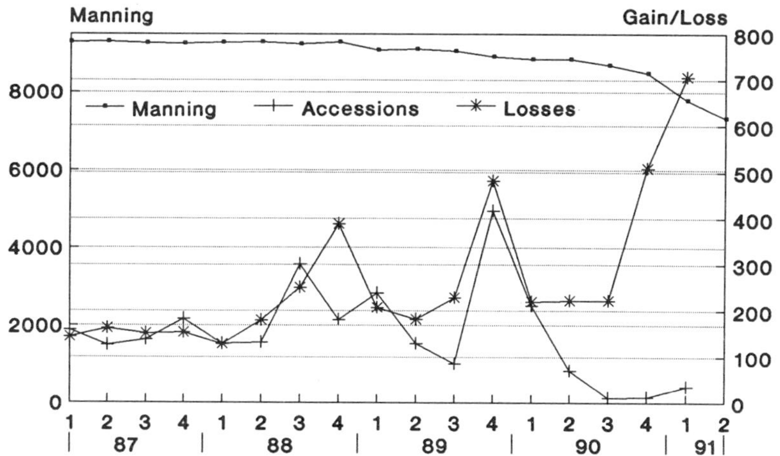

Figure 1: Mare Island Full Time Permanent Manning and Changes

discussions of the underlying model structure can be found in Niehaus (1979). The three types of scenarios which have been incorporated into the supporting Micro CAMAS (MCAMAS) support system are: (1) no hires, (2) force fit, and (3) best fit views of the future. The "no hires" case assumes there will be no replacement of losses from the outside with normal personnel flows permitted to continue within the organization. The "force fit" case assumes that workload requirements will be balanced precisely at each time period with adjustments accommodated through external additions or deletions to the workforce. Normal internal personnel flows are permitted to continue. The "best fit" case assumes the balancing of the workforce within each period as well as over time. This permits some management flexibility both in the internal movements and external additions or deletions to the workforce.

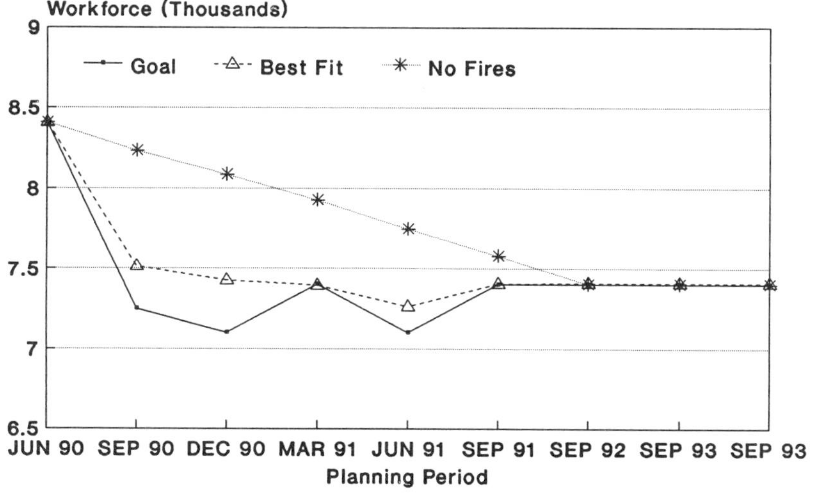

Figure 2: Mare Island Goals and Projected Workforce

Many model alternatives were run over the course of the Mare Island downsizing to help guide the shipyard from a personnel strength of over 9800 to 7200 at the conclusion of the 1990 RIF action. During the six months before the 1990 RIF, the model was run frequently as changes were proposed or made to the workload and on-board personnel. The no-hires and force fit results were used to obtain a quick read-out of proposed changes. The best fit results allowed shipyard management to smooth the workforce transitions by adjusting the peaks and valleys of the workload or personnel strengths as appropriate.

The next sections discuss the management and outplacement strategies and actions before and during a RIF, implemented in September 1990. This is followed by a summary of the decision support system which was discussed in the previous study. The final section examines the post drawdown actions and future directions to institutionalize the successful approaches used in a crisis.

Management Strategy

The management strategy for moving through this difficult period included:

o Using a flexible workforce,
o Using CAMAS flow models for projecting management actions to ensure management has considered long-term impacts of accelerating attrition,
o Using apprentice programs as a training pipeline,
o Implementing a comprehensive outplacement program., and
o Maintaining a computerized skills bank of data on exiting employees interested in returning to the shipyard for future work.

The shipyard has been modifying its employment practices for several years. Before the RIF action, 10% percent of the workforce was comprised of temporary and on-call employees. Twenty-five percent of the force was eligible for retirement (optional and early out). With this flexible group of temporaries, on-calls, and potential retirees, the shipyard was able to downsize with a much smaller forced RIF of the skilled core workforce.

As a continuing strategy, the apprentice program was maintained to provide a pipeline for producing skilled people needed in the mid 1990s as well as placement for some of the affected employees. Care was taken since excessive use of this program would have had too much of a short term impact on the shipyard's productivity ratios.

Dramatically increasing the size of the apprentice class to accommodate a large number of excess helpers and limited mechanics and projected needs in 1995 would cause overspending during downsizing and an over-supply of expensive employees in the longer term. Training mechanics for four years in an apprentice program makes sense only if you intend to get a return on your investment by retaining them. This logic was very important in planning for the downsizing.

Since the shipyard's resources come from a revolving fund, employment is directly driven by the workload (the number of ships assigned for overhaul or repair). Some increase in near- term (FY90-94) workloads could allow related increases in the apprentice classes to meet the workload increase in FY95 without making the shipyard's overhead cost too high. The increased apprentice classes would also allow the retention of more limited mechanics through FY90-94.

Optional early retirement was also offered at earlier stages of the downsizing to retain the recently trained workforce for the future. Early retirement allows those at least 50 years old with 20 years service, or at any age with 25 years service to retire.

The shipyard's outplacement program merits special discussion. The next section provides an in-depth review of the outplacement program, instituted at Mare Island.

Outplacement/Downsizing Program

One underlying assumption during downsizing is that assistance in career transition will leave positive feelings in all employees. The residual workforce will have less guilt and fear and the outplaced will have a more positive attitude toward a responsible employer. Downsizing raises many critical human resource issues deserving serious attention from top management. The shipyard's approach to the downsizing issue will impact its current and future performance and productivity.

At the beginning of the 1989/90 downsizing, the Personnel Operations Division met with senior management to inform them of the necessary actions for a least disruptive course of action. The decision support system, along with downsizing planning forms, were used to determine excess positions. The downsizing options discussed for trimming the workforce included: terminating temporaries, releasing on-calls, offering retirements where possible, using leave without pay and full-time to part- time actions, and implementing a comprehensive outplacement assistance program.

A strong communication program was initiated from the outset. It is in the organization's best interest to show the highest level of concern and ethics when downsizing. Effective communication is a critical step in showing concern and easing tension. As rumors spread, it is important that employees remain informed of current conditions. All available forms of communication media were used to maximum advantage.

The communications program focused on both in-house and public channels. The in-house Mare Island bi-weekly news publication *Grapevine* featured articles on RIF and outplacement issues. For example, one issue provided an entire pull-out section on downsizing. The public affairs office kept the local newspapers and TV stations informed of details which could be disseminated to a wider audience.

Monthly newsletters were sent to each employee's home address informing them of all the options available to them should they be affected. Several videotapes on the status of the downsizing were made for internal viewing. Senior management sponsored lunch time information sessions on a biweekly basis to keep all interested parties informed. This early and often use of all available communications media was one of the cornerstones of the success of the downsizing program. Shipyard management felt it was extremely important to employee morale to keep rumors to a minimum.

Supervisors were fully informed of every aspect of the RIF by videotapes, staff meetings, and handouts. A particularly useful videotape presented scenarios showing the right and wrong way to hand out RIF notices. The face-to-face and videos were supplemented by handouts such as one on common feelings experienced by employees who lose their jobs.

In an effort to allow employees a means of gaining and sharing job search information, "job clubs" were formed in organizations or occupation areas where extensive downsizing would occur. Each job club consisted of a leader (selected by the department and trained by the outplacement staff) and a small group of employees (10-20). In those shops/organizations with large numbers targeted for

Outplacement Staff

o Train Job Club Leaders.
o Provide Workshops to members.
o Sponsor Job Fairs and Employer Interviews.
o Facilitate weekly Job Club Leader Meetings.

Job Club Coordinators

o Receive information from Outplacement Staff.
o Disseminate information to Job Club Leaders.
o Serve as liaison between Outplacement Staff and
    Department Management.
o Attend weekly Job Club Leader meetings.
o Receive and disseminate weekly job vacancy packets.

Job Club Leaders

o Attend Job Club Leader training.
o Lead groups of 10-20 employees.
o Meet with Job Club weekly/biweekly.
o Coordinate workshop attendance of members.
o Provide positive reinforcement and encouragement.
o Attend Job Club Leader meetings weekly.

Job Club Members
(Limited to 20 Hours)

o Meet with leaders weekly/biweekly.
o Attend Job Search Workshops.
o Prepare Resume and SF-171.
o Review job vacancy information.
(Limited to 12 Hours)

o Attend Job Fairs and Interviews.
o Make employer contacts.

Figure 3: Job Club Responsibilities

downsizing, as many as 15 to 20 job clubs were formed. Each shop/organization then assigned a Job Club Coordinator who coordinated all activities with the various job club leaders in their area. Figure 3 summarizes the responsibilities of the various staff and members of the job clubs.

Informative and useful career workshops as shown in Figure 4 were conducted to assist targeted employees with their job search. The attendees recog-

o Federal Personal Qualifications   o Interview Techniques
    Statement (SF-171) Application   o Financial Management
    Completion   o Stress Management
o Resume Preparation.   o Hidden Job Market
o Starting Your Own Business.

Figure 4: Job Club Career Workshops

o Identify occupations of employees who will attend the job fair.
o Determine the job fair date.
o Locate a facility.
o Invite appropriate employers.
o Confirm employers participating (two weeks before the job fair).
o Send employers a reminder and entry instructions.
o Develop information for job fair attendees.
   - handout of employers attending.
   - map of the facility and the organizational layout.
   - evaluation forms.
o Prepare facilities for the job fair.
o Conduct the job fair.
o Evaluate employee/employer assessment of the job fair.

Figure 5 Job Fair Coordination Issues

nized that the labor market has changed considerably during the past five to ten years. They gained insight into the current approach to seeking a job.

Monthly "job fairs" were conducted on site where employees met with a wide variety of employers. Other Federal activities, local, state, national, public and private sector employers were represented. A total of six job fairs were held where 154 organizations shared occupational information with 3,128 employees. Figure 5 provides the types of issues that need to be addressed in coordinating job fairs.

One of the successful strategies in the downsizing was a variety of efforts to accelerate attrition. The decision support system was used to estimate the effects of controlling personnel movements within the shipyard to channel employees to available opportunities both within and external to the shipyard.

The shipyard was aided by a robust external labor market in the San Francisco Bay Area. Table 1 shows the results of various efforts to accelerate attrition. All the different efforts accelerated attrition and eased the impact of separations due to RIF. In the end, 460 employees were terminated through RIF action.

Table 1. Accelerated Attrition

ACTION		NUMBER OF EMPLOYEES
Termination of Temporaries		213
On-call Employees Put in Non-pay Status		267
Retirement Options		
Early Retirement	125	
Optional & Discontinued Service Retirement	146	
Total Retirement		271
Job Club Outplacement Efforts		
Offers Made	434	
Offers Accepted		350
TOTAL ACCELERATED ATTRITION		1,101

Job Club Hours

o Approved additional 10 hours per week for job search activities.

Individual Career Counseling

o Half hour sessions for separated employees.
o *Self Directed Search* was administered for skills assessment.

Employer Interviews

o Due to time constraints in the final month, efforts were directed to bringing in employers to do individual interviews rather than having another job fair.
o Public, Private, and Government Sector Employers were brought in to interview employees.

Case Management

o Develop short term career plan.
o Format and print copies of resumes.
o Maintain case file.
o Serve as liaison between employee and potential employer.

Outside Agency Referrals

o Local Private Industry Councils.
o State Employment Development Department.
o Mare Island Federal Credit Union.
o Small Business Development Center.

Figure 6: Post RIF Outplacement Activities

Once employees received RIF notices, a more concentrated effort was focused on those employees who would be separated from the shipyard. Figure 6 shows the types of services offered to individuals to assist with career planning issues.

Throughout the shipyard downsizing, the outplacement staff evaluated the success of program activity. Assessment continues in an effort to gain an accurate view of the impact of RIF and outplacement activities. Figure 7 provides a list of surveys used in assessing program activities. Separated employees are continuing to be tracked to ascertain their status in their post-RIF situation.

Attention is paid to the impact of the RIF on the workforce profiles by race or national origin and sex. Often, the civil service rules governing a RIF took precedence over EEO regulations. Where possible, positive efforts continue to be made to be an equal opportunity employer within the confines of the stronger retention regulations..

As mentioned earlier, the decision support system was used throughout the downsizing. The next section describes this system in more detail.

Decision Support System

The decision support system, developed at Mare Island, is aimed at integrating workload and workforce planning. This system has both "top down" and "bottom up" components. The purpose is to provide rapid evaluation of short and long term workload and workforce quality/quantity issues. Skills balancing

Outplacement Interest Form
o   Given to management to indicate outplacement interest.
o   Offered employees such options as LWOP, early retirement, change to
    part time, participation in job clubs.

Job Club Leader Weekly Report
o Leaders indicate meeting times, items discussed, offers made to members and
problems/concerns to be addressed by Outplacement Staff.

Offer/Resignation Form
o   Job Club members return form to Outplacement Staff when they have
    been offered and have accepted a position.

Job Fair Evaluation Form
o   Employees attending job fairs evaluated employers attending, handouts
    available, time allowed and overall impression.

Job Club Member Survey
o   Job club members were surveyed to determine how job club activities were
    going, if they found their leaders workshops and job fairs effective, and any
    suggestions for Outplacement Staff.

Outplacement Survey
o   Employees received survey with their notification of separation.
o   Employees were asked what companies and positions they were interested
    in, what obstacles they faced, and what assistance Outplacement could
    provide.

Priority Outplacement Questionnaire
o   After issuance of RIF notices, affected employees were asked if they had
    participated in job clubs and if they were interested in counseling sessions
    and job fairs.

Counselor Assessment Form
o   Employees who participated in career counseling sessions were asked for
    short range plans, outplacement activities they attended, and any special
    considerations.

Separation Survey - Job Club Leaders
o   Job club leaders were asked to update the status of separatees, i.e.,
    whether they had participated in outplacement, if they had received
    another Federal or private industry job, and if their notice had been
    rescinded.

Figure 7: Outplacement Program Assessment Surveys

strategies are developed at both the individual shop and cross- organizational levels. Particular attention is placed on identifying and tracking the core workforce.

The organization has established a common planning methodology. The key driver is the workload available to the shipyard. The Navy fleet maintenance, overhaul and nuclear refueling schedule is determined centrally to account for fleet operations, required maintenance cycles, and new ship additions. Periodically, there is a workload conference; participation includes all the naval shipyards to assure local input to shipyard workload balancing issues. These decisions are aided by long range workforce planning models using the microcomputer version of the MCAMAS.

The workload analysis part decision support system produces two types of reports. There is the workload forecasting model producing one to seven year studies by shop. These outputs are complimented by one to three year workload profiles by trade skill. The heart of the shorter range or one to three/four year workforce planning is total shipyard analysis using the types of MCAMAS model outputs briefly described at the beginning of this paper. Analyses are produced comparing "no hiring", "force-fit to goals" and "best-fit to goals". The system involves an eight period model which uses quarters to the end of the first full fiscal year and years thereafter. The shipyard-wide reports are extended to the shop level by deterministic models producing monthly workforce plans and trade level manning plans.

At the execution level, the shop level models can be used to produce proposed RIFs monthly before the RIF date based on the current workload and on-board count. These RIF data can also be calculated by trade skill.

Because of the need for MCAMAS results during the RIF, only part of the screen-driven user interfaces were complete. System operation required some intervention by a trained analyst for operation. While not difficult, the user needed

Outplacement

o Job clubs	o Communications
o Job fairs	- Newsletters
o Workshops and counseling	- Videos
	- Lunchtime sessions

Reduction in Force (RIF)

o Communications
o Training for managers on how to issue a RIF notice
o Weekly meetings with unions
o RIF point-of-contact for questions
o Early-out retirement
o Severance pay calculations on notice
o Issuing two notices (one in person and one by mail)
o Department of Defense Priority Placement Program

Shipyard Management

o No impact on production schedule
o Teamwork throughout
o Smooth check-out procedure for affected personnel

Figure 8: Efforts that Worked Well in 1990 Downsizing

to know several microcomputer packages such as LOTUS 1-2-3, LINDO, and Harvard Graphics following a fairly easy run sequence. This would initiate some executable computer programs to bridge between the packages.

More recently, the screen-driven version of MCAMAS has been completed. In this version, MCAMAS has a user oriented front end for the entire run sequence.This shell software allows running of the models from initial data file preparation to final report graphics in a manner similar to most microcomputer packages. This version of MCAMAS is being exported to the other naval shipyards and eventually to the larger field installations of the Department of the Navy.

Lessons Learned

The 1990 downsizing plan and results were analyzed by representatives from shipyard management, unions, and employees. Lessons learned were identified and process improvement teams were established to develop new downsizing strategies for further reductions which are on the horizon in 1991.

The downsizing efforts that worked well in 1990 are summarized in Figure 8. As might be expected, everything did not turn out as planned. Figure 9 shows some to the problems identified or efforts that didn't work during the 1990 downsizing.

Outplacement
o Not enough time
o Hard to stop attrition in technical areas

Reduction in Force (RIF)
o Vacancies left unfilled
o Mis-assignments
o Amendments created other problems
o Performance appraisals
o Impact on women and minorities
o Communications (Employees expected managers
      to know their fate)
o Official Personnel Files (OPFs)
  - Confusion of RIF process (bump and retreat)
  - Confusion about 30-day extensions
o Compensation
  - Severance pay with amendments
  - Numbers receiving severance
o Notice of Personnel Action (SF-50)
  - Not ready soon enough
  - Problems on the last day

Shipyard Management
o Managers needed earlier notification of results
o Employees being downgraded but performing same work
o Better coordination needed on placements
o Federal Employees Compensation Act (FECA)
  problems (workman's compensation for light duty employees)

Figure 9: Problems Identified during 1990 Downsizing

Major Improvements Planned in the Process

After the 1990 RIF was concluded it was learned that additional personnel reductions may be necessary as the planned workload was reduced even further. The continuing program to rebuild employee commitment to the shipyard's mission and future. The1991 RIF will be analyzed and coordinated largely though the use of computer- assisted support. This approach will shorten the length of process time. Also, it will allow enough time to conduct a simulated or "mock" RIF to give employees an earlier indication as to who will be affected.

Employees indicated for separation, reassignment or downgrade will be given at least sixty days notice. The notice period in 1990 was too short. It was difficult for the RIF team to complete RIF counseling within thirty days. At the same time the team had problems dealing with numerous changes and amendments required before the effective date of the RIF. Employees need to be given more time after an official notice to be able to decide about: shifting into private industry, accepting offers from the DOD Priority Placement Program (stopper list), or retiring. The minimum notice period should be sixty days.

The analysis of the impact of the RIF on minority and women will be a continuous process throughout the 1991 downsizing. There will be three different points in the RIF process for impact review: (1) after the first round of competition of the mock RIF, (2) after the completion of the mock RIF, and (3) after completion of the actual RIF analysis (before issuance of notices).

Outplacement will start after the conduct of the mock RIF. Employees proposed for separation from the mock RIF will be eligible for job clubs and other outplacement assistance. This will include voluntary early registration in the DOD Priority Placement Program.

The shipyard is committed to fostering teamwork at *all* levels. Continuing efforts are being made to keep all employees informed of the status of the RIF and associated outplacement assistance. Comprehensive communication efforts are being done using the following media: video presentations, newsletters, Shipyard newspaper pull-out sections, KMNS (530 AM) radio station, electronic marquees, weekly meetings with union/management/ rightsizing points of contact, and lunchtime information sessions.

The outplacement staff of the personnel office has been moved to the waterfront production shop area. Due to current economic conditions and recent increases in unemployment in the San Francisco bay area, the focus of outplacement has changed. Small group sessions are being conducted to provide hands-on assistance with: resumes and Federal employment application (SF-171) preparation, interview preparation and role playing, and telephone scripting. An employee job information center has been set up. A wide variety of job search material is provided to job club members for viewing and copying.

A career fair will be held prior to the issuance of mock RIF notices open to all shipyard employees. The purpose is to allow employees to gather information about future educational and career opportunities. A wide variety of organizations and educational institutions will be in attendance. A job fair is planned after the mock RIF notices are issued open to those identified for separation.

To deal with the concerns and issues of recovery and revitalization after the RIF action, a two-phase approach is being developed. The next section provides a program description.

Management Workshops

o Gaining management understanding and support for the recovery effort.

o Exploring new communication efforts with their employees.

o Understanding and coping with change.

o Supporting Total Quality Management (TQM).

Employee Workshops

o Understanding change and the factors creating the need for change.

o Managing Change.

o Reducing anxiety to due downsizing.

   - job burnout.

   - stress.

   - survivor guilt.

   - performance anxiety.

o Presenting the Shipyard's mission.

o Creating a vision of the future and generating a recognition that everyone
has a stake in and shares responsibility in making that vision a reality.

Figure 10: Issues in Workshops Recovery Phase

Recovery and Revitalization

A recovery and revitalization program has been designed to minimize impacts after the RIF and maintain and increase the shipyard's productivity ratio. The recovery phase is being designed to minimize the negative impact of downsizing on remaining employees. The revitalization phase will be a continuing program to rebuild employee commitment to the shipyard's mission and future. The revitalization phase is being delayed due to the impending 1991 reductions.

The recovery phase is being designed as an educational program on the environmental, economic, and social factors creating the need for change. Particular attention will be placed on reducing anxiety due to downsizing and on providing employees with an awareness of their value and contribution to the shipyard's mission and future. The shipyard's vision will continued to be shared through the total quality management (TQM) program and the shipyard's strategic plan. Workshops are to be developed for management and non-exempt employees. Management workshops will be held before employee workshops. Figure 10 provides the issues to be covered in the workshops.

The revitalization phase stresses the development of pathways for open dialogue between management and employees. Individual managers focus attention on the shipyard's vision of the future through identification of specific goals for their segment of the organization. Programs are being developed to increase workforce skills through cross-training, retraining, and job rotation. Effective human resource management is stressed with a focus on integrating business needs with employee needs.

The encouragement of career development is being done with emphasis on job satisfaction rather than promotion potential. A mentoring program has been established for employees in professional occupations. Employee participation has been cformally incorporated in the process as organizations are being restructured to fit the smaller size of the shipyard.

Conclusion

This report provides an operational example of the many considerations which can be used to try to make the best of a downsizing situation. Using decision and information support systems throughout the process is critical to provide early warnings and quick assessments along the way. Extensive communication early and often is extremely important. Positive employee oriented programs must be implemented at critical points as the downsizing proceeds. Equally important is the casting of all these programs with a view to the future. This will maintain a productive workforce to fulfill the organization's short and long term missions.

References

Aguilar, M., E.S. Bres, and R.J. Niehaus, "A Best Fit Planning Model for Managing Personnel Turbulence" in R.J. Niehaus and K.F. Price, Eds. *Human Resource Strategies for Organizations in Transition.* New York: Plenum Press, 1990

Bailey, G. and J. Szerdy, "Is There Life After Downsizing?", *The Journal of Business Strategy*, January/February 1988, pp. 8-11.

Bres, E.S., R.J. Niehaus, F.J. Sharkey, and C.L. Weber, "Use of Personnel Flow Models for Analysis of Large Scale Work Force Changes" R.J. Niehaus, Ed. *Strategic Human Resource Planning Applications.* New York: Plenum Press, 1987.

Bres, E.S., R.J. Niehaus, F.J. Sharkey, and C.L. Weber, "Coping with Occupational Structure Issues at Large Public Industrial Organizations". R.J. Niehaus and K.F. Price, Eds. *Creating the Competitive Edge through Human Resource Applications.* New York, Plenum Press, 1988.

Charnes, A., W.W. Cooper, and R.J. Niehaus, *Studies in Manpower Planning.* Washington, DC: U.S. Navy Office of Civilian Manpower Management, 1972. NTIS No. AD 055952.

Fisher, A.B. "The Downside of Downsizing", *Fortune*, May 23, 1988, pp. 42-52.

Jacobs, D. "Maintaining Morale During and After Downsizing", *Management Solutions*, April 1988, pp. 5-13.

Kuzmits, F.E. and L. Sussman, "Early Retirement or Forced Resignation: Policy Issues for Downsizing Human Resources" *SAM Advanced Management Journal*, Winter 1988, pp. 28-32.

Lawrence, A.T. and B.S. Mittman, "Preventionists, People-Pushers, and Parachute Packers: What Type of Downsizer are You?" *Management Review*, January 1991.

McLaughlin, D.J. "Managing the Downsizing", *Compensation & Benefits Management*, Spring 1988, pp. 237-243.

Niehaus, R.J. *Computer-Assisted Human Resource Planning.* New York: Wiley Interscience, 1979.

Niehaus, R.J. "Models for Human Resource Decisions", *Human Resource Planning*, Vol 11, No. 2, 1988.

Voluntarily Excessing Employees:
The Right Way to Downsize an Organization

R.B. STONAKER

Introduction

There is no good way to reduce staffing in an organization, with all the trauma which accompanies such a process, but there is a right way. A new strategic approach to this growing problem is not easy but is absolutely required if management hopes to maintain integrity and consistent productivity during and after the process. What one company has learned is that these ends can only be achieved through a new management mindset and considerable human resource strategic planning.

It comes as no surprise to many human resource professionals today that increased competition is forcing companies to do "more with less". A competitive advantage can be achieved by producing services or products of a higher quality with fewer employees. As a result, there are very few companies today who have not experienced downsizing or "rightsizing" or whatever term seems appropriate.

Depending on a company's culture, the experience of downsizing can range anywhere from the automatic to the traumatic. For those companies who historically have maintained a paternalistic approach toward their employees, the greatest stress on management is probably felt not only in implementing the process, but even in coming to the conclusion that such a process has to be considered. That stress level is pushed to extremes when downsizing has to occur in the home office rather than at the satellite operations. In this situation, statistics quickly become names and faces to those managers who have to make these tough decisions.

Metropolitan Property and Casualty in Warwick, Rhode Island, a small but emerging company in the property and casualty insurance business, downsized its home office in the latter part of 1990. Unlike many companies today who seem to be taking the position of "hunkering down," Metropolitan Property and Casualty is growing and growing rapidly. The company is working very hard at managing its top and bottom lines through this period of growth.

The size of the home office staff was at an all-time high. A recent merger had strained support services in the home office, prompting the company to bring additional employees on board the past several years. There was also a feeling by

R.B. STONAKER - Metropolitan Property and Casualty Company, 700 Quaker Lane, P.O. Box 350, Warwick, RI

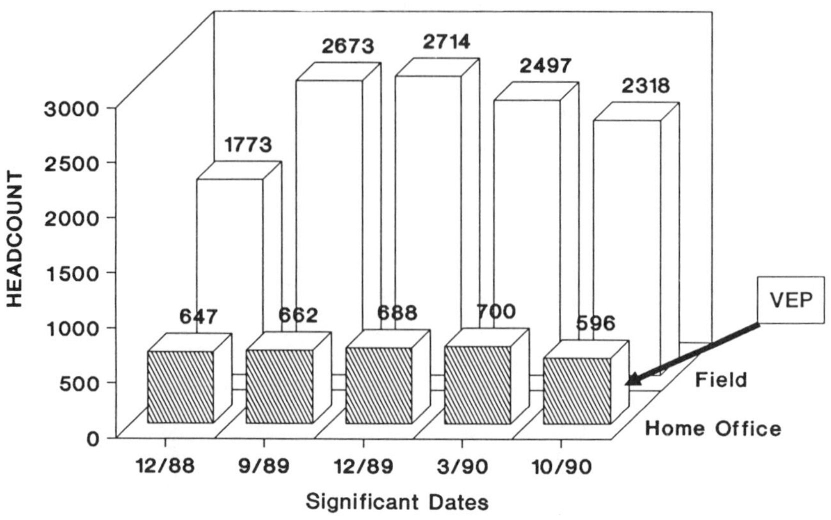

Figure 1: Home Office/Field Staffing Trends

management that the company should always be staffed to prepare for future growth.

What management did not monitor carefully enough, however, was the growing imbalance between home office support personnel and the size of the staff at the satellite operations. As the field began to downsize through improved efficiencies and increased technology, similar actions did not take place in the home office (Figure 1).

It is important to note here the real purpose of having home office personnel. Primarily, home office employees or corporate employees as they are sometimes called, tend to serve each other and usually provide support for some field operations. Typically, and very unfortunately, many corporate people do not have this perspective, and they tend to lose their true customer focus. These points were important and critical as Metropolitan Property and Casualty worked towards its crucial decision on downsizing.

Corporate staffing was beginning to become disproportionate to the decreasing levels in the field. The field operations had done an amazingly good job at becoming efficient while the reverse was happening at the central office. In all probability, many companies face this same situation today.

The circumstances confronting this company in the mid-to-latter part of 1990 will sound familiar to many human resource professionals: the organization struggles but is doing very well; to continue remaining competitive, employee reductions are needed; field office closings and hiring restrictions have already become part of the business routine; the necessary cuts must be made in the corporate office.

For those human resource professionals who have not experienced a downsizing effort, or particularly for those who have not had that happen in Corporate, some important points need to be considered and will be covered in this report.

Not in My Department

It is much easier to downsize at satellite operations than in the home office. In fact, the management team had become very skilled in closing or merging field offices, but collectively had never dealt with concurrent, substantial reductions in home office. The closer one gets to where the top decisions are made, the tougher it becomes. Throughout the preliminary discussion periods leading up to the decision, there was a shared feeling among senior management that some "fat" existed in the organization but it was always in someone else's department. As a result, discussions at that level usually led to subtle accusations, both public and private, but formal commitment or conclusions were nowhere to be found. Managers faced with the tough decision were not convinced it was necessary to take such action.

It is interesting to watch the process work. Usually there is denial such a condition exists; then when figures are presented to validate the direction, the credibility of the figures is questioned. Managers are sensitive human beings and do not want to face the prospects of terminating their own employees, particularly those with whom they interface during the workday.

The first step in coming to a decision was to have each manager who was head of a department give a presentation on how they might downsize. Very quickly, it was obvious only limited cuts were being proposed. Each manager could legitimately and honestly justify the need for practically every employee.

Despite allegations of "fat" in corporate, every employee was actively engaged in doing something for somebody. For the most part, only those who were recognized as "substandard" employees were considered expendable. However, in some cases, this finding was not even verified by ratings of their performance. It was rather evident, at this point in the discussions that decisions were being driven more by personality than by results.

Many companies never get beyond this point, and through sheer exhaustion they decide the pursuit is not worth the effort. Emotions during this period of time are high because personalities are still the overriding concern. Discussions tend to focus on evaluating people rather than their contribution to the organization.

Moving beyond the Stalemate

By changing focus, the group can move beyond the stalemate. Rather than concentrate on who the company was about to excess -- the focus should be on functions or services that management might be able to do without. This change in focus represented a major shift in management's thinking about the problem. At this point, managers would no longer consider who was performing the tasks but rather evaluate the relative importance of these tasks for the future.

Since most home office functions either serve each other or the company's field operations, each manager then described to the group those services or products his or her people were performing. Ultimately, the department managers evaluated services rendered and determined which of them the organization could stand to lose and remain effective. Managers were beginning to prioritize those essential services and non-essential services performed in the corporate functions.

Interestingly enough, through this process Met P&C management were compelled to fix their attention on the final customer, the person who purchases the product. The farther a particular unit's services were from that customer, the more acceptable downsizing became in that unit.

Choosing a Corporate Perspective

The group of managers also began to move away from viewing the problem through a departmental perspective, choosing in its place a corporate perspective. The decision was reached to begin the downsizing process after vested personal and departmental interests had lineally given way to corporate need. Although the Human Resources Department had been actively involved in this process by facilitating the discussion, it now became responsible for helping management come up with the solutions.

Met P&C's Human Resources structure is somewhat unlike that of other human resources departments. There is a Human Resources Strategic Planning Division whose primary responsibility is to present new approaches to old questions. Its responsibility is to help line management by presenting new alternatives from which management can select a given course of action.

This understanding is important because, without it, the management team probably would have handled downsizing as most companies do: employees would have been discontinued without much prior warning and with little explanation about why they were selected and others weren't. The process could have been very disruptive to their entire operation. There had to be a better way to reach sufficient staffing levels in the corporate office.

Partners in the Process

The concept of a voluntary approach was presented early in discussions by the Human Resources Strategic Planning Division. They felt that a voluntary program would fit the company's strategic plan and the vision of the organization. The plan would be structured so that employees could participate more as partners or shareholders in the organization. Partners not only enjoy the successes of the organization, but endure the hardships as well through thorough and effective communications. The division kept pressing the point that employees are adults who consistently make similar decisions in their lives outside the organization. In a sense, given the facts, employees will make the appropriate choices.

The concept was presented to the managers and summarily rejected; not once, but several times. Managers viewed such a process as uncontrollable, which meant they could not control who and how many left. Management was concerned about giving up their authority, power and control. The knowledge that they could choose a voluntary approach kept them from committing to an involuntary approach. They were caught between their sense of doing what was right and fair and their fear of losing control.

It's difficult to say exactly what finally convinced the manager's to choose the voluntary excess program approach. It may be that managers still want to do what's right and what's fair, and that they consider these values to be more important than the control they might relinquish. It truly represented a breakthrough for many of the people involved. There was a feeling they could now achieve the goal of reducing employees and maintain management integrity in the process -- but it would take work.

There were also things these managers did not want to do, which, in hindsight, were very appropriate. They did not want to duplicate voluntary programs touted by some other companies. Many organizations present their plans as voluntary ones, but some have strings attached. Several companies will announce a voluntary plan, but in actuality the company makes the final determination after receiving the employee's decision. This posture still maintains company control and power over employee decision making.

A program of that nature is, in essence, voluntary only when management says it is so. The Met P&C management team could not accept that premise in the spirit of having employees participate as partners in the process.

At that point, management turned to the Human Resources Department for the future development of the Voluntary Excess Plan. The actual mechanics of the process took three months to develop. During that period many meetings were held to update and validate direction. Demographics of the workforce in corporate were reviewed with the managers.

Enhanced Separation Benefits

If management were to be successful with a voluntary program, they would need to appeal to the largest representation of employees. They would also need to enhance separation benefits aligned with the demographics. As shown in Figure 2, there were two large groups in the corporate office. Such demographics are necessary to create the most effective plan.

It was determined that certain job functions and skills within those functions were considered essential to the future of the organization. Hence, these groups were excluded from participation in the plan. The thinking here was that replacements would have to be hired, and that didn't make good business sense. About one-third of the workforce was excluded; most were in the highly technical or professional categories.

Severance pay was improved because it was important for the employees to have enough incentive to leave. Due to regulations, however, there could be no enhancement of the retirement benefits.

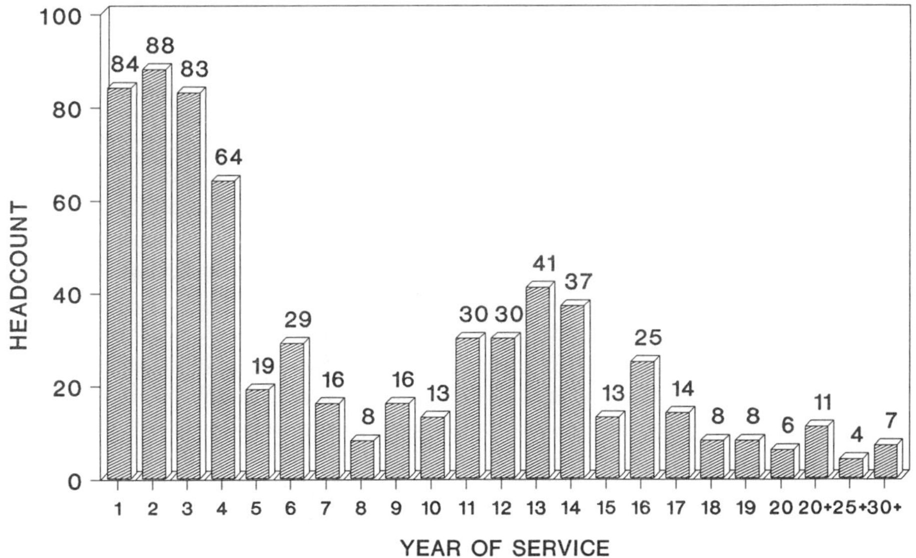

Figure 2: Length of Service - Home Office

8/21 (pm)	Plan announced to managers (off-site meeting)
8/22 (am)	Communications meeting announcement to staff President's letter sent HR back-up material sent
8/22-24	Team meetings provided specifics
8/22-9/19	VEP election period
9/19	Last day to elect VEP
9/19-10/5	Assessment & reorganization period
10/9	Minimal involuntary separations announced
10/12	Last day employed for those electing VEP

Figure 3: VEP Implementation Schedule

The normal out-placement and in-placement activities were begun, including counseling, job referrals and resume preparation. Most of this was done internally by human resources consultants to restrict costs. To facilitate these special services, a fully equipped conference room was converted into an "outplacement center" where employees either individually or in groups could receive specialized attention to their employment needs.

Flexible termination dates were among the unique features of the program. In a sense a "window of opportunity was opened with the full knowledge it would close on a prescribed date. Interestingly, most employees stayed until the window closed, even though they had given notice earlier.

After three months of discussion and preparation, and with the implementation schedule fully prepared, the group of managers was ready to communicate the process to employees. Rumors by now had become rampart, underscoring the need to explain the Voluntary Excess Plan as soon, and as comprehensively as possible (Figure 3).

The decision was to cover the program with managers first. These were the people charged with carrying out the program. It was imperative that they understand its purpose and design in order to intelligently and emotionally communicate it to their people.

In retrospect, that was a good move. Managers dealt with the problem as employees first, and as managers second. Therefore, talking about the specifics was very appropriate. By the end of the meeting, most of the participants understood and had made a commitment to their managerial responsibilities. The word "most" is quite appropriate because there were managers who were not affected at all, there were those who had their units dramatically&y reduced, and there were others who saw their present responsibilities no longer needed in the organization.

The next morning a major communication meeting was held with all employees. Everyone was advised of the reasons for the plan, told the basic details, and given the assurance they would have immediate meetings with their managers following that meeting. In the latter meetings, employees would learn what the structure of their unit would look like after the Voluntary Excess Plan and where their job titles fit into that unit.

For those units where several people had the same job description, the people were told that if the staffing levels were not reached as a result of the Voluntary

Table 1: Perception vs. Reality

Perception	Reality
Total predictability	Constant change
People are valued	People's skills are valued
Companies make money and add people	Companies make money and add and reduce people all at the same time

Excess Plan, an involuntary program would have to be implemented. Consideration would be overall ratings and seniority. It was hoped an involuntary program would not be necessary.

As the major communication meeting, concerns of employees were addressed by management. Employees were told that certain perceptions they held may be at odds with the way companies are forced to operate today. For example, as a result of intense competition and the forces of change, companies were moving away from some of the traditional values and beliefs held by some employees (Table 1).

Many people view a changing process such as downsizing as a threat. Their hope is to get through it and return to total predictability. What they needed to realize is that "normal" is constant change, as evidenced by tangible occurrences such as downsizing. Downsizing may happen in the future as a way of doing business.

Valuing Employee Skills

There also was a perception by many employees that people were valued in the organization. If that is the case, how can downsizing happen? They were told that employees are no longer simply valued as employees, but that their skills are valued even more. In a sense, "what you are" is more important than "who you are". Therefore, it is in their best interest to build continually their skills, and for the organization to help them do that.

Finally, the employees were confused. They were confused about how a company could make a rather large profit yet discontinue employees. The logic held by many employees is: if your company makes money, it adds people; lose money, discontinue people. The reality is that companies who both make and lose money add and reduce people all at the same time.

Initially, employees responded cautiously. Those few who immediately elected the Voluntary Excess Plan did so because they needed little impetus to leave -- they probably had been thinking about it anyway. Since management couldn't dictate who could take or not take the plan, there were a few initial surprises -- people the management staff thought would never leave. However, they left for many different reasons (e.g. return to college, graduate school, open up a business, etc.)

One of the benefits of a Voluntary Excess Plan was the employee force had a hard time distinguishing who was leaving the organization because "they felt they had to" or because "they wanted to". By having discontinued people leaving under both circumstances, any sense of humiliation or lost dignity was minimized.

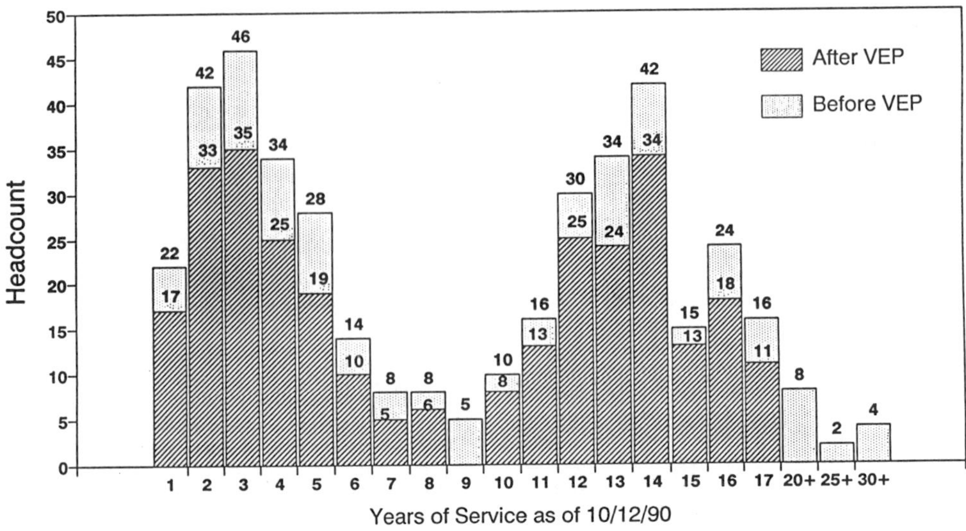

Figure 4: Yrs of Service - VEP Eligible Employees

Concern for Fellow Employees

There was also a deep concern about fellow employees in the process. People seemed to counsel each other, and care and concern were very evident. It's worth noting that employees were never critical of the Voluntary Excess Plan. Several were critical of the decisions to downsize, but not about the process itself. Even at the end of the communications meeting with the employees, management's approach was applauded -- not loudly but approvingly.

This should be contrasted with the high level of apprehension that is symptomatic of most downsizing programs. In this case, once employees had the information, they had control of their own destinies. This was a form of empowerment in a situation which usually generates the opposite reaction.

Goals Achieved

As a result of this process, 22 percent of eligible employees at Metropolitan Property and Casualty's home office chose to take the Voluntary Excess Program. The salary and benefits saved annually was $3.7 million, with one time costs estimated at $1.6 million. It was considered such a success that no involuntary program had to be introduced. The plan also achieved its goals of targeting the large population segments in the home office (Figure 4).

It is worth noting that following the election period, but before the date most employees left, there were parties held outside the office for those leaving by those not leaving. By this time counseling sessions were underway, and those who were leaving left with a great deal of integrity and dignity. Phone service and technical equipment such as computers were made available to the departing employees even after the final date of departure.

There should be no delusions at to what any downsizing process can do to an organization. Apprehensions remain about when it might happen again, and management decision making becomes subject to much more scrutiny. Employees' feelings need to be discussed and examined in any organization which has gone through such an effort. Opportunities for that to occur are already underway in many small sessions with employees and upper management.

The Voluntary Plan does create a more humane, enlightened and empowered method of downsizing. It is not for all companies and all situations. In the minds of the management at Metropolitan Property and Casualty, it represents a new way of managing organizations in turbulent time.

Implementing Organizational Change: An Ordinary Effort for an Extra-ordinary Situation

J.H. REYNIERSE and P.J. LEYDEN

Introduction

The Acquisition of Long Island Trust Company (LITCO) by The Bank of New York (BONY) in early 1987 more than doubled BONY's asset and deposit base in the vibrant Long Island market. The acquisition created a retail division with 79 branches, approximately 2.1 billion dollars in deposits, approximately 1.5 billion dollars in loans, and about 875 retail employees. In addition, another 175 employees from other BONY line and staff functions, e.g., Trust, had dotted line relationships to the Division and provided appropriate support. At the same time, the two banks' widely different cultures and immediate management problems resulted in deteriorating conditions that affected almost every aspect of the Long Island Division's operations.

Major problem areas as a result of the merger included high employee turnover, low employee morale, customer dissatisfaction, and an erosion of the Division's profitability, assets, and deposit base. In short, the merger was a traumatic event that adversely affected almost every aspect of the unit. In this paper we tell the story of this merger, the steps taken to address problem areas, and the rapid improvement that occurred following these efforts.

Background

BONY is a historical bank with roots in colonial times when it was founded by Alexander Hamilton. Its long service employees are proud of this heritage, have made a strong, personal commitment to the organization, and don't hesitate to work long hours or make personal sacrifices to meet the organization's expressed goals. The corporate culture at BONY includes a strong work ethic, highly visible ethical standards, an emphasis on lending and asset quality, highly centralized management decision making, and a strong financial focus emphasizing cost control

J.H. REYNIERSE - James H. Reynierse & Assoc., 320 Angus Road, Chesapeake, VA 23320; P.J. LEYDEN - Bank of New York, 245 Park Ave., New York, NY 10167

and bottom-line profitability. While these qualities have served BONY well at a corporate level, they undoubtedly contributed to some of the merger tensions that developed with the LITCO acquisition.

In February of 1987, BONY acquired LITCO from Banca Commerciale Italiana. At the time of the merger BONY was the 27th largest bank holding company in the U.S. with assets of approximately 21 billion dollars. Before the acquisition, BONY had a modest presence on Long Island with 32 branches in Queens, Nassau and Suffolk counties and with a deposit base of approximately $800 million. With the acquisition of LITCO, however, overnight BONY had a major presence with considerable potential for further growth.

Significant problems began immediately. LITCO operating management worked for an absentee owner who left them alone and gave them a considerable autonomy. Collectively they were highly resistant to the merger and resented the new relationship and the accountability imposed by BONY. This resistance was obvious during the transition period prior to the actual merger and little cooperation occurred during that time.

That the merger would be turbulent was signaled immediately on the day the two organizations officially merged and began operating as a single, BONY, entity. On the first day of the official merger 15 commercial loan officers quit and together joined a competitor bank. This deteriorated further over time as employees and customers became increasingly disenchanted with the situation.

While BONY's historical niche emphasized consumer and commercial lending, it is a selective lender in which credit quality is highly valued and a primary requirement for any individual credit. In contrast, LITCO was primarily a deposit-gatherer emphasizing the savings orientation of their Long Island market and customer base. LITCO made few consumer loans while their mid-market commercial lending group used liberal credit standards compared with BONY credit policy and standards. Many LITCO loans simply did not qualify using BONY credit guidelines.

For several years BONY had an aggressive Retail strategy that included: (a) building a national credit card unit that is one of the largest credit card processors in the country; (b) a commitment to automated teller machines (ATM's); (c) a growing mortgage banking subsidiary; and (d) an assortment of unique commercial products for mid-market commercial customers. LITCO was initially attractive to BONY since it provided an enhanced distribution system for marketing these products throughout Long Island. A competitive analysis of BONY's Long Island branch system supported this and indicated several inherent competitive advantages. Long Island management recognized this opportunity. Simultaneously with this exercise, they took the strategic step to develop consumer driven products that both fit this broader retail strategy and that were targeted for the mid-market customer base on Long Island. An overview and flow chart of the organizational model and basic elements is presented in Figure 1.

While the product and marketing strategy brought significant new services to LITCO customers, implementation in the marketplace was seriously flawed due entirely to Human Resource issues. Local, i.e., LITCO management and employees, resented the merger and refused to "buy-in" to the strategic game plan. In the final analysis it was HR issues, i.e., non- product issues, that stymied and frustrated senior management in Long Island. From a strategic perspective BONY Long Island was at a competitive disadvantage because its employees were unable, or unwilling, to execute the market and product strategy. There was a significant competitive deficit for the Human Resource link in their value chain.

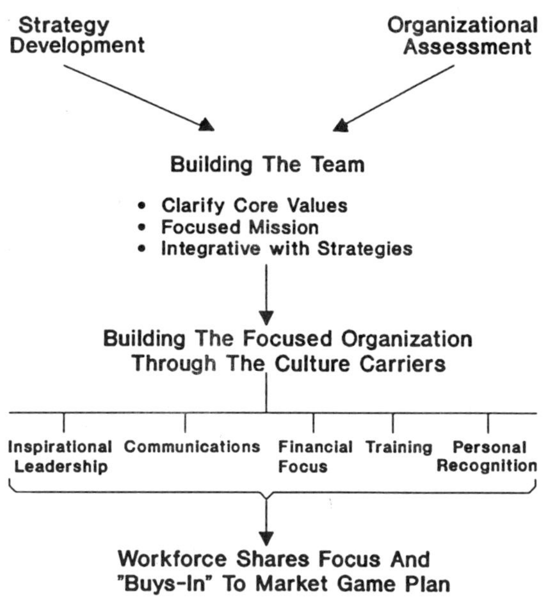

Figure 1: The Model for Organizational Change

Overview of the Reynierse Change Model and Intervention

Our approach is a top-down approach that begins with senior management in the client company, division, or strategic business unit (SBU). Our preferences, and recommendations, are to include the following general elements in the intervention, although we are flexible and usually deviate from the general approach depending on circumstances and the specific needs of the client.

Organizational Assessment

We prefer to start by taking an objective, snap-shot view of the broader organization. This approach helps to identify the strengths and limitations of the organization and those priority areas that need immediate attention. It makes the big issues stand out and provides direction to management regarding where to start.

We use several techniques including surveys, interviews, and focus groups for these organizational assessments. Our "organizational dynamics" survey (Reynierse & Harker, 1986) has been particularly effective. It provides an objective measure of the underlying cultural and business values for that organization, a primary focus of our approach. An advantage of using a survey assessment procedure is that it gets employees at every level involved as everyone has the chance to be heard. This is the first step in getting employees to "buy-in" and participate later when the stakes are higher. Our preference is to rely first on surveys with supplemental use of interviews and focus groups.

Focused Mission and Values

Next we help the management team to identify and clarify their core values and develop a focused mission. Our assumption is that when there is focus and the mission is clear, this can drive the entire organization. This stage is integrative with existing strategies. It also includes a significant team-building component where our values clarification process gains agreement for key priorities and direction and fosters the development of shared values and mission.

Down-Streaming to the Workforce

Our fundamental assumption is that a focused organization requires a workforce that shares this focus. The key to successful implementation is what action steps are taken to drive the process downward so that the entire workforce can "buy-in" and share this focused mission.

We have identified five broad implementation areas that sharpen the focus with employees and promote the core values and focused mission. These areas are integrated with our organizational dynamics survey. We call these the "culture carriers" and it is through these steps that senior management can shape the organization and reinforce the core values both consistently and frequently. In other words, the culture carriers" provide direction for marketing the core values and mission with all employees. The five culture carriers are summarized in Figure 2. Much of our action planning is directed toward developing specific implementation steps in each of these areas.

Inspirational Leadership

Our studies of corporate culture suggest that there are two ways that management stays in touch with what is going on in the company. They stay in touch by visiting work areas, being visible to their employees, and they exercise their inspirational leadership at this time. They also stay in touch through the balance sheet and their financial focus.

Visiting and talking with employees in the workplace is an opportunity to exercise a powerful leadership role and reinforce the core values and focused mission. This communicates what is important within the organization and what is expected of employees. When the Division head is leading the charge, everyone

Inspirational Leadership - Management is in touch with employees and operations.

Communications - People share information freely using both formal and informal channels of communication.

Financial Focus - Management is in touch with the balance sheet and business results.

Commitment to Training - Employees are well trained to enhance their career and work skills.

Personal Recognition - Employees are recognized and feel appreciated for their contributions.

Figure 2: The Culture Carriers

quickly picks up on this and any ambiguity regarding what is taking place is quickly removed. The results are multiplied when this leadership role is being exercised by the entire management team.

Communications

We recommend that management provide frequent communications with all employees during the entire time that new values are being introduced, employing formal and informal channels of communication. If there is a rule of thumb, it is that you can't do too much in this area.

Financial Focus.

How capital is invested and what activities are expensed carry important messages to employees. When promoting change, this financial focus can provide a resource allocation role that provides increased funding and resources to programs that support the core values and focused mission At the same time, there is a message in the denying (or at least the sharp reduction) of funds and resources to established programs that are less important. Our client's are faced with investment choices in which investment decisions are examined in terms of a strategic standard that includes their core values and focused mission.

Training

Training programs should be closely examined to insure that they conform to the organization's core values and focused mission. The first step is to provide for training program increases in those skill areas necessary to execute the mission and core values. In this way, a well trained and competent workforce is built in these areas. Second, it is critical to integrate the core values with the content of supervisory and management training programs. Managers and supervisors must set the example where the core values are concerned. Every attempt must be made to get this influential group to "buy-in" and embrace the core values and mission. This is particularly the case where change is taking place and many supervisors and managers are still marching to the beat of a different set of perceived values.

Recognition Programs

Our studies consistently show that this is one of the most powerful tools management can employ in motivating employees. We recommend that management link their personal recognition and reward systems with the core values; developing recognition programs that reflect the core values; and then provide frequent awards in these areas. Consistently and frequently applied, formal and informal recognition programs provide management with an effective and inexpensive tool to motivate employees to live the values and implement the focused mission.

The Problem Areas and Issues

The period following the BONY merger with LITCO was often adversarial and with a gradual decline in employee morale and performance in the Long Island

Division. For the division employee turnover for 1987 exceeded 45%, increased to over 70% during 1988, and in some branches was much higher, in some cases over 200%. High employee turnover at every level placed a disproportionate burden on an increasingly smaller number of highly trained and knowledgeable managers and platform employees.

Battlefield promotions to inexperienced personnel were necessary to provide minimum operational services but ultimately compounded the fundamental problem. This soon became a vicious circle as untrained, inexperienced personnel who were ill-equipped to service customers made up an increasing proportion of the workforce. Immediate, operational problems and putting together a permanent management team preoccupied management during this time.

The banking business also suffered. The Long Island Division showed progressive growth that matched other BONY retail units before the merger. This performance was immediately reversed following the merger. Almost 17,000 accounts were lost during the first four months after the merger and by year-end (1987) this increased to over 30,000 accounts lost. During this four month period this translated into a net loss of about $200 million in deposits and over $100 million in loan relationships.

Even more troubling were the indications of credit problems among LITCO customers and its loan portfolio. Overdrafts increased from an immaterial level (less than $1,000 per month) to over $235,000 within two months. Similarly, past due loans almost tripled within three months, non-performing loans more than doubled, and by mid-year gross charge-offs increased by a factor greater than ten. This trend continued during 1988 but at a lower rate.

By mid 1988 both employees and customers had voiced considerable dissatisfaction with what was occurring. It was clear that the perceived problems had to be addressed in some systematic fashion. BONY's first step was to contract with us as Human Resource consultants to evaluate the organization and examine employee attitudes and cultural perceptions.

As part of the organizational assessment an attitude survey was administered to all non-exempt employees while our organizational dynamics survey was administered to exempt employees. The attitude survey included conventional questions related to morale, satisfaction, and the administrative practices that affect employees. It was supplemented by several broadly cultural questions from the organizational dynamics survey.

Our organizational dynamics survey emphasizes broad cultural values and was supplemented by several attitude survey questions. These organizational categories are presented in Reynierse & Harker (1986) and, in a modest revision in Reynierse (1988). Both surveys also provided employees with the opportunity to make confidential comments and give a narrative account of their views and opinions.

Finally, the surveys were supplemented during a later stage with a large number of confidential interviews that included all senior and mid- level managers, and several small group meetings and focus groups. In particular, meetings with the top four executives in the Long Island Division and BONY Retail Sector executives reviewed retail strategies, organizational structure, market performance data, HRP plans, formal policies, etc.

The overall organizational assessment identified several important problem areas and as some areas of relative strength. Employees at all levels were critical of customer service levels and BONY's commitment to the customer. They were particularly critical of their training and often felt that they lacked essential knowledge and service skills for their jobs. Former LITCO employees were indiscriminate in their views about bank customers and were particularly resistant to BONY's strategy of targeting consumer customer segments and industry groups.

Customers surveyed in a parallel study conducted by a Market Research firm were also critical of service levels. The overall assessment was that there were operational and cultural problems that affected service levels. Any intervention would have to address day-to-day customer service practices as well as take steps to develop a supportive customer service culture.

Managers and officials were particularly negative, critical and reactive. Many were openly hostile and carried this message to their subordinates. In addition, they demonstrated an unhealthy competitiveness with each other. They were reluctant to make referrals, jealously guarded their own customers, and were often unwilling to service the customers of other BONY units.

Employees did not feel that they were valued by bank management. This included indications of low morale. Additionally, it included the feeling that they were not part of the team or a broader bank family, and that they were not valued as contributors to the organization's success. Similarly, employees felt that management was out of touch with day to day operations and what was happening throughout the branch system. In this regard, employees were highly critical of senior management's leadership.

There was evidence of a significant cultural gap separating former LITCO and BONY employees, especially officers. In particular, while they recognized BONY's strong financial focus and centralized management structure and decision making, they disagreed with and resisted them. Many employees saw little need for profitability or expense control and perceived that bank profitability was at the expense of customers and employees. Long service LITCO officers viewed BONY as cheap, unresponsive to customers, with unrealistic credit policies and restrictive management controls. Long service BONY officers viewed LITCO as wasteful, non-discriminating regarding customers and with liberal, out-of-control credit standards. Employees new to the merged organization largely shared the views of their managers. A summary of this culture gap and different cultural values is provided in Table 1.

On the positive side, everyone agreed that customer service was important and needed improvement. Similarly, there was general agreement that senior and middle management provided a considerable encouragement and recognition to individuals, and many LITCO employees saw career advancement opportunities within the larger BONY organization.

Table 1: BONY - LITCO Cultural Gap

BONY Employees view of LITCO	LITCO Employees view of BONY
1. Wasteful	1. Cheap
2. Liberal Credit Standards	2. Harsh Credit Standards
3. Employees & Customers Benefit at Shareholders Expense	3. Shareholders benefit at Employees & Customers Expense
4. Out-of-Control	4. Tight Management Control

The Intervention

The primary intervention was developed in a series of three retreats which gradually expanded the number of mid-management participants and were conducted over a 10 week time period. The first, a 1-day retreat, included 18 participants, primarily branch District executives, Commercial Loan managers, key staff members, and the division's senior management team. Each of these participants was aware of the macro survey results in addition to more detailed results for their subordinate organizations. The primary emphasis during this session was on survey review, prioritizing problem areas, open dialogue, and examination of some of the options. The discussion identified macro issues. There was also an emerging concensus for identifying a team focus, emphasizing the customer, and developing employee competence.

The second retreat was a 2-day, high intensity, team-building action planning effort that was expanded further to include 30 participants. Seventeen of the participants were originally from BONY, ten were from LITCO, and three were recent hires from other banks. The new participants were primarily branch area managers. They were added to both broaden the number of participants and in anticipation of their important role when the program would be down-streamed to all employees. The primary thrust of this retreat was to: (a) forge agreement within the group for a focused mission statement and (b) to develop action plans to address both priority problem areas and steps to down-stream the program to all employees.

Early during the retreat the group was broken down into seven groups and administered our proprietary values clarification exercise. This exercise consists of

Commited People - We value our employees as responsible individuals who deserve to be treated with respect and dignity. We strive for a team environment in which employees identify with and share in the success of the organization.

Professional Employees - We are committed to a well trained workforce that performs its duties in a knowledgeable, ethical,and technically competent manner. Career opportunities and added responsibility are given to those who consistently meet professional work standards.

Customer Focus - We value our customers and will make an extended effort to be responsive to their needs. It is our intent to provide quality financial products and services that are delivered with professional courtesy and pride.

Sales Focus - We believe it is imperative to grow within our marketplace, seeking new business relationships and an expanded customer base, while offering additional products and services to our established customers.

Profitability - We recognize the Bank's obligation to its shareholders and the advantages of being associated with a financially strong institution. We are responsible to all the Bank's stakeholders to return a fair profit for our services.

Figure 3: BONY Long Island Core Values - "Our Standards"

30 corporate values that are relevant (and credible) for business and industry. Each is defined and serves as effective probes, placing key issues on the table for discussion. Groups were given instructions to discuss the set of values and then select by concensus the five key values which, in their judgment, were most appropriate for BONY's Long Island Division. They were further instructed to prepare a brief presentation for the larger group. The purpose was to provide a rationale for each of the values selected including the group's reasons for rejecting any other values they considered particularly important.

In this regard, a case could be made for most or even all the values in this task. When we speak about core values we are dealing with many attractive virtues and our set of values is particularly virtuous. However, in our experience, an organization can give proper attention to only a few, e.g., 3-5, clearly stated core values. Gaining focus requires that the organization make some strategic choices and concentrate on some values to the conscious exclusion of others. Anything beyond this will be too diffuse and will only confuse employees as well as dilute management's efforts. This is analogous to the strategic concept of being "stuck-in-the-middle" (Porter, 1985).

Following the group reports there was a general group discussion and relatively rapid agreement regarding which core values should be emphasized. The core values identified were formalized as a statement of "our standard" which is presented in Figure 3. Similarly, this became the background for developing a focused statement of Mission and this is presented in Figure 4. While both statements were refined after this retreat, this became the focus and standard for all subsequent retreat activities and particularly the development of appropriate action steps.

Action plans were made with some urgency and the intent they be fully as quickly as possible. Some were implemented almost immediately while others were implemented after appropriate development work was completed, usually within a two-four month period.

A primary action was establishing five task forces and the addition of 30 more bank officers to the process. This included several individuals from other units with a dotted line relationship to the Long Island Division. The commitment to these

"The Bank of New York's Long Island Division is a leading provider of a broad spectrum of financial services to individuals, businesses and local governments throughout Long Island. Our extensive branch network provides convenience for our customers and promotes involvement in the communities we serve.

We understand the needs of our market and respond by providing an array of financial products and by tailoring services to meet special needs. We strive to provide quality financial products with professional customer service while simultaneously earning a fair profit.

We intend to grow and remain a leader in our marketplace through innovative services that are delivered by a professional and committed workforce."

Figure 4: BONY Long Island Mission Statement

Committed People Value
o   Increased Teller & CSR Salaries
o   Monthly Division Extra-Step Awards
o   Task Force on "Creating Unity in a Diverse Division"

Professional Employees Value
o   HRP Assessment and Developmental Plans
o   Commercial & Middle Market Lending Seminars
o   Credit School for Retail Branch Staff
o   Added a Second Teller School
o   Task Force on "Recruitment of Qualified Employees"
o   Task Force on "Development of Branch Progression"

Customer Focus Value
o   Review Loan Rejections
o   Product Knowledge Seminars
o   Customer Relations & Service Seminars
o   Telephone Etiquette Training
o   Monthly District Customer Service Awards
o   Task Force on "Credit Responsiveness"
o   Task Force on "Non-Training Customer Service Issues"

Sales Focus Value
o   Cross-Selling Seminars for CSR's
o   Retail Sector Sales Incentive Program
o   Monthly Promotional Sales Meetings

Profitability
o   Made Value Visible but Low-Key
o   Viewed Value as Emergent from Success with Other Values

Figure 5: Primary BONY Action Plans Summarized for the Core Values

task forces and the urgency of their task was communicated informally by freeing each participant to attend a one-day session that was scheduled only three days after the retreat. This insured that each task force began functioning very rapidly.

The primary action plans as related to the preferred core values, i.e., the Standard, are summarized in Figure 5. Similarly, since action plans also were designed to "downstream" the process to the entire workforce, the primary action plans as related to the "Culture Carriers" are presented in Figure 6.

The third retreat was for 1-day and consisted primarily of a progress review and refinement of the broad plan. This occurred about six weeks following completion of the 2-day planning retreat.

The action plans as identified for the core values (Figure 5) are self-explanatory. For the most part they are either a direct response to priority problem areas or action taken to demonstrate management's commitment to that value. They were steps taken to make the Values prominent and visible; to demonstrate systematically that these are the things that really matter.

The action plans for the "culture carriers" are applications of the consultant's model for organizational change. These are steps management can take to reinforce the core values both consistently and often. In our view organizational change occurs in small, discrete steps. Action steps require a corresponding series of small actions applied over and over again but with a consistent, focused message. In other words, management within BONY's Long Island Division used these tools to shape the Division.

Each individual action became an opportunity to deliver a message about the focused mission, to reinforce it, and build the entire employee base around it. Many of the action steps are repeated on a regular basis thereby multiplying the opportunity to send focused messages to employees and reinforce the values and mission.

Inspirational Leadership

The action steps taken provided senior management with many opportunities to meet with individual or small groups of employees and reinforce the values and focused mission. The two most senior executives in the Division made the commitment and visited every branch on an on-going basis. District and Area managers increased their visits and visibility in their branches. During the early stages of the process employees had a natural skepticism. These visits became an informal format to reiterate the Division's focus and respond to the concerns of employees.

Divisional and Regional kick-off meetings celebrated the values and were accompanied by a lot of hoopla and enthusiasm. At these meetings, employees received wallet-sized cards of the Standard and Mission, BONY coffee mugs emblazoned with the core values, and a pep-talk on the Division's focus and market expectations.

Communications

Survey results were reported to all employees in a series of Division and District employee meetings. The Division bi-monthly newspaper initially provided a preliminary report and later devoted an entire issue to survey results and management's response. Throughout, negative results and problem areas were presented honestly and this undoubtedly played a key role in reducing employee skepticism. The Values and Mission were also communicated systematically through meetings, frequent newspaper articles, and large, attractive signage that was prominently displayed in all work locations.

Financial Focus

Some of the intended action plans were big budget items that required high level management approval within BONY corporate. The two most far- reaching decisions had larger implications than the Long Island Division as they were implemented for the entire Retail Sector. The first was a marked salary increase for bank tellers and customer service representatives. This action was intended to attract and retain qualified employees and communicate the valued nature of these positions.

In the second, the Retail Sector made a major commitment to customer service, product knowledge, and sales training. These new programs were initially piloted in the Long Island Division and were later expanded to the entire Sector. More important, the Sector Training Department was created, given high visibility,

Inspirational Leadership

o   Senior Management Visits to every Work Location
o   District and Area Managers Increase their Visits
o   All Officer Meeting of Survey Results
o   Division Kick-Off Rally
o   District Kick-Off Rallys
o   Monthly Motivational Sales Meetings

Communications

o   Wallet-Sized Cards of Mission & Standard for Employees
o   Large Signage of Mission & Standard in Work Locations
o   Frequent articles in Bi-Monthly Newspaper
o   BONY Mug Displaying Values for all Employees
o   Update Internal Electronic Communications System

Financial Focus

o   Bankwide Commitment to Increase Teller & CSR Salaries
o   Expand Retail Sector Training Department

Training

o   Major Commitment to Training Area
o   Added a Second Teller School
o   Product Knowledge Seminars
o   Customer Service Seminars
o   Credit and Lending Seminars

Recognition Programs

o   Monthly District Customer Service Awards
o   Monthly Division Extra-Step Awards
o   Sector Sales Incentive Program
o   Monthly Nominee for Bank Quality Award
o   Commitment to give lots of "atta-boys" and "atta-girls"

Figure 6: Primary BONY Action Steps for the "Culture Carriers"

and significant budgetary support. Additionally, this department was assigned to a high ranking Retail Sector line executive.

Training

BONY's strategy for improving service quality included a significant investment in the training area. This included frequent seminars and workshops in customer service and product knowledge but also included increased credit and lending seminars. One of the first training decisions was to add a second Teller School in order to improve teller quality.

Recognition Programs

Three formal recognition programs were developed to recognize employee contributions linked to the Values. Just as importantly, they were designed to provide frequent awards rather than the one-shot programs and awards that occur with annual award ceremonies and recognition dinners.

The first, a Retail Sector sales incentive program that recognized sales production was developed but never implemented. However monthly sales meetings were initiated and provided frequent opportunity for public recognition of high sales achievers and demonstrated success to the entire group.

Second, a monthly Customer Service Award, was given in each District for an employee who made a particularly significant contribution in this area. Individual plaques were awarded to employee recipients while permanent plaques for customer service were displayed in the branch. This made both the award and BONY's commitment to the customer visible to other employees and customers.

Third, and directed particularly to the "Committed People" value, monthly "Extra Step" awards were presented by the Division head at a catered luncheon. These awards were for employees that made a special effort and took an "extra step" to fulfill the Division Mission statement. Besides the luncheon, a symbolic award was presented. In this case it was an attractive paperweight containing a statement of both the Standard and Mission, and about an hour of time that was used to praise the recipients. Everyone leaves these luncheons charged-up, feeling appreciated, and ready for the next challenge.

Finally, a commitment was made to submit at least one monthly nominee for a bankwide Quality award program and this also led to recognition for several employees. Recognition awards were made highly visible by public award presentations, articles in the newspaper, etc. The management discussion and reviews of nominated employees raised standards for performance throughout the organization by providing an informal "awards baseline" for expected performance.

The Bottom Line

The combination of survey participation, honest communication of results, enlarged employee participation in developing a game plan, and frequent reinforcement of the focused mission led to reversing the low morale and skepticism that earlier had characterized the workforce.

Employees quickly identified with the focused standard and Mission, "bought-in" to what was taking place, and became a positive force in achieving the market goals of the Division. Unhealthy competition with each other was transformed into a cooperative spirit and this competitiveness was redirected to the marketplace and BONY's external competitors. The charge was led by the approximately 60 officers who participated in the retreats and task forces and who became a strong voice for frequently reinforcing the Standard and Mission. The original apathy was quickly replaced by obvious enthusiasm.

Similarly, although the consolidations relating from the Irving merger led to reduced staffing levels, there was a dramatic decline in employee turnover for 1989. In addition, while turnover remained at the high levels of 1987, it was managed turnover. The commitment to build a professional workforce led to performance planning and termination or early retirement for many low producers.

The real test occurred, however, in the marketplace. Consider, however, that identifying objective measures of marketplace success is complicated by several factors. These include: the Irving merger, a restructuring that segregated consumer and commercial activities within BONY, deteriorating economic conditions during 1989 and 1990 in the Northeast and BONY's markets, as well as deteriorating conditions within the banking industry during this same time period. These latter two factors led to a very cautious lending posture and a sharp reduction in lending throughout the banking industry. Comparisons are necessarily tentative. Still, BONY- Long Island responded very favorably during this difficult period relative to both its external competitors and other Retail units within BONY.

Preliminary results were first apparent in late 1988 as the marked runoff of deposits and customer accounts was finally stabilized. By this time three events had occurred: (a) employee completion of the surveys, (b) management's introduction of new consumer products, and (c) management repeatedly linked these first two events as responses to acknowledged problems and indicators that a new era was just beginning. As the various steps in the intervention were implemented and there was increasing employee "buy-in" to the process there was a corresponding increase in account retention and deposit growth. During 1989 BONY Long Island more than recovered the deposits lost during 1987 and 1988 and was once again matching, or slightly exceeding, the rate of growth of other BONY retail units.

As suggested, it is more difficult to evaluate program effects for lending activities. Commercial lending in the Division held its own with loan quality now meeting BONY asset quality standards. Lending officers no longer resisted credit policy and lending practices were brought into accord with BONY credit policy and credit quality objectives. Consumer loans showed progressive growth.with increased credit training and a branch workforce now increasingly competent in consumer lending.

Market research surveys of customers were continued in both 1989 and 1990 and demonstrated significant improvement in customers' perceptions of service levels. Customers now viewed Long Island employees as both more knowledgeable and helpful than previously, reflecting perceived improvement in both tellers and customer service representatives. Most importantly, while former LITCO branches were below average in 1988, by 1990 their customer rating scores equaled or exceeded those of original BONY branches. Figure 7 provides a summary of primary, qualitative results that occurred following the intervention and implementation of the BONY Long Island focused mission.

The Irving Merger

This exercise was complicated somewhat by BONY's acquisition of Irving Bank, a large peer group bank in New York that enlarged BONY's asset base to about $50 billion. This required merging in an Irving subsidiary bank on Long Island, the usual systems conversions, and bringing the new employees on-board. Since there were now several existing programs, e.g., monthly sales meetings, new employee orientation materials built around the focused mission, established Customer Service and Extra Step recognition programs, etc., it became a simple matter to use these materials and extend the process to the new group from Irving. The ranking Irving executive on the BONY Long Island team cooperated fully and led the charge with this group. Without doubt, addressing the problems inherent in the LITCO acquisition and merger provided a sound base for an easier time and rapid success with the Irving merger.

This is not to imply that the Irving merger was without problems. Rather, at the time of this merger, BONY Long Island had corrected most of their internal problems and was a remarkably stable organization. It was now well positioned to

Employee Morale
Employees clearly enthusiastic and positive
Employees embrace Mission and Values

Turnover
Decreases to competitive levels

Customer Reactions
Perceptions of service levels improve
Below average LITCO branches now match
original BONY branches

Account Retention
Reversed high rate of account losses
New products attract new customers and
account relationships

Deposits
Deposit loss halted and replaced by deposit growth
Deposit growth matches that of BONY Retail

Loans
Significant consumer loan growth
Lending practices in accord with BONY credit policy
and asset quality

Figure 7: Post Intervention Improvements

handle any merger trauma and as assimilate this new employee group into a focused organization. BONY Long Island employees were positive and committed about their role in the organization and addressed merger problems in a positive and committed manner.

Bottom-up Impact on the Retail Sector

Success in the Long Island Division had important implications for the entire Retail Sector. Consumer products introduced on Long Island are now standard throughout the BONY system. Most importantly, the Sector has adopted a strong Customer Service focus which impacts line and staff functions in important ways.

The Retail Marketing monitors service quality very closely. As mentioned previously, the Sector Training area made a significant commitment to customer service and product knowledge. Seminars in both of these areas are now standard throughout the BONY system. Finally, the Sector now routinely acknowledges the key role recognition programs can play. Based on Long Island's success, each Division developed their own, local awards program and there is also an Exceptional Achievement Award at the Sector level.

Concluding Comment

Banking is a service business that is dependent upon the contributions of its employees to deliver these services in a knowledgeable and professional manner. It is unlikely that market driven strategies will succeed if the human resource link in the value chain is neglected.

BONY successfully overcame a difficult merger which was threatening the implementation of its strategy for the Long Island marketplace. To do this they had to address the weak human resource link in their value chain. Their success only came after management took the time to visit employees in their work areas, to communicate with employees, to inspire employees, and to recognize employees for their contributions. Management's biggest investment was their time. By taking the time they were able to show again and again that they were committed to the values and focused mission. This made it believable to almost everyone

Once the surveys were administered and the process begun BONY raised employee expectations. As the process was expanded in subsequent stages it began to feed on itself with snowballing effects of employee commitment and improvement. The process created an element of trust between employees and management that were necessary conditions to achieve later marketplace success.

References

Porter, M.E., *Competitive Advantage*. (New York: The Free Press, 1985).

Reynierse, J.H., "Corporate Culture and the Concept of Competition". in R.J. Niehaus and K. F. Price, Eds. *Creating the Competitive Edge through Human Resource Applications,*. (New York: Plenum, 1988).

Reynierse, J. H. and Harker, J. B., "Measuring and Managing Organizational Culture", *Human Resource Planning*, Vol. 9, No. 1, (1986), pp 1-8.

Staff Reduction and the Bottom Line: Less Is Not Always More

M.M. GRELLER and J.P. DORY

Introduction

Theory and practice sometimes diverge. The approaches businesses use to improve profitability in increasingly competitive markets are a case in point. Managers' actions seem to take place in a world separated from management theory and research. Under such circumstances the effectiveness of the approaches used are rarely assessed, taking their support from anecdotal evidence--evidence often provided by people with an interest in justifying their own past decisions.

Staff reduction's role as a tool for productivity improvement and profitability is a case in point. Restructuring, downsizing, and open- windows have become part of the business culture. They are justified by the simple mathematics which show that revenues not expended on labor "fall right to the bottom line." Dis-employment, systematically reducing the workforce to improve financial performance, is increasingly popular.

Human resource practitioners have reshaped their activities to accommodate these priorities. They discuss ways of facilitating staff reductions, making them more humane or efficient. There is talk of "right- sizing". Symposia are conducted on the best ways to downsize. Examples of human resource practitioners successfully slowing the rush to staff reduction are less common.

The trend has a moral tone to it. Advocates declare themselves to be delivering value to shareholders, making businesses more competitive and striking against the laxness of entrenched management (Pickens, 1986). To argue against "cutting the fat" is to risk the appearance of weakness. This could possibly subject ones corporation to takeover by raiders more willing to reduce staff as part of a restructuring. For the most part, critics of this approach have emphasized the risk to the business's long term well being and the human costs.

M.M. GRELLER - University of Wyoming, Laramie, WY 82071; J.P. DORY - Pace University, One Pace Plaza, New York, NY 10038
Acknowledgements: The authors would like to thank Michael Segalla, David Herold and Carol Schreiber for their comments on earlier drafts of this paper. The support provide by Personnel Strategies, Inc is gratefully acknowledged

Unfortunately, the heat generated by the value-tinged arguments revolving around long term versus short term and human cost versus corporate gain, have skipped over an important question. Does labor cost savings, as such, lead to improved corporate performance?

Research Questions

The answer to the question has been so thoroughly accepted in practice that it would hardly seem worthy of serious investigation. This common wisdom had its effect on the authors. Rather than look at the effect of downsizing on profit, a comparative approach was taken. Surely, downsizing would improve profit, but would it do so as well as an alternative, business building approach?

The impact of staff reduction was compared with an approach which is its virtual opposite: investment in R&D (research and development). R&D is a current expense made with the intent of securing future benefit. It is an investment in the business. Whether or not it is eventually beneficial, the immediate and certain effect is to reduce current earnings. Staff reductions work the opposite way. They reduce one expense almost immediately, while running the risk of limiting future capacity.

The effect of these two variables were examined over a short period, consistent with the time frame in which labor cost savings might be expected to show its effects. Companies' staffing levels and spending on R&D were monitored. The relationship between these two actions and subsequent profit were assessed, controlling for the magnitude of sales in the first year.

Three different results could be produced. First, if cost control is the most consistently successful approach, reduced staffing and reduced R&D should result in the greatest future profit. Second, if R&D is used to technologically replace workers either by creating more efficient processes or granting entry to less labor intensive businesses, R&D expenditures should have a positive relationship with future profit while increased staffing should have a negative relationship. The third possibility is that building ones business is the most effective route to future profit. In this case both R&D and staff growth should be related to future profit.

Methodology

Data were drawn from the *Business Week* "R&D Scoreboard." This survey provides comparative information about firms by industry group. The information used was sales, profit, R&D expenditure and number of employees.

Four industries (Chemicals, Electronics, Food & Beverage, and Information Services) were selected to provide a range of growth rates, technological intensities and labor practices (see Table 1). In the 1986 survey, 196 companies were in these industries. However, when companies not listed in the 1985 and 1987 surveys were eliminated the sample was reduced to 133 companies.

Profit in 1987 was used as the dependent variable. Other data taken from the survey included 1985 sales. This was used to control for size of company. R&D expenditures from 1984 to 1987 and the number of employees in 1985, 1986 and 1987 were determined. Some of these numbers had to be calculated from the information supplied. Specifically, 1984 R&D expenditures were calculated from the 1985 figure adn reported change since 1984. The number of employees was calculated by dividing the reported R&D expenses by dividing by R&D per employee.

Table 1: Characteristics of Industries Sampled

Industry Group	Number. Firms	Sales Growth Ratio	$R&D/ Sales	$Sales/ Employee
Chemicals (e.g., Dow, GAF, Olin)	38	0.0%	4.1%	$149
Electronics (e.g., Combustion Engineering, EG&G, Thomas & Betts)	52	8%	4.4	$74
Food & Beverage (e.g., Borden, CPC International, Quaker Oats)	19	11%	0.9%	$91
Information Services (e.g ,ADP, HBO, Lotus Development)	24	28%	7.7%	$848

Note: Classification based on 1986 *Business Week* survey

The difference in the number of employees between 1986 and 1985 was calculated. Positive values indicate growth in the number of employees, while negative ones indicate a decrease in workforce size. The interval 1984 to 1987 is interesting because it was a period of general economic growth, yet one during which companies continued to turn to staff reductions.

The choice to invest in the firm was indicated by tau (Greller & Herold, 1975), the rate of monotonic increase in R&D expenditures from 1984 through 1987. Companies which increased their commitment through the period would score highest on this index. ["Tau" is the linear contrast model. Tau = (-2)($R&D'84) + (-1)($R&D'85) + (+1)($R&D'86) + (+2)($R&D'87).]

Sources of Control and Contamination

Using sales as a control variable in a regression analysis removes the effect of size (in terms of sales volume) from change in employment and R&D expenditure as well as profit. To the extent companies with larger initial sales also have larger workforces and greater R&D expenditures, these effects will be removed by the control variable.

Using secondary sources meant we were not able to tailor the measures to reflect exactly the concepts that were being addressed. This was particularly true of downsizing. The change in the number of employees indicates a reduction or increase in staff size regardless of the reason. Such changes include ones other than "downsizing." Companies which exited business areas, reduced their operations or introduced innovations reducing the labor content of their product would show a reduced number of employees. Change in the number of employees does not differentiate companies which reduce staff for very sound reasons from those which have simply taken on a dis-employment strategy. Thus, the probability of finding

Table 2: Regression Models of R&D Trend, Change in Employment and and Sales on Profit.

	Total	Chemical	Electric	Food & Beverage	Information Service
R&D Trend	.17***	.17*	.16	.20	.21
Change Emp.s	.09***	.12	.17*	-.07	-.06
$Sales (85)	.84***	.86***	.84***	.81***	.80***
n	133	38	52	19	24
R^2	.86***	.86***	.83***	.84***	.73***

probability (* $p< .05$; ** $p< .01$; *** $p< .001$)

the popularly assumed outcome (i.e., staff reduction resulting in improved profit) is increased.

Results

In the analysis of the total sample (see Table 2), both R&D expenditures and *increases* in staffing were associated with greater profit. These two actions which most immediately create charges against earnings were associated with profit in a later year. The pattern of results support the notion that building ones business is the most consistent route to profitability. It draws into question the belief that staff reduction has an important role in improving corporate performance. The results were so thoroughly counter to common wisdom, other ways of representing the data were considered.

R&D expenditures were stable, correlations among the four years were .98 and .99. This suggested looking at initial R&D investment (in 1984) instead of the change as reflected in tau. Proponents of such spending might argue that this is a more appropriate test of R&D's effect for two reasons. First, it allows for a delay (four years) before the expected benefit to revenue is measured. Second, it considers the amount spent on R&D (controlling for company size), not the extent to which it was increased. The relationship between 1984 R&D expenditures and 1987 profit was of about the same magnitude as that for tau (b= .16, p< .05). However, the strength of the relationship between staffing and profit increased (b= .13, p< .001).

While overall workforce size was stable from year to year (correlations ranging from .92 to .99), the relationship between the two difference scores (e.g., 1986 - 1985 versus 1987 - 1986) was smaller, .51. It would be appropriate to examine whether the effects might be even more immediate, given that staff reduction produced the exact opposite result of that intended a year after the fact. What role does staff reduction play during the year in which it is implemented? When 1987 - 1986 changes in employment were used in conjunction with increases in R&D spending no relationship was found between employment and 1987 profit.

Table 3: :Regression Models for R&D Expenditures (1984), Change in Employment (1986 to 1987) and Sales on Profit.

	Linear Effects	**With Interaction**
Sales 1985	.78***	.92***
Change in Number of Employees	.08**	-.05
Research and Development Expenditure	.14*	.06
Interaction of Employment and R&D		.20***
R^2	.834***	.855***
R^2 Change		.021***

probability (* $p < .10$; ** $p < .05$; *** $p < .001$)

When the 1987 - 1986 employment numbers and 1984 R&D spending were used, the positive relationship between staff increases and profit remained significant. The independent effect of R&D was diminished (see Table 3). The interaction of staff size and R&D spending was tested, resulting in a significant increase in the variance explained (.021, $p < .001$). A similar result does not occur when using staff reduction from a previous year nor with tau. The interaction suggests the combination of R&D and immediate staff size changes may influence profit.

The next question was whether these results were supported in each of the industries. While there were no main effects for industry, it was possible that the dynamics of each industry might work differently. The results must be viewed with caution, as the samples within each industry group were small. The results can be seen in Table 2.

While the significance levels vary, the magnitude of the relationship between increased R&D expenditure and profit is consistent across industries. The relationship between staffing and profit was weaker than that for R&D in the analysis of the total sample, and this weakness is reflected by smaller standardized beta weights in the industry sub-samples. However, in no instance is there a significant relationship between staff *reduction* and profit.

Discussion

While staff reduction should not be rejected as one element in a profit improvement strategy, it is also clear that the simplistic formula which argues for it across the board is flawed. Of course, there are businesses which are run inefficiently and would benefit from staff reduction. There are strategic changes that require adjusting staff levels--although these may mean increases as well as decreases. (Herold, 1990) The problem is that staff reduction is not, of itself, a strategy. It is a tool, an action, and (for some) a knee jerk response. It does not reflect an integrated response to the environment. When a human resource department helps implement a staff reduction program, it is not always clear what strategic objectives it furthers. A more sensible framework is needed within which to consider the appropriateness of staff reduction.

In contrast with the role played by staff reduction, R&D illustrated the value of investing in ones business. As R&D was the only measure of investment in the business, even stronger results might be achieved if additional methods of increasing commitment to the business were included.

Staff Reduction as Part of a Strategic Response

Those who make considerable use of staff reduction, usually explain their actions in terms of cost control or expense management. Cost control is a sound practice in any company, regardless of strategy. It is the corner stone of some business strategies. However, staff reduction is not a necessary component of any of the major business strategies.

Porter (1980) describes three strategies: cost leadership, differentiation, and focus. Cost leadership creates the potential for price advantage. It is sometimes seen as the opposite of differentiation, in which the business secures advantage by offering something which is not available elsewhere regardless of price.

The attractiveness of an investment which achieves differentiation is dependent on how long the advantage can be maintained. (Henderson, 1984) If product cycles are short, the period in which to benefit from the investment is limited. As markets become more competitive, niches are redefined and technology changes; the length of time one may expect to hold a competitive advantage shrinks. Thus, managers are led to explore other strategic alternatives. This may explain the increased interest in staff reduction as the pace of business change accelerates.

With cost leadership managers have the luxury of more direct control over the major strategic variable. Expenditures are manageable--at least in so far as one must disburse funds. Conversely, uniqueness in the marketplace is dependent on the actions of competitors and the preferences (or perceptiveness) of the customer. If a cost cutting step does not improve profit, one at least has the sense of having done something.

Even those companies which are not compelled by debt or institutional owners to manage costs, still have an intellectual justification for selecting it as a strategic alternative. However, the method and targets for cost reduction may vary. It is not inevitable that staff must be reduced--a truth that may be at the heart of this study's findings. Reducing staff as part of a well thought out cost management strategy is one thing. Cutting head count as an alternative to strategy (dis-employment) is quite another.

The implications of major business strategies for labor cost savings are not clear cut. Particularly as the distinction between differentiation and cost leadership becomes less clear, it is important to recognize the limited certainty of the appropriateness of staff reduction for the strategy. Usually, differentiation does not result in true uniqueness, just distinctiveness. The product's cost continues to be a factor (Hill, 1988; Jones & Butler, 1988). Thus, even the company pursuing distinctiveness must manage costs, increasing the number of companies which may view staff reduction as an element of their strategy.

At the other end of the spectrum, a company in a mature business may achieve an advantage not just by cutting prices in the commodity end of its business, but by creating differences which deliver value to the customer. (Hall, 1980; Harrigan, 1980) Key among such differences are service level and continuity of relationships. Experience and expertise needs to be retained, and that experience resides within the same employee who would be the subject of a staff reduction.

The position that staff can be reduced continuously because employees learn more efficient ways to accomplish their tasks as they gain experience (Hirschmann, 1964), must be moderated by a careful consideration of the firm, its circumstances and other objectives. The value of eliminating employees who will be needed to achieve distinctiveness or to meet the performance requirements of projected growth has little economic value. In fact, it removes a strategic resource from the firm. Similarly, depending on the enhanced learning of remaining employees is itself suspect, as the most rapid gains on a learning curve occur during the early repetitions. Established organizations with stable workforces are less likely to see dramatic shifts due to the learning curve. Yet, these are the ones often subjected to a dis-employment in lieu of strategy.

Thus, knowing which major business strategy a company is pursuing will not determine what stance it should take regarding labor cost savings. While cost leaders will control their costs and firms following a strategy of differentiation may also be expected to control them. Both also have reasons to invest in their businesses. In neither case is staff reduction a necessary and sufficient route to appropriate economies. The results of this study suggest that the actual savings achieved by staff reduction are not generally adequate to offset the resulting costs and loss of productive capacity. So, a company needs more specific reasons if it is to expect staff reduction to yield profit.

R&D and Productivity

It is too easy to see R&D solely in terms of new products and new markets. These may be benefits of an R&D program. They would be consistent with the business commitment which R&D spending represented in this study. However, R&D has the potential to contribute productivity improvements which are both direct and indirect. Porter (1980) suggested that investment in R&D can improve competitive position and profitability either by reducing a firm's costs or through increasing differentiation, thereby permitting higher prices and margins. One might easily devise scenarios in which the competitive advantage secured through R&D (whether cost leadership or differentiation) produced larger market share, requiring additional staffing, while producing larger profits.

Cost control is a legitimate objective for a R&D program. Much R&D does focus on reducing product costs--producing the same functionality at lower cost. The interaction of R&D expenditure and staffing levels suggests that improvements in productivity may be an important factor in determining the appropriateness and consequences of staff reduction.

Whatever Happened to Distinctive Competence?

In seeking to identify the appropriate role for staff reduction in improving organization effectiveness, much of the thinking has focused on external markets and industry conditions (Barney, 1986). Yet, others have argued that companies can create advantage through product development or creating a unique capacity for production or service. (Nelson & Winter, 1982; Peters & Waterman, 1982)

A company's workforce can create a competitive advantage in several ways. It can be a highly motivated, well coordinated, high performing unit. It can retain high quality people. It may be flexible, communicative and adapt well to the requirements of change. If maintained and nurtured, these characteristics could be competitive advantages. Such strengths are unlikely to be realized in an organization which periodically reduces its ranks to achieve marginal increases in quarterly earnings per share.

The extent to which a firm's distinctive competence is dependent on its human resources was not measured in the present study. The criticality of human resources should be expected to play a key role in guiding decisions on staff size and investment in the workforce. Yet, it is not clear that this is the guiding principle in practice.

It is ironic that staff development and expansion often occur as a by-product of organizational slack--surplus and success that permit expenditures without threatening earnings expectations. Using periods of corporate abundance to increase the diversity of skill a company's workforce possesses is adaptive. It provides competencies which enable to the firm to explore new business directions (Gaertner, 1988). The reverse of this process is to reduce the investment in staff, skills and development when things become tight. This is precisely the time at which the added diversity has the greatest potential to be beneficial.

Forces Working Against Good Judgment

Given the ineffectiveness of dis-employment one might wonder why it seems so popular. Three factors may contribute. First, human resource professionals have not made a compelling case to the contrary (Cascio, 1991). Second, many corporations have placed themselves in situations in which cash flow considerations have become overwhelming. This may be carried to the point that delivering immediate cash is more important than any other business consideration. Third, human resources have not been scarce (hence critical) in the experience of most senior managers; thus, these issues do not figure prominently in their strategic thinking.

Two recent studies had the opportunity to demonstrate the role of effective human resource planning in corporate restructuring, yet neither was able to do so. In Schweiger's (1989) study of acquisitions, there was no evident effect from increased attention to human resource issues. The American Society for Personnel Administration's (Gray, Giacobbe, Wheeler & Quick, 1989) study of human resource practices among organization's in transition found no effects attributable to human resource programs and policies.

These studies revealed a failure of the programs provided by a range of personnel department's to make a difference. It may be more an indictment of the products of particular personnel departments or the use to which companies put their work, than it is an indication of limits to the potential contributions of good human resource management. There are reasons to believe that many human resource functions do offer management only limited vision of the costs and strategic consequences of the firm's personnel policy decisions (Nkomo, 1988). In reality, managers experience the products of real personnel departments and criticize them even if the failures would more properly be attributed to those managers' own misuse of the products.

On the financial side, public corporations face the demands of investors. While shareholder influence has been defuse and ineffectual in the past, increasing institutional ownership concentrates that power. This is felt in two ways. First, these are fiduciaries who are obligated to assume a risk avoidance posture. While there may be more and less risky elements in an institution's portfolio, they do value predictability. Second, the managers of the corporation are aware of their owners' interest in consistent performance, as reflected in regularly reported earnings, and they manage to that measure of performance. The effect is an orientation toward cost control and away from investment in the business. (Ellsworth, 1985; Graves, 1988)

While maximizing shareholder return, some businesses have placed themselves in situations which require increased, even excessive cost consciousness. Needham (1988) analyzed the mezzanine structure which finances many leveraged transactions. In the face of any adversity the debt would topple the firm. Thus, debt becomes the major environmental threat and reshapes the company's strategy (Greller, 1990). Pressed by owners demanding earnings and debt threatening their survival, over-leveraged firms reduce their investment in the future and manage costs (Hitt, Hoskisson, Ireland & Harrison, 1989)

With management so pressed, it is understandable that they would manage costs and cash flows. Why is labor cost so often the target of choice? There are other variable costs. One factor is the abundance of the human resource during the managerial careers of most current executives. Corporate leaders have little experience dealing with labor as a scarce resource. For the most part, they have been rewarded for forcing turnover of middle level people. This afforded them the opportunity to hire from a more abundant, better trained and less expensive entry level labor pool. (Greller & Nee, 1989, 1990) While these conditions may no longer obtain, it will take executives a while to factor the change into their strategic thinking (Bukszar & Connolly, 1988). This situation creates pressure on human resource planners to illustrate the scenarios resulting from different personnel policies (including staff reduction) and then link them to the strategic vision with which the firm identifies.

Limitations of the Study

We have performed a small study. Its greatest contribution may be that it sews doubt in an area previously controlled by unjustified certainty.

There is a temptation to discount such findings as a by-product method variance or reverse causality -- "Perhaps more profitable companies can afford to have all those people around." Regarding the employment data, this argument is contravened by the effects of time. The 1987 profit could not have determined the change in employment from 1985 to 1986. If profit creates a more casual attitude toward increased staffing, the relationship should have been strongest for the 1986 to 1987 employment changes, and it was not.

The results may be understated because of the crudeness of the measures. The data only show us how the number of employees changed. There is no way to tell how much effort was invested in their training and development. As mere head count was related to profit, a stronger relationship should be expected if additional data were available. This is true if such data indicated the strategy the business was following, it's intention in changing the size of its workforce, and investment in its people.

The most appropriate use of these findings may be as a caution. In practice, staff reductions are being treated as an easy technique which causes savings to "fall to the bottom line." Based on this nostrum, considerable change has been undertaken, disrupting individual lives, organizations, and business strategies. While discomfort might be an acceptable price for improved competitiveness, the improvement was not evident. The arithmetic may work, but the technique does not appear to do so.

References

Barney, J. B., "Types of Competition and the Theory of Strategy: Toward an Integrative Framework," *Academy of Management Review*, Vol. 11, No. 4, (1986), pp 791 - 800.

Bukszar, E., & Connolly, T., "Hindsight Bias and Strategic Choice: a Problem in Learning from Experience." *Academy of Management Journal*, Vol. 31, No. 3, (1988) pp 628 - 641.

Cascio, W. F. *Costing Human Resources: The Financial Impact of Behavior in Organizations.* 3rd Edition (Boston: PWS-Kent Publishing, 1991).

Ellsworth, R. R., "Capital Markets and Competitive Decline," *Harvard Business Review*, Vol. 63, No. 5, (1985, September-October), pp 171 - 183.

Gaertner, K. Managerial careers and Organization-wide Transformation," in R. J. Niehaus & K. Price Eds *Creating the Competitive Edge Through Human Resource Applications.* (New York: Plenum, 1988), pp 85 - 96.

Graves, S. B., "Institutional Ownership and Corporate R&D in the Computer Industry," *Academy of Management Journal*, Vol. 31, No. 2, (1988) pp 417 - 428.

Gray, D. A., Giacobbe, J., Wheeler, K. G., & Quick, J. C., "The Impact of Mergers, Downsizing and Acquisition: an ASPA/CCH Study," in *Perspectives in Human Resource.* (Alexandria, VA: American Society for Personnel Administration, 1989), pp 255 - 263.

Greller, M. M., "Post-acquisition Integration: the Structure of the Deal Determines the Human and Organizational Resource Requirements," in R. J. Niehaus & K. Price Eds., *Human Resource Strategies for Organizations in Transition.* (New York: Plenum, 1990), pp 301 - 309.

Greller, M. M., & Herold, D. M., "Sources of Feedback: a Preliminary Investigation," *Organizational Behavior and Human Performance,* Vol. 13, (1975) pp 44 - 56.

Greller, M. M., & Nee, D. M., *From Baby Boom to Baby Bust: How Business Can Meet the Demographic Challenge..* (Reading, MA: Addison-Wesley, 1989).

Fller, M. M., & Nee, D. M., "Human Resource Planning for an Older Work force," in M. London, E. S. Bassman & J. F. Fernandez Eds., *Human Resource Forecasting and Strategy Development: Guidelines for Analyzing and Fulfilling Organizational Needs.* (Westport, CT: Quorum Books, 1990), pp 181 - 193.

Hall, W. K., "Survival strategies in hostile environments," *Harvard Business Review*, Vol. 58, No. 5, (September-October, 1980), pp 75 - 80.

Harrigan, K. R., *Strategies for declining industries.* Lexington, MA: D. C. Heath, 1980)

Henderson, B. D., *The Logic of Business Strategy.* (Cambridge, MA: Ballinger, 1984).

Herold, D. M. "Using Technology to Improve our Management of Labour Market trends," *Journal of Organizational Change Management*, Vol. 3 No. 2, (1990) pp 44 - 57.

Hirschmann, W. B., "Profit from the Learning Curve," *Harvard Business Review*, Vol. 42, (January - February, 1964), 125.

Hill, C. W. L., "Differentiation versus Low Cost or Differentiation and Low Cost: a Contingency Framework," *Academy of Management Review*, Vol. 13, No. 3, (1988) pp 401 - 412.

Hitt, M. A., Hoskisson, R. E., Ireland, R. D., & Harrison, J., "Acquisition Growth Strategy and Relative R&D Intensity: the Effect of Leverage, Diversification and Size," in F. Hoy Ed., *Best Papers Proceedings Academy of Management*, Washington, DC, August 13 - 16, 1989, 22 - 26.

Jones, G. R., & Butler, J. E., "Cost, Revenue and Business Level Strategy," *Academy of Management Review*, Vol. 13, No. 2, (1988) pp 202 - 213.

Needham, N., "Son of LDCs: Banks are Borrowing Trouble with Loans to LBOs," *Barron's*, 26 December 1988, 13 - 30

Nelson, R. R., & Winter, S. G., *The Evolutionary Theory of Economic Change.* (Cambridge, MA: Harvard University Press, 1982).

Nkomo, S. M. "The Theory and Practice of Human Resource Planning: the Gap Still Remains," *Personnel Administrator*, Vol. 31 No. 6, (1988) pp 71 - 84.

Peters, T. J., & Waterman, R. H., Jr., *In Search of Excellence,* (New York: Harper & Row, 1982).

Pickens, T. B., "Professions of a Short-Termer" *Harvard Business Review*, Vol. 64, No. 3, (May-June, 1986) pp 75 - 79.

Porter, M., *Competitive Strategy.* (New York: Free Press, 1980).

"R&D Scoreboard", *Business Week* , June 23, 1986; June 22, 1987; and June 20, 1988.

Schweiger, D. M., "Human Resource Strategies for Implementing Mergers and Acquisitions." paper presented at Human Resource Planning Society Research Symposium, Salve Regina College, Newport, RI, May 30 - June 2, 1989.

Managing People

The five papers in this section provide discussions on several issues concerned with managing people. The first paper is concerned with how globilization is forcing a broader look at how management can and should be developed around the world. **Beres, Portwood, Latib, Timmons** and **Chowdhury** explore cultural differences among senior management of a single transnational corporation to determine if shared development and direct interaction lead to convergent attitudes. The findings suggest an improved strategy for the development of truly international managers.

Blanchard describes two situations where management and union worked together in an attempt to redesign organizations and work systems. This paper presents cases from the automotive and construction materials industries and discusses the implications for other organizations.

The Canadian government has taken an active role in attempting to help individuals in society resolve labor market adjustment issues within the firm, the community or on a sectional basis. **Butcher** describes what the Canadian government has done and the results obtained and how these results are being considered in the U.S., Eastern Europe, and South America.

Atchison and **Zumberge** describe how an independent bank conducted a study regarding employee pay preferences. The paper describes how the study was constructed and the results obtained.

Three dimensions of employee commitment are explored by **Bugbee and Davis**. They include: (a) business and human resource factors; (b) influence and impact of organizational communications; and (c) existence of any new "social contract " between the employee and the organization. The study undertaken for this paper was aimed at finding answers that could help as organizations strive for the elusive edge of maintaining a high degree of employee commitment.

A Cross Cultural Study of Managerial Attitudes toward Executive Development: Implications for Transnational Organizations

M.E. BERES, J.D. PORTWOOD, M.A.S. LATIB, M.J. TIMMONS, and J.M. CHOWDHURY

Introduction

Management literature in recent years has been replete with articles documenting the increasing importance of global markets. These writings warn of intense worldwide competition which may threaten the survival of organizations not well adapted to cope with this new environment (e.g. Aggarwal, 1987; Kantor, 1991b). Corporations have been encouraged to respond aggressively to these trends by restructuring themselves into more truly global or "transnational" forms (Bartlett & Ghoshal, 1988), and by developing cosmopolitan, globally focused management teams capable of operating effectively across national and cultural boundaries (Reich, 1991). While both of these recommendations have considerable merit, their implementation may well create an interesting dilemma for corporate human resource executives.

Implicit in the transnational model of organization is a diffusion of decision making responsibility out to various local or regional operations around the globe, so that they may develop strategies suited to their own unique situation. To insure local knowledge, it is often suggested that management teams be broadened culturally to mirror the range of markets across which the organization does business. This new form of organization, might then be characterized as a culturally diverse confederation where a significant portion of corporate strategy and practice develops as a result of negotiations among the various subunits (Taylor, 1991).

One issue which would be a likely subject for negotiation across the global network would be the nature and structure of any company-wide executive development and succession planning effort. Given considerable evidence that views on key management skills and preferred development techniques vary across

M.E. BERES.-. Leadership Systems, 1079D N. Jamestown Rd., Decatur, GA 30033; J.D. PORTWOOD - Temple University, Broad and Mongomery, Philadelphia, PA 19122; M.A.S. LATIB - Allentown College, Center Valley, PA 18034; M.J. TIMMONS - Dominion Textiles, Inc., 1950 Sherbrooke Street West, Montreal, Quebec HCH 1E7, Canada, and J.M. CHOWDHURY - University of Scranton, Scranton, PA 18510

cultures (Tung, 1982), gaining acceptance of an overall corporate strategy in this area could prove to be quite a challenge. Corporate human resource staff will need to find a way to balance local vs. global management needs in the firm.

A logical first step in preparing to deal with this problem would be to determine whether such an attitude gap exists within the organization. Studies reporting cross-cultural differences in management development strategies, have generally used data from different organizations, rather than different locations in the same organization. To test the possibility that such differences of opinion may be present within a single firm, the current study surveyed a culturally diverse sample of top executives from a large transnational organization. Results suggest that cultural variations in preferred management skills and development strategies can be found within a single firm. Implications of these findings for management development and succession planning in global firms is discussed.

The Changing Environment for Management Development

Differences in management styles and strategies across cultures have been studied in considerable detail. Comparisons have been made among the consensus oriented approaches in Asian cultures, the consultative approaches most characteristic of European countries, and the styles emphasizing individual initiative most common in North America. These differences in management style have also been paralleled by differences in how companies arising in these different cultures have tended to develop and promote management staff (Koster, 1988; Laurent, 1986; Portwood, 1989). Much greater emphasis, for example, is given to holistic (versus strictly skill) development in Asian firms (Granrose, 1988). European organizations, on the other hand, emphasize relational skills more heavily in their development efforts (Laurent, 1986).

As organizations moved into the global arena, they exported these organizational policies to act as a "cultural glue" to hold the organization together (Schneider, 1988). Human resource development efforts and promotion criteria were influenced by the need to support the prevailing corporate culture.

As market environments around the global have become more diverse and competitive, however, pressures have risen to shape the local management team to fit more closely the demands of each location. As one executive put it, "We can't have people abdicating their nationalities, saying 'I'm no longer German, I am international'." The world doesn't work like that. If you are selling products and services in Germany, you better be German!" (Taylor, 1991, p.94). To facilitate the process of customizing corporate approaches across markets considerable autonomy has been granted to national and regional units in many global firms. In these cases, national cultures have replaced a uniform corporate culture as the basis for operation. Personnel functions are one of the areas most frequently decentralized as part of this process (Koster, 1988).

Also, there is a compelling argument that significant competitive advantage may be derived from effective coordination across national business units (Kantor, 1991a), and that this coordination effort is best managed by executives with a global perspective and an understanding of the overall business. Such individuals must be, "Supranational corporate players, whose allegiance is to enhanced worldwide corporate performance." (Reich, 1991, p.77). Development of such individuals will require exposure to a variety of people and locations in the company. Managers must be made to confront and come to terms with different points of view and methods of operation, so they may develop both understanding and tolerance to deal with people both inside and outside the organization (Taylor, 1991). Such a process must be coordinated at the corporate level to insure sufficient balance and breadth are included.

Negotiating with multiple culturally diverse national units to devise such an overall development strategy will not be easy. Research on difficulties now being faced by international joint venture partners in arriving at mutually acceptable HR policies (e.g. Ganitsky & Watzke, 1990; Zeira & Shenkar, 1990) suggest that cultural differences can lead to substantial misunderstandings and resistance. Variations in such areas as time orientation (Ganitsky & Watzke, 1990), authority relationships (Granrose, 1989), and even learning styles (Hayes & Allinson, 1988) across cultures can effect both the acceptability and relative value of certain developmental strategies.

The purpose of this study is to determine the extent to which differences in HR attitudes continue to exist among the top executives of businesses that have been assimilated into a single transnational corporation. It could be that selection of executives for top positions, their participation in corporate-wide management development programs and involvement in corporate-wide strategic planning lead to convergent HR expectations. If so, selection, training and corporate-wide interaction offer solutions to the problems of cultural diversity. If, on the other hand, HR expectations continue to differ, new means need to be found for the effective integration of cultural differences.

The differences in HR attitudes can cover a wide range of issues including:

o perceptions of the role of managers,
o beliefs about the personal characteristics needed by managers,
o beliefs about the skills needed by managers,
o preferences for management development strategies,
o beliefs about the evaluation of management potential, and
o beliefs about the evaluation of management performance.

This study will examine differences in the first four of these areas.

In addition, culture is only one of several variables that could affect HR attitudes. Other factors include: (1) hierarchical level, (2) individual personality differences, (3) functional expertise, and (4) corporate business culture. This study will compare the relationship of culture to attitudes with the relationships of hierarchical level and individual personality differences.

The first objective of the study is to determine if differences in HR attitudes do exist among senior managers in a single transnational corporation and then to determine whether differences are related to culture or to some other factor. If differences related to culture do exist, then global competitors will need to commit resources to creation of culturally sensitive, management development strategies.

The Research Process

This study was conducted in a Canadian based, transnational corporation which operates in over 50 countries world-wide and has senior managers located in Canada, the United States and Europe. Information was gathered from 200 senior executives in corporate and business unit positions monitored for corporate succession planning. These managers are engaged in corporate strategic planning, have participated in corporate-wide peer meetings and in an intensive, corporate sponsored, strategic management development program.

Information was gathered by a survey faxed to respondents. The survey inquired about perceptions of: the role of senior managers, the skills and personal characteristics needed by senior managers, and strategies for developing senior managers.

A major challenge in development of the survey was to make it both simple to answer and culturally robust. Check lists were used for simplicity, but these lists suffer from the perennial problem of cross- cultural research. For the most part, HR content has been developed in the United States and reflects the U.S. management culture. To balance this cultural bias a few open-ended questions were included. Because the check lists emphasize the culture of one group of respondents, the study provides a conservative test of cultural differences.

The open-ended format was used to determine perceptions of the senior management role. Respondents were asked to "Describe the senior management role as you see it."

Perceptions of the personal characteristics and skills needed by senior managers were assessed by lists developed with corporate HR assistance. Respondents were asked to rate the desirability of the skills and personal characteristics on a five point scale labeled: Doesn't matter, Desirable, Preferred, Required, Absolutely Essential. The scale was pretested with MBA students at Allentown College to be certain that it would elicit varied responses.

Preferred management development strategies were also assessed by a list developed with corporate HR assistance. Respondents were asked to rank order five of thirteen strategies in terms of what would be most helpful for developing future senior managers and to check strategies currently being used.

Cultural orientation is not the only reason managers may have different beliefs and expectations about HR issues. For this reason, the study also examined the relationship that hierarchical level and personality have with HR perceptions. Cultural orientation was identified by two variables: geographic location and primary language.

At the present, the most of the corporation's senior managers are located in the region of their original culture: US managers are in the US, Canadian managers are in Canada, and European managers are in Europe. This placement reflects the emphasis on local management that characterizes today's approach to globalization. Primary language distinguishes between: English speaking Anglo-Saxons in the US, Canada and the British Isles; French speaking Canadians and French; and speakers of other European and Eastern languages.

All the respondents are in top management positions. They range in hierarchical level from staff managers to plant and general managers to managing directors, senior vice presidents and business unit CEO's. For purposes of the study, corporate HR grouped positions in terms of comparable hierarchical responsibility.

Individual differences have been identified by means of the Myers- Briggs Type Indicator of personality styles (Myers, 1987). This instrument distinguishes between people who are:

o externally (extroverts) or internally (Introverts) energized,
o are reality (Sensates) or idea (Intuitives) oriented,
o favor logical (Thinkers) or human sensitivity (Feelers) decision criteria,
o favor action (Judgers) or search (Perceivers).

Table 1: Attitudes about Executive Development: Scope and Number of Differences Found in Cross Cultural Study

Potential Causes of Differences

Attitudes	Culture	Hierarchical Level	Individuals
Perceived Role of Senior Managers	1 of 2 Dimensions	0	0
Skills Required	5 of 12 Skills	3 of 12 Skills	4 of 24 Skills
Personal Characteristics Required	7 of 15 Characteristics	1 of 15 Characteristics	4 of 30 Characteristics
Preferred Management Development Strategies	3 of 13 Strategies	4 of 13 Strategies	5 of 13 Strategies

Table 1 summarizes the areas of HR differences and potential causes addressed in this study, and indicates the number of significant findings for each analysis. There are significant differences in all four HR areas. There are more cultural differences in all areas except preferred management development strategies, where individual differences and hierarchical level account for more variance.

Respondents and Their Human Resource Attitudes

Interpretable surveys were received from 80 executives, a response rate of 40%. Table 2 reports the distribution of respondents by culture, hierarchical level and individual differences. Because there are so few 'feelers' and 'perceivers' among the respondents, the last two individual difference variables have been eliminated from further study.

Concerning the culture indicators, geographic location and language are associated. U.S. managers speak English, Canadians are equally divided between English and French backgrounds and two-thirds of the Europeans speak other languages. Because of this association and the skewed distribution of respondents by language, the present study focuses on geographic location as the primary indicator of culture.

The managers' culture, hierarchical level and individual characteristics are independent differences. Managers at every hierarchical level are located in all three geographic regions, speak a variety of languages and vary between extroverts and introverts and between sensates and intuitives. Likewise, there are introverts and extroverts, sensates and intuitives in every location. Because context differences are independent of each other, the results of this study can clearly indicate whether culture or hierarchical level or individual differences account for different attitudes about executive development among managers of the transnational corporation in this study.

Table 2: Executive Respondent Profile

Variable	Categories	Number	Percent
Culture	Canada	36	45%
	U.S.	27	34%
	Europe	17	21%
	English	49	61%
	French	19	24%
	Other	12	15%
Hierarchical Level	CEO,President Managing Director	27	34%
	General Manager Plant Manager	37	46%
	Manager,Staff	16	20%
Individual Differences	Introvert	21	39%
	Extrovert	33	61%
Available only for respondents who participated in the corporate development program	Sensate	36	67%
	Intuitive	18	33%
	Thinker	46	85%
	Feeler	8	15%
	Judger	4	7%
	Perceiver	50	92%

Table 3: Senior Management Role Descriptions

Dimension	Number	Percent
Type of Skill		
Conceptual/Technical	15	20%
Behavioral	8	11%
Both	52	69%
(Missing = 5)		
Scope of Responsibility		
Operations management	12	17%
Strategy implementation	29	40%
Strategy formulation	31	43%
(Missing = 9)		

Perceived Role of Senior Managers

Respondents were invited to describe the senior manager's role in their own words. This was an invitation to describe the work of senior managers and, by inference, what capabilities they need to develop. Inductive analysis of the descriptions identified two dimensions of variance. These dimensions have been labeled: Type of Skills and Scope of Responsibility. Table 3 reports distribution of responses in the survey.

The 'Type of Skills' dimension refers to the conceptual/technical or behavioral nature of the tasks identified in the description. In the conceptual/technical category respondents described work the senior managers themselves do. For example, this included "visionary, strategist, decision maker, risk taker, global thinker, problem solver." In the behavioral category, respondents described work involving other people. This included "motivate people to accomplish goals."

Descriptions that included both conceptual/technical and behavioral skills were classified as "both." Independent classification of responses by three raters resulted in complete agreement for 51% of the cases and agreement by two of three raters for an additional 32% of the cases for an agreement rate of 83%.

The "Scope of Responsibility" dimension refers to the magnitude of the managerial decision-making identified in the role description. Alternative responses were classified as:

o strategy implementation or the execution of change to meet new goals, or
o operations management decision making or the execution of set goals,
o strategy formulation or the creation of new visions, directions goals.

"The ability to meet consistently and improve standards" is an example of an operations management description. "Translate corporate vision and strategy to his/her area of responsibility and provide the leadership and motivation necessary to accomplish same" typifies a strategy implementation response. "Creator of vision (the business as it must be in the future), chief proponent of that vision, team builder (the right people in right positions), and ensure development of successes" exemplifies the strategy formulation category.

Brief, general statements using words like "leadership" were sometimes difficult to classify. Working independently, three raters achieved complete agreement in only 20% of the cases, however, two out of three raters agreed in an additional 52% of the cases, for a total of 72% agreement. Following discussion, the raters unanimously agreed on 66% of the cases. Concerning role descriptions, respondents tend to agree that senior management work involves both conceptual/technical and behavioral skills. Those who do emphasize one or the other skill are from diverse cultures, diverse hierarchical levels and differ in personality.

There is more variance in descriptions of the scope of a senior manager's responsibility as summarized in Table 4. These differences are related to culture as

Table 4: Cultural Differences in Perceived Management Role

Geographic Region	Scope of Responsibility
Canada	emphasize Strategy Implementation
United States	emphasize Strategy Formulation
Europe	emphasize either Operations Management or Strategy Formulation

Table 5: Characteristics Needed by Senior Managers: Ratings and Significant Differences

Characteristic	Mean Rating	Significant Differences
Integrity	4.68	Culture
Initiative	4.67	Individual Differences
Decisiveness	4.57	Culture
High performance expectations	4.51	Culture
Willingness to learn	4.43	-
Perseverance	4.32	Culture
Creativity	4.24	Individual Differences
Readiness to do whatever it takes	4.20	Culture
Emotional stability	4.15	Culture and Individual Differences
Risk taking	3.92	-
Sensitivity to others	3.90	Hierarchical Level
Interest in international work	3.87	Individual Differences
Tolerance for frustration	3.68	Culture
Career ambition	3.65	-
Sense of humor	3.24	-

indicated by geographic location. While some managers from each region gave descriptions identifying each degree of scope, 56% of U.S. managers focused on strategy formulation, 59% of Canadian managers focused on strategy implementation, and, among Europeans, 33% focused on operations management and 47% focused on strategy formulation.

The absence of a relationship between scope of responsibility and hierarchical level is one of the surprises of this study. One could expect managers to project their own scope of responsibility into descriptions of the role of senior managers. Instead descriptions appear to reflect a geographically prevailing management culture.

The Personal Characteristics and Skills Needed by Senior Managers

Senior management qualifications are another area in which HR attitudes may vary. Differences in this areas lead to differences in the selection of candidates for senior management, in the type of development they need, and in the focus of development programs. Respondents were asked to rate fifteen characteristics and twelve skills in terms of their importance for success in the corporation in the future.

Much longer lists could easily be generated from the myriad of selection and performance studies. The items included reflect the focus of the corporation's HR efforts and the intuitive judgment of the researchers. Tables 5 and 6 list the characteristics and skills in rank order of preference by the total respondent population. For personal characteristics, as shown in Table 5, mean ratings range from 4.68 to 3.24 (the higher the value the more important the characteristic).

Table 6: Skills Needed by Senior Managers: Ratings and Significant Differences

Skill	Mean Rating	Significant Differences
Vision of the whole	4.69	Culture and Hierarchical Level
Strategic Planning	4.49	-
Team building	4.44	Hierarchical Level
Ability to delegate	4.39	-
Problem-solving	4.38	Culture and Individual Differences
Listening	4.35	Hierarchical Level
Oral and Written communication	4.23	Individual Differences
Coaching	4.04	-
Networking	4.00	Culture
Negotiating	3.97	-
Language Capability	3.40	Culture and Individual Differences
Technical Expertise international work	3.25	Culture and Individual Differences

Respondents see more need for action characteristics, such as "decisiveness" and "readiness to do what it takes", and for work commitment characteristics, such as "integrity, high performance expectations, willingness to learn, and perseverance".

The respondents also see less need for innovative characteristics, such as "creativity, risk taking, sensitivity to others, interest in international work and sense of humor," and for psychological characteristics, such as "emotional stability, tolerance for frustration and career ambition." Apparently respondents value work performance over the innovation and sensitivity, yet the latter are the characteristics that facilitate cross-cultural management.

In terms of skills, as shown in Table 6, mean ratings range from 4.69 to 3.25. Respondents place a higher value on conceptual skills, such as "strategic planning and problem-solving," and on vertical skills, such as "visioning, team building and delegating." Less value is placed on interaction skills, such as "coaching, networking, negotiating, and language." The lowest rating is given to "technical expertise," a result consistent with the focus on senior management. In this area also, respondents value traditional management skills over the interpersonal skills that facilitate cross-cultural management.

Because five point scales were used to rate each characteristic, ratings above 4.5 indicate very little variation among respondents. Four characteristics and two skills were rated at this level. Nonetheless, there are significant differences between groups in ratings of these characteristics and skills.

Only four of fifteen characteristics and four of twelve skills are rated similarly by all groups of respondents. The characteristics are: "willingness to learn, risk taking, career ambition, and sense of humor." The skills are: "strategic planning, ability to delegate, coaching and negotiating." Clearly managers have are different attitudes about senior management qualifications. Culture, indicated by geographic location, accounts for half of the differences found (twelve of twenty-four). Culture is the most strongly related to personal characteristics due to high ratings by U.S. managers. U.S. managers rate "integrity, decisiveness, persever-

Table 7: Cultural Differences in Attitudes about Senior Management Qualifications

Cultural Difference	Type of Qualification
U.S. ratings > Canadian and Canadian > European	Emotional Stability (C)
U.S. ratings > both Canadian and European ratings	Integrity (C)
	Readiness to do what ever it takes (C)
U.S. ratings > Canadian	Decisiveness (C)
U.S. ratings > European	Perseverance (C)
U.S. and Canadian ratings > European	Vision of the whole (S)
Canadian ratings > both U.S. and European	Language capability (S)
Canadian ratings > U.S.	Networking (S)
Canadian ratings > European	High performance expectations (C)
	Tolerance for frustration (C)
	Technical expertise(S)
European ratings > both U.S. and Canadian	Problem-solving (S)

KEY: (C) = Characteristic; (S) = Skill

ance, readiness to do whatever it takes and emotional stability" higher than either Canadians or Europeans. U.S. managers emphasize action and commitment characteristics, which may reflect the southern location of the U.S. managers in this corporation.

Together with U.S. managers, Canadians rate "vision of the whole" higher than Europeans. This result is consistent with the role description findings described earlier. Canadians rate "high performance expectations, tolerance for frustration, and technical expertise" above Europeans, and they rate "networking and language capability" above U.S. managers. Canadians appear to value psychological commitment and balance and interaction skills.

Problem-solving is the only area in which European ratings exceed U.S. and Canadian. This finding may indicate a more conservative approach to ratings in general, another way in which culture can influence attitudes. Table 7 summarizes cultural differences in ratings of personal characteristics and skills. Culture relates to managers attitudes about the qualifications needed for senior management.

Hierarchical level and individual differences are also related to the managers' ratings. Hierarchical level is related more to ratings of skills and individual differences are related more related more to ratings of personal characteristics, an interesting finding in itself. These results suggest that managers project their personality onto the personal qualifications they value in others, while they project the management problems onto the skills they value in others. Table 8 summarizes these results. For this study the important finding is that, while managerial attitudes vary for a variety of reasons, culture is the strongest factor.

Table 8: Hierarchical and Individual Differences in Attitudes about Qualifications

Hierarchical Differences	Type of Qualification
Staff ratings > general manager and general manager ratings > managing director, CEO	Sensitivity to others (C)
	Vision of the whole (S)
	Team building (S)
	Listening (S)
Individual Differences	**Type of Qualification**
Introvert ratings > Extrovert	Initiative (C)
Extrovert ratings > Introvert	Creativity (C)
	Interest in international work (C)
	Problem-solving (S)
	Language capability (S)
	Technical expertise (S)
Sensate ratings > intuitive	Emotional stability (C)
Intuitive ratings > sensate	Oral and written communication (S)

KEY: (C) = Characteristic; (S) = Skill

In summary, cultural differences relate to the scope of responsibility identified in open-ended descriptions of the senior management role and to characteristics and skills believed important for senior management success. In terms of senior manager role and qualifications, there are more and stronger relationships between attitudes and culture than between attitudes and hierarchical level or individual differences.

Management Development Strategies Recommended for Senior Managers

Attitudes about senior management role and qualifications influence the content of development programs. The final component of this study addresses the development strategies or the process by which skills are enhanced. In this area the study provides contradictory results. Respondents were asked to rank five of thirteen development strategies. Table 9 reports the percent of respondents who ranked each strategy and significant differences in rankings. Corporate management development programs are the only strategy receiving very strong support. A majority of respondents favor executive seminars and personal development programs. On the other hand, very few respondents ranked cultural orientation programs and less than a third favor international assignments. Thus, while culture influences attitudes about management qualifications, managers see little value in development strategies that directly address this issue.

Table 9: Management Development Strategies Rankings and Significant Differences

Strategy	Percent Ranking	Significant Differences
Corporate Management Development Programs	75.0	Individual Differences
University based Executive Seminars	57.5	Individual Differences
Personal Development	53.8	Cultural, Hierarchical and Individual Differ's
Managerial counseling and coaching	42.5	Individual Differences
Cross-functional transfers	41.3	Hierarchical Differences
In-house skill	36.3	Hierarchical Differences
Cross-business transfers	35.0	Hierarchical and Individual Differences
Executive MBA	33.8	-
International assignments	30.0	Culture
Mentoring	17.5	-
Cultural Orientation	8.8	-
Exchange Programs	5.0	-

Culture appears to have little relationship with the preferred methods for management development. The only cultural differences are in an individualistic U.S. preference for personal development programs and an experiential Canadian and European preference for international assignments (See Table 10).

By contrast, hierarchical level and individual differences are related to several development preferences (See Tables 11 and 12). General managers favor work experience strategies, such as cross-functional and cross- business transfers. Staff managers favor in-house training and personal development programs. Apparently as far as hierarchical differences are concerned, as shown in Table 11, managers favor strategies that reflect the nature of their own work.

Table 10: Cultural Differences in Preferred Management Development Strategies

Cultural Difference	Strategy
U.S. preference > European and European > Canadian	Personal Development
Ranked by U.S. managers only	Sabbaticals (N = 3)
Canadian and European preference > U.S.	International Assignments

Table 11: Hierarchical Differences in Preferred Management Development
Strategies

Hierarchical Differences	Strategy
Staff rank > managing director, CEO and managing director, CEO rank > general manager	In-house skill training
Staff, managing director & CEO rank > general manager	Personal Development programs
General manager rank > managing director, CEO and managing director CEO rank > Staff	Cross-business transfers
General manager rank > managing director, CEO and staff	Cross-functional transfers

In terms of individual differences, more of the sensate managers selected educational programs, ranging from seminars to coaching, than did the intuitive managers. The reality oriented sensates appear to favor input strategies. On the other hand, intuitive managers placed more emphasis on cross-business transfers which provide direct experience. These findings as shown in Table 12 suggest that managers favor development strategies that fit their own learning styles.

The findings concerning strategies raise serious questions for management development in global corporations. The results suggest that managers favor development programs suited to themselves and see little value in programs that directly address differences. Managers' attitudes about managerial work do vary by culture. This combination of local focus in spite of global differences creates the kind of misunderstanding and mis-communication typical of cross-cultural interaction. In addition, a lack of awareness of differences keeps managers' from correctly identifying the source of the misunderstanding. In this environment differences are likely to produce competitive conflict rather than creative development.

Table 12: Individual Differences in Preferred Management Development
Strategies.

Individual Differences	Strategy
Intuitive rank > sensate	Cross-business transfers
Sensate rank > intuitive	Corporate Management Development Programs
	University based Executive Seminars
	Personal Development programs
	Managerial Counseling and Coaching

Culture and the Challenge of Management Development in Global Organizations

This study has found that cultural differences persist among senior managers who communicate with each other in the strategic leadership of a transnationalcorporation. The differences are subtle. They affect the way the management role is seen and the relative value placed on various management qualifications.

Senior managers in the U.S. focus on strategy formulation and place more value than Canadians and Europeans on personal work characteristics, such as integrity, and decisiveness. Canadian senior managers in this corporation focus on strategy implementation and place more value than U.S. or European managers on interactive skills, such as language and networking, and on psychological characteristics, such as tolerance for frustration. The European senior managers emphasized problem-solving more than others and focused either on strategy formulation or operations management.

While the weight placed on specific qualifications varies by culture the comparative rating of qualifications is similar for all managers. Similarities in rank ordering qualifications can easily obscure differences in the weight placed on specific qualifications. In these circumstances, managers are likely to find agreement when discussing general HR issues. It is in specific cases that differences emerge. For example, there are differences in conflicts over who to promote to a specific position, or the specific content of a development program, or the responsibilities of a specific position.

While culture affects the content of management development, it appears to have little direct relationship with process or strategic preferences for the managers in this study. Instead, managers' strategic preferences tend to match the learning styles of their personality and work environment. Reality oriented sensates prefer structured input in interaction settings. Idea oriented intuitives prefer an experiential setting. Staff managers prefer training and development programs. General managers prefer direct experience.

The similarity of strategic preferences across cultures may reflect homogenizing effects of corporate interaction. There is evidence to support this interpretation in the managers' role descriptions. Most of the U.S. and Canadian respondents participated in a corporate, Strategic Responses development program and their role descriptions have a strategic focus. Only a third of the European managers participated in the program and the European role descriptions include an operations management focus.

The subtlety of cultural influence may also be a factor in the overall agreement about general development strategies. In projecting their own learning styles into strategic development preferences, managers unconsciously assume that what works for them works for all. This is a natural, human assumption, but one that obscures awareness of interpersonal and intercultural differences. The assumption, however, that differences in interests are nonexistent or inconsequential is a major impediment to the constructive handling of differences (Adler, 1986; Fisher and Ury, 1981).

One major implication for Human Resource management is that senior level decision makers are unlikely to commit resources to understanding and dealing with cultural differences. This implication is supported by the low ranking given to cultural orientation programs (ranked by only 8.8% of the respondents) and international assignments (ranked by only 30% of the respondents). In addition, managers give the lowest ratings to personal characteristics and skills that deal interactively with differences, such as negotiating, language capability, sensitivity to others, interest in international work and tolerance for frustration. Thus, there may be little support for programs and program content that directly address effective cross-cultural interaction.

When culture is ignored in the design of management development programs, the culture of the designer becomes the standard for performance. The result, either intentionally or unintentionally, is a vertical approach to cultural integration. The designer's culture is established as the dominant culture. Where it conflicts with their culture, participants have to come to terms with the dominant approach. Such conflicts tend to be handled through a combination of public acquiescence and private competition to replace the dominant culture. The result is a diversion of energy from cooperation and productivity.

The federation, exemplified by ABB Asea Brown Boveri (Taylor, 1991), is an alternative, horizontal approach to cultural integration. This strategy can be pursued only by managers who recognize cultural differences and the conflicts they generate; and treat alternatives as equals. The implementation of such a strategy depends on collaborative, win-win negotiation of conflicts. Collaboration, however, involves major changes in management attitudes, skills, and behavior. If the changes are made, and the if is quite problematic, than the energies generated by conflict are actually directed toward cooperation and productivity.

Consciously or unconsciously, managers of global organizations will be choosing between these strategies. Managers who are unaware of cultural differences automatically choose the vertical approach as they project their preferences on everyone. Managers who recognize cultural differences will need to choose between vertical, cultural dominance strategies and horizontal, cultural federation strategies.

A Culture Sensitive Human Resource Development Strategy

Managers' awareness focuses their attention and directs their action, but it does not create reality. This study joins a host of others in documenting the existence of cultural differences. This concluding discussion offers a HR strategy for dealing with cultural reality when senior managers give little or no attention to cultural differences.

The recommended strategy:

o utilizes an action learning approach,
o focuses explicitly on performance problems,
o has inter-local, local and corporate components, and
o is orchestrated by a senior corporate HR person who recognizes and
    respects cultural differences.

The action learning approach responds to the learning preferences of participants. It combines the experiential component favored by intuitives with the input component favored by sensates. Cultural issues that are unrecognized by participants are surfaced both through the design of the learning process and through facilitator observations about experiences. The focus on performance problems relates the developmental strategy to the primary interests of the managers who create the program and participate in it. The explicit objective of the process is to generate solutions for performance problems. Surfacing cultural issues in this context not only generates awareness among managers, but it also illustrates how knowledge of cultural differences can improve performance.

At the inter-local and local levels the strategy involves facilitated cross-site visits. Visits are initiated by local management to facilitate solving of a local problem. They identify their own problem and select visitors and negotiate site(s) where the visitors guest observe, experience and compare. The objective is to heighten the visitor's awareness of similarities and differences in local issues and of relationships between local issues and local responses. Interaction with a facilitator is included to increase the visitor's understanding of reality, not to solve the visitor's problem. Following the visit, the visitor uses the new knowledge to solve his/her own local problem.

There are several unique features to this strategy. First, the emphasis on self-directed problem-solving. Managers are exposed to differences in order to generate creative solutions to their own problems. By contrast, visits are often used to solve the host's, or other's, problems. In the suggested approach differences are associated with positive results rather than obstacles.

Second, the inter-local visits involve peer managers who address related problems rather than upper level managers who visit either for visibility and information gathering or for evaluation. This difference reduces the threat of the visit and resulting defensive responses.

Third, the process uses managers' priorities to introduce them to unrecognized dimensions of the problem. Managers become involved based on problems they need to solve. In the process, they discover differences that are relevant. After the manager experiences the differences, facilitator interpretations can focus attention on issues that have escaped previous awareness.

The corporate level of the strategy can begin simultaneously with the inter-local and local levels. This component includes: cross-regional, senior management, action learning programs focused on senior management problems, and cross-regional peer gatherings for functional sharing and input. The Strategic Responses development program described at the previous conference (Portwood, Latib & Timmons, 1990), is an example of a corporate action learning process.

Managers are gathered from diverse regions to focus on relevant strategic issues. Through interaction they form relationships, increase understanding of the similarities and differences in their situations and generate creative solutions to problems.

Orchestration of this multi-level strategy by a corporate HR person who recognizes and respects cultural differences is essential. Corporate HR helps orchestrate the inter-local/local process by facilitating local problem identification, helping arrange visits and offering matching funds for financing the activity. Corporate orchestration is needed for three reasons. First, the culturally sensitive corporate person builds the cultural awareness dimension into the processes. Second, through central orchestration corporate can foster mutual development throughout the organization. Third, central orchestration provides corporate with information on the capabilities and developmental needs of the organization's managers. Matching funding fosters both local ownership in terms of funds the local unit commits and corporate incentive in terms of funds corporate commits.

The recommended development strategy enables HR to meet managers based on their conscious priority interests and, in the process, broaden awareness of relevant issues outside the managers' attention. The strategy also provides a learning context adapted to the preferences of different individuals and different level managers. For success, the strategy depends initially on the effectiveness of the corporate HR orchestrator.

In conclusion, through management development programs, HR plays a very significant role is the selection of corporate strategies. The attention HR gives or does not give issues shapes the thinking of managers and, in turn, the types of strategic visions they create. How HR handles the issue of cultural differences can significantly influence senior management's awareness of strategic choices available to them and, in particular, the selection of a vertical or horizontal approach to cultural integration of a global organization.

Corporate HR is not alone in addressing the choice between vertical, cultural dominance strategies and horizontal, cultural federation strategies. The U.S.S.R. Yugoslavia, Germany and Western Europe are among the regions of the world that are actively engaged in the struggle to choose between these strategies. The choices these political systems make combined with the choices of major global companies will shape the world in the next century.

References

Adler, N. J. *International Dimensions of Organizational Behavior*. (Boston: Kent Publishing Co.) 1986.

Bartlett, C. A. & Ghoshal S., "Organizing for Worldwide Effectiveness: The Transnational Solution", *California Management Review*, Vol. 30, Fall 1988, pp. 54-74.

Fisher, R. & Ury, W. *Getting to Yes: Negotiating Agreement without Giving In*. (New York: Penguin Books), 1981.

Ganitsky, J. & Watzke, G. E., "Implications of Different Time Perspectives for Human Resource Management in International Joint Ventures", *Management International Review*, Vol. 30, 1990, pp. 37-51.

Granrose, C. S., "Lessons for Western-based Global Enterprises from Career Management Practices in East Asia", Paper presented at the National Academy of Global Business, New Orleans, La., Nov. 1989.

Hayes, J. & Allinson, C. W., "Cultural Differences in Learning Styles of Managers", *Management International Review*, Vol. 28, #2, 1988, pp. 75-80.

Kantor, R. M., "Globalism vs. Localism: A New Human Resource Agenda", *Harvard Business Review*, Vol. 69 #2, March-April 1991(a), pp. 9-10.

Kantor, R. M., "Transcending Business Boundries: 12,000 World Managers View Change", *Harvard Business Review*, Vol. 69 #3, May-June 1991(b), pp. 151-164.

Koster, R. S., "International Human Resource Planning and Development: The Emerging Profession", in R.J. Niehaus & K.F. Price, Eds. *Creating the Competitive Edge Through Human Resource Applications*, (New York: Plenum Press), 1988, pp. 221-234.

Laurent, A., "The Cross-Cultural Puzzle of International Human Resource Management", *Human Resource Management*, Vol. 25 #1, Spring 1986, pp. 91-102.

Myers, I.B. Introduction to Type: A Description of the Theory and Applications of the Myers-Briggs Type Indicator. (Palo Alto, CA: Consulting Pyschologists Press), 1987.

Portwood, J. D., "Changing Corporate Realities: Considering Career Opportunities for U.S. Citizens in Foreign Owned Firms", Paper presented at the National; Academy of Global Business, New Orleans La., Nov. 1989.

Portwood, J. D., Latib, M., & Timmons, M. J., "Realigning Executive Development and Succession Planning Systems: Meeting the Management Needs of 'Global Organizations' in the 1990's", in R.J. Niehaus & K.F. Price, Eds.,*Human Resource Strategies for Organizations in Transition*, (New York: Plenum Press), 1990, pp. 233-244.

Pucik, V., "Strategic Alliances, Organizational Learning, and Competetive Advantage: The HRM Agenda", *Human Resource Management*, Vol. 27 #1, Spring 1988, pp. 77-93.

Reich, R. B., "Who is Them?", *Harvard Business Review*, Vol. 69 #2, pp. 77-89.

Schneider, S. C., "National vs. Corporate Culture: Implications for Human Resource Management", *Human Resource Management*, Vol. 27 #2, Summer 1988, pp. 240-245.

Shaeffer, R. G., "Matching International Business Growth and International Management Development", *Human Resource Planning*, Vol 12 #1, 1989, pp. 29-35.

Taylor, W., "The Logic of Global Business: An Interview with ABB's Percy Barneik", *Harvard Business Review*, Vol. 69 #2, March-April 1991, pp. 91-105.

Tung, R. L., "Selection and Training Procedures of U.S., European, and Japanese Multinationals" *California Management Review*, Vol. 25 #1 1982.

Zeira, Y. & Shenkar, O., "Human Resources and the International Joint Venture", *The International Executive*, March-April 1990, pp. 40-43.

Hourly Training Needs:
The Bottom Line Reaches the Leading Edge

P.N. BLANCHARD

Introduction

The business and labor environment of the 1980s and early 1990s has surfaced issues which have made traditional approaches to labor relations less effective. A slowing economy, increased domestic and offshore competition and the changing demographics of organized labor are resulting in cooperative and creative approaches to restructuring organizations, redesigning jobs, compensating hourly employees and providing job security. The responses of unions and management to this environment (downsizing, restructuring, job security, working conditions, etc.) impact the design of jobs and the corresponding skill and knowledge requirements for hourly workers.

In this paper, an automotive component plant and a regional business unit of an international construction materials manufacturer are used as examples. They show how union and management can work together to redesign organizations and work systems, meeting both company and union needs. The changed duties and responsibilities of hourly employees, the process of developing training components and the results of the training are described in the context of the redesigned work place. This paper concludes with a discussion of the implications of these case studies for other organizations.

Changing Union/Management Environment

The globalization of the American economy and recent recessionary trends have created great stresses on all sectors of American business. The competitive nature of the market has increased dramatically. The decline in U.S. competitiveness, and its corresponding economic impact has created a lack of confidence in traditional union/management relations. Several (Kochan, et. al., 1986; Lawler 1986; Yankelovich and Immerwahr 1983), have argued that significant improvements in the U.S. competitive capability are unlikely if the traditional management/labor relationship continues to prevail. Heckscher (p. 53)

P.N. BLANCHARD - Stratisys: Strategic Involvement Systems, 5520 State St., Ann Arbor, Michigan 48108 reports public opinion polls showing a lack of public confidence in labor leaders and organizations and an overwhelming belief that the country would be better off if unions had less power. Correlated with this loss of confidence are significant losses in membership (Handbook of Labor Statistics, 1985). As an example, according to a February 26, 1991 article in the Wall Street Journal, AFL-CIO unions organized 250,000 workers in 1990, but total membership fell by 15,000.

Changing Work Force

Younger members of the work force are more educated and see authority deriving from expertise rather than position (Bennis and Nanus, 1985; Heckscher, 1988). Ewing, as early as 1983 observed increasing concern about employee rights in all segments of the work force with hourly employees increasingly demanding more of a say in decision making. Hourly workers are more dissatisfied with their jobs and do not see the union as a source for remedying their concerns. Yankelovich and Immerwahr (1983) have described a "commitment gap". Workers are, by their own admission giving less than they are capable of giving to their jobs as a way of expressing their work dissatisfaction. Under current global market conditions the adversarial relationship, one giant controlling the other in a balance of power with walls deliberately constructed to separate workers from management (Heckscher, 1988), prevents appropriate adaptation to market demands and fails to address the needs of a changing work force.

These changing times are creating new labor/management paradigms. Labor and management have, in certain instances, begun to address these issues through more cooperative relationships. The Communication Workers, Auto Workers and Steelworkers have, in specific cases, all developed new relationships with their management counterparts. When these relationships have been appropriately structured and designed, the companies and their unions have achieved successes unrealized by others in the same industry. Evidence is accumulating that new approaches such as joint labor/management partnerships, QWL and employee involvement are helping both labor and management achieve their goals (Heckscher, 1988).

Coping Strategies

Information technology continues to advance at an exponential rate creating rapid market fluctuations. The work force demographics in the U.S. are also changing significantly. These turbulent market conditions and changing labor force characteristics are expected to continue through the 1990s. To compete in the rapidly changing global arena, management has had to reexamine operational, financial and human resource strategies. Downsizing, restructuring, retooling, and transforming became the management operatives of the last half of the 1980s (Drucker, 1991; Lawler, 1986, 1990; Peters, 1988; Kakabadse & Margerison, 1988; Twiss, 1988; Nelson-Horchler, 1988; Sheppeck & Rhodes, 1988). Most observers suggest that these activities are just the start of new ways of doing business.

Organizational Change and Flexibility

Organizations are moving from an old order of efficiency, conformity and authority to a new order of enterprise, marketing initiative and leadership (Hague,

1987; Peters, 1988; Sadler and Borham 1988). New products and new production processes will become critical mandates brought on by increasing sophistication in information technologies. The increased competitiveness of markets has driven many organizations to reduce management layers (becoming flatter) and the size of support staffs (becoming leaner). Organizations are faced with developing strategies that allow them to do more with fewer people.

Multiple Constituencies

Interpersonal relations between a manager, hourly employees, suppliers and customers can determine the success or failure of an operation. Opinions of customers and employees are increasing in importance as measures of management performance. More companies will be creating supplier and customer partnerships in the 1990s (Nelson-Horchler, 1988). Those who survive will have developed ways to translate continuously customer expectations and satisfaction into how the business operates.

High Involvement Organizations

Reduced costs and increased flexibility are the principle drivers of recent changes to organizational structure and design. Becoming flatter and leaner reduces costs. Flexibility can be addressed by creating a team based organization, with team members cross-trained to perform all aspects of the team's work. Companies in the 1990s will be primarily team organized and customer oriented (Peters, 1988; Nelson-Horchler, 1988). This, along with the movement to participative systems, creates the potential for fewer employees to meet increased demands. However, it also requires fundamental changes in management roles and the way work systems are designed. In unionized settings the labor can and should participate in shaping the design of reward, information and work systems. Lawler (1986) calls these redesigned companies "high involvement organizations".

Making the transition into a high involvement organization requires systems that distribute power, information, knowledge and rewards to the shop floor or "leading edge" of the company. I use the term "leading edge" to refer to the shop floor operations. It is here that the characteristics of the product the customer receives are last determined. The power to make decisions regarding quality, process improvements, cost savings, etc. must be incorporated in the employees who are closest to the work. Knowledge and skills need to be upgraded to manage adequately these decisions and these employees must have access to the information they require to make good decisions. Employees must be rewarded equitably for their contributions to the success of the organization (e.g., profit sharing, merit and gainsharing systems) for high involvement to work. The changes in design of the organization create corresponding changes in design of work.

Work Redesign

Traditionally, management has designed work and organized labor has reacted to the work design as it impacts contractual issues (e.g. classifications, wages, and safety). The basic model for both management and unions through the 1970s was an autocratic, hierarchically structured organization. Scientific Management principles (Taylor, 1911) were used to divide labor and define jobs.

This model puts power, rewards and information in the hands of a centralized management/union hierarchy. Jobs in this system are designed to narrowly focus the job holder on a few tasks that use a minimal number of skills. This results in job "classifications" that restrict organizational flexibility and limit satisfaction of employees' psychological needs. The changes in corporate culture, business strategies and design of organizations discussed above modify the job requirements of both management and labor; making traditional procedures for designing work inadequate for these "new design" organizations.

A significant aspect of work satisfaction comes from how well jobs satisfy the social and developmental needs of employees (Hackman & Oldham, 1980). Redesigning work from a set of simplified, individual tasks to a set of outcomes a team has responsibility for accomplishing is the key to making strategies such as organizational downsizing and employee involvement work. The theoretical and empirical literature surrounding work redesign (e.g. Champoux, 1980; Evans, Kiggundu, and House, 1979; Hackman and Oldham, 1980; Mroczkowski and Champagne, 1984; Sims and Manz, 1982) suggests that this approach meets the employee's social and developmental needs while improving the effectiveness of the organization.

The design of "team" or group work systems has gone under various aliases. Placing the words "work group" after each of the following provides a partial list of labels: semi-autonomous, self-managing, self- directed, self-regulating, cellular and composite. While some differences exist in methodology, the basic concept remains stable. The characteristics of jobs are changed to increase (a) the meaningfulness of the work, (b) the autonomy with which the work is performed at the group and individual level and (c) the knowledge of results provided to the group.

Jobs become more complex because a wider variety of tasks are included and more decision making is required by individual worker. This means that training must be provided to give employees the knowledge and skills necessary to deal with the added complexity of their responsibilities. People are asked to work in teams rather than as individuals. They must also receive training to enable them to develop positive group dynamics and manage their own group processes. Training then, becomes a critical component in the transition from a traditional work environment to a high involvement team environment.

Case Studies

As organizations in the 1990s attempt to become flatter, leaner and make greater use of teams they will need to focus on developing the skills of their hourly employees. An automotive component plant in the midwest and a regional business unit of an international construction materials manufacturer are undergoing transformation to high involvement organizations. They serve as examples of what redesigned work and training for hourly employees might look like during the 1990s.

The training in each case was a part of a larger organizational development effort aimed at redesigning work. The work was to be organized around teams that were to have responsibility for an end product (a finished component part, or a wallboard manufacturing process). A joint union/management steering committee working with an outside consultant designed and oversaw all aspects of the redesign and training. The two cases diverge in significant ways at this point and will be discussed separately.

Component Plant

The component plant is a part of a division of one of the big three U.S. automobile manufacturers and is located in the midwest. The move to autonomous work groups was an experimental venture at the component plant and involved workers in only a few production areas. The plant had been working in an employee involvement environment for several years, but retained traditional supervision and job classifications. The rest of the plant continued to operate in this mode while the experimental areas worked as autonomous teams.

A significant bureaucracy surrounded not only the area of the experiment but the plant in general. The experiment was only made possible through the efforts of the area manager, the Industrial Relations Manager and the Union Bargaining Committee.

A steering committee was formed consisting of cross-sectional slice of labor and management. This committee examined the production areas to determine sites that would be conducive to this team based approach. Once potential sites were identified, employees and supervisors were asked to indicate their desire to participate. The three areas indicating nearly unanimous desire to participate were chosen as the experimental sites. The few employees who did not wish to be a part of the experiment were offered positions elsewhere in the plant. One supervisor and two hourly employees chose this option. These were replaced by personnel in other areas who had indicated a desire to participate in the experiment.

Fifty UAW members and eight first line supervisors took part in the experiment and received training. Many of these employees had difficulty reading, writing and computing simple arithmetic problems while a few were working on bachelors or masters degrees. A separate program was in place providing basic reading, writing and arithmetic education. Those scheduled to be in the teams were encouraged to enroll in this program if they had skill deficiencies in these areas. The training was designed assuming minimal skill levels in these areas. Trainees received normal pay while they were being trained. Training took place in a conference room at the plant and was conducted during day shift working hours.

Training Purpose

The purpose of this training was to provide those involved with the skills and knowledge necessary to work as interdependent semi-autonomous groups. They were organized around a production process that produced an identifiable end product. Ultimately, they were to assume responsibility for all aspects of their operation. Based on the work design, the steering committee identified the skill requirements below.

Training Content

Eighty-eight hours of training were provided: 40 hours technical; 20 hours manufacturing/business; 12 hours interpersonal skills; 12 hours team building and 4 hours of problem solving (previous SPC training covered many aspects of problem solving). These training areas were seen as generic skills required of any set of employees involved in group based production systems where responsibility for the finished product rests primarily with those directly involved in its production. Training modules for team building, problem solving and interpersonal skills were developed by outside vendors with steering committee review and approval. Technical and manufacturing training were provided by in-house management personnel and equipment vendors.

1. *Technical Training.* Trainees were instructed in all the technical requirements of operating their automated equipment and learned to perform diagnostic analyses of that equipment. The technical interdependencies within their team were identified and each member of the team was trained in the operation of all the team's equipment and machinery.

2. *Business/Manufacturing Processes.* Trainees were given instruction in basic manufacturing processes related to their operation including all the support requirements (e.g. materials handling, maintenance, etc.). Trainees were presented with the nature of the inputs required for various operations, scheduling requirements, how their operation transformed the product and what their customer needs from the product. Techniques for evaluating the effectiveness of their processes and product in terms of profitability, and modification strategies (this may mean doing it themselves or knowing where to go to get it done) were also covered.

3. *Communication.* Effective communication skills and strategies were presented and practiced in relation to other team members, other teams, management, support groups, customers and suppliers. Communication that was nonthreatening, understandable and to the point was stressed. Vocabulary adequate to describe the manufacturing equipment, processes and product was introduced. Trainees were presented with and practiced techniques that would indicate their understanding of communication from others, allow them to seek clarification and would encourage others to share information required by the group. The trainees were presented with and practiced techniques for confronting undesirable behavior by others in a manner that was descriptive, oriented toward problem solving, clearly indicated the consequences of continued undesirable behavior and allowed the parties to move toward clearer mutual expectations.

4. *Conflict Management.* Trainees were provided with an understanding of how conflict arises, the positive and negative effects of conflict, their personal preferences for handling conflict and alternatives for managing conflict.

5. *Group Problem Solving Strategies.* Trainees were provided with and practiced problem solving activities while in a group setting. Techniques for problem solving (eg, Fishbone and Parieto Analysis, Brainstorming, Nominal Group and Delphi) were used for group or interpersonal problems and for mechanical and manufacturing problems.

6. *Team Building.* Trainees were provided with an understanding of individual differences and ways to use these differences to create and assign flexible team roles. The trainees received instruction in how to develop and set realistic goals and objectives and how to develop an operating plan to achieve those goals and objectives. The factors impacting group dynamics were presented and the trainees practiced techniques for improving group dynamics. At the end of this module, trainees developed a set of goals for their team and an implementation plan for achieving those goals.

Employees who had been selected to be members of these teams were assessed on the above set of skills and abilities. If a trainee scored above a predetermined level they were not required to take the training (but could if they desired). Trainees were assessed again at the completion of training. Trainees scoring lower than a predetermined level, were asked to retrain.

Training Evaluation

Only the interpersonal skills development, problem solving and team building training were evaluated. Trainees' scores improved an average of 49.4% from pre-test to post-test. One person showed no gain and one other person showed a drop. Two people showed gains, but did not reach the predetermined level of proficiency necessary to graduate from training. The remaining trainees showed gain and reached the required proficiency as measured by the post-test.

During the first year of operations, the manufacturing and business skills were less well developed than necessary for these teams. Remedial training was provided, again by in-house management personnel. At present, these teams are described by union and management as among the most effective operations in the plant. However, no additional teams have been created. The plant intends to use an evolutionary approach rather than a revolutionary one. That is, they intend to institute this work design as new products come into the plant and old products leave. The intent is that over time the entire plant will be designed in this fashion.

Construction Materials Business Unit (CMBU)

This business unit was a part of an international construction materials manufacturer that was moving from a centralized structure to a decentralized business unit concept. Each business unit had responsibility for structuring its organization and designing an employee involvement system. Each business unit manager was accountable to the Executive Vice President/General Manager for accomplishing this. The business unit under discussion consisted of two plants in the western U.S. There were 155 hourly employees, represented by the Teamsters at one plant and the Longshoremen at the other.

A joint union/management steering committee for the business unit, consisting of leadership from the two unions, the business unit and each plant, was formed and trained. This committee set parameters and guidelines for the plants to follow. Joint union/management design teams were created and trained at each plant. These design teams were to design an employee involvement process at their plant and modify plant systems to support the involvement process.

The design team at each of the plants chose to use a team approach to involvement with team membership based on the nature of the work they performed. Each team had responsibility for an entire process or product and included the first line supervision in that work area. Participation in the teams was voluntary, though training was mandatory. The teams, consisting of those employees choosing to participate, were expected to work together to identify and solve problems and work towards continual improvement in their area of operations. While participation was voluntary, employees who chose not to participate were required to abide by the decisions of the involvement teams.

The design teams and steering committee collaborated on the development of a training plan for the employees at both plants. The training needs were determined by (a) examining the expectations for the work teams, and the current duties and responsibilities of team members and (b) identifying new knowledge and skill bases required to meet expectations. The training plan called for the development of a "train the trainer" approach. Two union and two salaried employees from each plant composed the training group.

The consultant provided training to the training group. Once the trainers had been trained they trained the work teams. One union and one salaried trainer would, together, conduct the training for a single team. Thirty two hours of training were provided to the involvement teams organized into eight four hour modules. The training was designed so that teams were working on actual problems or improvement issues rather than simulations or hypothetical issues. The modules are described below:

1. *Team Building*: The team develops a statement of its purpose and philosophy. The team develops its structure, procedures and member roles.
2. *Goal Setting*: The team establishes its goals in specific, measurable terms. The team identifies and defines the problems related to achieving the goals.
3. *Problem Solving: Quick Fix* - The team develops a temporary solution that quarantines the problem until a permanent solution is found.
4. *Problem Solving:* The team identifies the underlying or root cause of the problem. The team generates and selects solutions and develops an implementation plan assigning individual responsibilities and time frames.
5. *Self Evaluation / Improvement Planning:* Team assesses its effectiveness to date and uses problem solving process to identify any internal problems and develops solutions and implementation plan. The team also examines ways to become more self sufficient in managing their operation.

No plans were developed to evaluate the training on a formal basis. On an informal basis, the two trainers would serve as consultants to the group that they had trained. If skill or knowledge deficiencies developed they would conduct additional training for the group. In addition, a "resource" team existed that any team could go to for assistance or access to organizational resources (expertise, finances, equipment, etc.).

Implications For Other Organizations

The global market is placing severe pressures on industrial organizations to adopt more efficient and flexible systems. The "high involvement team" approach to work design is rapidly gaining popularity. This approach promises to meet the needs of organized labor and management. As such, considerable training must be provided in conjunction with an overall planned change effort. Appropriate support systems, reward systems and information systems must also modified.

Team approaches require broader and deeper skill levels than in traditional job designs. For the first time, hourly employees are receiving training previously reserved for management. A side benefit of this training, is that hourly employees at these plants found the training to be of use in the factory and in their personal lives. The primary benefit to companies is the increased capability and flexibility of their work force, allowing them to do more with fewer people. For unions, the rank and file have more control over their work and are better able to satisfy their psychological needs. Fewer grievances and disciplinary hearings make life easier for union officials and committee members. These advantages are not without some cost.

Moving from traditionally designed work systems in which each person is required to perform only a few specialized tasks under close supervision to a team design is a fundamental change. These changes do not come without a price tag. Up front training costs are high and other organizational systems must be restructured to support a high involvement team approach. Both union leadership, first line supervisors and sometimes middle level management personnel are threatened by this approach. It is seen as reducing the need for their services.

As teams take on responsibilities for managing their work processes, management and staff support needs dwindle. As the team manages its group processes, grievances and disciplinary actions decrease, reducing the union and salaried staff personnel needed to oversee these actions. On the other hand, in organizations that have downsized, generally this approach frees up time for the first level and mid level manager to do more critical functions. Union leadership can now find time to deal with internal union issues that get ignored because of grievance overloads, discipline hearings, etc. These and other problem issues need to be addressed in a joint union/management forum before initiating a high involvement team approach.

It is clear from these two examples that much flexibility exists in how job redesign and training may be developed, organized and implemented. An important lesson here is that each company's unique circumstances must be considered in the work redesign process, training needs determination and developing implementation plans. At the automotive components plant the move to semi-autonomous work groups was an experiment involving only a small fraction of the total work force. As such, much more training could be provided (88 hours compared to 32 at the CMBU) because the total cost was less and the disruption of normal business was less.

Formal evaluation was possible because of the experimental nature of the work redesign in the components plant. At the CMBU the decision had already been made to move the entire organization in the direction of high involvement. Thus, formal evaluation of the training process was not seen as cost effective. The objective here was to make it work, rather than determine if it was working. The differences in the two organizations are also evident in their approaches to making the transition from a traditionally structured organization to a high involvement organization. The bureaucracy and size of the organization the component plant was a member of mandated a slower approach to change. The net result was considerably more political activity by both management and union. It reduced the ability to make changes in the system to support the semi- autonomous work groups and put management and union leaders supporting the experiment at professional risk.

In summary, in terms of flexibility, reduced layers of management and fewer salaried staff services, the potential advantages of the high involvement organization are achievable only when the knowledge and skill levels of the hourly employees are commensurate with the requirements of redesigned jobs. In most settings the redesigned jobs and higher knowledge and skill levels make hourly employees, as a group, a more critical factor in the success of the business. It is likely that this changed status will need to be recognized when issues of job security and compensation arise. In many ways, attainment of bottom line advantages through employee involvement requires a management partnership with the "leading edge".

References

Bennis, W., and Nanus, B. *Leaders.* New York: Harper & Row, 1985.

Champoux, Joseph. "A Three Sample Test of Some Extensions to the Job Characteristics Model of Work Motivation". *Academy of Management Journal,* 1980, vol. 23, 3, pp. 466-78.

Drucker, P. "Permanent Cost Cutting". *Wall Street Journal,* Jan. 11, 1991.

Evans, M. G., Kiggundu, M. N., and House, R. J. "A Partial Test and Extension of the Job Characteristics Model of Motivation." *Organizational Behavior and Human Performance,* 1979, Vol. 24, pp. 354-81.

Ewing, D. W. *Do it My Way or You're Fired.* New York: Wiley, 1983.

Hackman, R. J. and Oldham, G. R. *Work Redesign.* Reading, Mass.: Addison-Wesley, 1980.

Hague, Douglas. " The Development of Managers." *International Journal of Technology Management,* 1987, Vol. 2, 5-6, pp.699-710.

Handbook of Labor Statistics, U.S. Dept. of Labor, Table 64, June, 1985.

Heckscher, Charles C. *The New Unionism.* New York: Basic Books Inc., 1988.

Kakabadse, Andrew and Margerison, Charles. " Top Executives Addressing Their Management Development Needs." *Leadership and Organizational Development Journal.,* 1988, Vol. 9, Iss. 4, pp.17-21.

Kochan, T., Katz, H. and McKersie, B. *The Transformation of American Industrial Relations,* Basic Books Inc., New York, 1986.

Lawler, E. E., III. "The New Plant Revolution Revisited." *Organizational Dynamics,* Autumn, 1990.

Lawler, E. E., III. *High Involvement Management.* San Francisco, Ca: Josey-Bass, 1986.

Mroczkowski, T. and Champagne, P. "Job Redesign in Two Countries: A Comparison of the Topeka and Kalamar Experiences". *Industrial Management,* Nov/Dec, 1984, pp. 17-22.

Nelson-Horchler, Joani. "Performance Appraisals." *Industry Week,* 1988, Vol. 237, iss. 6, pp.61-63.

Peters, Tom. "Leadership Excellence in the 1990's: Learning to Love Change." *Journal of Management Development,* 1988, Vol. 7, 5, pp. 5-9.

Sadler, Philip and Barham, Kevin. "From Franks to the Future: 25 Years of Management Training Prescriptions." *Personnel Management,* 1988, vol. 20, 5, pp. 48-51.

Sheppeck, M. A. and Rhodes, C. A. " Management Development: Revised Thinking in Light of New Events of Strategic Importance." *Human Resource Planning,* 1988, Vol. 11, 2, pp. 159-172.

Sims, H. P. and Manz, C. C. "Conversations Within Self-managed Work Groups." *National Productivity Review,* 1982, pp 261-69.

Taylor, F. W. *The Principles of Scientific Management.* New York: Harper-Row, 1911.

Twiss, Brian. " Japan: Developing For the Future". *Industrial and Commercial Training,* 1988, Sept/Oct, pp. 3-8.

Yankelovich, Daniel and Immerwahr, John. *Putting the Work Ethic to Work: A Public Agenda Report on Restoring America's Competitive Vitality.* New York: Public Agenda Foundation, 1983.

The Industrial Adjustment Service:
A Canadian Model for Change Management

J. BUTCHER

The Context: 1963

Nineteen sixty-three was one of those "Very Important Years" in North America. Canadians elected a minority Liberal government under Lester B. Pearson. Twenty years later, with only a brief interruption, Liberals still ruled Ottawa. The first bombs of the FLQ exploded in Montreal. René Lévesque called for a "new Canada" in five years, or Quebec would separate. The Royal Commission on Bilingualism and Biculturalism was appointed.

Federal Finance Minister Walter Gordon's first budget contained provisions to limit U.S. control of the Canadian economy. They were soon withdrawn as unwise economically and counter-productive politically. Only legislation protecting Canadian banks against foreign ownership was enacted.

The Economic Council of Canada and the Canadian Union of Public Employees were established. "Pop art" made its appearance. The Shaw Festival was founded. Polls exploring values showed no differences between students and their parents. Gordie Howe scored a record 545th NHL goal; Wayne Gretzky was two years old. The Soviet Union bought 550 million bushels of Canadian wheat.

In the United States, the Senate ratified a nuclear test ban treaty with the Soviet Union. The White House/Kremlin hot line was hooked up, and the President authorized the sale of surplus wheat to Russia. Some 200,000 people participated in a civil rights march on Washington, where they heard Martin Luther King describe his "dream". George Wallace confronted Bobby Kennedy over integration of the University of Alabama.

Seventeen American soldiers were killed in South Vietnam that year. The United States proposed that all international tariffs be cut by half. Kodak unveiled the Instamatic camera. The Post Office introduced the zip code.

J. BUTCHER - Associates in Planning, P.O. Box 3638, Station "C", Ottawa, Ontario K1Y 4J8, CANADA

Acknowledgements: The author thanks Peter Brinton, Don DeJong, Ross Marshall, Chris Southin and Doug Robertson of Employment and Immigration Canada, Tony Zeigler of Kent State University, and Elaine Davis-Nickens of the United States Department of Labor.

Rachael Carson's *The Silent Spring* launched the ecology movement. In November, the Beatles began their U.S. tour. President Kennedy was assassinated. In a speech at Columbia University, James Reston remarked that "change is the biggest story in the world today" (quoted in Manchester, 1974, p. 1002).

Outlook for Business and Labour Market Change

Harvard Business Review reported in its January/February issue the outlook of American business leaders on 1963. The "profit squeeze" was their biggest headache. They worried that the rate of industrial growth in the Soviet Union and Western Europe was outpacing that in the United States. The Common Market was still an unknown quantity. Many wondered whether it was a precursor to other regional trading blocs.

Everyone hoped that lower tariffs and increased trade would spur productivity and job creation. Many feared economic disruption and job loss.

The computer was one of the new tools of "scientific" management. Firms were encouraged to take the medium- to long-term view in business and personnel planning. After all, their most important "inventory" was people. Forward planning was especially important in the face of technological change. Many firms professing to engage in long-term planning were actually, some said, only paying it lip service.

Many urged creation of a sounder labour-management relationship which could, with government's support, be used to resolve business issues. Just what was a "business" issue was subject to debate. Was retraining of workers displaced by technological change a responsibility of government, unions or business?

HBR's November/December 1963 issue, James R. Bright discussed "Opportunity and Threat in Technological Change". Bright saw new business opportunities in the provision of support to technological advances. Companies had to face up to "technological displacement" by superior products and services. Job security could no longer be guaranteed by traditional management practices, good marketing, sound financing and competitive costs and equipment. Government would intervene more in the management of technological change.

Opportunities and threats in technological change were also very much on the mind of the Economic Council of Canada. In its *First Annual Review* (1964), the Council observed (p. 201) that "progress produces casualties". This was an argument neither to halt change nor to leave workers, their communities and industries at its mercy. The task was to maximize the benefits of change, while minimizing its adverse effects.

However, from a labour market perspective, some of those benefits were difficult to pin down. While manufacturing output had grown by almost 80% since 1949, employment had risen by only 16%. In every sector - from resources to retailing - productivity improvements were driving down unit labour requirements. Demand for workers was growing fastest in the service industries.

By the early 1960s, Canada exported 50% of the goods it produced. It also imported large numbers of skilled workers, scientists and professionals from Europe (primarily Britain) and the United States. Canada was a country dependent on the international movement of products and labour. The trick would be to ensure that business adjusted rapidly to changing market demands, while maintaining a productive workforce readily adaptable to those demands.

Labour market inflexibility to change was, for the Council, a major threat to such goals as full employment, economic growth, price stability, and equitable distribution of rising incomes. Pursuit of those goals could not be left to any one segment of society.

As a result, the Council echoed the increasingly widespread view that adjustment to technological change was a shared responsibility of business, labour and government. Government's role was facilitative. That is, coordinated labour market and national economic policies; improved information on long-term trends in supply and demand; increased mobility of labour among occupations, industries and regions; and greater investment in education and training. The role of management and labour was to initiate vigorous firm-level adjustment programs.

A Change Model Is Born

The federal government had not waited for the Economic Council of Canada's views before launching its own program to encourage labour-management cooperation. A joint study by the Department of Labour and the OECD had already recommended establishment of a facilitating agency to help worker adjustment to industrial change (Woloschuk, 1970). On June 7, 1963, Cabinet created the Industrial Adjustment Service.[1]

Its rationale was described in the background Memorandum to Cabinet, dated May 31, 1963. At the time, the program was known as the "Manpower Consultative Service". This was changed to "Industrial Adjustment Service" in 1984. The title was to be both gender neutral and more descriptive. To avoid confusion, the newer title will be used throughout this paper.

Automation, technological and other industrial changes often require difficult and far-reaching manpower adjustments at the individual plant and community level. Occupational and geographic shifts must often be made if unemployment is to be avoided for workers affected. Management and labour, at the enterprise level, should be encouraged to assume more responsibility for developing effective manpower adjustment programs. This can be greatly facilitated through technical assistance and the provision of financial incentives to employers and unions by the government (quoted in Woloschuk, 1970, p. 45).

Newman and Gardner (1987) suggest more bluntly that there was great concern over the social and economic disruption in Britain caused by workers' resistance to technological change. The federal government hoped that, by encouraging advance planning with the full participation of employees, much of that resistance could be pre-empted.

The Industrial Adjustment Service (IAS) was operational by 1964. Consultants, as the Service's field representatives are called, were located in Halifax, Montreal, Toronto and Vancouver.

As with many new programs, IAS got off to a shaky start (Woloschuk, 1970; Economic Council of Canada, 1964). Coordination with other federal policies, programs and agencies was poor. There was little publicity. Only in 1968 did Employment and Immigration Canada's senior management really commit itself to IAS. By that time, a continuum of adjustment services - from labour market demand analysis to individualized employment counselling - had been put in place. IAS was ready to play a key role in that continuum.

Over the next 20+ years, IAS would broaden its activities, from an initial focus on firm-level layoffs to work with entire communities and industrial sectors. Its approach would remain consistent: labour-management cooperation was the surest road to durable and effective labour market adjustment.

Features of the Industrial Adjustment Service

Private sector use of the Industrial Adjustment Service is voluntary. IAS Consultants use their sources of local, regional and national labour market information to identify likely clients. The Consultants then promote the Service with management and labour representatives and, with other potential stakeholders. To be effective, the IAS Consultants must be highly entrepreneurial, tailoring their approaches and recommendations to each particular situation.

The decision to work with IAS is formalized by an agreement between the private sector participants and the federal Minister of Employment and Immigration. The purpose of the agreement is to establish a joint committee to plan and lead the private sector adjustment initiative.

The committee's membership is divided equally between management and labour. Other groups, such as provincial governments, may also participate. The IAS Consultant is an ex officio member, providing technical advice and liaison with federal programs and agencies. The committee hires a neutral chairperson to provide process leadership and administrative support. The chairperson also prepares the joint committee's final report to the Minister of Employment and Immigration on the results achieved through the IAS agreement.

The costs of committees are normally shared equally between the federal government, employers and any other institutional participants. Shared costs include research, chairpersons' fees and expenses, employees' wages while on committee business, and administrative support. Labour does not usually participate financially. Its contribution is in-kind, through the work of employee representatives on the joint committee.

At the time, the program was known as the "Manpower Consultative Service". This was changed to "Industrial Adjustment Service" in 1984. The title was to be both gender neutral and more descriptive. To avoid confusion, the newer title will be used throughout this paper.

The joint committee drives the diagnosis and response to the labour market adjustment situation. The focus is on research and planning, developing joint approaches supported by management and labour, and coordinating private and public adjustment measures. There are no pre-determined solutions. The key is to generate a shared sense of ownership of the situation and the actions to address it.

Over the years, three types of IAS agreements have evolved: firm- level, community, and association. Each has special features.

Firm-Level Agreements

These are the "bread and butter" of the Industrial Adjustment Service. Over 9000 such agreements have been signed since the program's inception. The annual volume is now some 700. The adjustment issues addressed by firm-level agreements range from lay-offs and workforce redeployment to plant expansions and quality of working life.

In 1989-90, lay-offs or threat of lay-offs generated 50% of these agreements. Plant expansion/start-up and technological change accounted for another 25%. Workplace problems, such as high turnover, absenteeism and low productivity, were behind 7% of firm-level agreements. Some 60% of such agreements, and 25% of the workers covered by them, were in the manufacturing sector (Industrial Adjustment Service, 1990). This level of IAS activity in manufacturing has declined only slightly since the early 1980s (Abt Associates, 1984).

Committees are encouraged to be as creative and vigorous as necessary to do the work required. In lay-off situations, committee members typically contact prospective employers personally on behalf of threatened workers. Skills inventories are prepared and distributed. Training, mobility assistance, counselling and other support can be provided.

Other adjustment situations generate other responses. Committees have carried out management studies on prospective business opportunities, have initiated employee-led buy-outs of failing enterprises, and have established quality of work life and productivity improvement programs. Once again, the key is the shared vision between management and labour on what needs to be done and how to do it (Case studies of firm-level adjustment measurs are available from the Industrial Adustment Service, Employment and Immigration in Ottawa)

Firm-level committees may operate up to one year or longer. IAS' maximum contribution is $200,000. Expenses are normally paid by the employer. IAS then reimburses its share. When the employer has no financial resources, IAS may pay 100% of the costs, to a maximum of $100,000. IAS can also advance operating funds to a committee. To ensure that IAS does not interfere with formal collective bargaining, firm-level committees are closed down if any industrial dispute breaks out.

Community Agreements

Some 4000 Canadian towns are dependent on a single industry. Many are in isolated areas. Others are more centrally located, with better prospects for economic diversification. Some communities are already diversified. They may be looking to attract other industries to enhance local development. Large sections of major metropolitan centres often depend on one or two dominant industries. In any case, labour market adjustment is a major issue in all such communities.

In 1989-90, the Industrial Adjustment Service signed 30 community- level agreements. Most such agreements are for two years and may be renewed for one year. The maximum IAS contribution, whether or not cost- sharing is in place, is $200,000. Joint committees may be composed of employers and workers, community representatives, and provincial or territorial government officials. Cost-sharing is normally divided among employers and the various levels of government. High in-kind contributions are typical.

When a community is struck by a major closure or a mass lay-off, workers are often caught between the need to move to other locales and their inability to replace the equity they have built up in their homes and businesses. Resolving this dilemma is often a major focus of the joint committee. When economic diversification is feasible, the committee also works in that direction. Sometimes, the town is closed and its population relocated. Uranium City, Saskatchewan, and Schefferville, Quebec, are two of the better-known town closures involving the Industrial Adjustment Service in this area. Activities were to range from macro labour market analyses to firm-level planning exercises.

Association Agreements

The most recent innovation in IAS agreements has been at the association or industrial sector level. Beginning in the late 1970s, the federal Minister of

Employment and Immigration signed human resource planning agreements with a number of national industrial and professional organizations. These ranged from the Mining Association of Canada and the Canadian Council of Professional Engineers to the Graphic Arts Industries Association and the Chemical Institute of Canada.

The purpose of the agreements was to publicize the need for improved private sector human resource planning. They also established a framework for industry-government cooperation in this area. Activities were to range from macro labour market analyses to firm-level planning exercises.

There was no funding mechanism to implement the agreements. The associations and the Employment and Immigration Canada officials who worked with them proceeded as best they could. Results were sometimes impressive, but more often limited. Many agreements were sources of frustration and embarrassment.

The Industrial Adjustment Service became the mechanism to pursue sector-level initiatives. In these cases, agreements may be for up to three years, renewable for one year. In shared-cost arrangements, IAS contributes up to $500,000. If no industry contribution can be made, the maximum IAS contribution is $100,000.

Some IAS agreements are preceded by sector studies. These are conducted by Employment and Immigration Canada's Labour Market Outlook and Structural Analysis Branch or by private consultants. The studies identify business and labour market issues, and help to initiate the cooperative labour-management process through a steering committee to oversee the work.

Major long-term IAS agreements have been implemented in such sectors as steel, automotive repair and service, and electrical and electronics manufacturing. Smaller-scale agreements have included geomatics (surveying and mapping), public health, logistics, roofing and engineering. Such agreements enable a coordinated approach to common labour market adjustment issues at the national level, while maintaining competitiveness among individual firms.

A major question in sectoral agreements is the ability of industry associations to encourage changes in human resource planning and adjustment practices among member firms. Another is whether labour representatives on sectoral committees are able to anticipate workers' reactions to the recommended adjustment measures. Sector-level strategies are both essential and practical in Canada's highly-concentrated economy. Firm-level action remains critical to successful labour market adjustments.

Three Sectoral Case Studies

The range of activities under sectoral association agreements can be illustrated through case studies of automotive repair and service, roofing, and logistics. These case studies follow.

Automotive Repair and Service

By the mid-1980s, a wide range of human resource management concerns had surfaced in the Canadian automotive repair and service industry. Rapid technological change gave increasing urgency to continuous retraining. There were no national standards to guide training and certification programs. The number of new apprentices was falling, while drop-out rates remained high. There were some

150,000 automotive repair and service technicians. Even so, shortages were expected to exceed 10,000 workers by the mid-1990s. A poor image, high costs and low wages deterred recruitment and made it difficult to retain existing employees.

A sector study (Woods Gordon, 1988) commissioned by Employment and Immigration Canada, and a follow-up national conference (Canadian Automotive Repair and Service Council, 1988), clarified issues and identified industry-led cooperative strategies to address them. The major outcome of the report and conference was the establishment of the Canadian Automotive Repair and Service (CARS) Council.

The Council regroups independent garages, dealers, manufacturers, wholesalers, educational and training institutions and automotive repair and service technicians. The objective of the CARS Council is to address short- and long-term critical human resource issues in the sector in a coordinated and strategic way.

The Council began operations in the Fall of 1988. Shared financial support was provided by the Industrial Adjustment Service. Industry provided both cash and high in-kind contributions. In March 1991, the Council became a permanent organization, with its operating costs fully funded by industry. It has made steady progress in resolving the sector's principal human resource issues.

Industry-wide communications and information networks have been established. National occupational and training standards for automotive repair and service technicians have been developed and approved. As a result, consistent inter-provincial approaches to training and certification are being put into place.

The Council is implementing strategies to attract more young people and to retain existing workers. Apprenticeship programs are being revamped. Industry will place state-of-the-art technology in community colleges. The Council's longer-term plans include innovative pilot apprenticeship programs and a literacy in the workplace initiative. Planning is underway to establish an institute of automotive repair and service technicians to oversee a program of testing and certification.

Roofing

The Canadian Roofing Contractors' Association (CRCA) represents just under 300 firms engaged in roofing and sheet metal contracting. Work is concentrated on new construction and re-roofing of non-residential buildings. The average firm has 36 employees during peak periods. Only 4% of member contractors have operations in more than one province. Most have annual sales under $2 million.

In September 1989, CRCA and the Industrial Adjustment Service signed an agreement to identify and recommend actions to resolve human resource issues in the industry. A joint committee of contractors and roofers was formed to implement the agreement, under the guidance of a chairperson from outside the industry.

Human resource issues range from the poor image of roofing as a dirty and dangerous trade to income fluctuations caused by unpredictable weather patterns. Training is ad hoc. Younger workers have little sense of career progression. Specialist workers are increasingly replacing journey status roofers. On the positive side, hourly wages are good, and the industry is relatively recession-resistant. Demand for roofers is high. Working conditions are improving as roofing materials become cleaner and easier to handle.

The joint committee concentrated on five general areas: recruitment, retention, training, upgrading and information. Most firms have a good supply of applicants for jobs. However, most firms lack systematic hiring procedures which provide realistic job previews and unearth candidates' skills, expectations and commitment.

Partly because firm-level orientation programs are rare, turnover within the first days and weeks of employment is high. To address this issue, the committee contracted with the Federal Business Development Bank to design a one-day orientation workshop for contractors and supervisors. The workshop covers interpersonal skills, leadership styles, and best practices in integrating new employees into the work team. The seminar will be managed by the Canadian Roofing Contractors' Association.

The committee worked with Employment and Immigration Canada to improve occupational definitions used in the Census, labour market studies, and immigration. A task group of roofers also helped to revise occupational analyses, which are the basis for inter-provincial standards and training curricula.

Several issues were left unresolved at the end of the committee's one-year mandate. Retention of experienced workers is a serious concern. Many in the industry are convinced that monthly and annual income fluctuations caused by work lost to weather force older workers into other employment. A follow-up IAS agreement signed in late 1990 will focus on the retention issue.

Logistics

Logistics is a group of services concerned with the movement of materials and information from source to point of consumption. It includes such fields as purchasing, production planning, inventory control, and warehousing. Some 400,000 people (3% of the Canadian labour force) work in logistics. Demand is expected to grow by 25% by the year 2000.

In 1985, Industry, Science and Technology Canada studied international freight forwarding, a component of the logistics field. The study concluded that human resource issues had to be addressed if the industry was to remain competitive. As a result, the Canadian International Freight Forwarders' Association (CIFFA) signed an IAS agreement in 1987. The joint committee recommended that a self-regulating logistics profession be established.

A follow-up IAS agreement was initiated in November 1989 to explore implementation of that recommendation. Signatories were CIFFA and the Canadian Institute of Traffic and Transportation (CITT), a national training organization in logistics. Industry, Science and Technology Canada also participated on the joint committee.

Industrial and professional development associations in logistics are highly fragmented in Canada. There are over 25 readily-identifiable groups. Many are small and lack professional staff. Coordinated planning and action are often problematic.

The joint committee realized very soon that it would have to bring those associations together to create consensus on just what were the principal human resource issues in logistics. Several associations made it clear that, unless they were part of the process, they would not support any actions recommended by the joint committee.

The committee took a facilitative approach to building consensus and participation. The vehicle was a series of forums bringing together industrial and professional development associations, post-secondary educators and federal government officials. Through these forums, and some representative working groups, the logistics community began to build a shared vision of its priority human resource issues.

Members of that community are now cooperating to establish a national coordinating body. Its activities will focus on education, training and professional status for logistics practitioners. It will also promote public awareness of the role of logistics in the Canadian economy. To help pursue this work, another Industrial Adjustment Service agreement - this one regrouping most of the major industrial and professional development associations - was signed in March 1991.

What the three case studies above show is the flexibility of the IAS approach. Each industrial sector is pursuing its own course at its own pace. While the human resource issues in the three sectors are very similar, no pre-packaged "solution" could work. A feature of IAS is that it is "content neutral". By focusing on process, IAS compels participants to take ownership of their human resource issues and to address them in ways that make the most sense from their perspectives.

Evaluation of the Industrial Adjustment Service

The latest comprehensive evaluation of the Industrial Adjustment Service was conducted for Employment and Immigration Canada by Abt Associates of Canada. The report was published in November 1984, and covered the 1982-83 fiscal year.

The evaluation examined only firm-level agreements. Sixty-five percent of them were in manufacturing. Most were in response to lay-offs or the threat of lay-offs - not surprisingly, since the period was one of economic recession in Canada. Twenty percent of the agreements were in small- to medium-size labour markets in remote communities.

Abt Associates concluded that "the IAS program has operated well in terms of its contribution to economic efficiency" (Abt, 1984). It reached this conclusion by comparing estimated savings in Unemployment Insurance payments ($25.5 million) with IAS program costs and employers' expenditures ($14.6 million). As well, Abt Associates felt that IAS' financial contribution had been incremental, and had not simply replaced private sector money.

The evaluation found that IAS had also met effectiveness standards. It had enabled the private sector to help displaced workers, and had aided firms in their adjustment efforts. It had also helped workers to accept change, and had improved labour-management relations. Other unmeasured benefits included reduced family and personal stress as a result of shortened periods of unemployment.

Abt Associates reported very high levels of satisfaction by employers, worker representatives and neutral chairpersons. While worker representatives were usually less satisfied than other participants, well over 90% felt that IAS would benefit other firms and their employees.

Only some 33% of the labour force as a whole, including public servants, were members of unions at the time. The evaluation observed that almost 45% of agreements were in unionized businesses. This most likely reflected the large number of unionized manufacturing facilities with IAS agreements. As well, unionized establishments had more experience in labour-management relations, and so may have found the IAS process less threatening.

Only some 10-15% of IAS Consultants' promotional contacts resulted in agreements. This was a cost of a voluntary program. The evaluation recommended that IAS be more proactive in encouraging private sector planning before lay-offs and other downside adjustments became necessary. While this had always been a feature of IAS, immediate problems, such as lay-offs, were more likely to result in agreements.

Several informal evaluations have also been done on IAS. In its 1987 statement, *Making Technology Work: Innovation and Jobs in Canada*, the Economic Council of Canada reiterated its long-standing support of the Industrial Adjustment Service. The Council found the Service fast, flexible and cost-effective. However, the Council also wanted IAS to be involved in the labour market adjustment process earlier, and recommended increased budget allocations and staff for the program.

In their report for the National Center on Occupational Readjustment, Newman and Gardner (1987) found IAS to be primarily reactive in practice. It was, however, trying to interest potential employer clients in longer- term strategic initiatives with labour.

Interestingly, two high-profile labour market study groups in the early 1980s paid practically no attention to IAS. The Task Force on Labour Market Development was an internal departmental group set up to report to the Minister of Employment and Immigration on labour market trends in the 1980s. Its report made only passing reference to IAS as a program which "could play a particularly effective role in facilitating change" (Task Force on Labour Market Development, 1981).

The Parliamentary Task Force on Employment Opportunities for the '80s was composed of seven members of the House of Commons from the three major federal parties. Despite a preoccupation with labour market adjustment issues, the Task Force overlooked IAS entirely. The Service was not mentioned in the Task Force's report (Parliamentary Task Force, 1981).

If Imitation Is Sincere Flattery...

Over the past ten years, labour market specialists in other countries have begun to examine the Industrial Adjustment Service. IAS Consultants have been loaned to countries in Eastern Europe and South America to assist them in their economic restructuring. The greatest interest has been in the United States.

That interest was sparked by an article by William Batt, Jr. in the July-August 1983 issue of *Harvard Business Review*. "Canada's Good Example with Displaced Workers" reported that IAS worked "very simply, effectively, and fast". Batt described the program's "prompt, responsive, uncomplicated, and voluntary format that pools everyone's efforts..."

His proselytizing on behalf of the IAS approach to managing lay-offs led the U.S. Department of Labor to establish in 1985 the Canadian- American Plant Closing Demonstration Project. It was directed by the Bureau of Labor-Management Relations and Cooperative Programs and the National Governors' Association. The Project had three phases (General Accounting Office, 1989).

In March 1986, representatives from 34 states attended a seminar on Canadian assistance strategies. This was followed later that Fall by visits of officials from nine states to observe IAS joint committees. Then, in November 1986, six states were selected to organize labour- management committees.

The purpose of the Project was to "demonstrate the effectiveness of the labor-management-neutral (chairperson) system for state dislocated workers programs ... patterned along the lines of the Canadian Industrial Adjustment Service, with the addition of several domestic features including job clubs and self-directed job search" (General Accounting Office, 1989). Batt had recommended that such enhancements be added to the program (Batt, 1983).

In its review of the Canadian-American Plant Closing Demonstration Project for the House Committee on Education and Labor, the General Accounting Office (1989) found that the labor-management committees had assisted workers to find new jobs and to cope with job loss. The committees were most effective when their assistance strategies focused on individual workers' needs. Early intervention and coordinated services and communications were also key. Strong state intervention and sustained committee involvement, even after the lay-offs took effect, were other elements in effective interventions.

The General Accounting Office noted that, in the United States, labour, management and government were unaccustomed to working together voluntarily. "They are, to a large degree, unnatural partners." Even public agencies were often reluctant to cooperate.

The cost of that reluctance to work together was growing. The General Accounting Office estimated that one million American workers lost their jobs each year. The average period of unemployment was 14 weeks. Lost productivity per worker was some $4500.00. The total annual loss to the U.S. economy was $9 billion. At the same time, less than one-third of employers provided any job placement or counselling assistance to laid-off workers.

What the pilot joint committees had shown was that cooperation among labour, management and government could reduce periods of unemployment and improve workers' ability to cope with job loss. The economics of lost productivity aside, those results meant less family violence, drug and alcohol abuse, divorce and suicide. These are the social and personal effects of involuntary unemployment and isolation in the labour market not captured in the economic statistics.

Even while pilot projects to test the IAS approach in the U.S. context were going on, legislation was being drafted to formalize that approach in the management of lay-offs. In 1988, Congress enacted the Worker Adjustment and Retraining Notification (WARN) Act and the Economic Dislocation and Worker Adjustment Assistance (EDWAA) Act. Each was based on lessons learned from the Industrial Adjustment Service (General Accounting Office, 1989; Zeigler, 1989).

WARN requires employers to give 60-days notice of mass lay-offs or plant closures. For violation of the law, the Federal Court may fine employers or direct them to compensate their employees, but may not prevent the lay-off or closure.

EDWAA was intentionally positioned as a separate piece of legislation. It covers the actual assistance available to laid-off workers. While modeled on IAS, EDWAA incorporates U.S. divisions of political authority and practice. What stands out about the legislation is how comprehensively it involves all the stakeholders in major lay-offs and closures - from the U.S. Secretary of Labor and state Governors to local service providers and joint committees of employers and workers.

The Act provides the mechanism to transfer federal funds to enable states and "substate" areas to respond to mass lay-offs and closures. Broadly-representative State Job Training Coordinating Councils advise their Governors on the designation of substate areas and local coordinating organizations. These, in turn, prepare plans for the Governor outlining the services, delivery vehicles, coordinating and consultative mechanisms and other features of their lay-off response system (Zeigler, 1989).

Each Governor then submits a two-year plan to the U.S. Secretary of Labor. Those plans contain commitments in several areas. States must serve eligible dislocated workers regardless of their residence. State units are to be established to ensure rapid response, coordinated action and the provision of technical assistance to local organizations. Labour bodies are to be consulted on services to their members. Labour-management cooperation is to be fostered.

The transfer of federal funds is based on a formula which ensures a division among adjustment activities and locales. The Secretary of Labor reserves 20% of the EDWAA budget allocation for emergencies, demonstration projects, industry-wide initiatives, and activities covering several states.

EDWAA stresses rapid response focused on joint labour-management committees with neutral chairpersons. Committees provide individualized adjustment services to affected workers, and ensure coordination and communication among private and public sector organizations. Cost-sharing, the catalytic role of state officials, and private sector leadership in the actual adjustment measures are critical ingredients. While the Act focuses on lay-offs, provisions for demonstration and industry-wide projects leave open the possibility of more proactive initiatives in the future.

Assessing the Change Model

The mission statement of Employment and Immigration Canada is explicit. The burdens of economic adjustment will not be borne exclusively by workers or any other single group (Employment and Immigration Canada, 1989). Adjustment is a shared responsibility of all the beneficiaries of the economic system - the general public (through their governments), employers and labour.

The Industrial Adjustment Service provides the framework for beneficiaries to assume their responsibilities. Government's funds, technical expertise and programs are used to support private sector initiatives. Those initiatives are driven by joint committees of stakeholders. Neutral chairpersons provide process facilitation which enables stakeholders to identify their individual and collective needs and act cooperatively to meet them.

IAS is based on a simple principle of change management: change is best managed by the people it affects most directly. The underlying assumption is that people will accept and work together to implement change, provided they can set its pace and direction.

For governments in North America, the IAS approach is both wise and brave. Its wisdom lies in enabling governments to focus their direct interventions at the margins of the labour market, where self-management initiatives such as IAS are not feasible. Many groups and individuals face chronic difficulties in employment and adjustment: they are the proper focus of governments' heaviest expenditures and most caring efforts.

The IAS approach is a brave one because it vests with stakeholders outside governments' control an increasing sense of their own ability to manage labour market adjustments. The risk for governments is that they may not be able to respond in their roles as quickly, effectively and efficiently as the private sector requires. The experience with IAS so far makes that risk worthwhile.

For all participants in the adjustment process, IAS demands great personal commitment and accountability. Joint committees are not composed of consultants, gurus or public servants. They are made up of the people with the problem. If they are unable or unwilling to act, nothing happens. There is no one else to blame.

The strength of IAS is that people learn how to manage change themselves. Because the learning is process-oriented, it is portable to new situations (Schein,

1987; Moss Kanter, 1989). The process can be used to address both immediate "pain" and long-term adjustment strategies (Sashkin, 1989). Its flexibility leaves people to focus on the problem to be addressed, rather than wrestle with structures (Beer, Eisenstat and Spector, 1990).

In the end, the IAS approach allows governments and the private sector to do what they should do best (Porter, 1990). Government catalyses and challenges. The private sector innovates.

References

Abt Associates of Canada, *Evaluation Study of the Industrial Adjustment Service (IAS) Program: Final Report* (Ottawa: Employment and Immigration Canada, 1984).

Batt, William L., Jr., "Canada's Good Example with Displaced Workers", *Harvard Business Review*, Vol. 61, No. 4 (July-August, 1983).

Beer, Michael, Russell A. Eisenstat and Bert Spector, "Why Change Programs Don't Produce Change", *Harvard Business Review*, (November-December, 1990).

Bothwell, Robert, Ian Drummond and John English, *Canada Since 1945: Power, Politics and Provincialism*, (Toronto: University of Toronto Press, 1981).

Bright, James R., "Opportunities and Threat in Technological Change", *Harvard Business Review*, Vol. 41, No. 6 (November-December, 1963).

Canadian Automotive Repair and Service Council, *Proceedings Of Human Resources Workshop, May 31 and June 1, 1988*, (Ottawa: Canadian Automotive Repair and Service Council, 1988).

Canadian Roofing Industry Adjustment Committee, *Building Our Workforce*, (Ottawa: Canadian Roofing Contractors' Association, 1990).

Economic Council of Canada, *First Annual Review: Economic Goals Canada to 1970*, (Ottawa: Queen's Printer, 1964).

Economic Council of Canada, *Making Technology Work: Innovation Jobs in Canada*, (Ottawa: Economic Council of Canada, 1987).

Economic Dislocation and Worker Adjustment Assistance Act, United States Public Law 100-418, August 23, 1988.

Employment and Immigration Canada, Annual Report 1988-1989, (Ottawa: Employment and Immigration Canada, 1989).

Employment and Immigration Canada, *Employment Manual, Chapter 44, Adjustment Service*, (Ottawa: Employment and Immigration Canada, 1988).

Goodman, Earl A., and Yvon Lacaille, *The Industrial Adjustment Service: A Self-Instruction Manual*, (Ottawa: Employment and Immigration Canada, 1985).

Harvard Business Review (Editors), "Management Problems in 1963", Vol. 41, No. 1 (January-February, 1963).

Industrial Adjustment Service, *A Chairperson's Guide to Adjustment Service (IAS) Committees*, (Ottawa: Employment and Immigration Canada, undated).

Industrial Adjustment Service, *Annual Report - 1989-90*, (Ottawa: Employment and Immigration Canada, 1990).

Industrial Adjustment Service, *Manpower Consultative Service Handbook*, (Ottawa: Employment and Immigration Canada, 1981).

Industrial Adjustment Service, *Terms and Conditions*, (Ottawa: Employment and Immigration Canada, undated).

Logistics Industry Adjustment Committee, *Working Together*, (Toronto: Canadian Institute of Traffic and Transportation, 1991).

Manchester, William, *The Glory and the Dream: A Narrative History of America 1932-1972*, (Toronto: Little, Brown and Company, 1974).

Moss Kanter, Rosabeth, *When Giants Learn To Dance*, (New York: Simon and Schuster, 1989).

Newman, David G. and William Gardner, *Business Closings and Worker Readjustment: The Canadian Approach*, (Washington, D.C.: The National Center on Occupational Readjustment, Inc., 1987).

Parliamentary Task Force on Employment *Opportunities for the Work for_Tomorrow*, (Ottawa: House of Commons, 1981).

Porter, Michael E., "The Competitive Advantage of Nations", *Harvard Business Review*, (March-April, 1990).

Sashkin, Marshall, "From the Special Guest Editor", *Human Resource Planning*, Vol. 12, No. 4 (1989).

Schein, Edgar H., *Process Consultation* (Volume II), (Don Mills: Addison- Wesley Publishing Company, 1987).

Task Force on Labour Market Development, *Labour Market Development in the 1980s*, (Ottawa: Employment and Immigration Canada, 1981).

United States General Accounting Office, Human Resources Division, *Dislocated Workers: Labor-Management Committees Enhance Reemployment Assistance*, Report to the Committee on Education and Labor, House of Representatives (GAO/HRD-90-3, November 1989).

Woloschuk, B.Z., *The Manpower Consultative Service: A Self-Instruction Manual*, (Ottawa: Department of Manpower and Immigration/Employment and Immigration Canada, 1970).

Woods Gordon Management Consultants, *Canadian Automotive Repair and Service Industry: A Human Resource Study*, (Ottawa: Employment and Immigration Canada, 1988).

Worker Adjustment and Retraining Notification Act, United States Public Law 100-379, August 4, 1988.

Zeigler, Anthony G., *Plan for the Implementation of EDWAA*, (Kent State University: Northeast Ohio Center for the Advancement of Labor/Management Cooperation, 1989).

Employee Pay Plan Preferences in a Bank

T. J. ATCHISON and C. ZUMBERGE

Introduction

The past ten years have seen a revolution in American industry. This revolution is a result of our lost competitiveness in the international marketplace. In attempts to regain their competitiveness, American companies have focused on increasing productivity in many ways. One of the most talked about ways has been to make drastic changes in the way human resources are managed within the organization (Grayson and O'Dell, 1988).

Compensation administration is one of the areas of human resources management that has been overhauled in the past ten years. For over fifty years before the 1980s, compensation practices in American companies had remained virtually the same. Pay was awarded for time spent on the job. Most organizations claimed that they had a merit pay plan for wage increases; but these plans, when examined closely, granted pay increases more for seniority than for performance (Heneman, 1989). Thus, the major focus of compensation was on equity, both internal and external. In order to align compensation administration practices with the changes in today's competitive strategies, organizations have made renewed and serious attempts to develop "pay for performance" systems. In these systems pay is related to individual, team or organizational performance. In aligning compensation with new team-oriented production, compensation systems have been developed to relate pay to employee skills (Wallace, 1989).

The purpose of these new compensation systems is to tie compensation practices more closely to organizational strategy. This is done in several ways. The first is by relating pay to organizational performance, as gainsharing plans do. The second is to place a portion of the employee's pay "at risk," as most incentive plans do. The value of this is to make a portion of labor costs into variable costs, allowing organizational performance to vary without having to reduce the work force. The third way is to attempt to increase employee work flexibility by paying for skills. This last way is an important adjunct to changing a production system to a group orientation, such as in a self-managed work team.

T. J. ATCHISON - School of Business Administration, San Diego State University, San Diego, CA 92182-0096; C. ZUMBERGE - BankTemps, 4379 30th Street, San Diego, CA 92104

A major feature of all these changes is that they have been initiated from the top of the organization. They are attempts to make employees more productive from management's perspective. This would be the normal way in which change is attempted in organizations. In an era in which change is supposed to be made in a participatory fashion and employees are to be empowered, making changes in something as important as pay with little or no input from employees is indeed strange.

Not involving employees in changing the compensation system risks failing to make the most out of the change. If the new system pays employees in a manner that they feel is unfair or undesirable, dysfunctional consequences are bound to follow. As a first step, organizations might find out how employees feel about the systems used to determine how much they are paid. This is the subject of this paper.

Organizational Justice: Distributive and Procedural

Human resources management has to do mainly with the employment relationship. As in any relationship, in employment there are concerns with fairness and equity. This concern for justice has two aspects, distributive and procedural. Distributive justice is the perceived fairness of the amount of compensation that employees receive, and procedural justice is the means used to determine those amounts (Folger and Kanovsky, 1989). Most studies of pay are concerned with distributive justice issues: how much of the pie does each party get? These studies ask whether employees feel fairly paid in terms of the amount of pay they receive. From the results reported, we know that employees prefer more rather than less and that they feel they should receive an amount equivalent to that received by others who have the same level of contribution to the organization (Berkowitz, et. al., 1987).

During the past ten years, employees have felt inequity in distributive justice. Wages have not kept up with the economy, so employees are worse off today than they were ten years ago. Employees are also worse off in comparison with all the other claimants for organizational income. Executive pay is way up, stock prices have risen, and more income than ever is going toward paying off high levels of corporate indebtedness.

Even employees who receive a "good" income may still feel that justice is not being served if (a) they do not know how it is that they are receiving that income, or (b) they do not agree with the criteria or method of determining the amount. This is the issue of procedural justice that is the topic of this paper -- an aspect of organizational justice about which much less has been studied.

One aspect of this issue that has been studied is the communication of information about how pay rates are set. The findings in this area are clear: employees feel that the system is fair if they know how their wages are set (Jenkins and Lawler, 1981). Allocative procedures are important because they engender strong attitudes among employees. They can "facilitate or hinder the attainment of individual and collective goals. . . (and those procedures) which facilitate important goals are evaluated favorably while those which interfere are evaluated negatively" (Leventhal, Karuza and Fry, 1980, p. 189).

Other studies have touched on the topic of criteria for establishing pay rates. Here the evidence seems to support the ideas that employees prefer performance (or merit) to be the major factor. They feel that the organization does not make enough or good use of this criterion (Lawler, 1966). In addition, feelings of fairness about wage setting are related to other variables, such as trust and commitment (Greenberg, 1987).

A Case in Point

The inspiration for this study came from two sources. One author was concerned about this top-down imposition of new compensation programs on employees. The concern was that if employees' feelings of procedural justice were violated, the effectiveness of these new compensation systems would be diminished.

The second author had administered an employee opinion survey at an independent commercial bank, attempting to gauge employee attitudes. This was part of an effort to improve teamwork and involve employees in strategic goal attainment. When results of the survey were analyzed, the issues involving pay were found to have received the least favorable responses. The employees' feelings were particularly strong for questions relating to how their pay was set. Before moving forward to make changes in the compensation system, it was felt that more information should be collected regarding employee preferences for different pay practices. This became the impetus for the design of a pay practices preference questionnaire.

Methods

The question that we wanted answered was, "How do you want to be compensated?" This is not a simple question. There are many aspects to it, including the criteria for setting pay rates, the levels and structure of pay, pay increases, and the form that pay should take.

The Questionnaire

The questionnaire which was developed, following a couple of pre- tests, consists of seventeen questions. In each question the respondent is given four options and required to pick the one that he/she most prefers and the one that he/she least prefers. Figure 1 is an example of one of the questions. This procedure was used in order to force respondents into selecting only one choice when presented with other positive and/or negative choices, since a compensation system must be designed using a limited number of options.

The seventeen questions fell into four categories of pay practices: wage setting, pay policy, increase decision, and the pay form. The topics were mixed in

---

My pay should be based upon. . .

_______ (a) my job duties and responsibilities.

_______ (b) the product or output of my work.

_______ (c) my performance, how well I do my job.

_______ (d) the skill and knowledge that I possess.

Figure 1. Example of Question

order, rather than grouped. Demographic information regarding age, sex, and officer/non-officer status was also collected.

The Respondents

Of the bank's 100 employees, 88 completed the questionnaire. When the questionnaires were checked for completeness, seven had to be deleted, leaving 81 for analysis. As could be expected in a bank, women constituted over two-thirds of the group, and 50 of the respondents were non-officer level employees. The ages ranged from under 25 to over 55.

Procedures

Copies of the questionnaire were distributed during work-unit staff meetings. A representative of the human resources department introduced the questionnaire as a follow-up to the results of the previous year's employee opinion survey results. The directions for completing the questionnaire were read aloud and any related questions were answered. A period of time was allowed for everyone in attendance to complete the questionnaire, and then all copies were collected by the administrator. A comments session was encouraged following the completion of the questionnaire. All comments were recorded in writing.

Analysis

Data in this study are presented in the form of profiles for the most desired and least desired pay practice choices. For each question, the option with the highest number of positive responses was recorded as the most desired pay practice. The one with the highest number of negative responses as the least desired pay practice. When the data were analyzed, it was found that in some questions one option was clearly desired (or not desired) whereas in others, two options were desired to a substantial degree. In the latter case, both options were included in the high or low profile.

Results

Results are presented here for the total sample in four categories as outlined earlier: wage setting, pay policy, increase decision, and the pay form. For each category a profile is presented, along with a description of the response to each of the questions in that category. Next, a comparison of officers and non-officers is described. This allowed us to examine the different preferences that members of management might have from other employees.

Wage Setting

The results detailed in Table 1 indicate the choices made by employees from the four possible choices listed in each of the seven questions about wage setting. (See questions 1,2,3,4,5,7 and 8 in the Appendix) In summary, employees chose factors relating to wage setting that are performance based or competitive with other organizations as most desired. They chose factors regarding the organization's current pay, work output and financial impact as least desired.

Table 1. Most and Least Desired Profile for Wage Setting

Most Desired	Least Desired
pay based on performance (38+;1-)	pay based on product or work output (8+;33-)
pay based on importance of job to organization (25+;5-)	pay based on other organizations' pay (21+;32-)
pay based on comparable jobs in other organizations (50+;7-)	pay based on the employer's ability to pay (4+;39-)
pay level compared to like jobs in similar organizations (43+;9-)	pay level compared to like jobs throughout the country (3+;58-)
future pay decisions based on pay in other organizations (33+;15-)	future pay decisions based on current pay in this organization (9+;39-)
salary grade based on KSA's required by job (38+;5-)	salary grade based on job's financial impact (12+;52-)
relative pay determined by jobs in other organizations (32+;11-)	relative pay determined by current pay in this organization (8+;33-)

KEY: (number of "most desired" responses; number of "least desired" responses)

Pay Policy

The profile for pay policy preferences follows in Table 2. (See questions 6,14,15 and 17 in the Appendix) In summary, in the area of pay policy the bank employees desire open information about pay; competitive wages; and broadly defined job groups with room to advance through pay ranges. When asked who should determine the proper pay level for a particular job (the human resources department, the supervisor, a committee of top managers, or a committee of peers), the employees gave an especially strong negative response to the peer committee concept.

Table 2. Most and Least Desired Profile for Pay Policy

Most Desired	**Least Desired**
competitive wages (75+;2-)	below-market wages with profit sharing (2+;40-)
completely available information about pay (29+;30-)	complete confidentiality of pay information (17+;47-)
job's pay level to be determined by supervisor (32+;10-)	pay level to be determined by a committee of peers (6+;43-)
broadly defined job groups with wide pay ranges (27+;11-)	no pay ranges or job groups; market pricing of jobs (7+;38-)

KEY: (number of "most desired" responses; number of "least desired" responses)

Increase Decision

Table 3 shows the responses to items regarding increase decision. (See questions 10, 11, 12 and 16 in the appendix.) The results reported in Table 3 are based on strong responses that salary increases should be tied to performance rather than to other factors.

Pay Form

Results from the questions in the area of pay form are reported in Table 4. (See questions 9 and 13 in the appendix.) Again the results were strongly in favor of using performance as the key factor on which to base compensation decisions, in this case for determining bonuses. In the question about compensation mix, employees chose average wages and benefits over the following other choices: high wages with low benefits; low wages with high benefits; and low wages with average benefits and bonuses.

Comments

Over 50 individual comments were recorded in the comment sessions that were encouraged following the completion of the questionnaire. The largest group of comments (eleven) pertained to the questionnaire itself. Included were phrases like these: "I wanted to be able to combine or overlap the options" and "I felt unprepared to answer these questions; I hadn't thought about different forms of pay." The next largest group of comments, (nine) had to do with the performance factor in determining pay. Five employees singled out performance as the most

Table 3. Most and Least Desired Profile for Increase Decision

Most Desired	Least Desired
special pay increase as reward for good performance (37+;2-)	non-monetary reward for good performance (1+;68-)
raises based on performance (66+;2-)	raises based on "my need" for a raise (2+;38-) OR on the company's ability to pay (1+;37-)
salary increase $ pool to be divided among employees according to performance (51+;3-)	salary increase $ pool to be given at same $ amount to each employee (2+;38-)
salaries should move up within ranges based on performance steps (52+;1-)	salaries moving up based on seniority steps (6+;34-) OR only by bonuses (0+;33-)

KEY: (number of "most desired" responses; number of "least desired" responses)

important factor in determining pay and increases. Another person said, "Average and poor performers shouldn't be rewarded; it seems like we give everyone something," and was echoed by the comment, "A person who is not performing 'above and beyond' should not receive anything other than a cost of living increase."

There were eight comments about the mix of benefits in the compensation package, mostly stating that the desired mix of benefits and pay depends on the individual employee's age and family status.

Table 4. Most and Least Desired Profile for Pay Form

Most Desired	Least Desired
average wages and average benefits (61+;2-)	low wages and high benefits (4+;29-)
bonuses based on individual performance (52+;6-)	bonuses based on employee cost savings (4+;36-)

KEY: (number of "most desired" responses; number of "least desired" responses)

Another eight comments evaluated current overall pay practices at the bank, varying from, "By and large, wages here are very fair," to "My own personal pay situation does not seem fair; I need to discuss it with someone." The remainder of the comments had to do with cost of living increases (which three people felt should automatically adjust the base pay and be separate from merit increases), the importance of paying what other organizations within the market pay, and requests for more information regarding the bank's current compensation system.

Officer/Non-officer Differences

Only four of the seventeen questions produced noticeable differences in results of most fair/least fair choices between officers and non- officer employees. Of those who responded to the item asking about basing pay upon "the value of my skills," twice as many non-officer employees selected the item as most fair as opposed to least fair; officers chose the item as least fair over most fair at the rate of almost four to one.

Three of the other questions that yielded differences between officers and non-officer employees had to do with the concept of cost of living. Among those non-officer employees who responded to the item, "My pay should be based upon the cost of living," over 80% felt the item to be most fair rather than least fair. Only three of the total group of officers felt that the item was most fair. Second, when asked if "The most important information that should be used to decide on future pay rates is the cost of living," over 75% of the non-officer employees responding to this item felt that it was the most fair.   Only four of the total group of officers selected it as most fair. Third, in response to the item, "Pay raises should be based upon the cost of living," non- officer employees who responded chose the item as most fair over least fair by a ratio of five to one; only two of the total group of officers selected it as most fair.

Finally, the question about dissemination of information about pay practices showed that non-officers felt information should be available to all employees regarding all pay ranges. Officers wanted to restrict this information by allowing the employee to have only the range of pay for his or her job.

Discussion

In this study we have tried to find out how employees of an independent commercial bank feel regarding alternate compensation practices. Although the answers on a whole are moderate in tone, three major ideas come across as important factors for the bank employees in their perceptions and preferences of pay practices

First, there is repeated emphasis on performance. Bank employees feel that performance should be the basis for decisions regarding their pay, their pay raises and relative increase sizes. They also feel that salaries should move up through ranges based on performance and that bonuses should be based on individual performance. But do these employees understand what performance really means? According to their responses to the first question, they do not equate performance with "the product or output of my work." How exactly do these employees define performance? Their responses say that individual performance is very important, but they balk at the idea of basing pay on group performance or organizational performance. It is clear that the organization needs to define what performance is, how it is measured, and how performance contributes to the ability of employees to receive salary increases.

It appears that these answers regarding performance suggest a conservative response to the question of how wages should be set. As indicated by the strong preference given to the concept of everyone getting some amount of increase (varied according to performance levels), these employees are probably not ready for a salary-increase policy tied strictly to performance.

This leads into the second important theme of the data: the bottom line results of the company are not very important to employees in their selection of fair methods of setting pay. For example, only 15% of the employees selected the financial impact of a job as being most important when comparing jobs for pay purposes, and these were bank officers. The employer's ability to pay was rejected as a fair way to determine pay, as was the level of wages currently paid in the organization. When asked about determining bonus amounts, employees did not chose employee cost savings or company profits as factors to be used. In fact, neither of these items received over 25% response as most fair. A further comment on the current level of wages paid in the organization is in order. This may be a response based upon perceived sex discrimination. In other samples, this has proved a major difference between males and females, reflecting the feelings of women that current wage structures in organizations are biased against women.

The third major idea to emerge from the bank data was the importance to the employees of other organizations' pay levels. These bank employees want pay for jobs that is competitive with pay for comparable jobs in other similar organizations. The factor of what other organizations pay was perceived as relatively more important than the bank's current pay or its ability to pay. This feeling was especially strong among the non- officer group. In addition, the cost of living was an issue, particularly with non-officers. In both questions involving the cost of living, comparisons with other organizations took first place, with the cost of living close behind. In both cases, however, non-officers were much more likely than officers to prefer the cost of living as a standard. Some other minor points emerged within the data, including the following: pay levels should not be decided by peers; non-monetary rewards are not relished; an average mix of wages and benefits is preferred to some other mix.

Conclusions

Banks, like many other organizations, are installing "pay for performance" compensation plans in order to enhance their competitiveness in the marketplace. The plans usually involve bonus formulas based on measurable outcomes. The results of our study show that one particular group of bank employees is probably not yet ready for this type of plan, although they endorse the general concept of "pay for performance." Management would do well to take a step back and investigate what it is that people perceive as performance. An educational program needs to be undertaken in order to inform employees about how and why their compensation is tied to individual, work-group and company results.

Launching into "pay for performance" means a re-ordering of compensation goals (Atchison, 1990). The purpose of these plans is to increase productivity through increased motivation of the employee. The current system, which the employees reflect in their answers, focuses on equity and market competitiveness. This latter is a very different goal than motivation, and the two are not congruent. Thus the organization is faced with making some choices about which goals are to be optimized by the compensation program. Making a change of this magnitude requires bringing the employees along so that they understand and buy into the program; and, even then, the goal of equity will not be as well served.

As a last comment, we have developed profiles of most and least preferred compensation practices. These are not universally desired by all persons in the sample. An examination of the data shows just how varied were the responses to all the questions. On no question was there unanimity or even very close agreement. (On only nine of 68 items did the score for "plus" or "minus" exceed 50%.) It would seem that the probability of developing a compensation program that meets all employees' requirements is slim indeed.

References

Atchison, T. J., "What Should We Pay For?" in R. J. Niehaus and   K. F. Price, *Human Resource Strategies for Organizations in Transition* (New York: Plenum Press, 1990), pp. 107-122.

Berkowitz, Leonard, Colin Fraser, F. Peter Treasure, and Susan Cochran, "Pay, Equity, Job Gratifications, and Comparisons in Pay Satisfaction," *Journal of Applied Psychology*, Vol. 72, No 4 (1987), pp. 544-551.

Folger, Robert, and Mary A. Konovsky, "Effects of Procedural and Distributive Justice on Reactions to Pay Raise Decisions," *Academy of Management Journal*, Vol. 32, No. 1 (1989), pp. 115-130.

Grayson, C. J., and C. O'Dell, *The Two Minute Warning* (New York: The Free Press, 1988).

Greenberg, Jerald, "A Taxonomy of Organizational Justice Theories," *Academy of Management Review*, Vol. 12, No. 1 (1987), pp. 9-22.

Heneman, Robert L., *Working Paper Series: Merit Pay Research* (Columbus: OSU School of Business, 1989).

Jenkins, G. Douglas, Jr., and Edward E. Lawler III, "Impact of Employee Participation in Pay Plan Development," *Organizational Behavior and Human Performance*, Vol. 28 (1981), pp. 111-128.

Lawler, Edward E. III, "Managers' Attitudes Toward How Their Pay Is and Should Be Determined," *Journal of Applied Psychology*, Vol. 50, No. 4 (1966), pp. 273-279.

Lawler, Edward E. III, *Pay and Organizational Effectiveness: A Psychological View* (New York: McGraw-Hill, 1971).

Lawler, Edward E. III, "The New Pay," USC Center for Effective Organizations, 1985.

Leventhal, Gerald S., Jurgis Karuza, Jr., and William Rick Fry, "Beyond Fairness: A Theory of Allocation Preferences," *Justice and Social Interaction*, ed. G. Mikula (New York: Springer-Verlag, 1980).

Price, James L., and Charles W. Mueller, *Handbook of Organizational Measurement* (Boston: Pitman, 1986)

Wallace, M., *Alternative Reward Systems* (Scottsdale, AZ: American Compensation Association, 1989).

Appendix

Pay Practices Preference Questionnaire

In this questionnaire, we would like you to express your preference for various ways in which your wages and benefits may be determined. For each set of four items, please indicate the ONE choice that you feel would be most fair with A + and the ONE you feel would be least fair with A -. There are no right or wrong answers.

1. My pay should be based upon...
_____ a) my job duties and responsibilities.
_____ b) the product or output of my work.
_____ c) my performance, how well I do my job.
_____ d) the skill and knowledge that I possess.

2. My pay should be based upon...
_____ a) what people in other organizations are paid for doing the same job.
_____ b) the importance of my job to the organization.
_____ c) the value to the organization of my job compared to other jobs.
_____ d) the value of my skills.

3. My pay should be based upon...
_____ a) my employer's ability to pay.
_____ b) comparable jobs in other organizations.
_____ c) the cost of living.
_____ d) the supply of and demand for labor.

4. The pay level for my job should be determined by a comparison to like jobs...
_____ a) in the local area.
_____ b) in the state.
_____ c) throughout the country.
_____ d) in organizations similar to the one I work in.

5. The most important information that should be used to decide on future pay rates is...
_____ a) what people in other organizations are paid.
_____ b) internal comparison of jobs.
_____ c) the cost of living.
_____ d) current wages paid in my organization.

6. My company should pay...
_____ a) higher-than-competitive wages and lay off workers if labor costs get too high.
_____ b) competitive wages and lay off workers only in emergencies.
_____ c) wages that are lower than the competition and give a small bonus if the company makes a good profit.
_____ d) much lower wages than the competition and tie workers in to a substantial share of the profits.

7. The comparison of jobs for pay purposes in my organization should be
determined by looking at...
_____ a) job responsibility.
_____ b) knowledge, skills and abilities required by the job.
_____ c) decision making and discretion required by the job.
_____ d) the financial impact of the job.

8. The relative pay for jobs should be determined by a comparison of...
_____ a) jobs within the organization.
_____ b) jobs in other organizations.
_____ c) information from wage surveys.
_____ d) current wages paid within the organization.

9. Employees should be paid in the form of...
_____ a) high wages and low benefits.
_____ b) low wages and high benefits.
_____ c) average wages and benefits.
_____ d) low wages, average benefits, and bonuses.

10. Good performance should be rewarded by...
_____ a) a pay increase given with the annual performance appraisal.
_____ b) a special pay increase.
_____ c) a bonus.
_____ d) non-monetary recognition.

11. Pay raises should be based upon...
_____ a) my performance.
_____ b) the cost of living.
_____ c) my need for a raise.
_____ d) the company's ability to pay.

12. If my supervisor were given a pool of money to be used for pay raises in our
area, he/she should...
_____ a) give each employee the same dollar amount increase.
_____ b) give each employee the same percentage of salary increase.
_____ c) give large increases to top performers and no increases to average or poor
        performers.
_____ d) give everyone some amount of increase, but vary according to
        performance levels.

13. Any bonuses paid should be based on...
_____ a) individual performance.
_____ b) work-group performance results.
_____ c) company profits.
_____ d) cost savings by employees.

14. Information about the organization's pay practices...
____ a) should be kept confidential.
____ b) should be shared with each employee regarding the pay range for his/her
        own job only.
____ c) should be available to all employees regarding all pay ranges.
____ d) should be completely available to all employees.

15. The proper pay level for my job should be determined by...
____ a) the human resources department.
____ b) my supervisor.
____ c) a committee of top managers.
____ d) a committee of my peers.

16. Assuming that there is a specific pay range for each job, an employee's salary
should move up through the range by...
____ a) steps based on seniority.
____ b) steps based on performance.
____ c) matching his/her performance to salary based on an open range.
____ d) receiving bonuses rather than salary increases.

17. Often similar jobs are placed together in job groups that have assigned pay
ranges. The organization should have...
____ a) broadly defined job groups with wide pay ranges, resulting in few (but
        meaningful) promotional increases.
____ b) narrowly defined job groups with narrow pay ranges and frequent
        opportunities for small promotions.
____ c) no job groups at all, but individual pay ranges assigned to each job.
____ d) no pay ranges or job groups, with pay rates set solely according to what
        the competition is paying.

Please answer the following questions about yourself.

Age: ____ under 25; ____ 25-39; ____ 40-54; ____ 55 or over

Sex: ____ female; ____ male

Position level: non-officer____; officer____

Employee Commitment: The Elusive Edge

P.L. BUGBEE and D.J. DAVIS

Significant Background

The landscape of American business changed dramatically during the 1980s. As companies and organizations look to the rest of the 1990s, most are trying to adjust to a host of different forces. For some, this translates into finding ways to simply survive. For others it means focusing on the impact of globalization. For still others it may mean merely improving already strong business results to stay competitive.

American business has also created a dilemma for its employees. The actions taken to be more competitive have seriously impacted the work force and are requiring employees to act different -- radically different sometimes. Organizations now expect employees to eagerly and immediately adopt new technologies, productivity improvement programs, quality improvement initiatives, and other forms of change. They also expect employees to accept bravely all the uncertainty that this and other change engenders. In short, employees are expected to be more committed than ever to totally new ways of doing business with far less in the way of traditional support and reinforcement.

Given the premises that a high level of employee commitment is critical for companies to succeed in the 1990s; that commitment now appears to be eroding in many organizations and that it is in need of a different focus, a limited participant study was undertaken to explore the issue of effectively building and maintaining employee commitment.

While leaders of many organizations perceive a need to have a high level of employee commitment, finding and honing that competitive "edge" has proven to be a difficult task. This study was aimed at finding answers that could help as organizations strive for this elusive edge.

In this study, we explored three dimensions of employee commitment. These included:
1. The business and human resource factors that appear to have the most impact on employee commitment -- both positively and negatively;

P.L. BUGBEE and D.J. DAVIS - TPF&C, 1200 17th Street, Suite No.1200, Denver, CO 80202-5812

2. The influence and impact of organizational communications activities on enhancing employee commitment. Activities that were explored included:

-- effective articulation of the organization's vision, mission and business strategies;
-- formal and informal lines of communication up, down, and across the organization; and
-- external media/communications; and

3. The existence of any type of new "social contract" between the employee and the organization, and the role it plays in building and maintaining employee commitment.

The Process for the Research Study

The research process involved with this study included three action steps. These action steps were as follows:

o   Conducted a literature search of periodical articles, books and other print materials on the subject of employee commitment; and

o   Interviews and discussions with and a review of relevant research conducted by selected members of the academic community who have done considerable work on employee commitment. The interviews were conducted either over the phone or in person to gather their thoughts and perspectives on the issues around employee commitment. Individuals interviewed included: Fred K. Foulkes, Boston University School of Management; Bonner Ritchie, Brigham Young University, and Quinn Mills, Harvard University. Relevant research conducted by several members of the academic community was also reviewed. Included in this review was research conducted by Lee Dyer, Cornell University, and David Ulrich, University of Michigan School of Business Administration.

o   Held management interviews and focus groups in a selected group of companies. The firms selected were identified as organizations that are either (a) doing an excellent job of maintaining commitment or (b) have applied unique approaches to build or rebuild it in recent years. Also, we wanted to look at both large and small companies to see what, if any, different approaches were being employed to foster a higher level of commitment.

The following companies were included in the study:

-- Ben and Jerry's Homemade, Inc.
-- Intermountain Health Care
-- Mrs. Fields, Inc.
-- Union Pacific Railroad Company
-- US WEST

The research approach in this step involved asking interviewees and focus group participants selected questions from a questionnaire prepared in advance. The questions centered on three themes that form the basis of this study: (a) positive and negative business factors influencing commitment, (b) the role of internal and external communication and (c) the presence of a social contract.

General Findings

Based on the information gleaned from the literature search and research review and input from the interviews, several general findings quickly came to the surface. These include:

o There is universal agreement that a high level of employee commitment is essential to organizational success.

o There are lower levels of employee commitment today in most organizations than there was five years ago.

o Efforts are being undertaken (either directly or indirectly) to enhance employee commitment, but little seems to be working.

o Social contracts are seen as having been broken, but not much has been done to put something new in place.

Need for High Level of Employee Commitment

Executives in the organizations we talked with unanimously believe the level of commitment an employee has to the organization and their job will be critical as organizations cope with the myriad of changes they will be facing during the 1990s.

Many of those individuals interviewed were also quick to make a distinction in definition of terms between "loyalty" and "commitment." Most define loyalty as an unguided, emotional attachment to an organization with little regard to why or how these feelings are attained. John F. Welch, Chairman, General Electric Corporation, summed up many executives' feelings about loyalty in a *Wall Street Journal* article when he said, "Loyalty to a company, it's nonsense."

The executives of the companies surveyed prefer to build and maintain a strong level of commitment -- meaning developing employees who are focused, recognize the realities of the relationship that they have with their organization, and come to work each day dedicated to doing the maximum.

There are a host of different factors that seem to either positively or negatively impact the level of employee commitment someone has. However, there is common agreement that commitment is very important for organizations to succeed.

Supporting these qualitative observations are the results of a variety of studies embarked on in recent years that look at issues related to employee commitment. For example, a 1990 survey conducted by Heidrick and Struggles of chief human resource executives of *Fortune 500* and *Fortune Service 500* parent organizations, showed that next to controlling employee benefit program costs, the most critical issue they faced was building and keeping a qualified work force (read a committed work force). Another study, led by David Ulrich, a specialist in human resource management at the University of Michigan's School of Business Administration, found that a premium, in the future, will be placed on the skills needed to help a company manage change. According to these study findings, managing change involves at least three aspects, one of which is building long-term relationships between the company and employees based upon trust.

Lower Levels of Employee Commitment Today

Despite the need for a much *higher* level of commitment among employees in order for organizations to accomplish their business goals and objectives, this study reveals that commitment levels appear to be lower than ever. For example, in a national study conducted by TPF&C several years ago, roughly one-third of the respondents indicated they were less committed to their employer than they were in the past.

Many of the executives interviewed in this study pointed the finger of blame for these lower levels of commitment at three factors. These included:

o *New worker values* - employees now looking for different types of
    satisfaction and challenge, and have new priorities in their lives, different
    from their fellow workers of the 1960s and '70s;
o *A work / business environment that has gone from highly predictable to
    highly unstable* - organizations across the board (particularly larger
    organizations) are very differently focused and oriented today versus even
    five to seven years ago. This has created a sense of insecurity and
    instability among employees, and;
o *The speed and complexity of change* that organizations are experiencing is
    impacting employees' abilities to feel a sense of commitment.

The exceptions concerning falling levels of commitment appear to be isolated within two types of organizations. The first concerns organizations that have traditionally had employees with very high levels of commitment and who, as an organization have remained stable. An example here would be Federal Express. Based on our study, the key appears to be the combination of both a high level of commitment initially, and relative stability within the organization over a period of time (also coupled with continued growth).

The other type of organization that appears to have little, if any, decline in the level of commitment, is in certain service organizations that have a very focused work force. An example here would be hospitals. Many health care organizations have structurally undergone extensive change in recent years, and many have also faced significant staff reductions. The remaining employees are able to sort through the other events that are going on and continue to focus on the effective delivery of health care services.

Efforts to Enhance Employee Commitment

In each of the organizations included in the study, members of management were quick to articulate programs and activities that either have been or are being undertaken to enhance a new definition and level of employee commitment. These efforts ranged from revamped compensation programs to better articulated visions and missions to highly focused training and skill development activities. However, among the executives interviewed, many expressed a skepticism about just how well some of their efforts were working. Focus groups that were held to accompany the interviews in a couple of organizations further substantiated this finding. It is clear that many of the activities that are being embarked on are simply not working.

The primary problems identified by both executives and employees included:

o *Program-itis* -- A host of different programs were put in place to deal with
    very specific aspects of commitment, but there appeared to be a "let's throw
    a program at it to solve the problem" mentality.

o *Disconnectedness of the efforts* -- While some individual efforts were perceived as effective (e.g., revised reward systems), there did not appear to be adequate linkage, or alignment among the efforts, thus leading employees to be confused about what was being done and why.

o *A "say/do" gap* -- A number of the executives interviewed as part of the study perceived that what was being said to be important in their organization, was not necessarily being followed-up through day-to-day actions and deeds. This was creating a "say/do" gap that formed a level of frustration and confusion for employees.

View of Social Contracts

For years there was in place, in most organizations, an implicit "social contract" between the company and the employee. The company more or less offered lifetime job security, and in return, the work force pledged steadfast allegiance. Most argue that this type of arrangement is now gone. Without a doubt, the participants in this survey - both executives and employees - perceive that it is gone as well. The concern, however, revolves around the fact that some type of "contract" will be necessary in order for employees to believe their efforts have meaning. With few exceptions, our research indicates that attempts to develop and implement meaningful new social contracts, are few and far between.

Within the three major themes explored in this study, let's look more closely at specific findings around each.

Specific Findings

Business Factors that Negatively Influence Employee Commitment

In looking at the business factors or conditions that can influence employee commitment, we first explored through the survey those factors or conditions survey participants felt were a negative influence. Several surfaced that appear in much of the literature on employee commitment. These include:

o the impact of overall organizational change;

o turnover within the organization (including downsizing, staff reductions, and ordinary employee turnover);

o lack of job security and job permanence;

o obsessive focus on profitability, enhanced financial results, etc.; and

o perceived lack of trust between management and employees.

Throughout the interviews that were conducted as part of this study, many of the executives cited one or more of these factors as being a particularly negative influence on commitment -- and some of them indicated that these factors are in operation in their own organization.

Along with these commonly perceived negatives, several of the interviewees pointed to others. For example, Dick Davidson, Executive Vice President-Operations at Union Pacific Railroad Company, felt that the actions of members of management, particularly senior management, could do the most damage to employee commitment, depending on how well these people performed. "Today's manager, to be good, must literally be a clone of Jesus Christ," explained Davidson.

"Everyone expects a manager to be good at everything. Otherwise, they're not doing their job. I don't think this is realistic, but my sense is that it *is* reality in the minds of our employees," continued Davidson.

Scott Parker, President and Chief Executive Officer of Intermountain Health Care, sees the issue of fairness as an extremely important factor or condition that can negatively influence commitment, if not handled appropriately. "The person in the trenches must sense that there is a strong level of 'fairness' -- fairness with all things across-the-board, in order for there to be commitment," explained Parker. "For example, in our organization, nurses don't seem to feel society values them highly. They translate this feeling into a sense that our organization doesn't value them as much either, thus, leading to a sense of a lack of fairness. These are all perceptions, mind you," continued Parker, "but I think they impact how committed an employee is."

Business Factors That Positvely Influence Employee Commitment

While a study of the issue of employee commitment can quickly unearth many negatives that impact employee commitment, it's much harder to pinpoint those business factors or conditions that positively influence commitment. In the course of our interviews and research; however, we were able to glean several positive influences. These include:

o Effective communication of the vision and direction of the organization -- providing employees with a point of focus with which they can move forward; (More information about the impact of effective communication on commitment is included in the next section of our specific findings.)
o Managers who truly are leaders and posses outstanding skills in communicating and motivating employees;
o A work environment that fosters employee involvement, both with regard to local and organization-wide decision making;
o An organization's culture, vision, mission and business strategies that are all aligned and not working at cross-purposes;
o A "turned on" work force as reflected by a strong level of volunteerism;

"In my mind, the key to employee commitment is the degree of 'how turned on' an employee is," said Michael H. Walsh, Chairman, Union Pacific Railroad Company. "If employees are turned on -- willing to do more than what is expected of them -- then you can tap into their level of volunteerism, and you're well on your way to a truly healthy and successful organization. Volunteerism is critical," continued Walsh, "but, you can't buy it, you can't order it; you've got to work with your employees to make it happen."

o A clear focus on helping employees develop and enhance career skills;

Unlike the old notions of developing new and better job skills, some companies today are completely changing the focus and are working with their employees through training and development programs to enhance basic career skills. They are focusing on skill enhancement that will enable the employee to grow and advance, both within the company they are now with, and to be highly marketable outside the firm, should their or the firm's needs change. "One big key to building employee commitment in the future," says Connie McArthur, Executive Director of Human Resources at U S WEST, "will be the extent to which we can help employees develop and maintain state-of-the-art skills that are highly portable and transferable. If an employee feels he or she has the skills to be sought after, both within their own company and in the outside marketplace," continued McArthur, "then that employee is likely to be more committed to the organization they're with. They can see a win/win situation for both themselves and their company."

Other major organizations have also adopted this career skill enhancement approach to help foster employee commitment. These firms include General Electric and Xerox.

o   Finding and fostering ways for employees to have fun;

One aspect of corporate life that has gotten very little focus in most organizations today, is fun. Some managers believe having fun is simply inconsistent with doing a good job.

However, there are many lessons that can be gleaned from smaller organizations and their effectiveness at engendering extremely strong employee commitment. Some of this success comes from taking the time and setting processes for employees to have fun. For example, at Ben and Jerry's Homemade, Inc., a host of different activities are held both regularly and on an ad-hoc basis to underscore the "fun" nature of employee work. For example, the company has quarterly all-employee meetings where there is a dual focus -- partly on communicating what's happening in the business and why, and partly to get all employees together to have fun -- ranging from testing new ice cream flavors, to belly-bumping contests. At Ben and Jerry's, an employee "fun committee" also evaluates what should be done to enhance fun and how effective past measures have been.

Numerous articles have been written over the years about the need to inject more humor and fun into the day-to-day business world. However, most organizations have moved little, if any, in this direction. While a firm of fewer than one thousand employees can more easily embark on fun activities (such as Ben and Jerry's), the benefits of infusing fun in the work place are many, including tension reduction, an enhanced spirit of camaraderie, and a bonding that can be very powerful in helping employees feel a stronger level of commitment.

o   Creating an environment of commitment;

Throughout many of the interviews, executives we talked to in this study pointed to some specific "work environment" points they felt can positively influence commitment. For example, several of the executives touched on the need for a high level of trust to exist between employees and management in order for appropriate levels of commitment to exist. Others pointed to a need for open communication between the leadership of the organization and employees.

o   An organizational operating style that limits bureaucracy hierarchy;

In some of the companies included in the survey, extensive efforts have been made in recent years to trim bureaucracy and related hierarchy. At Union Pacific Railroad Company, for example, the operating department, which constitutes over 80 per cent of the railroad, went from eleven layers of management to three, within a six-month period of time. This effort resulted in much more responsibility being pushed down to first-line supervisors and employees. The result was a faster and more effective communication process, leading over time to higher overall employee commitment.

Many other organizations have also trimmed layers of management. They are looking for the same types of results, as indicated by the level of activity around downsizing and restructurings that are still going on in business.

o Impact of effective communication.

One area that we looked at closely in conducting this study, was the influence on employee commitment of various internal and external communications activities. Our reasoning was that, if there is a strong correlation between effective communication and good employee commitment, then a clear, definable area of opportunity exists for organizations to focus on as they attempt to enhance the level of commitment.

Our study findings verified our initial premise -- that is, there are some communication steps that can be taken that do positively influence employee commitment. Based on our study findings, the types of communication activities that appear to net the most value are:

o   A clearly articulated and well communicated vision, values and business strategies;

These types of communications were most often cited by both executives and employees as being extremely valuable in enhancing commitment. Helping employees understand the focus of the business, where the organization is going and how they fit in, are seen as extremely critical. These types of communication efforts also must involve both effective initial communication and constant reinforcement with employees in order for the effort to work.

At Mrs. Field's Cookies, for example, each year each store receives a poster that lays out: (a) a definition of who the customer is, (b) a definition of the qualities the organization is looking for from each employee, (c) the mission statement for the organization, (d) that year's goals, and (e) a reference to what is commitment. All these communication elements revolve around Mrs. Field's overall vision of providing the highest quality products, and focusing intensely on the customer and satisfying their needs.

Another example of clearly articulating a vision and strategy for achieving it comes from Union Pacific Railroad Company. The company has identified their change and growth process as encompassing two chapters -- Chapter One which involved four very intense years of fundamental cultural change, while Chapter Two will include accomplishing a set of goals that will help the company become world class competitive. The Chapter Two goals or business objectives revolve around quality of service, market growth, cost of quality, supply effectiveness, asset utilization and management, and overall management effectiveness.

A comprehensive set of communications tools and media were used to underscore the messages around the introduction of Chapters One and Two. These communications included printed booklets, teleconferenced townhalls, and articles in the company's regular employee publications.

o Perception that the organization really listens;

In order for employees to feel a sense of commitment and belonging, it's clear to many of the executives we interviewed (and the literature on the subject, as well) that an open atmosphere conducive to employee feedback and listening is extremely important. While unique new vehicles for gathering mass input (employee townhall meetings, interactive telephone surveys, randomly selected employee focus groups, etc.) can serve as excellent feedback instruments, the most powerful and effective listening, through the eyes of the executives in this study, comes from the actions of the manager and supervisor. They must serve as a conduit for upward movement of information.

"If you're going to have *real* commitment in an organization," says Mike Chapman, Regional Superintendent in the operating department at Union Pacific Railroad Company, "a lot of energy and effort must be focused on building the supervisor/employee relationship so that both parties feel a sense of power and an opportunity to communicate. A supervisor must understand the vital roll he or she plays in listening, as well as communicating downward," according to Chapman.

An organization may have a variety of listening activities in place. Numerous surveys conducted by TPF&C over the years indicate that employees may not value these listening vehicles if they do not feel their immediate work-related and work environment issues are being addressed. Repeatedly, in response to survey questions, employees in a variety of organizations have indicated that they do not view an organization as doing a good job of listening if they have concerns that are going unaddressed or are simply not acted upon.

Thus, listening, while critical to building employee communication, must be carefully evaluated and understood within each organization.

o A continuous improvement focus on the communication skills of leaders
   within an organization; and

Throughout the interviews conducted for this study, it's clear that a critical communications link to developing and maintaining employee commitment comes from having a management team that has and uses effective communication skills. The role management plays in building an appropriate environment of communication -- critical to employee commitment -- must be heavily focused on within an organization.

Communication skill enhancement, in the eyes of these executives, must go far beyond traditional communication skill training efforts. Tomorrow's effective business leaders must not only have effective communication skills, but also the understanding behind why effective communication is so important to the overall success of their business. Understanding the why, and being able to effectively transmit that to employees and create an environment of effective communication, will require unique developmental efforts within organizations.

There are numerous pilot efforts underway in companies we talked with in this study to address some of these needs. For example, at Union Pacific Railroad Company, work is underway to develop a unique manager communication skills training effort based around a curriculum developed and refined by a selected group of managers. The use of interactive video and the delivery of the training at the job site, rather than in group meetings, highlight several of the planned program features.

o   The presence of a new "social contract."

Much has been written and discussed about the breaking of the old social contract that used to exist between an employee and an employer. As common thinking has it, in the past, an employer provided job security, stability, predictable pay increases, and numerous other support mechanisms. In turn, the employee offered to the company a level of loyalty and commitment bound together by a level of trust and perception of fairness. With the tremendous upheaval and number of changes that have taken place across the landscape of American business in recent years, most people feel this implied social contract has been broken. Most people also feel it must be replaced by some type of new social contract between an employer and the employee, that can provide a foundation on which an individual can develop a level of commitment.

Through our study, we queried representatives of the five companies about whether or not they felt they have in place such a new social contract. Most of those interviewed indicated they did not feel they have in place a new contract, at least as we defined it (some type of implied set of operating values around which the company and the employee could agree, and which could serve as a stimulus for strong levels of employee commitment). Of the five companies included in this study, only in one, Ben and Jerry's Homemade, Inc., did the members of management perceive themselves as having in place a social contract that addressed the current and future needs of both the employees and the organization. In all the other firms included in this survey, members of management perceived themselves as working on articulating and developing the framework of a new social contract, but they weren't yet there.

"Here at U S WEST, we're trying to create an environment where we have committed employees, and as part of that focus we want the employee to understand fully and accept what we'll do for them and what we're expecting from them," said Connie McArthur of U S WEST. "Our approach is to instill in our work force the understanding that we will provide the skill development opportunities necessary to make them the best at what they do, with the idea that this will make them more valuable within U S WEST. It will also position them to be most valuable in the marketplace, should our business needs change and their services are no longer required." "As I see it," continued McArthur, "this is the type of framework all organizations are going to need to establish in building some type of new social contract between the company and employees. Firms can't and won't offer the same ingredients in a contract as we saw there 15 or 20 years ago. But we do need to have some type of framework."

In terms of laying out a new type of social contract, David Rhodes, TPF&C, recently wrote in a *Journal of Business Strategy* article,
"New social contracts in some organizations will focus on increasing employees' ability to balance work, family, and other personal responsibilities. Employees will be attracted to these organizations because they will offer flexible employment opportunities that fit in with career, personal, and financial expectations."

"Watch for these employers to use all kinds of flexible work arrangements," continued Rhodes, "such as flex-time, job sharing, job banks, retiree work programs and project staffing. Watch also, as progressive employees turn to these companies because the actions of these corporate parents will be consistent with employees' own aspirations."

Lessons from This Study

Based on the results of this study, it's clear that a dilemma exists for the management of most corporations and organizations. On the one hand, they want and need a committed employee work force. On the other hand, there are many business and social pressures that are pushing, tugging, and pulling employees to feel less committed than ever before. If an organization is to improve and be successful on an continuing basis, it must find ways to build and maintain employee commitment -- to find and hone that elusive edge.

There are several lessons that the leadership of an organization can take from the data in this study. These lessons revolve around five touchstones. These touchstones are:

Focus If employees are going to build a high level of commitment, they have got to see and feel they are a part of a focused organization. They have got to believe their organization has a clear vision, mission and strategy, and has communicated it well throughout the organization. Employees must also feel focused concerning their role and responsibilities within the organization, and have a sense of focus about the value added of their actions.

Fairness Employees must believe that they work within an environment where trust and fairness abound. It's clear through the research conducted in this study and others, that most employees are *never* going to feel everything is completely fair. They must believe they work for an organization that operates with a foundation of basic fairness in treatment of customers, treatment of employees, and an emphasis on ethical actions.

Flexibility If employees don't perceive the organization or unit they work for is flexible and adapts well to changing business conditions and internal needs, then they themselves are not going to do what they need to be flexible in approaching their work or role in the organization. Flexibility also relates to the immense need for organizations to create flexible working environments that help employees better balance personal and work lives.

Future security One of the most challenging undertakings organizations will face in the near term is to paint a new picture for employees of what future job security means. The best picture will most likely involve helping employees changing their perceptions from that of looking for old-fashioned job security with their existing organizations, to building future security through personal skill enhancement that can be useful in either their existing company or within other organizations in the marketplace. If companies and employees can begin to view the individual as a valuable asset that needs developing but with a goal of skill enhancement beyond the employer's existing environment in mind, employees will have the confidence to place a level of commitment with that company. Loyalty based on job security will be gone, but replaced by a whole new focus for commitment around overall skill enhancement.

Fun There is an old cliche that goes something like "life stinks and then you die." If employees only perceive that an organization is focused on serious gut-wrenching problems, higher and higher financial hurdles, and tougher individual and unit goals from year to year, one doesn't need to go very far to determine whether employees in this setting would be committed. Introducing some if not more fun into the day-to-day work environment - at all levels of an organization - and reinforcing through the leadership that the organization is committed to a balanced perspective regarding work, goal achievement, and attention to personal needs, can go a long way toward heightening the level of employee commitment.

Conclusion

Employee commitment -- maintaining it is a little like keeping a sharp edge on the blade of a knife. By not taking care of a knife -- trying to cut the wrong things with it, letting it get wet and rust or cutting on the wrong surface -- the blade gets dull and doesn't work well. Organizations that don't focus on and foster employee commitment -- keeping the employees and the firm focused, building an environment of trust and fairness and having a little fun along the way -- will find the level of commitment dulls very quickly. In some cases, just like with an ill-cared-for knife, it can't be fixed.

The good news based on this study is that there is both a recognition of the strong need for a high level of employee commitment and several special action steps that can be taken to enhance commitment. Maintaining commitment, like keeping a knife blade in great shape, requires frequent attention and the right combination of action steps.

A high level of employee commitment can be a powerful edge in today's business environment. Finding that elusive edge is possible.

References

Barling, Julian; Bill Wade and Clive Fullagar. "Predicting Employee Commitment to Company and Union: Divergent Models", *Journal of Occupational Psychology*, Vol. 63, No. 1 (1990) pp 49-61.

Boyett, Joseph H. and Henry P. Conn. *Workplace 2000*, (New York, NY: Penguin Books, 1991).

Davis, Stan and Bill Davidson, *2020 Vision*, (New York, NY: Simon and Schuster, 1991)

Drennan, David. "How To Get Your Employees Committed", *Management Today*, (Oct 1989) pp 121+.

Goman, Carol Kinsey, "Earning Employee Loyalty: New Values Demand New Approaches", *Management World* Vol. 18, No. 2 (Mar/Apr 1989) pp 40+.

Kanter, Rosabeth Moss, *When Giants Learn To Dance*, (New York, NY: Simon and Schuster, 1989)

Kotter, John P., *The Leadership Factor*, (New York, NY: The Free Press, 1988)

Miller, Gordon P., "Understanding Values -- Your Own and Theirs", *Supervisory Management*, Vol. 34, No. 4 (Apr 1989) pp 43-45.

Rhodes, David W. "Employee Loyalty Is An Attainable Goal", *The Journal of Business Strategy*, (Nov/Dec 1989)

Romzek, Barbara S., "Employee Investment and Commitment: The Ties That Bind", *Public Administration Review*, Vol. 50, No. 3 (May/June 1990) pp 374-382.

Solomon, Jolie, "Diverse Makeup of Work Force Poses Challenge", *Wall Street Journal*, March 1, 1989, pp B-1, B-5

Tichy, Noel and Ram Charan, "Speed, Simplicity, Self-Confidence: An Interview with Jack Welch", *Harvard Business Review*, No. 5, (Sep/Oct 1989) pp 112-119.

Tornow, Walter W., "Contract Redesign", *Personnel Administrator*, Vol. 34, No. 10 (Oct 1988), pp 97-101.

Measuring the Impact on the Bottom Line

This section provides insight into measurement issues related to human resource programs. In the first paper, **Walker** and **Bechet** define and describe effectiveness and efficiency measures used in various HR programs. This paper is an overview and a review of the approaches used.

One of the least measured jobs in an organization is that of the Chief Executive Officer, according to **Schneier, Beatty,** and **Shaw**. In their studies, only 14% of companies evaluate CEO's individual performance, the majority relying instead on the total company financial results to infer how effectively the CEO performs. The authors argue that the CEO's individual performance impacts a company's performance and culture, and hence can, and should be measured.

Based on a three year study of over 500 large public companies **McLaughlin, McLaughlin** and **Lischick** conclude that successful companies appear to have distinctive values and beliefs. They argue that a company's values and beliefs are pivotal in its survival and success. They also describe the role that values and beliefs can play in corporate revitalization.

Verdin and **Pagano** describe how quality programs have become a central part of doing business in both manufacturing and service industries. This study explores the types of quality programs being offered by firms in manufacturing and service industries and determines what role HR managers have taken in these . This study was sponsored by the Human Resource Planning Society and funded by Weyerhauser and The Equitable Corporation.

Teigland describes, in a case history, how New York State, since 1988, has come a long way in developing the capacity needed to conduct long range HR planning and analysis. This case talks about the development of a comprehensive workforce information system. It goes on to describe several applications that have a clear impact on the "bottom line."

The final paper in this publication outlines what current research and practice show about the relationship between employee commitment or attitudes as measured by employee surveys and on-the-job performance of a workforce. The paper, by **Hinrichs**, illustrates how the level of employee commitment can have a significant impact on bottom line results. It goes on to describe criteria for effective employee surveys.

Defining Effectiveness and Efficiency Measures in the Context of Human Resource Strategy

J.W. WALKER and T.P. BECHET

Introduction

Well managed companies that address important business issues through the implementation of human resource strategies often seek to measure performance of the human resource function in terms of both effectiveness and efficiency. Effectiveness relates the results of activities to the achievement of objectives (i.e., "are we doing the right things?"). Efficiency relates the yield of outputs to the energy, time, or resources applied as inputs (i.e., "are we doing things right?") (Drucker, 1973).

Human resource staff functions need to measure both efficiency and effectiveness. Some companies attempt to measure the efficiency of the human resource function (often relying on a series of quantitative measures). Few companies adequately measure their effectiveness in relation to implementing human resource strategy and achieving specific objectives. Efficiency addresses the relationship between key results and short term human resource activities. Effectiveness addresses the relationship between key results and longer term issues and strategies.

The focus of many effectiveness and efficiency measures is on the performance of the human resource staff function, as a service unit within a company. The concept of measuring effectiveness and efficiency could be applied to any or all human resource functions, including those performed by line managers. Measures of effectiveness and efficiency can be applied to human resource staff performance. They can also be used to measure human resource management efficiency and effectiveness throughout an organization. As a result, measures may be as useful to operating managers as they are to staff managers.

This paper presents a framework for defining effectiveness and efficiency measures. It describes how such measures are applied in practice in four companies studied. The companies included a diversified services company, a consumer products company, an industrial and aircraft equipment component manufacturer, and an oil exploration and production company. Our findings are based on knowledge developed through consulting relationships with these companies.

J.W. WALKER and T.P. BECHET - The Walker Group, 3713 E. Equestrian Trail, Phoenix, AZ 85044

The Human Resource Planning Context

All the companies studied develop human resource strategies on an ongoing basis (see Figure 1). The process begins with a review of business plans and strategies, definition of external and environmental changes, and definition of internal organizational issues. Analysis of this "strategic context" includes the identification of the critical human resource issues and implications inherent in the environment, plans, strategies, and organization issues. These human resource issues are typically defined in detail and ranked by priority (Schuler and Walker, 1990; Walker, 1990).

Next, companies define the human resource strategies that can best address the most critical human resource issues and implications. These strategies tend to be longer term (i.e., longer than one year) directional plans that usually require the application of significant resources. Sometimes several strategies may be required to address a single issue. Similarly, a single strategy may address more than one issue.

The specific human resource actions, programs, and activities needed to carry out each strategy are then planned and implemented as required. Throughout the planning period, strategies and activities/programs are modified as necessary to ensure that critical issues are being addressed adequately. Finally, the results of the activities that are implemented are measured and documented.

The "upstream" elements of human resource planning (i.e., issue identification and strategy development) are oriented toward line managers as "customers". These upstream activities are conceptual and of a long term nature. As the process unfolds, "downstream" elements of the human resource planning process (i.e., activity development and implementation) are more directly related to the human resource function itself. These downstream activities tend to be transactional, tangible, and immediate.

Human resource planning helps a human resource function manage strategically. When this approach to human resource planning is applied, all the human resource activities and programs that are implemented are linked directly to the resolution of business needs. The approach helps management ensure that all important issues are being addressed and that all actions are aligned with the strategies. Through human resource planning, human resource activities are better integrated as well. For example, the recruiting aspects of various strategies can be combined to create a coherent strategy for recruiting needed talent throughout the organization.

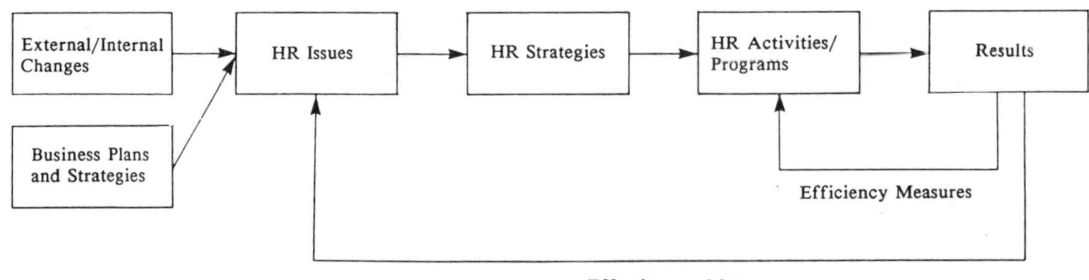

Figure 1: Human Resource Planning Context

The manufacturing company studied used a human resource planning process to define specific issues, strategies, and actions in nine areas of human resource management: commitment to corporate mission and values, labor relations, union-free facilities, global management perspective, recruitment and staffing, compensation and benefits, organization design and improvement, training and development. The specific actions planned include:

o Introduce the use of attitude surveys to monitor and avoid potential union issues,
o Provide managers with briefings on international topics,
o Develop specific retention tactics for all key technical and high potential employees,
o Use employee groups to help design benefit changes to increase "buy in", and
o Develop compensation programs for technical employees to encourage technical growth and contribution.

These specific actions guide human resource activities on an ongoing basis and provide a specific set of objectives for the unit against which results and performance could be evaluated. Besides these more strategic, longer term activities, the function provides day to day services in specific, functional human resource areas which are also subject to evaluation.

Measuring Human Resource Efficiency

Implicit in human resource plans is the intent to achieve intended results at minimum cost and at optimal speed. In companies where the performance of the human resource function has been measured, typically measures of "productivity" or efficiency are used. These measures have included those relating to response time (e.g., average time required to fill an opening, time required to respond to a request for a job regrading), work volume (e.g., the number of applicants interviewed), and cost (e.g., cost per hire, cost per training hour).

Applications of cost-effectiveness measures have been a focus of research and company practice in recent years (Tsui and Gomez-Mejia, 1988). Efforts have also been made to apply utility analysis, a cost- benefit modeling process concerned with employee selection decisions, to the human resource function as a whole (Boudreau, 1988). Definition of measures, however, has not been consistent nor gained general acceptance. Many companies, including smaller companies, still do little if any measurement in human resource management.

By their very nature, efficiency measures are stated quantitatively, usually in terms of cost, response time, and output volume. Some companies concentrate on measures of efficiency simply because they can readily gather, analyze, and present the necessary data. It is also a common mindset of managers to look at such measures. As one executive stated, "If you don't know what else to measure, measure efficiency."

Companies use efficiency measures by comparing the current value of the indicators to past values (current performance to past performance), looking for such improvements as reduced cost, reduced response time, or increased volume. They also use these measures to compare performance across units (e.g., different divisions or with the company as a whole). Companies also compare measures with

COST

Source cost per hire
Cost per hire for specialized or minority recruiting programs
Total cost per interview (management and staff time included)
Cost per relocation
Ratio of compensation expense to total operating expense
Benefit cost per employee covered (measured for each type of benefit)
Ratio of benefits costs to total payroll costs
Ratio of benefits expense to total operating expense
Processing costs per benefit claim
Administration costs per employee covered
Administration costs per benefit claim
Direct and indirect hiring and internal replacement costs
Cost per trainee per program
Cost per training day

QUANTITY

Number of hires
Number of special hires (e.g., minorities, females)
Number of interviews conducted to get one call back
Number of positions filled vs. open
Ratio of filled positions to authorized positions
Number of appraisals completed
Percent of appraisals completed
Percent of jobs having formal, current job descriptions
Percent of jobs with current evaluations
Number of unevaluated positions or positions awaiting regrading
Total claims processed per staff member (for each type of claim)
Number of training days

TIMELINESS

Response time (between requisition and a candidate interview)
Fill time (between requisition and start date for candidate)
Number of late appraisals
Time between benefit claim submission and payment
Elapsed time to develop and deliver a training program
Time required to develop/generate human resource information reports

Figure 2: Efficiency Measures Used in Human Resource Functions

those of other companies where there is commonality of measures (e.g., through a benchmarking process). Companies in some industries regularly share information on such measures, often through association surveys or informal contacts. The Society for Human Resource Management sponsors a survey data base on selected human resource performance measures.

In the context of human resource planning, efficiency measures relate results achieved to specific human resource actions (see Figure 2). Efficiency is expressed in terms of results achieved in relation to the resource inputs. Various activities and programs (e.g., training, recruiting, and salary administration) are examined considering the results achieved (e.g., cost per trainee, cost per hire, and time needed to re-evaluate a position).

RECRUITING AND SELECTION

Number of candidates interviewed per position
Ratio of offers accepted to offers extended
Number of "good" hires (tenure or performance after the first year)
Distribution of "good" hires per source
Ratio of call backs per interview per source
Average tenure per hire of hires who stay for a minimum desired
period of time
Percent of hires who are outstanding second year performers
Cost per hire that stays three or more years

INTERNAL PLACEMENT/STAFFING

Job posting response rate (applications per posted job)
Job posting hire rate (percent of posted jobs filled with candidates
   identified through the posting process)
Internal hire rate (e.g., percent of jobs filled internally)
Number of candidates selected from a succession plan

PERFORMANCE MANAGEMENT

Distribution of performance ratings
Percent of objectives that are clear and well-written
Extent performance objectives are linked to business plans
Extent performance objectives are met or exceeded
Extent to which stated development activities are implemented
Extent to which management and employee self ratings coincide
Average rating history/trends by unit/function

COMPENSATION

Percent of employees over salary grade maximum (e.g., red circles)
Percent of individuals under salary grade minimum
Extent to which managers feel they attract the talent they require
Extent to which actual salaries match the salary grid/salary model
Extent to which turnover is based on salary issues
Extent to which no one leaves to take higher paying jobs elsewhere

TRAINING AND DEVELOPMENT

Training hours per employee
Extent employees/managers feel training meets development needs
Difference in performance ratings before and after training
Depth of management talent "benchstrength"
Number of qualified successors per position

Figure 3: Measures of Effectiveness

To increase efficiency when necessary, companies change human resource activities or programs (such as changing training course structure in order to reduce cost per training hour or focusing recruiting on the most productive sources). Because companies are seeking to reduce staff expense, opportunities to improve efficiency are considered very important.

Efficiency measures can be defined for each functional area of human resources. A list of measures used in the companies surveyed is shown in Figure 3. They include such measures as average cost per hire, cost per training hour, and average time required to fill openings. There are numerous publications describing such measures and their application (Fitz-enz, 1984; Spencer, 1986; Cascio, 1982).

Overall measures of the efficiency of the human resource function are also used by companies. Some define trends (usually expressed as ratios) that relate human resource costs to profit, revenue, or other business indicators (Dahl, 1988). The interpretation of such measures is difficult, however. Conceptually, spending on recruiting, training, or other human resource activities could be reduced to zero (thus increasing efficiency drastically) but the effect of such reductions would be disastrous in the longer term. Another frequently used measure of overall efficiency of the function is the ratio of professional (exempt) human resource staff to total employees in the organization. The analysis and interpretation of this measure can be influenced by several factors, however (e.g., differences in human resource activities performed by staff in the units measured) (Walker, 1988).

Efficiency measures help functions measure their contribution to the business, but only in terms of immediate resource utilization. Efficiency measures relate most directly to the day to day activities and actions of the function.

Measuring Human Resource Effectiveness

Effectiveness is the extent to which the human resource function supports the successful implementation of long term business plans and strategies. In practice, companies define the human resource strategies needed to address critical human resource issues that arise from the environment or business plans and strategies. The criticality of these issues and appropriateness of strategies may change as priorities and conditions change (Walker, 1990). Hence the definition of effectiveness in each company depends on the focus of its issues and strategies.

Effectiveness measures relate results achieved to human resource issues and strategies (i.e., the effect of human resource activities on the achievement of business objectives). Results of various activities and programs are examined in terms of how well human resource issues are being resolved (i.e., "Are the issues going away?")

One company studied suggested that the most effective function is one that sees that there are no pressing human resource issues concerning management. The most proactive, strategic approach to managing resources anticipates and addresses emerging issues before the "pain" is felt. Usually, however, there are issues to be addressed. Through human resource planning, the function may bring these issues to management's attention and create a sense of urgency for action.

In contrast to efficiency measures, effectiveness measures are usually judgmental and qualitative. They are defined and used in terms of management expectations and perceptions. They represent a higher order of performance evaluation, but evaluation of the performance of the human resource function, nonetheless.

The Service Dimension

Many of the activities of a human resource function are services provided to customers, internal or external. These multiple "constituencies" have expectations of the function which shape the definition of effective performance. In these cases, the functions that are most effective are those that consistently meet or exceed the expectations of their constituents.

The results of our study track closely with those of a study by Anne Tsui (Tsui, 1987). Several criteria for evaluating the effectiveness of the human resource function were identified through discussions with senior managers:

- o Level of cooperation from the function,
- o Line managers' opinions regarding the effectiveness of the function,
- o Quickness and effectiveness of responses to each question brought to the function,
- o Rating of quality of information and advice provided to senior management,
- o Satisfaction and dissatisfaction of clients, managers and employees,
- o Degree to which the department has a strategy to support local management business plans in relation to human resources,
- o Average time to fill requisitions,
- o The degree to which the function is open and available to employees to deal with problems, and
- o Employees' trust and confidence in the human resource function.

This varied mix of factors indicates that customers of the human resource function define service quality in many ways. It is little wonder, then, that human resource functions vary widely in the ways they define and measure their effectiveness. Where a company-wide "total quality management" process exists, a staff group can define more rigorously its internal customers' expectations and standards. Subsequently it can measure how well it is meeting those expectations. It also provides a basis for ongoing dialogue and negotiation among staff and client users of staff services. None of the companies studied had such a process in place, although quality processes are being introduced or more fully developed in each.

Management Perceptions

One of the best ways to measure human resource effectiveness is to obtain the perceptions of managers regarding the quality of services provided by the human resource function. In each company studied, human resource staff has solicited perceptions of managers regarding the effectiveness of the function. In two, formal studies were conducted that involved interviews done by an outside consultant. In the others, regular discussions with managers are held on an continuing basis that solicit inputs, concerns, and feedback. Examples of each of two of these approaches are described below.

One company surveyed managers in detail regarding their perceptions of more than 80 defined activities of the human resource staff. The survey gathered managers' perceptions of the level of effort expended on each activity by human resource staff (i.e., amount of time and resources devoted) and their opinions regarding the results attained (i.e., extent to which their needs had been met). The survey also asked for narrative comments on opportunities for improvement (e.g., the most significant human resource challenge facing the organization, activities on which HR should spend more/less time on, the one change that should be made in the way the HR staff operates to increase effectiveness). Finally, the survey asked managers to rate the extent to which the staff has demonstrated specific capabilities "relative to your needs", in these specific terms:

- o Knowledge of the business (e.g., business perspective, external relations, strategic perspective, financial perspective, information management);

o Management of change (e.g., vision, planning and organizing, decision making, managing performance, communicating, adaptability); and

o Human resource practices (i.e., capabilities to perform the various activities listed earlier).

The human resource staff serving those units also completed the survey, indicating the level of effort that they perceive they expend, the results they perceive they achieve, and the extent to which they demonstrate required capabilities. The survey responses from managers were summarized by unit and compared with the aggregate response of the human resource staff serving that unit. Differences in perceptions provided a basis for staff discussion and planning in an off-site retreat. Through the survey, human resource staff gained insights into management views of the effectiveness of the function and addressed areas requiring improvement.

Another company restructured and repositioned the human resource function in response to concerns raised by managers in several senior management meetings. A task force comprised of line managers and human resource representatives conducted a detailed review of the function's activities and priorities and established a series of clear expectations that would be used to assess staff effectiveness:

o Human resources are largely decentralized and oriented to the business units;

o Authority and responsibility for human resource actions are clearly defined for business units;

o Changes in employee benefit programs are effectively communicated and implemented;

o Relocation policies effectively support management moves;

o The job evaluation system gives appropriate weight to technical, managerial, and other factors;

o Management looks inside the company for talent before recruiting outside;

o Performance and development reviews are fulfilling their intended purposes;

o Appropriate and adequate supervisory training is provided;and

o Appropriate and adequate information on career development opportunities is provided professional and managerial employees.

The human resource function was then reorganized to better meet these expectations. Six months after the restructuring, the task force surveyed managers across the company to determine the extent to which these expectations had been met (e.g., Had the concerns been resolved?). These questions addressed the effectiveness of the function. The survey also gathered opinions regarding changes in the quality, quantity and timeliness of staff services (poorer, about the same, improved, etc.) in order to assess the efficiency of the function. Specific ratings were obtained for each functional area of human resources.

The survey provided a quantitative assessment of the effectiveness of the function in terms of specific dimensions defined by the task force as important. The survey also provided a benchmark for subsequent assessments, fostering the planning of continual improvement.

Implications for Measurement and Evaluation

All of the companies strive to relate human resource activities and programs to their business needs. However, they measure the impact of activities and programs (and thus the effectiveness of the human resource function) in different ways, according to the business focus.

Development of sales skills through training may directly increase sales. Organizational and job redesign may improve customer service, reduce the cost of doing business, or accelerate new product development. Changes in human resource policies and procedures may lower turnover rates. Each of these results (i.e., improved service, lower costs, and accelerated product development) may be measured in specific, quantitative terms. However, the specific contribution of human resource activities to them requires subjective judgment by managers.

However, all quantitative measures of effectiveness or efficiency have subjective elements -- in the nature of the data (e.g., opinion), in the collection of information at the source, or in the formulation or interpretation of the measure itself. A figure, a ratio, or a change in measures alone tells little. Interpretation or analysis of the measure must be based on comparisons to standards, over time, among units, or with benchmarks, thus bringing an element of judgment (or subjective evaluation) into play.

Often quantitative measures appear to be objective, but on closer examination both have significant subjective elements. Performance ratings are often numeric and companies sometimes perform quantitative analyses (such as averaging or creating rating distributions). Yet the rating itself is based on a manager's subjective opinion regarding individual performance. Similarly, the results of surveys are analyzed statistically and in great detail, but responses, though numeric, reflect the subjective opinions of the respondent. This does not detract from the prospective usefulness of the measures, it is merely acknowledgment of fact. Many financial indicators and reports are based on similarly subjective judgments and estimates (e.g., depreciated asset values, bad debts, inventory).

Human resource actions may be highly efficient (e.g., an extremely low cost per hire) yet at the same time ineffective (e.g., if those hires do not possess the skills required for the business). In one company studied, cost per hire was considered an inadequate measure of efficiency because a large number of employees were leaving soon after being hired or turned out to be poor performers. Instead, the cost per "good" hire is measured, with "good" defined subjectively in terms of desired minimum tenure (e.g., staying with the organization for at least three years) or performance rating (e.g., achieving at least a "meets expectations" rating after two years).

An "efficient" source of new hires (defined in terms of cost per hire) may indeed be quite ineffective when many of the employees that are hired do not stay with the organization for an adequate length of time. In these cases, the cost per hire was low, but the cost per hire that reaches minimum tenure was high. Similarly, cost per hire could be low, but if those employees do not perform adequately, the cost per employee achieving an acceptable performance rating in two years could also be quite high (if the bulk of those hires are poor performers).

Other similar measures of effectiveness and efficiency include the number of employees remaining in position for 18 months (critical to maintaining customer contact), the number of managers capable of completing supportive, well-documented performance plans (as opposed to simply measuring the number of plans completed or discussions held), and the number of qualified backups in management development pools (as opposed to simply counting the number of candidates).

As these examples show, the analysis of even highly quantifiable measures of effectiveness and efficiency must include a subjective, judgmental interpretation. As a result, the companies studied acknowledge that there is no absolutely objective measure of either human resource effectiveness or efficiency. They recognize that overemphasis on measurement can block views of the purpose of evaluation. Much like some company efforts to win the Baldrige award, companies strive to score well, not substantively improve quality.

Conclusion

Because the human resource function has multiple roles and constituents, it provides ongoing services which must be delivered efficiently. The function also provides leadership in defining and addressing human resource issues and developing human resource strategies required to implement business change.

The human resource function is increasing its use of both effectiveness and efficiency measures as diagnostic tools in managing these services. Efficiency and effectiveness measures, particularly information obtained from managers as customers, are useful in identifying needed improvements in human resource practices.

Efficiency measures are primarily quantitative (e.g., cost, response time, and output volume) and relate results to short term human resource activities. Effectiveness measures are primarily qualitative and relate results to the resolution of critical issues and the implementation of strategies. Both involve subjective judgment and perception by managers.

While objective measures are desirable, quantification alone offers no sure basis for evaluation. Companies have found that the best test of effectiveness lies in managerial perceptions of the human resource function's fit with strategic issues and plans, its service quality, and level of expense. These perceptions can be measured and presented quantitatively but must be interpreted using sound business judgment. Narrative comments of managers often provide greater insight into effectiveness and the subtleties of evaluation than do the statistics.

References

Boudreau, John W., "Utility Analysis," *Human Resource Management: Evolving Roles and Responsibilities* (Washington: Bureau of National Affairs, 1988), pp. 125-186.

Cascio, Wayne F., *Costing Human Resources: The Financial Impact of Behavior in Organizations* (Boston: Kent Publishing Col., 1982).

Dahl, Henry L., Jr., "Human Resource Cost and Benefit Analysis: New Power for Human Resource Approaches," *Human Resource Planning* (Vol. 11, No. 2), pp. 69-78.

Drucker, Peter F., *Management: Tasks, Responsibilities, and Practices* (New York: Harper & Row, 1973), pp. 45-46.

Evans, Paul A. L., "The Strategic Outcomes of Human Resource Management," *Human Resource Management*, Spring 1986 (Vol. 25, No. 1) pp. 149-167.

Fitz-enz, Jac, *Human Value Management* (San Francisco: Jossey-Bass, 1990)

Fitz-enz. Jac, *How to Measure Human Resource Management* (New York: McGraw-Hill, 1984)

Schuler, Randall S. and James W. Walker, "Human Resources Strategy: Focusing on Issues and Actions," *Organizational Dynamics* (Summer 1990), pp. 4 - 19.

Spencer, Lyle M., *Calculating Human Resource Costs and Benefits* (New York: John Wiley & Sons, 1986)

Tsui, Anne S., Defining the Activities and Effectiveness of the Human Resource Department: A Multiple Constituency Approach, *Human Resource Management* (Spring 1987), 35 - 70.

Tsui, Anne S. and Luis Gomez-Mejia, "Evaluating Human Resource Effectiveness," *Human Resource Management: Evolving Roles and Responsibilities* (Washington: Bureau of National Affairs, 1988), pp. 187-227.

Walker, James W., "Human Resource Planning, 90s Style," *Human Resource Planning* (Vol. 13, No. 4), pp. 229 - 240.

Walker, James W.,"How Large Should the HR Staff Be?" *Personnel* (October 1988), pp. 36 - 42.

Walker, James W.,, *Human Resource Planning* (New York: McGraw-Hill, 1980).

Why Measure the CEO's Performance

C.E. SCHNEIER, R.W. BEATTY, and D.G. SHAW

Introduction

A recent survey (Sibson, 1990) of 644 companies found that only 14 percent bother to evaluate their CEO's performance via any systematic process. Evidence also suggests that, for CEOs, negative consequences (i.e., dismissal, drastically lower pay) associated with poor performance are almost nonexistent (Jensen and Murphy, 1990). Finally, the relationship between CEO pay and company performance "is weakening" (Crystal, 1990; p. 94). Fifty five percent of the variance in CEO pay is not accounted for by company performance, size, business risk, company geographic location, or even CEO tenure.

Without relevant measures of performance, clear evidence that there are consequences for poor performance, and a close linkage from performance to pay, shareholders do not know *how* they are paying arguably the person in the most critical position in their companies; *what* they are paying for, and *why*.

The purpose of this paper is to review the state of CEO performance measurement and management (PMM). We argue for a definition of CEO performance that transcends measurement of company financial outcomes. The role of the CEO has broadened. It must include, for example, the inputs to financial outcomes, such as articulating and communicating a vision for the company. We provide a perspective on what type of performance should be measured at the CEO level and how it can be measured. Examples from specific companies are cited and discussed. A case study of a durable goods manufacturer is provided to illustrate our CEO PMM model.

Why Measure a CEO's Individual Performance?

A CEO's individual behavior influences, but is not the same as, his/her organization's performance. For any organization, the issue is not whether to measure CEO performance. It is what to measure, how to do so, and what to do with the results of the measurement. Financial performance of companies is, of course,

---

C.E. SCHNEIER and D.G. SHAW - Sibson & Company, Inc., 212 Carnegie Center, Princeton, NJ 08543; R.W. BEATTY - Institute of Management, Rutgers University, P.O. Box 5062, New Brunswick, NJ 08903-5062.

Bottom Line Results from Strategic Human Resource Planning
Edited by R.J. Niehaus and K.F. Price, Plenum Press, New York, 1991

TYPE OF PERFORMANCE MEASURE	LEVEL OF PERFORMANCE MEASUREMENT *	
	Organizational: **How well the organization performance**	**CEO (Individual):** **What the CEO does/directs**
Direct Financial	EPS ROE Revenue growth	Meet budgets Award stock options Add/eliminate staff
Nonfinancial	Product quality Customer satisfaction Corporate culture	Set strategic direction Develop "bench strength" Articulate values

Figure 1: Organizational and CEO (Individual) Performance, Mutual Influences. *Illustrative, not Exhaustive

always measured and the CEO's performance is hence inferred from financial performance. Organizational performance is not the same as the CEO's (individual) performance. As Figure 1 shows, a distinction can also be made between financial and non-financial performance. The items in the four cells of the figure do, however, influence each other. For example, increasing quality could impact budgets, which in turn could impact returns, which in turn could require elimination of staff, which could, in turn, affect "bench strength."

The interactive nature of Figure 1 would seem to complicate the CEO appraisal picture. However, the real issue for measuring individual CEO performance, as distinct from organizational performance, is to focus on what the CEO individually does or directs to be done or not to be done. Anything on the right side of Figure 1 could be part of the CEO's individual performance. The behaviors/

CEO INDIVIDUAL BEHAVIORS/DECISIONS	IMPACT ON ORGANIZATION PERFORMANCE *		
	Indirect (Culture)	**Direct (Income Statement)**	**Direct and Immediate** (Balance Sheet)**
	Communicating vision/values	Increasing prices	Repurchasing shares
	Setting succession criteria	Setting R&D budget	Decreasing dividend
	Personally providing recognition	Downsizing	Acquiring assets

Figure 2: The Impact of CEO Behavior/Decisions on Organizational Performance. *Illustrative, not Exhaustive. **Typically Involve Board

LEADERS	MANAGERS
Set direction	Plan and budget
Align people	Organize and staff
Motivate people	Control and problem solve

Figure 3: What Leaders and Managers Do (After Kotter, 1990)

decisions of the individual CEO all affect organization performance, but in varying degree of immediacy and directness (see Figure 2).

CEO leadership is not the same as management. Organization observers and scholars (e.g., Zalesnik, 1977; Kotter, 1990) have differentiated between leadership and management. Management is rational, systematic, and planning oriented. Data is critical to a manager's success and the manager's many systems provide data. Hence, performance measurement can be a rational and orderly process, as comparing actual to budgeted results. Zalesnik (1977) explains:

> It takes neither genius nor heroism to be a manager, but rather persistence, tough-mindedness, hard work, intelligence, analytical ability and perhaps most important, tolerance and good will (p.6). The influence a leader exerts in altering moods, evoking images and expectations, and in establishing specific desires and objectives determines the direction a business takes (p.9).

Nadler and Tushman (1990) include more traditional aspects of management (e.g., controlling, rewarding, structuring) in their notion of "transformational" leaders and Kotter (1990) argues that leadership "compliments" management. Based on the above descriptions, few would argue that management is more easily measured than leadership (see Figure 3).

Leadership "counts": organization performance is impacted by individual behavior. Leadership remains one of the most intensively researched areas in the management literature, with data emerging from thousands of experiments (see e.g., Bass, 1989, for a comprehensive review), as well as in-depth observations (see e.g., Vancil, 1987).

One of the most controversial streams of leadership research relates to the issue of whether and to what extent a leader impacts organization performance. A landmark 1972 study (Lieberson and O'Connor, 1972) found that mattered little, and was reinforced by subsequent research (e.g., Salancek and Pfeffer, 1977). Recent studies (e.g., Weimer, 1978; Thomas, 1988) have found that the results of the Lieberson and O'Connor research were artifactual. It is essentially dependent on the order variables were entered into the statistical analysis.

More important, however, for the purpose of this paper, recent work strongly supports the notion that leadership counts. As an individual CEO's decision making style, business strategies, and influence tactics are observed, differences in his or

Table 1: A CEO's Vision and Organization Performance: Examples from Some Visible CEO's (Source: *Business Week*, April 1990)

CEO	COMPANY	VISION	ROE (%)*	INDUSTRY AVERAGE ROE (%)*	PERCENT GREATER THAN INDUSTRY AVERAGE
Bill Marriott	Marriott	Service	21.6%	9.2%	134%
Ray Vogelos	Merck	Invest in R&D for long term	44.8	23.8	88
Jack Welch	GE	Boundaryless, small company culture	18.9	15.8	20
Bob Crandall	AMR	Business traveler service	12.5	7.6	64
J. B. McCoy	BancOne	Customer service; new technology	15.8	10.3	53
Don Kearns	Xerox	Total quality	14.0	8.9	57

her organization's performance have been seen (e.g., Bennis and Nanus, 1985; Kotter, 1988; Peters and Austin, 1985). CEO's with a clear and well communicated "vision" for their organizations, translated easily into observable behavior, have been able to drive both culture change and resultant financial results (see Table 1).

Visible CEO behavior has a profound impact on the direction their company's take. For that reason, the performance that direction yields, a CEO's individual performance should be assessed.

CEO RESPONSIBILITY	ILLUSTRATION
Chief Culture Change Agent/Catalyst	Jack Welch, GE "The winners of the nineties will be those who can develop a culture that allows them to move faster, communicate more clearly, and involve everyone in a focused effort to serve ever more demanding customers." (Fortune, March 26, 1990)
Chief Values Communicator	Robert Haas, Levi Strauss "It's the ideas of a business that are controlling, not some manager with authority. Values provide a common language for aligning a company's leadership and its people. My personal philosophy is to suboptimize business decisions. When you do that, suddenly the traditional hard values of business success and the nontraditional soft values relating to people start blending. (Harvard Business Review, Sep.–Oct., 1990)
Chief Organizational Architect	John Reed, Citicorp "We've come up with a way to deal with Japan, Europe, and North America as a seamless market with no geography, a truly global approach to corporate business." (Harvard Business Review, Nov.–Dec., 1990)
Chief Competitive and External Environmental Monitor	Alain Gomez, Thomson "A CEO has no specialty. An organization is neither an island nor inert. It is a living system interrelated to a set of wider systems. The CEO's task is to monitor how the company is attuned to the outside world (and how it is renewing itself internally)." (Harvard Business Review, May–June, 1990, parentheses added)
Chief Manager of Systems and Performance	T. J. Rodgers, Cyress Computer "Most companies don't fail for lack of talent on strategic vision. The fail for lack of execution . . . At Cyress, our management systems track . . . performance so regularly and in such detail . . . We don't go over budget — ever." (Harvard Business Review, July–August, 1990).

Figure 4: The Emerging Role of the CEO: Some Examples

Table 2: Board Member Views of CEO Performance Measurement

	PERCENT OF BOARD MEMBERS RANKING CRITICAL TO CEO SUCCESS
QUALITATIVE PERFORMANCE MEASURES	
Establishing Strategic Direction	86%
Building Management Team	84
Leadership Quality	79
Providing for Succession	75
Implementing Strategy	64
QUANTITATIVE (FINANCIAL) PERFORMANCE MEASURES	
EPS Over Two to Five Years	64
Total Shareholder Return	56
Return on Invested Capital	41
Return Measure Trends	40
Return on Equity	33

*Boards, Company Performance, and Executive Pay (Princeton, NJ: Sibson & Company, Inc., 1988), n = 600+.

The CEO role has broadened beyond financial and strategic decisions to chief values communicator and culture change agent. There have always been CEO's who set a change agenda. Recently, however, the emphasis on the (large company) CEO as secluded, unapproachable, and steeped in strategic and financial plans is giving way. By their own admission, many CEO's see themselves as strategic actors, not merely strategic thinkers, as architects of cultural change, and as the key single person who must articulate the vision and values of the company (see Figure 4).

Jack Welch of GE, Robert Haas of Levi Strauss, and Rod Canion of Compaq Computer are notable examples. These CEO's view their jobs as setting a cultural and change agenda, not just a strategic and financial one. They are sensitive to the power of their behavior and the message it sends. They use their visibility, approachability, and actions to send their message.

For all the talk about keeping stock prices up and quarterly earnings growing, CEO's themselves view other, non-financial issues as important, according both to what they say (e.g., Table 2) and survey results. A 1990 Business International survey found that 53 percent of the CEO's see customer satisfaction as their greatest priority, with being a leader in quality second. In a 1989 Korn/Ferry and Columbia University survey, "strategy formulation" was the top ranking CEO skill needed in the year 2000, with "human resource management" ranking second. The chief concern of CEO's of large companies in a 1990 *Industry Week* survey was "quality."

Our research (see Schneier, 1991) shows that Board members rate the importance of four non-financial aspects of CEO performance above that of any of the financial aspects. Establishing a strategic direction and building a management team and the performance areas most often cited as critical or very critical to evaluating CEOs (see Table 2).

Table 3: Current Practice in CEO Performance Appraisal

INDUSTRY	PERCENT OF COMPANIES WITH NO FORMAL CEO APPRAISAL PROCESS
General Industry	86%
Durable Goods	83
Nondurable Goods	83
Services	91

*Facts and Issues in Executive Compensation (Princeton, NJ: Sibson & Company, Inc., 1990), n = 350+.

The State of CEO PMM

Is a measurement process used? For most large, publicly-held companies, a CEO's performance is not separated from that of the (short- term) financial performance of the organization. The percentage of companies of various industries that do not use a formal appraisal process for their CEO's is very high (see Table 3).

What is measured? Company financial performance seems to be the most common actual CEO performance measure, although Boards and leadership experts (see e.g., Eccles, 1990) argue for a much broader set of measures, as discussed above. In cases where non-financial measures are used, they are not weighted as high as financial measures (see Table 4).

Some CEO's have made it difficult for their Boards to rely solely on short-term financial objectives as they have gone public with a non- financial agenda. Jack Welch of GE has made public (e.g., Tichy and Charam, 1990) his personal dedication to changing GE's culture via his Work-Out initiative. He has even reported progress on the effort to financial analysts. Jim Robinson of American Express changed the corporate bylaws to name himself Chief Quality Officer. (How effectively Mr. Robinson and the company performs in the quality arena may not easily escape the Board's eyes at performance evaluation time.)

The CEO of Whirlpool has an appraisal system that includes both financial and non-financial measures. Scientific Atlanta's CEO has both financial and non-financial objectives on his appraisal screen and is assessed on strategic leadership and organizational changes.

Evidence is available indicating that CEO's could improve on the non-financial components of their job mentioned above. A recent survey reported in the *Wall Street Journal* found that 82% of the CEO's felt they effectively communicated strategy to their executive team. Less than one- third of the COO's and VP's who execute the strategies agreed. Nevertheless, organization-level, financial performance measures are the norm at the CEO levels.

Top executives at several companies are evaluated on non-financial performance criteria. Ashard Oil uses safety records, Aluminum Company of America uses environmental sensitivity, and Chemical Bank uses customer rating of service. Reuben Mark of Colgate-Palmolive evaluates his subordinates on

Table 4: Weighting of CEO Performance Measures

	PERCENT OF COMPANIES		
INDUSTRY	**Financial Measures Weighted More Heavily**	**Nonfinancial Measures Weighted More Heavily**	**Both Weighted Equally**
General Industry	70%	2%	28%
Durable Goods	74	0	26
Nondurable Goods	73	5	22
Services	71	13	26

*Annual Executive Compensation Report (Princeton, NJ: Sibson & Company, Inc., 1990), n = 350+.

individual and qualitative, non-financial measures (e.g., developing woman and minority managers). Constantine Nicandos of Conoco measures environmental action. Paul Allaire of Xerox ties business to customer satisfaction. All these companies' CEO's would have a difficult time ignoring non-financial criteria at their own level, given the data base evaluations of their direct reports provide.

Is performance tied to compensation? A key to effective individual performance measurement systems is a link from the results of the assessment to rewards, including compensation (Lawler, 1990; Beatty and Schneier, 1988). As noted above, most CEO appraisal practices violate this condition (see e.g., Crystal, 1990). However, the relationship between CEO performance and pay requires some explanation. Most of the data supporting a weak relationship between CEO pay and "CEO performance" indicate that organization-level and financial performance, not what an individual CEO does or does not do, as the primary performance criterion (e.g., Crystal, 1990; Jensen and Murphy, 1990).

The strongest correlate to pay was organization structure, not performance, in one study of 100 corporation's over a four-year time period (Leonard, 1990). Companies with more layers paid more at the top. Crystal (1990) studied company financial performance, stock price volatility, company size, geographic location (i.e., Manhattan-based or not), CEO tenure, and industry pay levels. Unexplained variance in CEO pay was higher than the variance explained by the model's variables noted here. Jensen and Murphy (1990) studied the sensitivity of CEO pay changes on company performance in the 430 largest public corporations and found CEO pay relatively insensitive or changes in company performance.

Why the CEO Individual Performance Measurement Process Is Weak

Qualitative aspects of performance are more difficult to measure. Few would argue that earnings per share is more easily measured than "strategic leadership." Accounting and finance departments must collect and scrutinize financial data regardless of CEO performance measurement considerations, and they have perfected their craft. Companies are novices at measuring the less obvious aspects of performance.

Boards are seldom in a position to observe individual CEO behavior. As the late Harold Geneen of ITT pointed out, "How can they form a fair judgment if nearly all their information comes from the Chief Executive himself?" Particularly for outside directors, they rarely see the CEO in action except at board meetings.

Board members are often CEO's themselves: The fox is guarding the hen house. Confronting the CEO is not part of most boards' culture or politics. Jensen and Murphy (1990) cite studies showing that in only 20 of 500 cases was a CEO actively fired for poor performance. There was little difference in dismissal percentages between high and low performing companies. Lockheed is an instructive case here. Despite obvious poor corporate performance (i.e., three-year average annual total return to shareholders = -1.9%), directors entrenched management (and themselves) further via stock ownership, a "poison pill" defense, and charter provision changes that "removed all accountability of the management to shareholders" (*Business Week,* April 16, 1990). Lockheed's board consisted of two former CEOs and of course the current CEO. None were likely to criticize the policies they developed. Many board members owe their prestigious and lucrative board seats to their relationship with the CEO, a fact tough to ignore at CEO appraisal time.

Interlocking directorates are commonplace. A CEO appraisal system too candid, too closely tied to a CEO's "style," too subjective, and which ties CEO pay too closely to company performance could be simply too easily copied at the board member's own company. This may not be perceived as a welcomed trend by many CEOs, often beneficiaries of rather insensitive appraisal systems.

Case Study: Measuring the Performance of the Head of a Durable Goods Manufacturer

The Business. A long-standing midwestern business (to be called "Transport"), with overseas operations and revenues in excess of one billion dollars, saw a change in the top job two years ago. Financial performance was unstable during the 1980's, with severe problems occurring in the recession of 1982 and a subsequent downsizing of half the exempt labor force. The late 1980s show Transport's workforce at 1500 exempt and 6000 nonexempt. The business manufactured a limited number of very large, technically complex products for the transportation industry, with one product group accounting for the vast majority of the revenue. Substantial revenues also came from sales, service, and leasing.

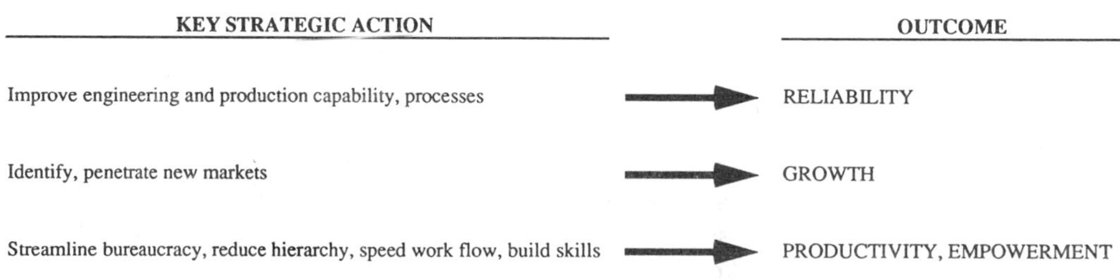

Figure 5: Transport's Goals

Heroes	Expend enormous effort
Way to Win	Lowered costs, reduced quality
External Customers	The enemy
Internal Customers	Insensitive
Suppliers	Source of cost savings
Reliability	Not at expense of cost
Management Style	Benign neglect, with fiefdoms
Communication	Give orders down, filter messages up
Conflict	Ignore
Cooperation	Within not across functions
Authority	Based on position/title
Accountability	To identify scapegoats
Failure	Blame others

Figure 6: Transport's Culture

The Business Issues. Over the last decade, Transport, partly because of its cash-poor position and hence low investment in development, lost its once significant technological competitive advantage. In addition, its inability to invest in plant and equipment, its outmoded production facility, and its failure to attract bright new engineering and manufacturing talent, hurt product reliability. Customers, themselves financially pinched, began to look not only at Transport's prices, but also their products costs over the life of their use. Poor reliability drove those costs beyond that of the competition.

On the human resource side, years of downsizings and inadequate recruiting left the workforce shaken and insecure, with key skills missing. In short, Transport was a classic Rust Belt company with its once glorious past all but forgotten, hanging on to solvency by a thread. High start-up costs deterred competitors, and investors with deep pockets provided Transport much needed capital to continue operations.

The Business Objectives. The new business leader saw cultural, financial, and production imperatives (see Figure 5). The corporate culture was seen as the biggest obstacle to success (see Figure 6) and hence was the first target for change. However, it was obvious that culture change would be slow and customers and investors had little patience.

Developing Transport's Business Leader Performance Measures: Strategy Execution. The business leader saw both financial and non-financial goals as equally important. Relying solely on short-term, financial problem "treatments" (e.g., across-the-board budget cuts) could lower costs but would not fundamentally augment Transport's capability to compete. Longer-term, cultural "cures" had to be

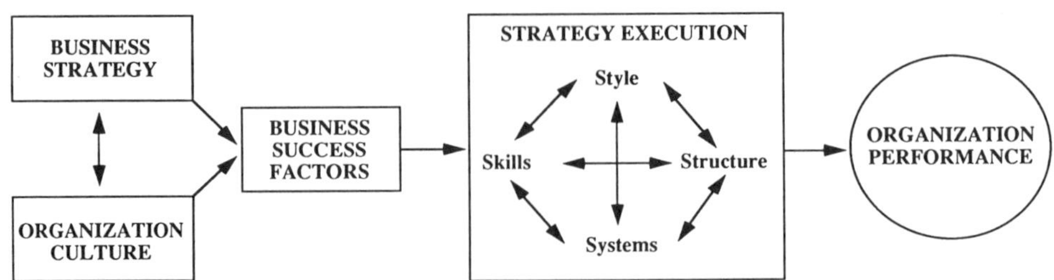

Figure 7: CEO Performance Based on Strategy Execution

addressed as well. In arguing for a balanced approach, the business leader viewed his role as "Chief of Strategy Execution."

Strategy dictated a set of "Business Success Factors" - factors necessary to execute strategy and succeed as a corporation. Because these were at the organizational level, they were appropriate as the performance measures for the business leader. Each of the four areas Transport deemed essential to execute strategy (see Figure 7). The business leader's major objective was to impact the "Business Success Factors" via leading the organization as it executed strategy.

For example, he changed the compensation and performance appraisal systems in the sourcing unit to recognize and reward choosing suppliers based on quality, not the historical measure of lowest price. He redesigned the organization structure to require specialists in engineering and manufacturing to work with those in marketing and sales to assure that what was sold could be built at the right margins and on time. He revamped the delivery system for skills development from training for functional expertise to process-mapping and continuous improvement.

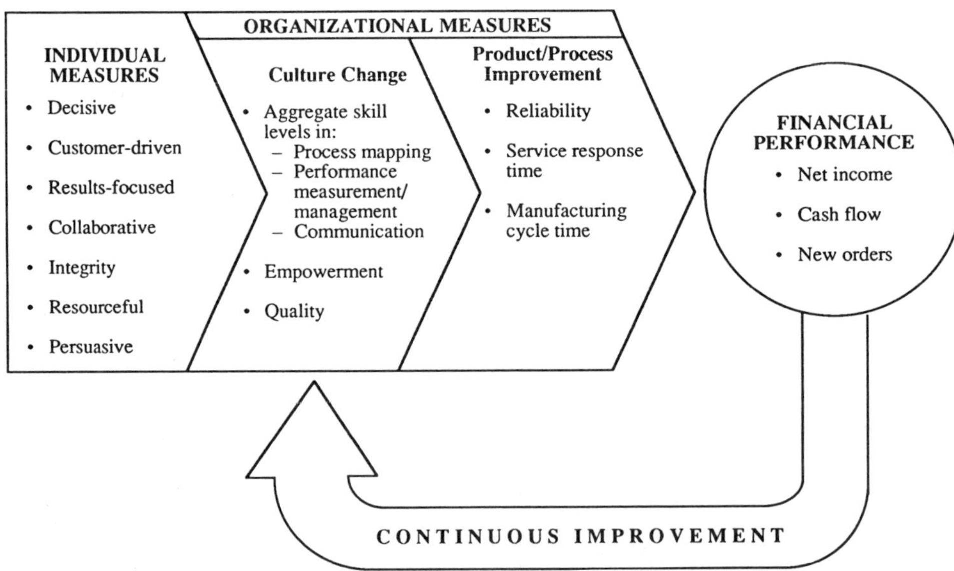

Figure 8: Transport's CEO Performance Measurement and Management System (Specific mesurement targets and methods were developed for each criterion; lists are illustrative, not exhaustive)

He defined the high-trust, candid, high discretion style he wanted, and practiced it himself. The resultant CEO appraisal system from a leadership in strategy execution perspective appears as Figure 8.

How the System Worked. The effectiveness of Transport's business leader PMM system must be evaluated on several levels. First, did individual and organizational performance improve? The business leader's subordinates were given a survey instrument to assess his behavior change. Marked improvements were noted by them after one year. Culture change was assessed via survey and focus groups, with market improvements seen even after 18 months. For example, 59% of those surveyed said they were using the process improvement tools they had learned. Ratings of the leaders' communication style and effectiveness, as provided by their subordinates, showed considerable improvement. Product and process improvements were also notable. As an illustration, one key product component required an average of 8.6 hours of rework before process improvement and only 2.8 hours after the process was redesigned. Defects in the main motor of the product were reduced by 63%. Service response time went from 75% of responses within 14 days to 75% responses within 72 hours.

A second aspect of the new PMM system was whether the system had a positive impact on other, related systems. Because of the business leader's insistence on using both financial and non-financial performance measures at his level, a heretofore marginal performance management system throughout Transport was revitalized. New performance measures, based on Business Success Factors and the business leader's culture change objectives, were injected into the appraisal criteria of all managers.

These measures provided relevance and specificity, as well as higher performance hurdles for teams and individuals. Knowing the boss is taking appraisal seriously provides needed credibility for the performance management process at all levels. Since the business leader's annual incentive pay was linked to financial and non-financial of appraisal criteria, tying performance to pay at all levels was more effective.

Did the system assist the organization execute its strategy? Transport's organizational-level indicators in product/process improvement and financial performance indicated successful strategy execution. As Figure 7 shows, strategy execution is made possible by changes in structure, systems, skills, and style. At least in part because the business leader was being measured on a variety of criteria, changes in these four areas were made possible, if not imperative. For example, if the business leader is being measured on improvement and communication, his subordinates' style comes into question. As discussed above, each was changed to some extent, at the initiative of the business leader and others, in order to meet the performance targets.

CEO PMM Systems: Necessary Conditions for Success

At the best-run companies, CEO performance is more than just a numbers game. Companies that have broadened their CEO PMM systems beyond financial criteria have certain characteristics in common. Some of them are no doubt necessary for any PMM system to work, at any level in the company. Others are necessary for organization change to succeed. Still others are unique to the CEO position. Key CEO PMM success factors are:

1. *Board of Directors involvement.* It is the Board, or a Board Committee, that evaluates the CEO. Key Board accountabilities include their: (a) understanding of what should be measured in order for both the CEO and the company to succeed, (b) skill at the PMM process (e.g., data gathering, performance review), and (c) willingness to be candid and constructive regarding how well their CEO is doing.

2. *Linkage of individual CEO performance to consequences.* There is an obvious relationship between CEO individual behavior and performance and a company's performance. At least part of the CEO's rewards should be based on how well he/she does at the critical tasks of, for example, building "bench strength" and communicating vision. In any given quarter, or even year, these efforts may not show up on the income statement or balance sheet. If they are not rewarded, it is too easy to de-emphasize them and hence hurt the long-term viability of the business.

3. *A compelling need to change current PMM practice.* Most companies still rely exclusively on financial measures for CEO PMM. Their CEOs and their Boards need to see a reason to change. Poor financial performance often provides motivation to fix the financials. Little interest in non-financial performance measures may be seen in times of financial crisis. Visionary CEOs like David Kearns of Xerox and Jack Welch of GE have seen the imperatives of both culture change and financial performance for their companies. Without the latter, there is no present, without the former, there is no future. A visionary CEOs passion, a strategic shift, a merger or acquisition, or a similar need is hence required to change the CEO PMM status quo.

4. *Specific and quantifiable performance data from multiple sources.* In order to make CEO PMM work using non-financial measures, data must be gathered from subordinates, customers, board members, and other relevant constituents. A typical CEO has a penchant for data. Non-financial CEO measures will have little credibility with the CEO or the Board unless they are more than anecdotal. What evidence is there that strategy and values have been communicated, are understood, and are being acted upon? The CEO PMM system must provide accurate evidence on CEO performance. Without it, the Board will be loathe to confront its CEO or powerless to help him/her improve.

5. *Linkage to PMM systems below the CEO.* PMM at the CEO level is without a context or foundation unless it is carried out at levels below the CEO. To continue the example cited above, developing successors is something not only the CEO but other executives must do as well. If those below the CEO do not develop successors, too few candidates will be available high enough in the hierarchy for the CEO to develop.

6. *Relevant company best practices.* Partly because most Boards are made up of at least some CEO's and partly because non-financial aspects of CEO PMM are often breaking new ground, other companies' experiences can be not only instructive but also reduce concerns about the process. Board

members' own companies are a potential source of best practices. Most CEOs have relationships with peers in other companies and can obtain some suggestions and cautions from their colleagues.

7. *Measures that facilitate strategy execution.* The CEO PMM system's non-financial measures should be driven by what is required to execute strategy and sustain competitive advantage. If product reliability is a "business success factor," the CEO's role in communicating its importance, committing resources to it, and holding executives accountable for improving it should be measured. A laundry list of generic executive "traits" is far less credible than a carefully developed, small set of measures that truly drive success in a specific organization. Like all members of organizations, the CEO's performance is continuously evaluated. The key decisions relate to: on what basis, according to what standards, by whom, by what mechanism, and for what purpose. The Board and CEO must ask and answer these questions. Quarterly company financial measures are necessary, but not sufficient. They rarely tell the whole story at the CEO level.

References

Annual Executive Compensation Report (Princeton: Sibson & Company, Inc., 1990).

Bass, B. M. *Stogdill's Handbook of Leadership* (NY: Free Press, 1990).

Beatty, R. W. and C. E. Schneier, "Strategic Performance Management Issues," In R. Schuler and S. Youngblood (Eds.), *Personnel and Human Resource Management* (St. Paul: West, 1988), 256-266.

Bennis, W. and B. Nanus *Leaders* (NY: Harper Row, 1985).

Bere, James F. *The CEO's Job: The Difference Between Motion and Movement,* (Chicago: A. T. Kearney, Inc., 1986), 18.

Burchman, Seymour J. and Craig E. Schneier, "Assessing CEO Performance: It Goes Beyond the Numbers," *Directors & Boards,* 13, (2), 15.

Crystal, Graef, S., "Seeking the Sense in CEO Pay," *Fortune,* June 5, 1989, 90104.

Crystal, Graef S., "The Great CEO Pay Sweepstakes," *Fortune,* June 18, 1990, 94102.

Deutsch, Claudia H., "Using Money to Change Executive Behavior," *New York Times,* May 20, 1990.

Dobrzynski, Judith H. and Eric Schine, "Lockheed's Lesson: It's Open Season on Yes-Man Boards," *Business Week,* April 16, 1990, 25.

Eccles, Robert G., "The Performance Measurement Manfesto," *Harvard Business Review,* January February 1991, 131137.

Howard, Robert, "Values Make the Company: An Interview with Robert Haas," *Harvard Business Review,* September October 1990, 133144.

Jensen, Michael C. and Kevin J. Murphy, "CEO Incentives - It's Not How Much You Pay, But How," *Harvard Business Review,* May June 1990, 138153.

Kotter, J. P. *A Force for Change,* (NY: Free Press, 1990).

Kotter, J. P. *The Leadership Factor* (NY: Free Press, 1988).

Kotter, John P., "What Leaders Really Do," *Harvard Business Review,* May June 1990, 103111.

Lawler, E. E. *Strategic Pay* (SF: JosseyBass, 1990).

Leonard, J. S., "Executive Pay and Firm Performance," In R. G. Ehrenberg (Ed.), *Do Compensation Policies Matter?* (Ithaca: ILR Press, 1990), 1329.

Lieberson, S., and J. F. O'Connor, "Leadership and Organizational Performance," *American Sociological Review,* **37,** 1972, 117130.

Nadler, D. A. and M. L. Tushman, "Beyond the Charismatic Leader," *California Management Review,* **33,** Winter, 1990, 7797.

"Pay Stubs of the Rich and Corporate," *Business Week,* May 7, 1990, 56108.

Peters, T. and N. Austin *A Passion for Excellence* (NY: Random House, 1985).

Rodgers, T. J., "No Excuses Management," *Harvard Business Review,* July August 1990, 8498.

Salanick, G. R. and J. Pfeffer, "Constraints on Administrator Discretion," *Urban Affairs Quarterly,* **12,** 1977, 475498.

Schneier, Craig E. "Executing Strategy: The New Battleground in Business Competition," In C. E. Schneier (Ed.), *Human Resource Strategies for the 1990's* (NY: American Management Association, 1990), 115.

Schneier, Craig E. "Measuring and Assessing Top Executive Performance," In M. Rock and G. Berger (Eds.), *Compensation Handbook,* 3rd ed. (NY: McGraw Hill, 1990), 521532.

Thomas, Alan Berkeley, "Does Leadership Make a Difference to Organizational Performance?," *Administrative Science Quarterly,* **57,** 1988, 388400.

Tichy, Noel and Ram Charan, "Citicorp Faces the World: An Interview with John Reed," *Harvard Business Review,* November December 1990, 135144.

"Today's Leaders Look to Tomorrow," *Fortune,* March 26, 1990, 3036.

Vancil, R. F. *Passing the Baton* (Boston: Harvard Business School Press, 1987).

Webber, Alan M., "Consensus, Continuity, and Common Sense: An Interview With Compaq's Rod Canion," *Harvard Business Review,* July August 1990, 115123.

Weiner, N. and T. A. Mahoney, "A Model of Corporate Performance as a Function of Environmental, Organizational, and Leadership Influences," *Academy of Management Journal,* **24,** 1981, 453470.

Zaleznik, Abraham, "Managers and Leaders: Are they Different?," *Harvard Business Review,* May June 1977, 112.

Company Values:
A Key to Managing in Turbulent Times

D.J. McLAUGHLIN, B.C. McLAUGHLIN, and C. WILCOX LISCHICK

Introduction

The recent war with Iraq taught us many lessons, not the least of which is the power of belief. Shortly after the war ended a front-page article in *The New York Times* observed:

> The war provided a clarity and passion to Mr. Bush's leadership that had been missing. It was striking that Mr. Bush appeared to be acting from strong, unequivocal beliefs. The power of principle, the stark and vivid definition of purpose, allowed Mr. Bush to reverse the conventional wisdom, and turn a conflict that no one wanted at the outset into the most popular American war since the one he fought in (Dowd 1991).

The major themes of our paper are: (a) a company's values and beliefs are a pivotal element in its survival and success; (b) formal statements of values and beliefs include a wide range of philosophical and pragmatic material that can be analyzed and compared within an industry and across industry lines; (c) organizations with strong values -- companies that are truly value-driven -- out perform their competitors; and (d) successful companies appear to have distinctive values and beliefs.

The paper is organized in four parts. Drawing upon a three-year study of 555 large public companies, the first section describes the approaches companies take to state formally their values and beliefs. The second section summarizes the available evidence on the relationship of values and beliefs to performance. The third section presents preliminary findings on the differences in the prevalence and scope of the values aspired to by the most and the least successful companies in four industries. The final section covers the unique role that values and beliefs can play in corporate revitalizations. An illustration is given of the prevalence of statements of values in companies that achieved a turnaround between 1985 and 1989.

D.J. McLAUGHLIN, B.C. McLAUGHLIN, and C. WILCOX LISCHICK
McLaughlin & Company, Inc., 19 N. Main Street, P.O. Box 365, Essex., CT 06426

Formal Statements of Values

In 1987, two of us were invited to the People's Republic of China to lecture for a week on human resource policies and strategies of successful American companies (McLaughlin 1987). In our preparatory meetings with the Chinese representatives, discussions of human resource strategy or best HR practices bogged down in a cross-cultural mire caused by radically different political, social, and economic systems. It was not until we got to a higher level of abstraction -- core human values, basic assumptions about people, overall management philosophies -- that we began to lay the groundwork for a meaningful exchange.

To prepare for our lectures in China, we surveyed the extensive literature on company culture and corporate values (in particular, Schwartz and Davis 1981; Deal and Kennedy 1982; and Kilmann, Saxton, and Serpa 1985). We also contacted the top human resource executives in twenty multibillion-dollar U.S. corporations, and asked them to identify the values and beliefs that underpinned their human resource and business strategies. Many of the companies included formal belief statements with their replies; the results of our survey were so intriguing that we decided to launch a broader research effort at some future date.

In 1989 we began a study of values and beliefs. Our initial focus was on very large industrial and service businesses with at least $1 billion in sales and financial institutions with at least $10 billion in assets. During the second stage of the data collection, we contacted all publicly held companies listed by Standard & Poor's in five industries (chemical, electrical/electronics, food, paper, and pharmaceutical).

Table 1: Financial Profile of Survey Group (94 Companies)

	CHEMICAL	ELECTRICAL/ ELECTRONICS	PAPER	PHARMACEUTICAL
NUMBER OF COMPANIES	30	23	25	16
Total Employment	628,000	1,028,000	416,800	460,000
Median Sales (millions)	$2.3	$1.5	$1.7	$4.2
Five-year Average Returns (1985-89)				
Operating Income as % of Revenue	15.1	11.6	16.9	23.8
Return on Shareholders Equity (percent)	13.4	13.3 *	15.4	23.3
Return on Invested Capital (percent)	10.9	9.4	8.0	18.1

* Excludes companies with negative return

By 1990 we had contacted a total of 850 public corporations and received data on the values and beliefs of 555 companies (a 65 percent response rate). (Table 1 shows summary financial data on 94 companies in four industries.) The documents that the responding companies felt best captured their core values and beliefs are classified in Table 2. The breakdown of material within most industries is similar to the all- industry profile. (Table 3 presents types of documents by industry.)

We discovered early on that company values and beliefs cover a wide array of subjects, which we ultimately grouped into six principal categories: business values, human values, social values, management philosophy, company style, and human resource beliefs. (Examples from the categories are given in Figure 1.) Companies that used formal mission statements (fewer than two out of five) included descriptive material about their businesses (captured in a company business section) and stated their future goals (captured in a company vision section).

Based on material from the first 200 companies, we developed a research instrument that we are now using for an extensive analysis of each company. To date we have analyzed the values and beliefs of 94 companies in four industries. These industries were selected because they are representative and because we had a high number of responses in these sectors.

Contrary to the popular belief that corporate value statements all say the same thing, the written material we collected demonstrates a wide range of distinctive company philosophies. Formal mission statements and credos are usually not "the corporate version of the boy scout oath" (Olins 1990). They vary in format from full books (over a dozen) to booklets to one-sentence slogans. Some companies focus exclusively on one area, such as management philosophy. Others present an extensive moral and philosophical rationale for the corporation and its role in society. In general, the large companies in our survey espouse 122 distinct value concepts in a wide variety of combinations.

All the stated values, of course, represent aspirations. Actual company practice often falls far short of intent. However, formal statements of values and beliefs are the best available sources of what senior managements intend as the philosophical foundations for their corporations. Formulation of the statements usually takes months of consensus building; in one company the process took 21 months. What is finally produced is considered a unique document by most chief executives, setting forth not only the foundation of the personnel philosophy but a

Table 2: Breakdown of Values and Beliefs Material by Type

Document	Number of Companies	Prevalence
Mission Statement	202	36.4%
Credo	111	20.0
Other Material*	242	43.6
Total	555	100.0%

*Annual reports, company brochures, ethics booklets, CEO speeches,
  in-house publications, books, policy statements, Newcomen addresses.

Table 3: Comparison of Most Important Values and Beliefs Material,
Ten Representative Industries Vs. All Industries

INDUSTRY	NUMBER OF COMPANIES	MISSION STATEMENT	CREDO	OTHER RELEVANT MATERIAL
Aerospace	14	50 %	14 %	36 %
Business & Personal Services	20	40	25	35
Chemical	31	32	26	42
Commercial Banks	33	30	33	37
Computer	18	44	28	28
Electrical/Electronics	24	38	24	38
Food	29	41	31	28
Paper	25	36	8	56
Pharmaceutical	17	35	24	41
Retailers	34	32	12	56
All Industry	555	36 %	20 %	44 %

basis for leadership (Hsieh, 1990). Formal statements of values are central to the presentation of the corporate image (Gray and Smeltzer 1985) and strategic marketing (Badovich and Beatty 1987). Evidence of the importance management attributes to these statements is that over one- third of the companies we surveyed supplemented the material they provided with a personal note and sometimes several pages of commentary.

Mission Statement Study Approach

Data Set

Over the past three years we mailed letters and a one-page questionnaire requesting information on company values and management philosophies to the CEOs of approximately 850 companies. All were publicly held industrial or service businesses with over $1 billion in revenues or financial institutions (commercial banks, savings and loans, diversified financials, and insurance companies) with assets over $10 billion. Later we collected data on all companies listed by Standard & Poor's Compustat with primary SIC codes in the chemical, electrical/electronics,

MAJOR CATEGORY	EXAMPLES
BUSINESS VALUES	• PROVIDE SUPERB CUSTOMER SERVICE • PROVIDE QUALITY PRODUCTS • OPERATE AT LOWEST COST
HUMAN VALUES	• SHOW INTEGRITY • BE TRUTHFUL • SHOW COMPASSION
SOCIAL VALUES	• SUPPORT COMMUNITIES • PROMOTE WORK FORCE DIVERSITY
HUMAN RESOURCE BELIEFS	• PAY FOR PERFORMANCE • PROMOTE FROM WITHIN • RESPECT THE INDIVIDUAL
MANAGEMENT PHILOSOPHY	• DECENTRALIZE • STRESS TEAMWORK • CONTROL COSTS
COMPANY STYLE	• ENCOURAGE PARTICIPATORY MANAGEMENT • MANAGE BY WALKING AROUND

Figure 1: Examples of Values and Beliefs

food, paper, and pharmaceutical industries. We ultimately received material from 555 of the 850 companies contacted, a 65 percent response rate.

Depending upon the initial response, an additional follow-up was often necessary to obtain the requested information. Our letter specifically requested documents containing statements of fundamental and enduring corporate values, of the company's vision for the future, and of values that distinguish the company's approach to the marketplace, as well as statements about the treatment of employees. The materials collected included formal mission statements, corporate credos, and an extensive array of CEO speeches, annual reports, employee handbooks, policy statements, and so forth.

Each company was assigned an identification number; the company name was removed wherever it occurred to ensure anonymity during the coding process. Some of the materials received included portions of irrelevant text that did not fit into any of the 122 categories of the mission statement research instrument (MSRI). The irrelevant materials were deleted and the usable data for each company was copied and bound in a spiral notebook for the coders' use.

Coding Team

The coding team consisted of one male and two female graduate students working on their doctoral dissertations in psychology at Rutgers University, New Jersey. The coders' average age was 43.3 years, with a range of 43 to 47 years. They had held a variety of business and academic positions, that directly aided and contributed to their knowledge and familiarity with the content of the study. In addition, the coders were trained over a two-month period using authentic company materials (which were deleted from the actual study due to our sample cut-off criteria) and various versions of the coding instrument.

Definitions

A separate set of definitions, corresponding directly to the MSRI concepts, was developed in tandem with the MSRI itself. The MSRI concepts were operationally defined for used in the coding process. The definitions were formulated using general management, human resource, and psychology textbooks as well as the authors' experience in management and management consulting. Examples and applications of the concepts were also included wherever possible. Among the definitions are:

> *Mission Statement:* A formal document that presents an overall vision and purpose for an organization, defines its business, and describes its scope of operation in product and market terms. It often embodies some aspects of a company's business philosophy. Taken in its totality, the mission statement presents a broadly defined framework for strategic decision making and an enduring description of the organization's distinctive character.

> *Credo:* formal statement of an organization's most important business principles, core values, and beliefs. It may describe, in general terms, the company's approach to the marketplace, its management principles, and its overall human resource philosophy. It often includes a statement of purpose as well as a description of the organization's responsibilities to its various constituencies.

> *Distinct Value Concept:* a specific value (such as trust), management practice (such as decentralization), or goal (such as customer orientation) embodied within a credo, mission statement, or other formal material used to communicate company philosophy. We identified 122 distinct value concepts in our study. Each concept was defined and given a variable label that distinguished it from other values and beliefs surveyed.

Mission Statement Research Instrument

The MSRI used for data collection by the coding team contains categories involving concepts of interest for a comprehensive study of the core values and management philosophies behind companies' growth and successes. The various concepts were grouped together as follows: business values (BV), including 23 separate subcategories; human values (HV), including 12 separate subcategories; social values (SV), including 15 separate subcategories; human resource beliefs (HRB), including 20 separate subcategories; management philosophies (MP), including 13 separate subcategories; company style (CS), including 20 separate subcategories; company business (CB), including 11 separate subcategories; and vision (V), including 8 separate subcategories.

The development of MSRI concepts required a literature review and examination of the categories that were found to be relevant in recent studies of corporate values and beliefs (Germain and Cooper 1990; David, 1980; Byars and Neil 1987; Pearce and David 1987; Cochran and David 1986). The MSRI was expanded further by randomly reviewing approximately 200 sets of company materials for concepts that were important based upon their frequency of occurrence, their uniqueness, and their intensity.

The MSRI went through approximately seven revisions, including three coding trials. We ultimately achieved reliability coefficients for the scale scores that range from .7763 for human values to .9031 for business values. The coding trials were designed to give the coding team maximum exposure to a variety of types of documents; to a broad scope of applications of the 122 MSRI concepts; and to the process of coding with a structured format using specific rules designed to ensure consistency of approach, selection, and objective rating.

The information collected for each concept included a record of the number of times the concept was mentioned; a Likert scale for rating the degree of elaboration of individual references; and a Likert scale for rating the degree of intensity of the individual references. In addition, a separate set of Likert scales at the end of the "vision" section required coders to make an overall industry comparison on five different dimensions. Finally, the coders highlighted the most intense, uniquely stated passages and statements about corporate "vision."

Values and Company Performance

One test of the significance of written statements is whether better performing companies give more emphasis to values and beliefs than companies that perform more poorly. There is considerable anecdotal evidence that strongly stated, unique values influence company success.

Many of the legendary business leaders of this and earlier eras have been driven by their beliefs. A few formalized these beliefs, usually in times of transition or crisis, for the next generation of management. The founder of J.C. Penney articulated the "Penney credo" at the time the company first offered shares of its stock to the public (Penney 1907). David McConnell, the founder of Avon, issued his "statement of principles" over a hundred years ago when the company started to expand (McConnell 1990). Those companies lucky enough to inherit a forceful set of beliefs attribute much of their success to them. Thomas Watson, Jr., who succeeded his father as chief executive of IBM, captured the idea effectively: "Any organization -- one that has lasted over the years -- owes its resiliency, not to its form of organization or administrative skills, but to the power of what we call beliefs and the appeal these beliefs have for its people" (Watson 1963).

Despite eloquent testimony to the importance of values, there have been few attempts to study the link between values and performance. One of the first quantitative studies of mission statements (Pearce and David, 1987) showed that better performing companies had a stronger "self concept." Socially responsible behavior correlates with several aspects of financial performance (McGuire 1988).

Most of the studies that have been made, however, use limited measures of performance. We wanted to include multiple measures of performance and examine the values/performance link by industry over an extended period. We also wanted to try to identify which of the scores of values and beliefs are linked to sustained superior performance. In addition, we wanted to study how values relate to different business strategies and situations.

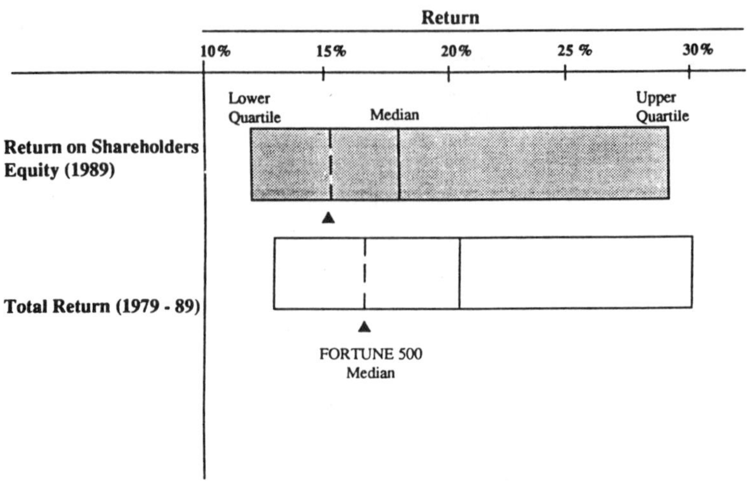

Figure 2: Results Achieved by Companies with Outstanding Credos
and Mission Statements (45 Companies)

The preliminary results of our study confirm that the performance of value-driven companies is well above average. (Figure 2 shows 1989 return on shareholders equity and total return [from 1979 to 1989] for the 45 companies [out of the total survey group of 555] with the most forceful and comprehensively stated values and beliefs.) The median 1989 return on shareholders equity for the value-driven companies was at 17.0 percent a full two percentage points higher than the Fortune 500 Industrial median; the upper quartile achieved a stellar 23.5 percent. The ten-year total return (stock price appreciation plus dividends) enjoyed by the shareholders of these 45 value-driven companies was also dramatically higher. (The median total returns of 20.1 percent and upper quartile returns of 25.9 percent far exceeded the Fortune 500 median of 16.3 percent.)

Our preliminary analyses of performance differentials within industries also provide compelling evidence of the strong link between values and performance. We ranked the companies within each industry by operating income margins, return on shareholders equity, and return on total invested capital over the 1985-1989 period. Then we compared the emphasis placed on values by calculating the total number of references to specific values and beliefs, using the 122-item research instrument. (Figure 3 shows the results for the chemical industry.) The top one-third performers gave 21.6 percent more emphasis to values than the average company, while the bottom one-third gave 15.8 percent less emphasis to values. The differences were pronounced in three of the four industries studied. The exception was the paper industry, where credos are not as frequently used (8 percent of paper companies use credos, compared to 20 percent of all companies).

In summary, all available evidence confirms the importance of values and beliefs in building and sustaining a successful company. Are strong values enough? Of course not. If strong and distinctive values alone could guarantee success, Peoples Express would be flying today. Great and venerable companies like Pillsbury would not be in foreign hands. Companies with distinctive cultures, like Sears Roebuck, would not flounder for years.

Values need to be sustained, and company beliefs (particularly business and human resource principles) need to be updated periodically. When James Burke became chief executive of Johnson & Johnson, he initiated "challenge sessions" to test the credo formulated by the company's founder, General Johnson (Tedlow and Smith 1985). A successful company must also be blessed with leadership that embodies its best values and has the skill to sustain the business. An important part of our research has been to try to develop a better understanding of how values fit into the formula for success.

Values of Most Profitable Companies

In the early stages of our research we formulated a series of hypotheses about the differences in values of the most and the least profitable companies. This research is based upon our consulting work and a review of the culture and management literature. One of our theories was that successful companies would have clearer and more powerfully stated visions of their desired future state.

"Vision" has been conceptualized by business experts as the starting point for forming corporate strategy and building organizational commitment (Drucker 1974; Bartlett and Ghoshal 1990). So far we have not found any evidence that the most profitable companies make greater use of formal vision statements. Only about one out of three companies employs a mission statement, the preferred vehicle for expressing business vision. Part of the reason may be that describing vision in a compelling, inspirational way is not easy to do. (During our research we found over a dozen companies struggling with this.) More fundamentally, many companies appear to feel that the sum total of their stated values and beliefs is their enduring vision.

We did find that the most profitable companies gave more emphasis to every category of values except company style (Figure 3). Their statements of business and human values were more extensive than those of poorer performers. On the

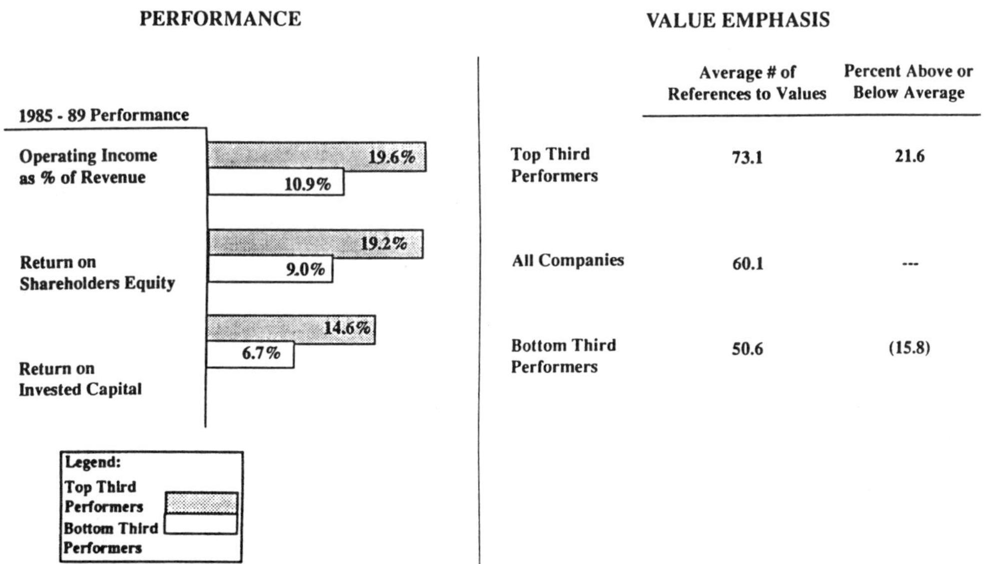

Figure 3: Relationship Between Corporate Values and Performance
in Thirty Chemical Companies

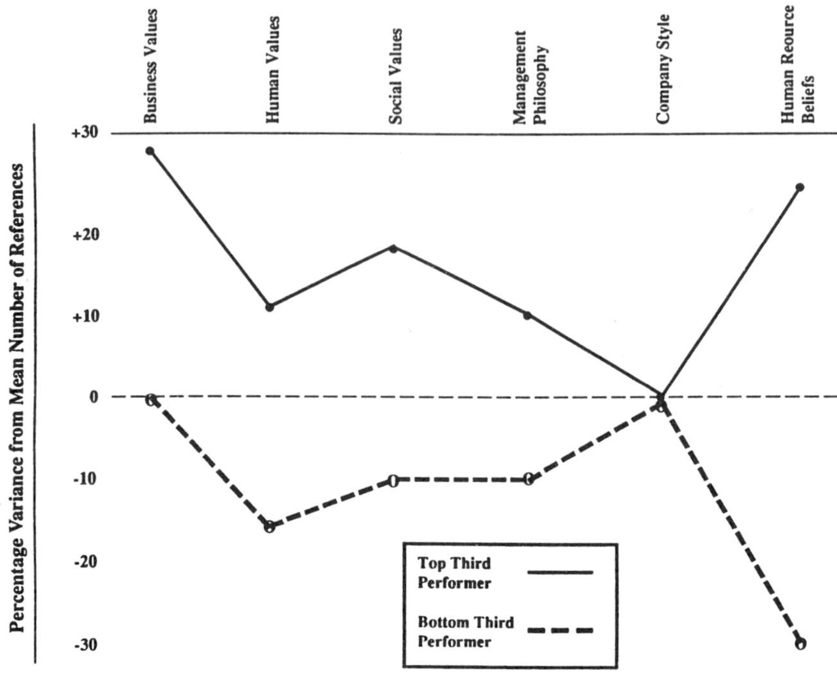

Figure 4: Relative Emphais Given to Values and Beliefs in Most and Least Profitable Companies (94 Companies)

other hand, the best performers used fewer "precepts" such as "manage by walking around." Such formulas often reflect management fads. We hypothesize that better performing companies stress more enduring values.

We have found that the most significant difference between the most and least profitable companies is the emphasis they give to human resource beliefs and accompanying HR policy statements. (Figure 4) shows a dramatic difference between the top and bottom third performers.) Top performers not only mentioned human resources more frequently but were also more likely to include an HR statement as part of corporate philosophy. (Figure 5)shows the occurrence of human resource beliefs in the values statements of companies in the electronics industry.) Six central HR beliefs were articulated significantly more frequently by top performers than by bottom ones; the commitment to training was particularly noteworthy.

The survey companies as a group put more emphasis on business values than on any other category of values. Table 4 shows the distribution of references to values (an average of 61 per company) by category.

Although all companies stressed business values, the top third gave them more emphasis than the bottom third. (Business values most closely concern the strategic positioning of the company.) The differences in the particular business values top and bottom performers emphasized are significant (Table 5). The best performers stressed their commitment to quality, customer orientation and innovation. The bottom stood out from the average in only one area: the importance they attributed to growth. This differentiation in business values supports the evidence that "negotiated belief structures" influence a firm's strategic decisions (Walsh and Fahey, 1986).

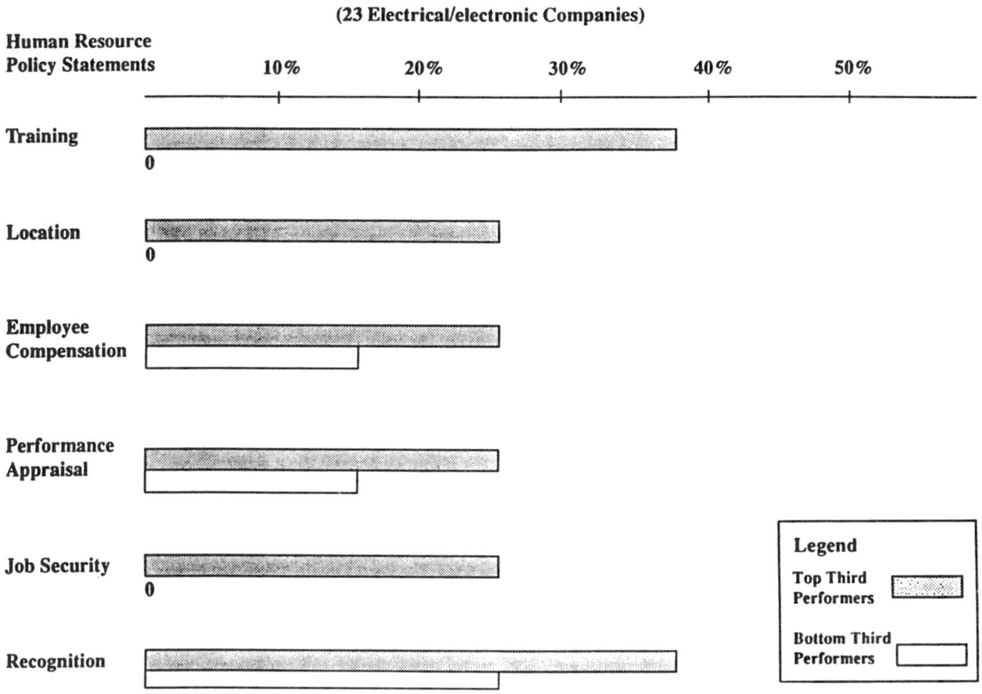

Figure 5: Prevalence of Statements of Human Resource Beliefs
(23 Electrical/Electronic Companies)

There is some evidence that successful companies practice both "hard" and "soft" management simultaneously (Beer 1990). In our study the most profitable companies combined a comprehensive, deeper commitment to human values and humanistic HR policies with greater emphasis on performance. The stress on performance was demonstrated by greater competitiveness and human resource strategies that discussed individual accountability, pay for performance, performance appraisal, and advancement based on merit.

Table 4: Areas of Emphasis in Corporate Value Statements

Category	Prevalence
Business Values	44%
Management Philosophy	19
Human Resource Beliefs	11
Company Style	9
Social Values	9
Human Values	8

| | TOP THIRD PERFORMERS | | | BOTTOM THIRD PERFORMERS | |
VALUE	NUMBER OF REFERENCES	PERCENTAGE CITING	VALUE	NUMBER OF REFERENCES	PERCENTAGE CITING
Quality	88	84 %	Growth	42	65 %
Customer Orientation	73	75			
Innovation	57	78			
Productivity	42	69			
Competitive Orientation	42	59			

Revitalized Companies

We identified fourteen companies (11 percent of the total) whose performance improved dramatically from 1985 to 1989 as shown in Table 6. We analyzed the values of the revitalized companies to see if there was a distinctive pattern. We found that mission statements or credos were more prevalent (used by ten revitalized companies or 71 percent, compared with 56 percent of all 555 companies). The revitalized companies also gave special emphasis to human values as indicated in Table 7.

Evidence of the importance of human values in company turnarounds will not surprise HRPS members who attended the 1991 conference in San Diego. In a keynote address, Warner-Lambert's Ray Fino (vice president of corporate human

Table 6: Performance of 14 Revitalized Companies

Measure	1985	1989
Operating Income as % of Revenue	10.8	16.3
Return on Shareholders Equity (percent)	8.3	19.5
Return on Invested Capital (percent)	6.8	12.5

Table 7: Human Values Cited by Revitalized Companies

Values	Number of References	Percent of Companies Citing
Integrity	20	64.3
Openness	16	64.3
Creativity	14	57.1
Respect for the Individual	12	71.4
Fairness	12	50.0

resources) and Melvin Goodes (recently named chief executive officer) described their company's successful revitalization. According to Fino and Goodes, the development of the Warner-Lambert creed, which emphasizes human values, was the starting point for the company turnaround because "business plans and decisions flow from commitment to values" (Fino and Goodes 1991). Warner-Lambert was one of the fourteen revitalized companies identified in our study.

Ongoing Study of Values

We expect to provide more fact-based insight into the importance and unique role of values and beliefs as our analysis progresses. We plan to complete the data entry for six additional industries over the summer and complete more extensive analysis of this larger sample by the end of the year. Using our findings, we are fine-tuning several analytical tools we employ in our consulting work on strategy implementation and the management of change. We are particularly excited about a value gap questionnaire we have developed to measure the extent to which a company practices the values it espouses. All of our experience confirms the advice given by Melvin Goodes in San Diego: "If you want to build company value, build values."

References

Sharon E. Beatty, "Shared Organization Values: Measurement and Impact Upon Strategic Marketing Implementation," *Journal of the Academy of Marketing Science*, Vol. 15, No. 1 (Spring, 1987) pp 19-26.

Bartlett, Christopher and Sumantra Ghoshal, "Matrix Management: Not a Structure, a Frame of Mind," *Harvard Business Review* (July-August, 1990) pp 138-145.

Beer, Michael, *The Critical Path to Corporate Renewal*, (Boston, MA: Harvard Business School Press, 1990).

Byars, L. L. and T. C. Neil, "Organizational Philosophy and Mission Statements," *Planning Review* , Vol. 16, No. 5 (1987) pp 32-35.

Cochran, D. and F. David, "Communication Effectiveness of Organizational Mission Statements," *Journal of Applied Communication Research*, Vol. 14, No. 2 (1986) pp 108-118.

David, F. R., "How Companies Define Their Mission," *Long Range Planning*, Vol. 22, No. 1 (1989) pp 90-97.

Deal, T. E. and A. A. Kennedy, *Corporate Cultures: The Rites and Rituals of Corporate Life*, (Reading, MA: Addison-Wesley, 1982).

Dowd, Maureen, "A Different Bush Conforms to Nation's Mood," *The New York Times* (March 2, 1991) pp 1-7.

Drucker, Peter F., *Management : Tasks, Responsibilities, Practices*, (New York, NY: Harper Row, 1974).

Fino, Raymond M. and Melvin R. Goodes, "The Transformation of Warner-Lambert 1980-91," Paper read at the Human Resource Planning Society annual conference, April 15, 1991, in San Diego, CA.

Germain, R. and M. B. Cooper, "How a Customer Mission Statement Affects Company Performance," *Industrial Marketing Management*, Vol. 19 (1990) pp 47-54.

Gray, Edmund R. and Larry Smeltzer, "Corporate Image -- An Integral Part of Strategy," *Sloan Management Review* (Summer, 1985) pp 73-78.

Hsieh, Tsun-Yan, "Leadership Actions," *The McKinsey Quarterly* No. 4 (1990), pp 42-58.

Kilmann, Ralph H., Mary J. Saxton, and Roy Serpa, *Gaining Control of the Corporate Culture*, (San Francisco, CA: Jossey-Bass Publishers, 1985).

McConnell, David, "Statement of Principles," *Avon Annual Report* (1990).

McGuire, Jean B., Alison Sundgren, and Thomas Schneeweis, "Corporate Social Responsibility and Firm Financial Performance," *Academy of Management Journal*, Vol. 34, No. 4 (1988) pp 854-872.

McLaughlin, David J., *Personnel Management in the People's Republic of China*, (Princeton, NJ: Sibson & Co., Inc., 1987).

Olins, Wally, *Corporate Identity: Making Business Strategy Visible Through Design*, (Cambridge, MA: Harvard Business School Press, 1990).

Pearce, John A. II and Fred David, "Corporate Mission Statements: The Bottom Line," *Academy of Management Executive*, Vol. I, No. 2 (1987) pp 109-116.

Penney, J. C., *The Penney Idea* (1907).

Schwartz, H. M. and S. M. Davis, "Matching Corporate Culture and Business Strategy," *Organizational Dynamics*, (Summer, 1981) pp 30-48.

Tedlow, R. S. and W. K. Smith, "James Burke: A Career in American Business," Harvard Business School Case 9-389-177 (1985).

Walsh, James and Liam Fahey, "The Role of Negotiated Belief Structures in Strategy Making," *Journal of Management*, Vol. 12, No. 3 (1986) pp 325-338.

Watson, Thomas J., Jr., *A Business and Its Beliefs: The Ideas That Helped Build IBM*, (New York, NY: McGraw Hill, 1963).

Quality of Output Programs
for Manufacturing and Service Industries

J.A. VERDIN AND A. PAGANO

Introduction

Quality programs have become an integral part of doing business in both manufacturing and service industries. Not only are firms marketing their quality programs as part of their general advertising campaigns (eg., Ford Quality Number One), but the use of automated manufacturing systems, just-in-time inventory systems, and interactive data bases requires a high level of precision and data accuracy.

Manufacturing firms are requiring their suppliers to meet stringent quality specifications (Miller, 1988), and consumers have increased their expectations with regard to the quality of the goods they purchase and the service they receive. Retailers such as Nordstom's have successfully entered new markets, in part because of their reputation for providing a high level of customer service. Many companies such as Rockwell International, have developed quality improvement programs based on customer input (Goldstein, Howe, and Gaeddert, 1988).

Another aspect of the quality issue is the introduction and awarding of the Malcolm Baldrige Award, established in 1987 by an Act of Congress (Glover, 1988). Some firms require their suppliers to apply for the Malcolm Baldrige Quality Award. This may mean that the suppliers must implement quality programs and procedures, incorporate quality considerations into their current processes, and fill out the rather lengthy application forms. If a firm wins, they are sure to emphasize their award in their advertising and public relations. Although first established for manufacturing firms, the Baldrige Award has recently been extended to service industries as well.

Human resource managers have become involved in the development and implementation of quality programs (Segalla, 1989). Although traditional quality programs focus on job and work design, statistical process control, and various customer service efforts, many human resource programs are also involved (Guzzo, 1983). For example, training efforts related to the traditional programs are often

J.A. VERDIN - Decision Technology Associates, Inc., 81 East Elm Street, Chicago, IL 60611; A. PAGANO - University of Illinois at Chicago, College of Business Administration, Chicago, IL 60680

administered through the human resource departments, and performance appraisal and reward systems which incorporate quality measures are usually developed and overseen by human resources. However, the actual role of human resource managers is unclear (Keating, 1990; Roth, 1988).

In order to explore the types of quality programs being offered by firms in manufacturing and service industries and to determine what roles human resource managers have taken in these firms, a study was sponsored by the Human Resource Planning Society and funded by Weyerhauser and The Equitable Corporation. This paper outlines the results of that study.

Research Questions

Research questions were developed in conjunction with an advisory panel representing the HRPS Research Committee, Weyerhauser, and The Equitable Corporation. These include:

1. How are organizations currently ensuring the continued production of high quality products and services to their customers?
2. What programs are organizations planning to implement in the near future which have as one of the primary goals the output of high quality products and services?
3. What role has the human resource department taken in these efforts?

3a. Have HR professionals played the role of initiator, facilitator, supporter, or resistor with regard to the implementation of changes aimed at improving the quality of output?
3b. Has the strategy of human resource professionals been reactive or proactive in moving their organizations in this direction?
3c. What is foreseen as the human resource role in the near future?

4. What factors act as facilitators in increasing the human resource manager's role? What factors act as barriers to developing this role?

Methodology

With input from the advisory panel, a letter describing the study and a questionnaire addressing the research questions were developed. These were sent

Table 1: Characteristics of Sample Firms

	Total	Manufacturing	Service
	(53) 100%	(33) 62%	(20) 37%
Average # Employees	34,249	32,066	37,851
Average Sales (Billions)	4.61	4.66	4.53

to HRPS Corporate Members as well as other members of the society throughout the country requesting participation in the study. A phone survey was then conducted using this questionnaire. A total of 53 interviews were successfully completed.

The interviews centered around the following areas: background of the interviewee and the company, approaches to improve quality, and human resource management's role in the quality programs at the company.

Survey Results

Sample Description

The 53 companies that participated in the study were divided into manufacturing (62%) and service sectors (38%). Table 1 summarizes their characteristics with respect to average number of employees and average sales.

Current Approaches to Quality Improvement

Figure 1 describes the approaches the respondents used to improve the quality of their products and services. Training programs were mentioned by 85% of the firms and workflow changes by 79%. The inclusion of quality as a criterion in performance appraisal systems was cited by 68% and linking compensation to quality performance was indicated by 60%. Job design changes were a part of the program for 59% of the companies and 51% used some type of team management approach. Quality circles were only mentioned by 11% of the respondents. (Because of the small number of companies using quality circles, further analysis of these programs was not done.)

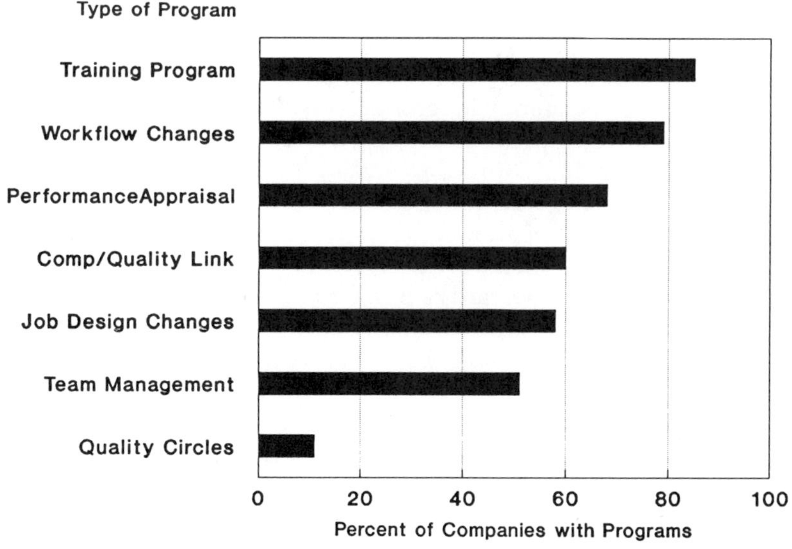

Figure 1: Types of Quality Improvement Programs (Total Sample)

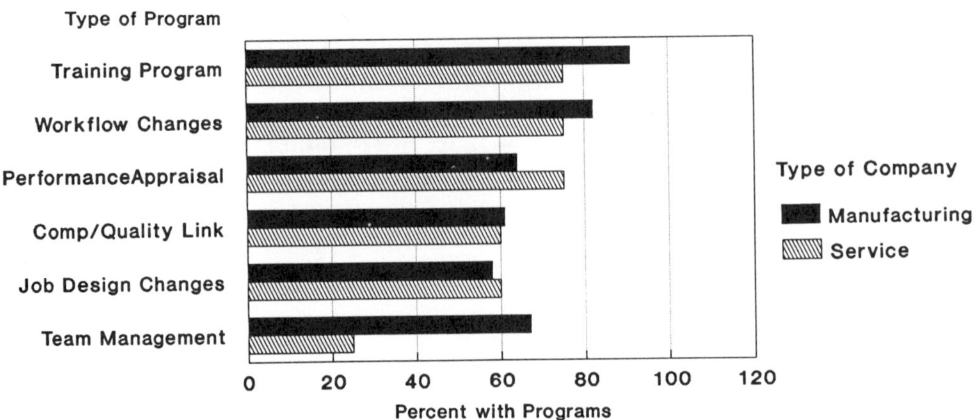

Figure 2: Types of Quality Improvement Programs
(Manufacturing Versus Service)

An analysis of the percentage of manufacturing firms as compared to the percentage of service industries using each type of quality improvement program is shown in Figure 2. Ninety-one percent of the manufacturing firms reported having training programs, 82% reported making changes in workflow, and 64% included quality measures as part of their performance appraisal systems. Seventy-five percent of the service firms reported using each of these programs. The only other difference concerned the utilization of team management programs. Sixty-seven percent of the manufacturing firms used this approach while only 25% of the service firms used it. Reasons for Implementation of Current Approaches.

The respondents were asked why their firms implemented the various approaches aimed at quality improvement. The results are displayed in Table 2. The implementation of all of the programs depended to some extent on the top management philosophy of the firm. This was particularly true with regard to training programs and the inclusion of quality in the performance appraisal system.

The results also indicate that the approaches can be logically grouped with regard to the reasons for implementation. In the first group are training programs which address the areas of competition (particularly domestic competition) and customer service. Improvements in product quality and productivity are less frequently mentioned as reasons for developing training programs.

The second group includes workflow and job design changes which are used to address product quality, cost reduction, productivity issues, competitive pressures, and the need for improved customer service. Over 33% of the respondents mentioned the need for improved productivity with respect to workflow changes and 42% felt productivity was an important reason for making job design alterations.

The third group of programs combines performance appraisal and linking compensation with quality performance. The respondents mentioned linking quality with rewards and the philosophy of paying for performance as reasons for these programs. In addition, approximately 20% of the respondents mentioned domestic competition and improved customer service as reasons for including quality as part of the performance appraisal process.

Finally, team management appears to be implemented as a result of domestic competition, the need for improved product quality, and to increase employee

Table 2: Reasons for Implementing Quality Improvement Programs
(Percent of Respondents Implenting Each Program)

Reason for Implementation	Training Prog	Workflow Changes	Perform Appraisal	Comp/Qual Link	Job Design	Team Mgmt
Top Management Philosophy	33%	17%	28%	16%	19%	18%
Develop Quality Culture	9			12		
Foreign Competition	18	14			13	
Domestic Competition	49	33	19		48	26
Customer Service	38	31	22			32
Improve Product Quality	11	17			29	15
Reduce Recalls		14				
Buyer Specifications		12				
Improve Productivity	16	33	11		42	
Reduce Costs		12				
Reward for Quality			17	31		
Pay for Performance			28	53		
Increase Employee Involvement						70

involvement. The desire for increased employee involvement was mentioned only in conjunction with this approach

Resistance to Implementation of Quality Programs

The phone survey instrument also probed whether resistance was a problem and the reasons for resistance to a program. As can be seen in Figure 3, the most resistance was found when the program involved workflow or job design changes. A moderate amount of resistance was reported for training programs and team management efforts, and the least resistance was found when quality was included in the performance appraisal process or when it was linked to compensation.

The reasons for resistance were further explored and are summarized in Table 3. More specific reasons for resistance include lack of communication, inertia of the employees, and fear that authority or control will be lost. It is important to note, however, that the only programs where the fear of job loss was mentioned are those directly affecting the work, ie., workflow and job design changes.

Table 3: Reasons for Resistance to Quality Improvement Programs
(Percent of Respondents Implementing Each Program)

Reason for Resistance	Training Program	Workflow Changes	Perform Appraisal	Comp/Qual Link	Job Design	Team Mgmt
Lack of Communication	16%			12%	13%	
Inertia of Employees	11	17			19	
Job Loss Fear			10		13	
Team Management						11

Evaluation of Quality Improvement Programs

The respondents were asked if quality programs were evaluated. The results are displayed in Figure 4. Approximately 80% of the training programs and team management programs are evaluated in some way. Sixty-nine percent of the workflow change programs and 64% of the job design programs are evaluated. Slightly fewer of the performance appraisal programs (53%) and the programs linking compensation and quality (56%) are evaluated.

The methods used to evaluate the programs are summarized in Table 4. Follow-up monitoring of some type was mentioned as being used by one-third of the training programs, 16% of job design programs, and 25% of the other quality improvement approaches.

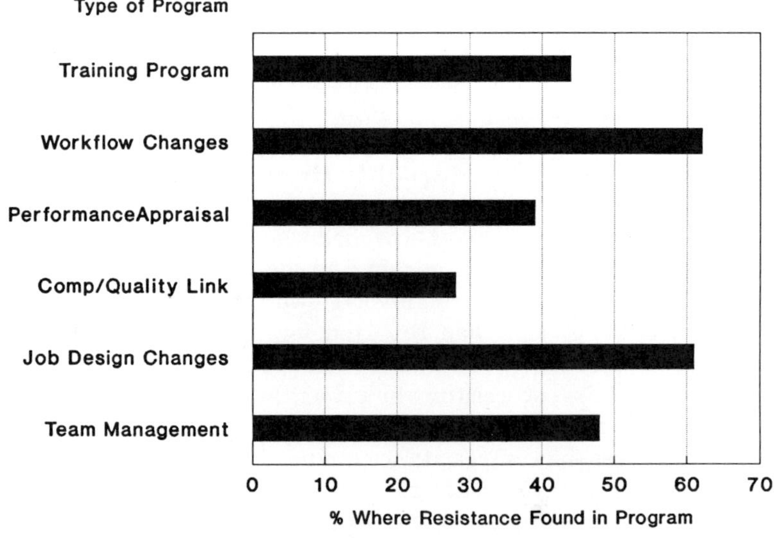

Figure 3: Resistance to Quality Improvement Approaches

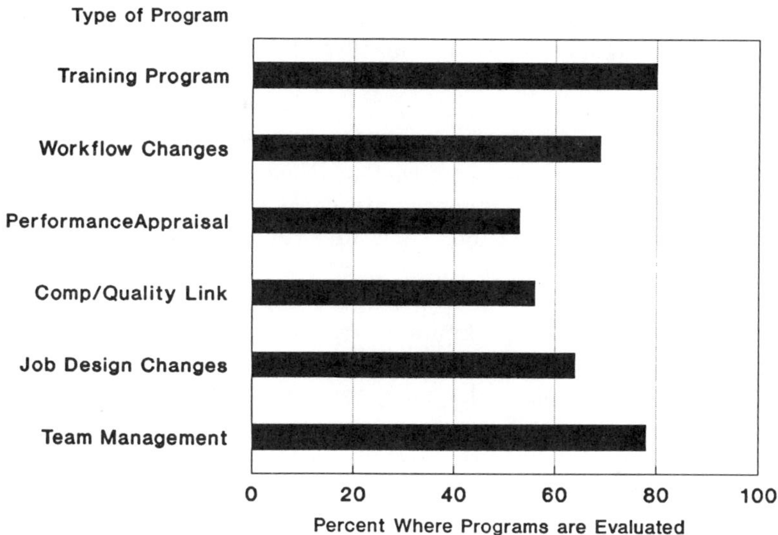

Figure 4: Evaluation of Quality Improvement Programs

Table 4: Methods of Evaluation Used for Quality Improvement Programs
(Percent of Respondents Implementing Each Program)

Methods of Evaluation	Training Program	Workflow Changes	Perform Appraisal	Comp/Qual Link	Job Design	Team Mgmt
Customer Reports	22%	12%	14%		19%	
Follow-up/Monitoring	33	26	25	25	16	26
Quantitative Measures						
Productivity		14			16	
Cost Savings		12			16	
General Measures	13					18
Number of Rejects	11					
Employee Retention				12		
End of Program Evaluation	27		14			
Compare to Standards	11					
Meet Set Goals		9	19		19	22

Training programs are also evaluated using customer reports and end of program evaluations. Quantitative measures, comparison against standards, and meeting specific goals are utilized to evaluate training programs by less than 15% of the firms.

The methods to evaluate workflow changes and job design programs are similar. Productivity measures and cost savings are used for both of these approaches, and 19% of the respondents with these programs mentioned meeting set goals as a criterion for evaluation. Customer reports are also used to evaluate the success of these efforts.

Performance appraisal is evaluated using customer reports and end of program evaluation by 14% of the firms incorporating quality measures into this process. Measures of employee retention are part of the evaluation process for programs linking compensation with quality performance.

Eighteen percent of the firms with team management programs indicated that quantitative measures were used to evaluate these efforts. In addition, 22% of the firms indicated the success of their team management programs was measured against set goals.

Future Plans for Expansion of Programs

Figure 5 indicates the percent of respondents who indicated their firms have plans to expand their current quality improvement programs. The greatest amount of expansion is anticipated in training programs and workflow change programs, with over 50% of the firms expecting growth in these areas. In addition, approximately 40% of the respondents indicated plans to incorporate quality into their performance appraisal systems and expansion of programs addressing job design changes. One-third of the respondents expected increased linkages between compensation and quality performance, and 22% expected to increase their team management programs.

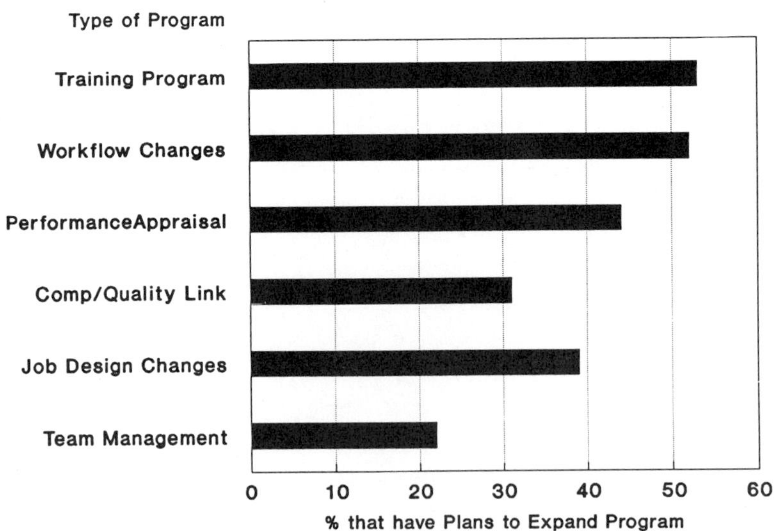

Figure 5: Plans to Expand the Programs in the Future

How Quality Improvement Programs Are Managed

Forty percent of the respondents indicated their firms had one person or group in charge of quality improvement programs. The responsibilities include overseeing the entire quality improvement program, coordinating efforts among various organizational units, and facilitating units during implementation.

Employee communications programs are also important in the effort to disseminate top management's philosophy regarding quality and to build quality into the organizational culture. Written communication vehicles such as memos, newsletters, and quality specific publications are used by many of the firms. In addition, one-third of the respondents used audio or video tapes to present information on their quality improvement programs. Speeches and seminars as well as training programs also served to communicate with various employee groups. Finally, nonmonetary awards were given by 28% of the firms. Only three companies used monetary awards for quality.

Role of HR Management in Quality Improvement Programs

Human resource managers have a variety of roles with respect to quality improvement programs. As indicated in Table 5, over half of the respondents indicated they had a consultative or training role. Although the specific impact on corporate quality programs may vary, it appears that the majority of the respondents characterized their role as supportive and/or reactive in nature.

One-third of the respondents indicated the HR managers at their firms were involved in the implementation of quality improvement programs, and 15% were involved in the planning of the programs. In general, these roles were more direct and proactive with respect to the company's quality efforts and focus on the longer term. Finally, 15% of the respondents indicated that HR managers had a minimal role with respect to quality improvement programs.

The responses of manufacturing versus service firms regarding the aspects of HR management's role in quality improvement programs were analyzed. The current role of HR managers, described in Table 5, is similar for both manufacturing

Table 5: Current Role of Human Resource Management

Current Role in Quality Improvement Programs	Total Sample	Manufacturing	Service
Consulting Role	62%	64%	60%
Training Role	53	49	60
Implement Quality Programs	32	33	30
Manage Supportive HR Programs	23	21	25
Planning	15	12	20
Minimal Role Regarding Quality	15	15	15

Table 6: Role HR Should Play Regarding Quality

Role HR Should Play	Total Sample	Manufacturing	Service
Consulting Role	59%	67%	45%
Manage Supportive HR Programs	43	39	50
Training Role	30	27	35
Develop Quality Oriented Culture	23	24	20
Planning Role	15	15	15

and service firms. Over half indicated they currently take on a consulting and training role, and one-third are involved in the implementation of quality improvement programs. Only 12% of the manufacturing firms indicated they were involved in the planning of quality programs, while 20% of the service firms currently had a planning role.

Table 6 summarizes the responses to the question of what role *should* HR managers play with respect to their firms efforts regarding quality improvement. Fifty-eight percent indicated that HR should play a consultative role, 43% felt they should support related HR programs, and 30% felt the training role was appropriate.

Twenty-three percent felt HR managers should be involved in developing a quality culture at the firm. This is an area which indicates a longer range view of the quality issue, and had not previously been mentioned as a role HR managers are currently playing. In addition, 15% felt the planning role was appropriate, again focusing on the future and implying a more proactive role.

The perceptions of the respondents from manufacturing firms regarding what the HR management role should be is different from those from service firms as can be seen in Table 6. Respondents from manufacturing firms focused on the consulting role, with some emphasis on management of supportive HR programs. The service industry respondents put somewhat less emphasis on the consulting role (45%) and more emphasis on the training role. The notion that a quality oriented culture needs to be developed was mentioned by about one-fifth of the respondents in both groups.

Facilitators and Barriers to HR Role in Quality

Table 7 summarizes the respondents perceptions of factors which can act as facilitators and barriers to the HR management role in quality improvement programs. With respect to facilitators, 47% of the respondents cited HR managers' knowledge of the business as a key factor in enhancing their role. In addition, the credibility of the HR managers in the firm was indicated by 38% of the respondents. The notion of an organizational culture incorporating quality was mentioned by 32% and the existence of good management systems by 26%.

Barriers to HR playing an active role in quality programs are just the obverse of facilitators. The most important barrier to HR managers' involvement in quality

Table 7: Facilitators and Barriers to HR Management
in Quality Improvement Programs

Factors Facilitating the HR Management Role in Quality	Total Sample	Manufacturing	Service
Knowledge of the Business	47%	39%	60%
Credibility of HR Managers	38	42	30
Quality Oriented Culture	32	33	30
Good Management Systems	26	27	25

Barriers Keeping HR Management from Being Involved	Total Sample	Manufacturing	Service
Lack of Knowledge of the Business	36%	39%	30%
Lack of Credibility of HR Managers	55	48	65
Lack of Quality Oriented Culture	15	15	15
Poor Management Systems	26	27	25

improvement efforts is lack of credibility of the HR function, mentioned by 55% of the respondents. Thirty-six percent mentioned a lack of knowledge of the business as being a problem. The lack of adequate management systems was indicated by 26% and a problem with quality not being a part of the overall organizational culture was mentioned by only 15%.

Table 7 also indicates that respondents from manufacturing firms see high credibility of HR managers as a facilitator to increasing the HR role in quality improvement programs to a greater extent than those from the service industry. On the other hand, knowledge of the business was cited as a facilitator by 60% of the service firm respondents versus 39% of those from manufacturing.

Some divergence in what is perceived as a barrier was also indicated. In particular, lack of credibility of HR managers was felt to be a greater barrier to those from service firms than those from manufacturing.

From this analysis, it appears that to enhance HR management's role in quality improvement programs, it is extremely important to have knowledge of how the business operates combined with developing a high level of credibility for the HR function.

Conclusions

The organizations included in this study have adopted a variety of strategies to address quality improvement problems. Those programs most directly related to the work itself are workflow and job design changes. The remainder of the programs support quality improvement efforts and can be classified into three major groups. The first includes training programs supporting quality improvement programs throughout the firm. The second group includes quality measures in performance appraisal programs and linking compensation with quality performance. The third approach incorporates team management with a primary goal of increased employee involvement. Future plans included continuing to expand these types of quality improvement programs.

Human resource managers currently take on a variety of roles with respect to quality improvement programs. Consulting and training roles are most frequently mentioned. Relatively few HR managers mentioned taking on a planning role which is more future oriented.

To enhance human resource managements' role in quality improvement programs, it is important for HR managers to develop expertise and understanding of the operations of the business itself. In addition, a high level of credibility of the HR department was frequently cited as a facilitator for this increased involvement.

References

Glover, M. Katherine, "Malcolm Baldrige National Quality Award-- `The Quest for Excellence,'" *Business America*, Volume 109, Number 25, December 5, 1988, pp. 2-5.

Goldstein, Sam, Howe, Roger, Gaeddert, Dee, "Rockwell's Approach to Improving Quality," *Personnel Journal*, Volume 65, Number 7, July, 1988, pp. 44-47.

Guzzo, Richard A., "Sizing Up the Impact of Human-Resource Productivity Programs," *National Productivity Review*, Autumn, 1983, pp. 376-385.

Keating, Bernard L., "Viewpoint: Welcome Aboard the Quality Team," *Personnel Journal*, Volume 67, Number 7, July, 1990, pp. 36-37.

Miller, William H., "'Technology Fix' to Quality Passe, Says Pole," *Industry Week*, August 1, 1988, p. 16.

Roth, William F., Jr., "The Great Quality Shell Game," *Personnel*, December 1988, pp. 53-58.

Segalla, Ellen, "All for Quality, and Quality for All," *Training and Development Journal*, Volume 43, Number 9, September, 1989, pp. 36-45.

Workforce Analysis and Turnover Forecasting: Building Capacity in New York State Government

C.L. TEIGLAND

Introduction

Economic, demographic, educational and technological trends are dramatically reshaping the labor force available to both the public and private sectors. As a result, New York State government, one of the nation's largest employers, is facing the reality that there will no longer be the steady supply of skilled workers they have come to expect.

The late 1980's were marked by a proliferation of books describing the changing demographics and predicting a shrinking labor pool (e.g. *Workforce 2000* issued by the Hudson Institute, 1987). While overall shortages have not yet occurred on a global basis, the trends are evident in a growing number of occupations and geographic areas in New York State. Though the impact of the current recession has slowed the emergence of projected shortages, the underlying demographics remain as a critical factor in the labor market. When the economic downturn ends, the state will again be faced with labor force problems stemming from emerging trends.

Like many large organizations, personnel costs dominate the government's cost of doing business, exceeding 80 percent of the state operations budget. It has become critical to deploy a workforce in a way that is both productive and cost efficient. Over 200,000 employees having an average length of service of 10.7 years and an average annual salary of $30,000 represent a major investment for the state. With the recognition that human resources are a real key to fiscal control, strategic planning for human capital becomes a bottom-line necessity.

Workforce Planning in New York State

In 1988, Governor Mario M. Cuomo set up a major new workforce planning initiative in New York State. Since that time, the government has come a long way in developing the capacity needed to conduct long-range workforce planning and analysis.

C.L. TEIGLAND - New York State Department of Civil Service, State Office Campus, Bldg No.1, Rm 158, Albany NY 12239

Bottom Line Results from Strategic Human Resource Planning
Edited by R.J. Niehaus and K.F. Price, Plenum Press, New York, 1991

A key component of this effort was the establishment of a technical Workforce Planning Analysis unit. The structure of this unit represents a unique combination of resources committed to the area of human resource planning in government. It is indicative of the seriousness ascribed to this effort. Directed by a Ph.D. economist, the unit was initially staffed with an econometrician, statistician, demographer, operations research specialist, public policy analyst and several research specialists. The staff have extensive computer skills and experience with database, statistical and graphics software. This combination of education and experience committed to the problems we face now and through the year 2000 allows us to respond in a more rigorous fashion to these complex issues. Importantly, this unit gives the state the analytical tools necessary to develop proactive programs and policies to respond to emerging workforce crises.

New York State published its first annual *Workforce Plan* in 1989, followed by another in 1990. Following the format of the first two documents, each will provide a detailed demographic and occupational profile of the state government workforce. Significant trends will be outlined and discussed. Key issues facing the state which impact the effective recruitment, retention and deployment of a capable workforce will be documented. Projections of those occupational areas where shortages or surpluses are expected to occur, and estimates of the number of replacements needed by title and geographic location, will be specified. Remedial policy initiatives will be proposed, and specific future action plans will be described.

The Need for a Comprehensive Workforce Information System

One of the most practical and far-reaching efforts of the workforce planning initiative has been the development of a comprehensive Workforce Information System. The report issued by the Commission on the Skills of the American Workforce, "America's Choice: high skills or low wages?", received nationwide attention (National Center on Education and the Economy, June 1990). The report proposes a broad-based approach for solving the severe labor force problems faced by the nation. A key component of the approach stressed the need for "a comprehensive labor market information system to project the demand for labor in all fields." New York State government is moving toward that objective.

A scan of the environment which precipitated the need for this focused effort is presented below. The Workforce Information System will then be described in some detail, including several applications which have had a clear impact on the "bottom line" in New York State. The final section of the paper focuses on turnover analysis and modeling, which we feel has significant savings potential. This research was given high priority in the Governor's 1991 State of the State Message.

This effort has taken on even greater significance in the current fiscal environment--the state is facing a projected budget deficit of over $6 billion in fiscal year 1991-92. One goal of workforce planning is to ensure that the hard choices are made with the benefit of information, about both possibilities and potential outcomes.

Scanning the Environment

A review of the current economic and demographic environment in New York State reveals that human resource planning will become more concerned with training potential job candidates, and attracting and managing a workforce that is highly diverse in terms of background, age, country of origin, needs and values.

The development of workforce profiles and trend data has proven to be one of the most pragmatic uses of the Workforce Information System. As the demographic profile of the state changes, we must focus on two critical areas. First, how will the demand for services change, and how will that impact the demand for workers. Second, how must human resource programs and policies change in order to be responsive to the emerging labor force.

The Changing Composition of the Workforce

It is important to monitor trends in the workforce, such as age, gender and ethnic make-up, to ensure programs and policies are aligned with the needs of current and future employees. The ethnic composition of the state is changing rapidly as New York's diversity is increasing. The state government workforce is already more diverse than the state's labor force as a whole, with minorities representing nearly 23% of the government workforce, and about 16% of the state's labor force. Minorities will make up a large share of the expansion of the labor force from now to the year 2000. Furthermore, New York State becomes home to 25 percent of all immigrants admitted to the United States.

While male and female employees are now evenly represented in the state government workforce, closer analysis reveals major differences in employment. For instance, women represent approximately three-quarters of the part-time workforce. Moreover, three out of four women are in the childbearing age group (age 15- to-49). Within this range, 32% are in the 18-to-34 age cohort most likely to have children, and hence to go on leave, often with pay (New York State Department of Civil Service, 1990).

There are not only more women working, but increasing numbers of women working in non-traditional occupational areas. There has been a steady increase in the number of women holding previously male-dominated job titles over the past several years. The changes are especially noticeable in administrative, professional and technical titles, and in such occupational fields as law, accounting, computer programming and investigations. For example, in the field of law, the statistics reflect nationwide increases in numbers of women enrolling in law school (e.g. women now hold 40% of the Associate Counsel jobs, compared to 19% in 1984).

A breakdown by age group reveals much about the composition of the future workforce. The number of female employees among officials and administrators has increased by almost 80% since 1984, expanding their representation to nearly 25% in 1991. However, among younger employees the progress is most noticeable; nearly 48% of officials and administrators in the 18-to-34 age group were female.

This type of information serves to pose a multitude of questions for policy makers. Whatever is undertaken in the way of employment practices--including policies affecting recruitment, retention, attendance, leave time and work schedules--must be measured against the needs of existing and potential workers, who are increasingly women and minorities.

Geographic Diversity

New York is a large state, encompassing several very different economic and demographic regions, and state government has employees located in every geographic area. Of particular significance is the New York City area, which accounts for about 61.5% of the state's population and has a labor force larger than that of 42 states. With 32% of the state government workforce (over 66,000 employees), nearly 50% of which are minorities, the region clearly warrants special attention and study.

Workforce problems in New York City tend to be more severe than in other areas of the state. Furthermore, because of its significant role in the national and international arenas, the city is on the forefront of technological and economic activities which are changing the work place. The area bears watching not only as a vehicle for learning about work force problems and solutions, but as a precursor for the rest of the state.

Unlike many private sector organizations, state government generally does not have the option to "move out"--there will continue to be functions and services that are critical to the area. Competitive solutions must be found to address problems in the recruitment and retention of skilled workers.

Occupational Profile

Compounding the dramatic demographic changes, the occupational profile of New York State's labor force was transformed by major structural changes in the 1980's. The blue collar sector, particularly in the manufacturing industries, suffered from severe job losses. On the other hand, the knowledge and information processing sectors experienced massive expansion over the last decade (Ehrenhalt, 1990).

For example, IBM discovered, after installing millions of dollars of computers in its Vermont factories, that it had to teach thousands of workers high school algebra. These people are the "blue-collar" workers of the past, who now must know algebra and advanced mathematics, read blueprints, and perform complex operations to be competitive and do their job (Nussbaum, 1988).

The knowledge and information sectors show large concentrations of highly skilled professional, managerial and technical workers; hence, these three occupational groups will experience significant growth in the 1990's. They are projected to account for over 40% of job openings due to growth, while the clerical sector, which experienced rapid growth in the 1970's and 1980's, will post future growth rates well below average (New York State Department of Labor).

Not surprisingly, changes in the New York State government workforce have tended to mirror these trends. The state experienced considerable growth in the professional occupational group. However, the area of largest growth demonstrates how major policy changes in government affect the deployment of the workforce. The protective service group increased by 40.7% due to the tremendous expansion of the correctional service system over the past five years--the Department of Corrections alone added over 10,000 employees, a growth of 48.3%. The managerial category held constant as a proportion of the workforce, but all other occupational groups declined. Administrative support, technicians, skilled crafts workers, service maintenance and paraprofessionals all represent a smaller share of the overall workforce.

Some of the specific titles with the largest expected job growth through 1995 are titles for which state government will be in direct competition with the private sector, including registered nurses, janitors and cleaners, accountants, secretaries, and computer programmers (U.S. Dept. of Labor, 1986). All of these are among the twenty largest job titles in New York State, which together comprise 45 percent of the workforce.

This analysis demonstrates the necessity for New York State to be able to estimate the demand for and supply of workers in these occupations. The loss of traditional blue collar jobs, increasing skill levels of emerging jobs and declining skill levels of available workers all indicate that state government will continue to experience a general shortage of qualified applicants on an occupation-specific and regional basis.

The Link: Environmental Data and Strategic Direction

These workforce trends, compounded by the fiscal crisis, have made the need for information more critical than ever before. These data demonstrate that New York State must begin to understand and plan for structural changes in its workforce arising out of demographic trends, labor supply and demand, fiscal uncertainties and shifts in agency programmatic needs. The annual workforce plan documents are intended to provide an agenda, anchored in what the data reveal, for such actions. The workforce database is the foundation of this research and strategic planning effort.

Like most organizations, the automation of human resource information has had low priority in the past. That attitude, however, can "weaken internal cost controls, erode overall operating efficiency and lead to decisions not supported by sound analyses" (Richter, 1991).

Data analysis has become a critical part of the workforce planning process in New York State. The state has recognized that we must develop the capacity to forecast workforce trends and to conduct rigorous, ongoing analyses of government's labor supply and demand. To accomplish this, the state must have accurate and complete information about the major forces that affect its workforce. The system designed to fill this need is described below.

Developing a Large-Scale Workforce Information System

The Workforce Information System puts basic information on every employee into a relational database, which allows quick and flexible access to the information. The new database contains a wealth of demographic and fiscal information on the workforce. It will contain current and historical data on active and inactive incumbents of positions. The availability of consistent and comparable historical data will allow us to track people and expenditures over time. Besides snapshots of the workforce taken at specific points in time (e.g. quarterly), the information will be accumulated on a fiscal year basis.

A significant feature of the database is the ability to integrate, for the first time, information from several independent systems. Processes have been developed to update much of the information on a weekly basis, though some of the data are updated less frequently. The database contains basic human resource information on people and positions from the Department of Civil Service personnel system, and incorporates ethnic and protected class information. It integrates comprehensive fiscal data from the Office of the State Comptroller, the agency which maintains payroll information on salary and other components of compensation. It integrates key retirement data from the New York State Retirement System, another separate organization. Finally, it gives a more complete look at the entire state government workforce by retrieving information from several agencies/organizations which maintain independent personnel and payroll systems and, hence, would otherwise be excluded from analyses (e.g. Department of Labor, Thruway Authority).

The development and definition of the workforce database proved to be a difficult task. The extensive thinking about the relationships and logic in the database led to a thorough review of numerous personnel transaction policies by organizational staff. Ironically, various divisions discovered they had differing perceptions of how a particular transaction worked. It often turned out than none were exactly correct. Therefore, the development of the database led to a review and updating of outdated or improperly functioning personnel policies and procedures.

The personnel system in New York State is derived from the Civil Service Law, which sets out the rules of the merit system of government. Because of the legal complexities of administering this system, the information and relationships maintained in the database are more complicated than would typically be required for a workforce information system.

For example, instead of one initial appointment date, employees also have a classified service seniority date, date of last permanent appointment and competitive service date, as well as others. In addition, dates will be created and stored in the new database, such as appointment to current title and appointment to current salary grade level. The latter will be used to compute "time in title" and "time in grade." This information will be valuable for research purposes, such as plateauing studies.

The salary information is also quite complex. The cost of numerous premium compensation items (e.g. salary differentials such as location pay, geographic pay, inconvenience pay, hazard/safety pay and overtime) will be accumulated on a quarterly and annual basis. This will allow for the analysis (and eventually projection) of "total" compensation and its components paid over the fiscal year to various groups of employees.

This broad-based integration of information allows for a wide range of sophisticated workforce analyses not heretofore possible. It creates the capacity necessary to conduct comprehensive research on the entire classified service branch of government, including cross-section and time-series analyses.

One example of a useful application of this new system is a study produced for the NYS Budget Division, which included cost estimates of changes in the salary grade distribution over time (i.e. "grade creep"). By factoring out increases due to the implementation of pay equity, we were able to estimate how much reallocations and reclassifications have historically cost the State. Further, we compared these percentage increases and rates of promotion over time and across agencies, geographic areas, occupational groups and collective bargaining units. Based on past experience, it will be possible to project the future costs of changes in the salary grade structure. These steadily increasing labor costs are not readily observable, as are annual raises and performance advances. The degree by which increases in salaries exceed increases in pay rates is important to know.

The Integration of HR Planning and Fiscal Planning

As is true in many organizations, the functions of human resource planning and fiscal planning have been relatively independent in New York State. Prior capability to address simultaneously these issues did not exist. As a result, fiscal resources available to agencies did not always support human resource needs, especially from a long-range planning perspective. The cost of various policy initiatives could only be estimated or guessed at. As warned by the Commission on Work Force Quality and Labor Market Efficiency, "absent research, policy will be based at best on intuition and, at worst, on special interests" (U.S. Dept. of Labor, 1989).

By integrating demographic and fiscal information on the workforce, the potential costs and benefits of alternative policy and program initiatives may be determined. The value of the capacity to inform the decision making process in this way is immeasurable. Only by linking payroll to personnel data can we accurately answer questions such as:

o What would a one percent increase in salary cost? What would it cost to increase location pay by one percent?
o What would the fiscal impact be of extending certain pay differentials to new groups of employees?
o How much money did employees choosing an early retirement incentive option receive for unused leave credits?
o How did the age distribution of the workforce change following the implementation?, and
o What is the distribution of employees leaving state government by geographic area, job title, salary, gender and ethnicity?

The ability to produce quickly such reports gives policy makers realistic estimates of the actual costs connected to alternative policy decisions within the time frame of making the decision. It allows for the simulation of current and longer-range outcomes of various proposals.

This new capacity has proven its strategic value during the current fiscal crisis faced by New York State. The emerging workforce problems described above combined with an unprecedented budget deficit have presented a very difficult scenario. With state government negotiating a new three-year contract with its major unions, the database has been relied on extensively.

Turnover Analysis

Why is turnover analysis so important? According to the U.S. Merit Systems Protection Board, "The dynamics of employee turnover can impact on the ability of the government to effectively and efficiently fulfill its public service responsibility." They have issued a report "Who is Leaving the Federal Government?" which contains a comprehensive analysis of turnover. The Federal government has also responded to a 1988 General Accounting Office study, which calls for an ongoing and systematic assessment of separations from the Federal public service.

Consistent with efforts of the Federal government, New York State has begun to analyze turnover. Useful information about the number and types of employees who leave state service has not been readily available. The creation of the database has made such information accessible, and allows for great flexibility in the analysis of turnover.

Employee turnover is very costly to the state, and knowledge about who is leaving can provide useful information about the degree to which turnover is detrimental. By looking at turnover in various ways, one can uncover potential problem areas. For example, the fiscal year 1988-89 turnover rate for the

Department of Correctional Services was 6.3%, over four percentage points lower than the overall state government rate of 10.7%. The initial reaction would probably be that turnover is not a problem. Further analysis reveals that several facilities within the department have very high turnover rates (e.g. Sing Sing with a rate of 12.7% and Taconic with a rate of 17%).

The Value of Historical Turnover Data

Historical data are useful in many ways. They allow for the identification of annual trends and seasonal patterns in turnover. Historical information is also a useful tool to measure the effectiveness of various incentive programs designed to encourage employees to remain on the job. A comparison of separation rates before and after implementation of such a program provides a good measure of success. Perhaps most importantly, historical data provide government-wide benchmarks against which to assess the nature and severity of turnover experienced within state agencies.

It is often instructive to look deeper into the numbers to discover potential problems or significant trends. A review of historical turnover rates reveals no surprising or significant trends. Similarly, historical retirement rates, a component of turnover, have been stable over time. The lowest rate of 1.2% in fiscal year 1984-85 followed a year when an early retirement incentive program had been offered, which explains why the rate is relatively low (see Figure 1).

This quiet surface, however, can hide significant changes in turnover patterns. An analysis of the percentage of turnover due to retirements reveals a very clear, steady upward trend. That is, out of the total number of employees leaving state service, the proportion leaving due to retirement has increased from 11.1% in fiscal year 1984-85 to 18.9% in 1989-90 (see Figure 2). This substantiates projections of increasing numbers of employees retiring, and provides evidence that this trend has already begun.

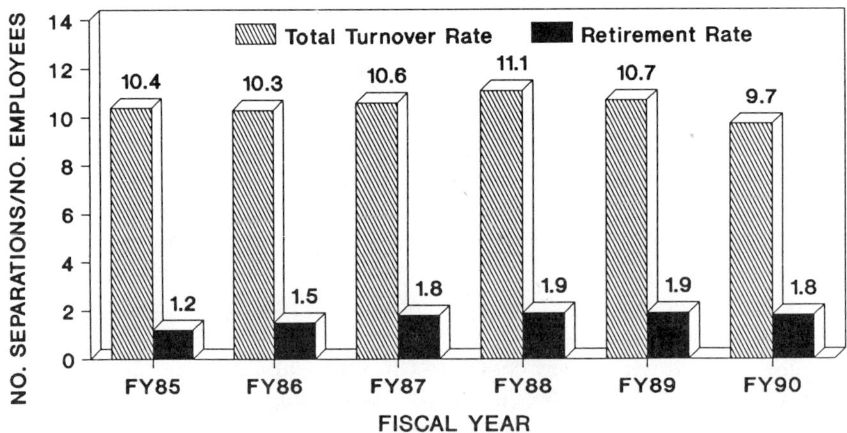

Figure 1: Annual Turnover Rates. (Rates Based on Incumbents of Permanent Positions Only.)

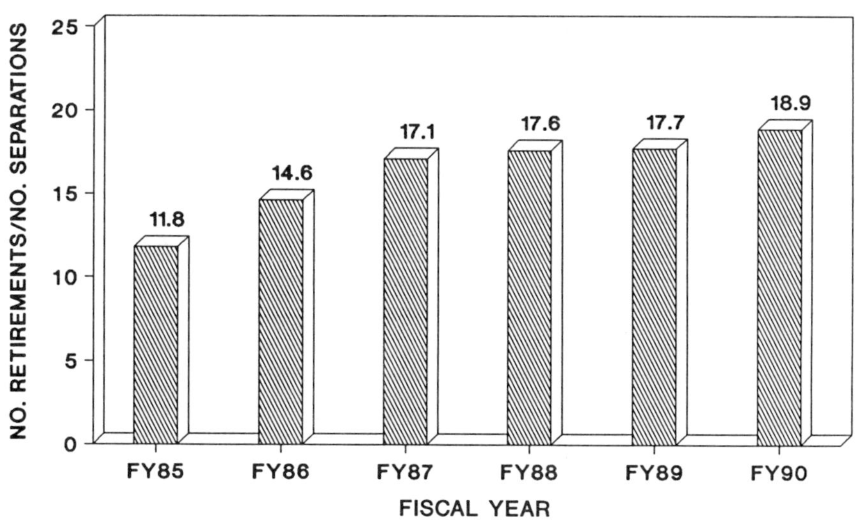

Figure 2: Proportion of Turnover Due to Retirements. (Rates Based on Incumbents of Permanent Positions Only.)

As baby boomers near retirement age in larger numbers, these "hidden" patterns will become more evident (Lewis, 1991). This analysis demonstrates how raw turnover rates may be hiding real problems. Program managers will want to know where there may be potentially large numbers of employees retiring in a particular job title, occupation or program area. The state will want to know where potential problem areas may be in order to develop a statewide policy response. The challenge facing New York State is to identify those segments of its workforce which require attention and to allocate its resources accordingly.

Recent Turnover Experience in New York State Government

Given that recruitment of skilled labor is becoming increasingly difficult, the need to retain current employees becomes critical. A careful study of employee turnover will provide a means by which the state can assess its loss of quality workers. Knowing who is leaving state government and when, human resource managers may ask three questions: 1) is the turnover significant? 2) if so, what are the causes? and 3) what can be done to alleviate the problem of undesirable turnover?

From a macro-level perspective, the overall turnover rate has remained quite stable over the past five fiscal years, ranging from a high of 11.1% in fiscal year 1987-88 to a low of 9.7% in 1989-90 (see Figure 1). However, the number of permanent employees who leave government each year is not insignificant. A total of 19,445 employees left state service in 1988-89; the 17,757 employees who left in 1989-90 represented the fewest departures in the past six years. Importantly, this turnover does not occur uniformly across all agencies and all titles.

Looking beneath the surface, a key fact that emerges is that the highest rates of separation occur among employees who have worked for the state for less than one year. For 1988-89, this rate was almost 42%. This rate is excessively high relative to the average rate of separation. It is also high compared to the Federal government, which reports a 25% turnover rate for this group of "new hires." Beyond the first year, turnover rates steadily drop as length of service increases, but start to rise again at the twenty years of service point to another peak of 25.8% for those with 35 or more years of service.

Given that the highest rates of turnover occur at both ends of the length of service spectrum, it makes sense that those are two areas in which New York State should focus its efforts to reduce the rates at which employees leave. For example, if further research revealed that the losses occurring during the first year are the result of poor selections, the state would be advised to examine its selection and placement procedures.

We have already collaborated with some agencies to put the right people in the right jobs. For example, the separation rate for therapy aide trainees in the state mental health institutions exceeds 42%. In an attempt to reduce this extremely high turnover, candidates now watch a pre-test video depicting a typical day on the job. This video is intended to serve as a screening device for those who would be likely to leave because the job duties were not consistent with their expectations.

At the other end of the length of service continuum is the group of employees who are nearing retirement. Their numbers are increasing rapidly, and agencies could be in precarious situations in some instances where large numbers of workers with institutional memory and acquired skills which are difficult to replace are projected to retire.

The age distribution of the state government workforce is shifting dramatically; the average age has increased from 39.9 years in 1984 to 41.6 years in 1990, which is older than the labor force as a whole (with an average age of 36 years). To the extent that turnover rates increase with age, large numbers of employees will be leaving due to retirement over the next ten years.

A more discrete analysis reveals several occupations, agencies and titles that face potentially large and critical losses. For example, over 20% of the state's officials and administrators are retirement eligible; Department of Labor employees have an average age of 46.4 years and an average length of service of 15 years, much higher than statewide averages; the average age of civil engineers is 44.5 years, the average length of service 21.4 years. There is a high probability that nearly all these engineers will retire over the next ten years.

The examples cited demonstrate the exigency of studying these trends--the state must plan now to prepare its workforce to fill vacancies left by departing employees. Providing agencies with the projected number of employees with a high likelihood of leaving, broken down by title and location, will give managers the lead time to respond in a timely and cost effective manner to such departures.

An analysis of turnover by geographic area reveals a striking difference between upstate and downstate rates. The downstate rate of 14.7% surpasses the upstate rate by over six percentage points. While 32% of the workforce is in the downstate region, a disproportionate 47% of the turnover occurred there.

A review of turnover rates for the twenty most populous titles illustrates specific instances of disparity between upstate and downstate rates. Correction officer, the most populous title in the state, has a low statewide turnover rate of 3.8%. The downstate rate of 10.4%, however, is over 7 percentage points higher than the upstate rate of 3%. Titles which fall within the clerical field tend to exhibit wide differences in turnover rates. For example, keyboard specialists have an upstate turnover rate of 10.7% as compared to a downstate rate of 17.4%; stenographers downstate leave at nearly twice the rate of their upstate counterparts. The intense competition for a shrinking pool of qualified workers is a major reason for this loss of employees, but it is important to investigate other causes.

"Total" Turnover

In order to get a complete estimate of turnover from an agency perspective, one must look not only at employees leaving state government employment, but the numbers transferring to other titles or agencies within the state. These vacated positions represent a job which must be filled at the organizational level (assuming the position is retained), even though it is not turnover for the state as a whole.

For example, the job title Nurse 1 had 739 positions in fiscal year 1989-90. The "total" turnover for that title was 76.2%. The turnover rate due to separations was 25.6%, which was high relative to the statewide average. Additionally, 374 employees who were in this title moved into a different job title over that same time period, a rate of 50.6%. The alarming fact that over three-fourths of these positions turned over within a one-year period warrants further investigation.

The Value of Turnover Forecasts

With the growing costs of recruiting, testing, getting people into jobs and training them on one end, and increasingly high severance costs on the other, it is clear that taking steps to reduce excessive turnover will produce significant savings for New York State. One of the major ways in which workforce planning will increase the state's ability to meet immediate and long-term staffing needs is by using analytical tools and data resources to develop models of the workforce. These models will project turnover, including separations, transfers, promotions and retirements. The forecasts will provide estimates of the demand for labor by occupation and geographic area. They will also help to identify occupations in which shortages and surpluses are likely to occur.

Employee turnover is influenced by many environmental factors. These include the state of the economy, the current labor market, the nature and location of the job, demographic characteristics, values and expectations of employees, and other factors specific to a job or agency.

An optimal model of turnover will incorporate as many of these factors as is practicable. We are using a statistical modeling tool, regression analysis, to build forecasting models based on these factors. For example, preliminary results have shown that aggregate employee turnover is inversely related to the rate of unemployment. This is not surprising--when the unemployment rate is high, the number of external opportunities will be relatively small, and fewer people are likely to leave their jobs. Alternatively, there is a strong positive correlation with the NYS Industrial Production Index, a key measure of economic activity. Again, as external opportunities increase and competition for workers intensifies, aggregate turnover will increase as employees accept better offers.

Other quantifiable variables that have been shown to have a statistically significant impact on the number of people leaving at more discrete levels (e.g. job title, individual) include: age, length of service, gender, geographic area, agency size, title size, and past experience (i.e. lagged turnover rates). A forecasting model which measures the impact of changes in these factors on turnover rates will produce more accurate and efficient predictions than a basic trend line projection. Indeed, the dynamics of the workforce can be forecast with a high degree of reliability through the use of econometric modeling techniques (Bres, Niehaus, Sharkey and Weber, 1987)

Applying the Data

Comprehensive turnover data are essential to the workforce planning process, but are merely a starting point. Because turnover is influenced by many factors, without a detailed analysis it is impossible to separate the contribution of each factor to turnover.

Information on turnover can help identify problem areas and guide the search for causes. However, in order to get the most use out of turnover rates to diagnose retention problems, further research is necessary. For instance, the Volcker Commission asserted that the Federal civil service is losing high quality employees due to declining relative pay in government (1989). While this is true for some titles and locations in New York State, salaries are generally quite competitive; we must search deeper for the underlying causes of high turnover.

Consider, as an example, the case of civil engineers. Is the turnover rate in New York City higher at particular times of the year? Is it higher or lower than that of other kinds of engineers in the same geographic area? Is it possible that the way an agency structures its engineering work is a larger contributing factor to turnover rates than are salary levels? Titles with high rates of transfer with no change in salary might indicate such a situation. The next step is to investigate whether the moves are the result of the new agency's having better working conditions, a better location, increased promotion opportunities or a combination of these.

Conclusion

The turnover data reveal the areas in which New York State should focus its efforts to reduce the rates at which employees leave. By analyzing current turnover trends and projecting future problem areas, we can begin to identify and isolate retention problems in critical occupations. A thoughtful review of this information leads one to ask questions which, in turn, better define the problems. Using this information as a vehicle for problem clarification and solution development, human resource managers, program managers and budget managers can actively participate in developing cost-effective initiatives to resolve retention problems.

References

Bres, E.S. III, R.J. Niehaus, F.J. Sharkey, and C.L. Weber, "Use of Personnel Flow Models for Analysis of Large Scale Workforce Changes", in *Strategic Human Resource Planning Applications*, ed. by R.J. Niehaus, (New York: Plenum Press, 1987).

Commission on the Skills of the American Workforce, *America's Choice: High Skills or Low Wages!*,(Rochester, NY: National Center on Education and the Economy, June 1990).

Cuomo, Mario M., *Message to the Legislature*, (Albany, NY: January 9, 1991), p. 41.

Ehrenhalt, Samuel M., *New York Trends and Prospects: The Dynamics of Jobs and People*, (Paris, France: International Statistical Institute, August, 1989).

Johnston, William and Arnold Packer, *Workforce 2000*, prepared for U.S. Department of Labor, (Indianapolis, Indiana: Hudson Institute, June, 1987).

Lewis, Gregory B., "Turnover and the Quiet Crisis in the Federal Civil Service", *Public Administration Review*, (Vol. 51, No. 2: March/April, 1991), pp. 145-155.

New York State Department of Civil Service, *New York State Work Force Plan 1990: Building a State Work Force in the 1990s*, (Albany, NY: 1990).

New York State Department of Labor, Division of Research and Statistics, *New York State Occupational Needs in the 90's, 1990-1992*, (Albany, NY: July, 1989).

Nussbaum, B., "Needed: Human Capital", *Business Week*, (September 19, 1988), pp. 100-103.

Richter, M.J., "Now's the Time to Computerize the Personnel Department", *Governing*, (February, 1991), p. 77.

Teigland, Christie L. and Lori K. Hewig, "Projecting Workforce Needs in Government: The Case of New York State", in *Human Resource Forecasting and Strategy Development*, ed. by Manuel London, Emily S. Bassman and John P. Fernandez, (Westport, CT: Quorum Books, 1990).

U.S. Department of Labor, *Employment Projections for 1995: Data and Methods*, Bulletin 2253, (Washington, D.C.: U.S. Government Printing Office, April, 1986).

U.S. Department of Labor, Commission on Workforce Quality and Labor Market Efficiency, *Investing in People. A Strategy to Address America's Workforce Crisis*, (Washington, D.C.: September 4, 1989).

Survey Data as a Catalyst for Employee Empowerment and Organizational Effectiveness

J.R. HINRICHS

Introduction

The employee attitude and opinion survey has been around business and industry for a long time. For well over fifty years since World War II, the survey process has been tried by most companies on at least one occasion. The focus has been on morale -- to identify the things that are causing people to be dissatisfied and to try to smooth out the low spots.

From the perspective of fifty years of activity it's clear, however, that many companies have had less than resounding success in their experiments with morale surveys. Traditional surveys usually have asked question after question about administrative topics such as satisfaction with pay and benefits, working conditions, or the food in the cafeteria. Then the task of sorting out the issues and "doing something" about negative results fell to Administrators -- Personnel or Human Resource people. Thus, the survey was often seen as a staff exercise with little relevance to the "real" concerns of the business.

In many forward-thinking organizations over the last few years, however, the employee opinion survey process has changed its role dramatically. It has evolved from a passive monitor of morale to a proactive tool for supporting the implementation of human resource strategy. The methodology has evolved to one which -- if implemented with care -- has been demonstrated to yield significant productivity gains, and bottom-line return.

We'll outline this methodology shortly. First, it's important to understand why the employee survey is a management strategy whose time has finally arrived.

Traditional Viewpoints

In years past, the driving assumption underlying most management decisions to embark on a survey has been that there is a direct association between

---

J.R. HINRICHS - Management Decision Systems, Inc., 397 Boston Post Road Darien, CT 06820

employee satisfaction or "morale" and productivity. Presumably, employees who like their jobs should feel grateful to their employer and work harder, and employees who dislike their jobs will feel resentful toward their employer and work less hard. This view spawned a sort of "happiness-orientation" in thinking about people at work. Like Snow White's seven dwarfs, the thinking went, productive employees whistle while they work.

Through these same decades, organizational psychologists searched -- without luck -- for this direct relationship. The evidence is now overwhelming that this assumption is wrong (Organ, 1977). There is no direct association between overall satisfaction or morale and productivity. High morale can equal low productivity and vice versa. Research, and a logical analysis help to explain why.

For example, it's not uncommon to find companies whose employees are euphoric -- like pigs in mud. They have beautiful work surroundings, wonderful benefits, and secure jobs. Management goes out of its way to treat them well. Still, many are not doing much productive work. Sometimes, we've observed, they're not doing much of anything except socializing and taking literally the advice to "have a nice day!"

In other companies -- a die-casting plant with smoke in the air and hot metal on the floor comes to mind as a specific example -- the screws may be down tight. Management is riding herd and closely monitoring production and quality. There is no time for the niceties of good human relations pleasantries. Yet ambitious production quotas are invariably met. The workers are not very happy, but their productivity is high.

The problem is that both of these actual situations are less than ideal from the point of view of the long-term health of the firm, and for the future of U.S. industry to compete in today's environment. On the one hand, non-producing, pampered workers will bleed the firm dry. On the other, a harassed and over- driven work force will, before long, display serious and costly symptoms of turnover, conflict, and ill-health effects of stress.

Today's View

The new view about job satisfaction, backed by recent research findings, does confirm that employee attitudes are extremely important contributors to productivity. They indicate, however, that our traditional view of the satisfaction-performance relationship has been too narrow. Instead, we must think in terms of relatively-focused attitudes or perceptions about specific aspects of work -- not global "morale" or job satisfaction. Perceptions drive behavior, often through indirect channels. For example, performance -- and thus productivity and ultimately profitability -- have been found to be related to factors such as these:

o Perceptions about elements which may be restraining the organization's ability to compete in a changing marketplace.

o Opinions about the responsiveness of the organization in providing the necessary tools, facilities, or information so that employees can do their jobs effectively.

o Attitudes about the sincerity of management's commitment to provide quality products and customer service.

o Feelings about what rewards there are for productive effort and how equitably these are distributed -- what's in it for me if I produce at superior levels.

o Views about the potential for long-term job security and opportunities
to grow on the job and within the organization.

o Beliefs about management's willingness to listen and respond to
employee concerns and constructively try to solve problems.

Knowing something about the state of such attitudes can point an organization's way to significant improvements in operating effectiveness. Also, rather than looking for a direct one-to-one tie between general morale and performance, current research is showing that such specific patterns of attitudes often have an impact on organizational effectiveness through indirect channels.

For example, a major retail chain found through surveying employees and customers of a large number of its stores that employee commitment to providing responsive customer service directly affected the satisfaction of customers with their shopping experience at the store. The analysis further showed that where customer satisfaction was high, the profitability of the store was significantly higher than where customer satisfaction was less favorable. There was little direct tie between overall employee satisfaction and store profitability.

Thus, it has become clear that overall employee satisfaction and dissatisfaction usually do not show up in just one behavior such as performance, but that specific patterns of attitudes may impact many different types of outcomes, any of which can have an impact on the bottom- line return of the enterprise. Today's forward-thinking organizations are searching for more systematic ways to understand and harness the power of employee commitment in driving a diversity of outcomes which contribute to the success of the enterprise.

The Stakes Are High

The stakes can be large in such efforts to enhance work-force commitment. Most human resource people have some intuitive sense of this when they deal with problems of turnover, absenteeism, or employee conflict. They have seen data in their various publications and conferences suggesting that a reasonable cost of turnover for an average employee can be at least $10,000; a low estimate calculates the cost of a day's unauthorized absence at $100. Further, HR people know that many of these costs are tied to attitudes -- what goes on in people's heads to make them concerned about quality, loyal to the business, willing to come to work, or exert effort to be productive.

To illustrate, recently we have been working with a manufacturing organization which has been experiencing 6% average absenteeism in its hourly work force; across multiple locations the rates vary from 4% to an intolerable 13%. By highlighting that this 6% absence rate reflects 500 people off the job on any one day, management has demonstrated the real cost of low job commitment in this work force. Interestingly, the union has gone further to grab the attention of its members by equating daily absence of 500 rank and file to potential outright closing of an entire plant. By aligning both management and union around a common objective of reducing absenteeism to some tolerable minimum -- even if the underlying driving force for one revolves around profitability and for the other around job security -- this organization stands a good chance of really impacting commitment to enhance the organization's business prospects.

Another example illustrates the potential bottom-line return from addressing constraints to work-force commitment simultaneously on several fronts. This firm is a rather typical 2,000-person manufacturing company with $150 million in sales, gross payroll equal to 40% of sales, and 5% pre-tax profits. They also have monthly turnover running at 1.5%, 2.7% absenteeism, their cost of finished quality runs roughly 10% of sales, and latent unused productivity potential based upon employee survey results is equivalent to over 300 person-years. When expressed in annual dollar equivalents, based upon trends from many studies of the cost of turnover (Cascio 1982; MDS 1984; Mercer 1988), absenteeism (Klein 1985; MDS 1985; Mirvis & Lawler 1977), or quality (Crosby 1979), that translates to $28 million tied largely to employee commitment of one form or another.

Let's assume that by focusing on the departments and locations where these direct costs are most severe, and their primary causes, this company can achieve a modest 10% improvement. That is $2.8 million savings direct to the bottom line; this $150 million company would have to increase sales by over $55 million to net this additional return.

Thus the leverage from enhancing work-force motivation is substantial -- so much so that human resource professionals tend to shy away from speaking in such financial terms fearing they will lack credibility. However, it's time to speak out, because operating executives need to realize how high the stakes are and how great the potential leverage is.

Today, fortunately, more and more executives in forward-thinking organizations are recognizing just how high this potential for productivity leverage is. They are recognizing that this bottom-line leverage comes not just from traditional objectives pursued by most HR departments -- reduction of turnover, better control of absenteeism, more harmonious labor relations, or better overall "morale" -- but from a host of positive work-force attitudes which translate into bottom-line payoff through sometimes unclear channels. Research shows, for example, that:

o   Employee commitment to customer service does impact customer
    satisfaction, and this, in turn, does enhance unit profitability, as
    outlined above, rather than a direct linkage between employee attitudes
    and profits.
o   Employees who like their jobs are more likely than those who don't to
    engage in beneficial "organizational-citizenship" behaviors (Bateman
    and Organ 1983), such as helping co-workers, keeping others informed,
    or participating in meetings and other company activities.
o   In a recent study, the willingness of employees to participate in a major
    corporate move was not driven by their overall satisfaction with the
    company or their jobs. Instead, their perception of the company's desire
    for them to stay and the steps being taken to facilitate the move
    determined their subsequent willingness to go along.
o   Despite an organization's professed concern about producing quality
    products and services, as an example, until employees perceive that
    management by their actions considers quality to be an overriding
    objective, employees won't take it to heart. When quality does becomes
    number one, positive performance results can be dramatic.

The Role of the Employee Survey

That is where the employee survey comes in. It is the only way to pin down the real diversity of people-oriented constraints to productivity -- and profitability -- within a specific organizational setting, and then take steps to correct it.

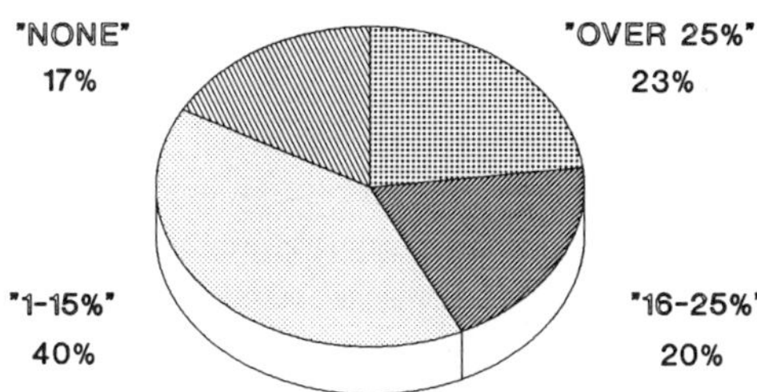

Figure 1: Response Rate to Expected Productivity Increase Question

As an illustration, some major manufacturers recently included a question in their regular employee surveys asking: "If conditions on the job were right, to what extent could you increase the amount of work you get done?" As shown in Figure 1, of roughly 25,000 employees from 25 very diverse companies, on average 40% said they could increase their productivity by at least 15% if conditions were right An astounding 8% said they could be at least 50% more productive. When these results were weighted and totaled, it was evident these employees were telling their management that there was latent productivity of over 4,000 person- years waiting to be tapped in these companies. This is the equivalent of a 16% increase in headcount, at no additional payroll cost as summarized in Table 1.

Most of these companies took active steps to realize this productivity potential by using their survey results as a catalyst for discussion and problem-solving in a series of small group meetings with employees at all levels. In the process, they were careful to push accountability for taking constructive actions down to the lowest level possible. This fostered joint ownership by department management and employees for dealing with the survey issues. The process generated significant energy and creativity for improvement at the grass roots level where, after all, most productivity enhancements must be implemented.

In these organizations, each department had access to its own results and comparison benchmarks with the rest of the company. The focus of each meeting

Table 1: Response to Productivity Potential Question

	Response %	Number People	People Equivalent
"None"	17	4,250	0
"1-15%"	40	10,000	800
"16-25%"	20	5,000	1,025
"26-50%"	15	3,750	1,425
"Over 50%"	8	2,000	1,000
	100%	25,000	4,250

was to get specifics out on the table and to brainstorm solutions for their particular situation. Then, a process was put into place to be sure feasible suggestions were implemented and appreciation expressed for employees' commitment and involvement. In follow-up, the organizations reported a wide diversity of improvement actions with tangible payoff.

This process shows very tangibly that employee perceptions --in this instance the latent productivity potential in the work force -- can energize and focus a diversity of organizational improvement efforts, with significant bottom-line payoff.

Surveys as a Management Tool

Without doubt the most systematic and cost-effective way for any organization to understand and enhance its work-force motivation in areas such as this is through a well-designed employee survey process. Today's surveys serve multiple roles which go well beyond the traditional objectives of merely measuring attitudes. Surveys can:

o Dramatically focus the attention of all members of an organization in each of its segments -- levels, functions, locations, etc. -- on key strategic issues important to organization effectiveness.

o Spotlight specific problem units and identify targets of particular improvement opportunity.

o Open lines of two-way communication, at all levels, involving managers and employees as partners in action planning and problem resolution.

o Create a catalyst for change by "unfreezing" stagnant situations and creating momentum.

o Provide a set of techniques and a forum for problem identification and resolution.

o Build employee involvement and commitment to support the organization's strategic objectives.

o Tangibly assign accountability for constructive action steps to all managers at all levels, while pushing specific items of accountability down to the lowest level feasible.

The essential aspect of all this is tied up less in the actual process of administering a survey -- collecting the data -- and more in what happens after the results are in. The key is the data feedback process at the individual departmental level.

Feedback of survey results is the catalyst for complete involvement. The technology for survey feedback has evolved to the point where we know something about what makes for an effective feedback process as follows:

o First, surveys must be designed with feedback in mind. This means that most if not all the items in a survey should deal with issues that are under local control and where employee involvement can make a difference to enhance organizational effectiveness. Such factors as job assignments, supervisory recognition, teamwork, and adequate communication channels fall into this category. Factors beyond the immediate control of intact work groups, such as market strategies, long-range corporate plans, or benefit programs, may be appropriate survey topics, but they probably contain little potential for much constructive employee involvement. One way to test whether survey items can be involving is to have managers and employees rate them in terms of potential actionability at the local department level, before deciding to include them in a questionnaire.

o To a considerable extent surveys should be open-ended to ensure that they cover what's on the minds of employees. While from a data processing point-of-view open-ended items may present some difficulties in large scale surveys, we're seeing them used more extensively. Careful precoding schemes or sampling can reduce the processing load.

o Anonymity of survey respondents has always been a concern. This becomes particularly important where there is heavy emphasis on feedback and breaking results down to the local department. Strict procedures are needed to preserve respondent anonymity, and data analysis must never be so granular that what any one individual says can be determined.

o Providing useful feedback and involving employees requires skill. Increasingly we're seeing training for feedback leaders in how to give feedback effectively. Behavior modeling and role play can be used for skill building. The feedback leader may be the manager of the group himself or herself (probably an ideal situation, this takes a considerable skill and perhaps a thick skin), a key employee, or a professional feedback giver. Keeping the responsibilities for coordinating the feedback process within the departmental team is usually preferable to calling on an outsider for help.

o Increasingly there is a structured discipline for use of survey results. Ideally, this flows out of the feedback meeting into an administrative system where suggestions are captured and circulated for review and action and accountability for taking action is clear -- within the team itself whenever possible. A tracking system to follow and resolve any open recommendations ensures that there is adequate response to the input provided by employees in the survey and feedback session.

In the Final Analysis

Organizations that fail to discover sources of employee dissatisfaction or tap employees' ideas and suggestions for performance improvement will harm themselves by being unaware of issues before they become crises and by being unable to correct problems and capitalize on opportunities. The long-term result may well be that employees take actions which harm both the management and the company. An employee survey is a serious and powerful intervention to prevent that eventuality. Done clumsily or incompletely, it can do more harm than good; done well it can yield enormous benefits.

The employee survey process is a long-standing and proven technology. Most surveys have a thoroughly modern mission: employee involvement and productivity enhancement. For any company that wants to move into this new and growingly pervasive arena of employee involvement and empowerment, the attitude survey, with comprehensive feedback, is an ideal catalyst to help make it happen.

References

Bateman, Thomas S. and Dennis W. Organ. "Job Satisfaction and the Good Soldier: The Relationship Between Affect and Employee Citizenship." *Academy of Management Journal*, Vol. 26, No. 4 (December, 1983) pp. 587-595.

Cascio, Wayne F. *Costing Human Resources: The Financial Impact of Behavior in Organizations*" (Boston: Kent Publishing Company, 1982).

Crosby, Philip B. *Quality is Free: The Art of Making Quality Certain* (New York: McGraw-Hill, 1979).

Klein Bruce W. "Missed Work and Lost Hours," May 1985. *Monthly Labor Review* (Nov. 1986) pp. 26-30.

Management Decision Systems, Inc., *Relationship Between Department Level Job Satisfaction and Absence Rates* Darien, CT: MDS, Inc., (1985) (Internal Report).

Management Decision Systems, Inc., *Survey-Measured Intention to Leave and Subsequent Turnover* Darien, CT: MDS, Inc., (1984) (Internal Report).

Mercer, Michael W. "Turnover: Reducing the Costs." *Personnel*, Vol. 65, No. 12, (1988) pp. 36-42.

Mirvis, Philip H. and Edward E. Lawler, III. "Measuring the Financial Impact of Employee Attitudes." *Journal of Applied Psychology*, Vol. 62, No. 1 (1977) pp. 1-8.

Organ, Dennis W. "A Reappraisal and Reinterpretation of the Satisfaction- Causes-Performance Hypothesis." *Academy of Management Review* Vol. 2, (1977) pp. 46-53.

Contributors

MARY AGUILAR is Head, Personnel Operations, Mare Island Naval Shipyard

THOMAS J. ATCHISON is Professor of Management, San Diego State University

DONALD M. ATWATER is Principal, William M. Mercer, Inc., Los Angeles

RICHARD W. BEATTY is Professor in the Institute of Management and Labor Relations, Rutgers University

THOMAS P. BECHET is a Partner, The Walker Group

MARY ELIZABETH BERES is an independent Leadership and Organization Development Consultant, Leadership Systems

P. NICK BLANCHARD is an Organization Consultant, Strategic Involvement Systems

PETER L. BUGBEE is Vice President, TPF&C, Denver

JOHN BUTCHER is President, Associates in Planning

JAFAR M. CHOWDHURY is Assistant Professor of Management, University of Scranton

DAVID W. DANNER is Director, Organizational Planning and Development, Hahnemann University

DEBRA J. DAVIS is at TPF&C, Denver

JOHN P. DORY is Chairman, Management Department, Graduate School of Business Administration, Pace University

KAREN N. GAERTNER is an Associate Professor, School of Business Administration, Georgetown University

NORMAND W. GREEN is Senior Vice President, Boyden World Corporation

MARTIN M. GRELLER is a Professor, College of Business, University of Wyoming

WALTER H. GRIGGS is a Principal, GriggsManring, Inc.

JOEL H. HEAD is Regional Practice Leader, Communication Consulting, Ernst & Young

JOHN R. HINRICHS is the President, Management Decision Systems, Inc.

RONALD S. KOSTER is Director, Corporate Strategic Planning, Boehringer Ingelheim Corporation

MOHAMED A.S. LATIB is Assistant Professor of Business, Allentown College

PAUL J. LEYDEN is Senior Vice President and Group Executive, The Bank of New York

CYNTHIA WILCOX LISCHICK is a Project Manager at McLaughlin and Company and a doctoral candidate in Psychology at Rutgers University.

SUSAN L. MANRING is a Principal, GriggsManring, Inc.

BRADLEY CRAWFORD McLAUGHLIN is Vice President and Director of Research at McLaughlin and Company, Inc.

DAVID J. McLAUGHLIN is President, McLaughlin and Company, Inc.

ALAN M. MILLER is Chief Administrative Officer, Borden, Inc.

JACK A. NELSON is a Consultant, William M. Mercer, Inc., Los Angeles

RICHARD J. NIEHAUS is Assistant for Human Resources Analysis, Office of the Chief of Naval Operations

STANLEY D. NOLLEN is an Associate Professor, School of Business Administration, Georgetown University

ANTHONY PAGANO is an Associate Professor, University of Illinois at Chicago

JAMES D. PORTWOOD is Professor of Human Resource Administration, Temple University

KARL F. PRICE is a Principal, Towers Perrin, Philadelphia

JAMES H. REYNIERSE is President, James H. Reynierse & Associates, Inc.

CRAIG ERIC SCHNEIER is Managing Principal and National Director, Sibson & Company

DAVID M. SCHWEIGER is an Associate Professor, College of Business Administration, University of South Carolina

FRANCIS S. SHARKEY is Director of Industrial Relations, Mare Island Naval Shipyard

DOUGLAS G. SHAW is a Principal, Sibson & Company

ROBERT B. STONAKER is Vice President, Human Resources, Metropolitan Property and Casuality Company

CHRISTIE L. TEIGLAND is Director of Workforce Planning Analysis, New York State Department of Civil Service

BARRY THOMAS is a Senior Vice President, Frank Russell Company

MICHAEL J. TIMMONS is Vice President, Human Resources Corporate Group, Dominion Textiles, Inc.

JO ANN VERDIN ia a Principal, Decision Technology Associates, Inc.

JAMES W. WALKER is a Partner, The Walker Group

CATHY ZUMBERGE is Vice President, BankTemps, San Diego

Index